Fatal Glamour

Fatal Glamour

THE LIFE OF RUPERT BROOKE

PAUL DELANY

McGill-Queen's University Press

Montreal & Kingston • Ithaca

ISBN 978-0-7735-4557-1 (cloth)
ISBN 978-0-7735-8277-4 (ePDF)
ISBN 978-0-7735-8278-1 (ePUB)

Legal deposit first quarter 2015
Bibliothèque nationale du Québec

Printed in Canada on acid-free paper that is 100% ancient forest free
(100% post-consumer recycled), processed chlorine free

McGill-Queen's University Press acknowledges the support of the
Canada Council for the Arts for our publishing program. We also
acknowledge the financial support of the Government of Canada
through the Canada Book Fund for our publishing activities.

Library and Archives Canada Cataloguing in Publication

Delany, Paul, author
Fatal glamour : the life of Rupert Brooke / Paul Delany.

Includes bibliographical references and index.
Issued in print and electronic formats.
ISBN 978-0-7735-4557-1 (bound). – ISBN 978-0-7735-8277-4 (ePDF).
– ISBN 978-0-7735-8278-1 (ePUB)

1. Brooke, Rupert, 1887–1915. 2. Poets, English – 20th century –
Biography. I. Title.

PR6003.R4Z628 2015   821'.912   C2014-907647-9
                                         C2014-907648-7

Contents

Acknowledgements

My first debt is to those members of the Rupert Brooke generation, or their children, who have now passed away: Quentin Bell, Bob Best, Christopher Cornford, David Garnett, Richard Garnett, Catherine Gide, Sophie Gurney, Angela Harris, Sir Geoffrey Keynes, Cathleen Nesbitt, Frances Partridge, Dr Benedict Richards, and Mary Newbery Sturrock. For access to family archives I am specially grateful to Val Arnold-Forster, daughter-in-law of Ka Cox, and to Pippa Harris and Tamsin Majerus, granddaughters of Noel Olivier.

I thank those who provided invaluable insights through personal reminiscences, private documents, or other help: Val Arnold-Forster, Anne Olivier Bell, Michael Hastings, Elizabeth Hollingsworth, Lucilla Shand, Michael Holroyd, H.A. Popham, Sophia Popham, and Julia Rendall. Many others have added pieces to the story, whether in letters or conversation: Peter Ackroyd, Anna Anrep, Nicholas Barker, Lorna Beckett of the Rupert Brooke Society, Alan Bell, Justin Brooke, Keith Clements, Sophia Crawford, Jenny Dereham, Helen Duffy, George Gomori, Keith Hale, Dr Tony Harris, Paul Levy, Ann Radford MacEwan, Angus Macindoe, Perry Meisel, Howard Moseley, Lois Olivier, Peggy Packwood, Tristram Popham, David Pye, Mark Ramage, S.P. Rosenbaum, the Laird of Rothiemurchus, John Schroder, Frederick Schroder, Robert Skidelsky, David Steel, and James L. West III. For archival sources, I am specially indebted to Peter Monteith at the Modern Archive, King's College, Cambridge.

Stephane Roumilhac provided a memorable lunch and tour of the Château de Prunoy, Yonne; Mr and Mrs J. Finlinson showed me their home, formerly The Champions, at Limpsfield; Mary Archer invited me to the Old Vicarage, Grantchester. The librarians of Rugby and Bedales, and the housemaster of School Field, Rugby, took me over their ground.

In Tahiti I should thank Mareva Poole at the Mairie de Teravao, Moorea; Tipari Gooding; John Taroanui of the Académie Tahitienne; and my partner in detective work, Colette Colligan.

For ideal surroundings in which to work, I am grateful for residencies at Clare Hall, Cambridge, and Playa Summer Lake, Oregon.

For permission to quote from copyright materials, I am indebted to the Trustees of the Rupert Brooke Estate, Jon Stallworthy, and Andrew Motion.

At Simon Fraser University, Dean John Craig gave financial support to my research. Helen Wussow helped with the Virginia Woolf connection. My agents, Georges Borchardt and Andrew Gordon, kept the book on course with their confidence and sound advice. Jonathan Crago and Joanne Muzak at McGill-Queen's University Press recognised the need for speed.

In these times we are reminded constantly of the nightmare of 1914–18, and especially what it meant for British civilians and combatants alike. All living memory of those times has now gone, and it is disappearing daily for those who came after them in the Second World War. In memoriam Paul Lawton, 4th Battalion, Coldstream Guards, 1944–45.

Vancouver, British Columbia
October 2014

Mrs Brooke with Rupert (left) and Alfred, 1898.
(Modern Archive, King's College, Cambridge)

Hillbrow School, c. 1901. Mr Thomas Eden, the pedophile headmaster, at centre. Rupert in fourth row, second from right; James Strachey in third row, sixth from right. (Hillbrow School)

Rupert at Rugby School in 1903, hair still cut short.
(National Portrait Gallery, London)

Rupert in the Rugby Cadet Corps, 1906, at age eighteen.
The antelope badge belongs to the Royal Warwickshire Regiment.
(National Portrait Gallery)

School Field House, Rugby, autumn 1906 (detail). Denham Russell-Smith, fifth from right in top row. Alfred Brooke, second from right, top. Charles Lascelles may be below Denham to right, with broad collar.
(Rugby School Archives)

Olivier sisters, c. 1912. From left: Margery, Brynhild, Daphne, Noel.
(Private collection)

Brynhild Olivier, 1909. (George Bernard Shaw collection, London School of Economics)

Ka Cox as a Young Fabian – a model for Mary Datchet in
Virginia Woolf's *Night and Day*. (Private collection)

Camp at Clifford Bridge, Dartmoor, summer 1911. From left: Noel Olivier, Maitland Radford, Virginia Woolf in gypsy headscarf, Rupert. (National Portrait Gallery)

Noel Olivier at Rothiemurchus, 1913.
(Private collection)

Justin Brooke in Bedales fashion, around 1914.
(Private collection)

Lytton Strachey, 1913.
(National Portrait Gallery)

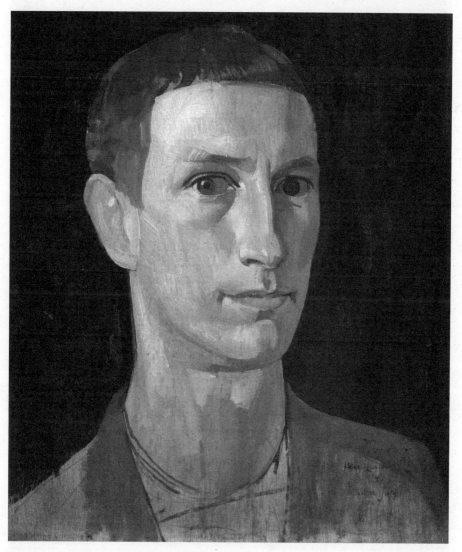

Henry Lamb, self-portrait, 1914.
(National Portrait Gallery)

Jeune Fille au Fox Terrier, 1910. Elisabeth van Rysselberghe, painted by her father. (Private collection)

James Strachey, becoming a Freudian, around 1918.
(National Portrait Gallery)

Cathleen Nesbitt, 1913. (National Portrait Gallery)

Rupert with Duncan Campbell Scott, Ottawa, 1913.
(National Portrait Gallery)

A young friend of Chief Tetuanui, Mataeia, 1914.
Rupert's Mamua? (From Frederick O'Brien, *Mystic Isles
of the South Seas*, 1921)

Group in front of the guesthouse at Mataeia, March 1914. Tataamata at left, Rupert at right. (Modern Archive, King's College, Cambridge)

Fairy Gold, Phyllis Gardner's self-portrait, 1913, now at King's College, Cambridge. (By kind permission of the Provost and Scholars of King's College, Cambridge)

Eileen (Wellesley) Orde, 1921.

Rupert Brooke by Sherrill Schell, 1913.

Olivier sisters on the beach in Cornwall, c. 1914.
From left: Margery, Brynhild, Noel, Daphne.
(Private collection)

Officers of the Hood Battalion, 1914.
Rupert in front of the window.

Fatal Glamour

Introduction

In writing a life, the biographer lives with two questions: Why does this person matter to the world? And, why does this person matter to me? In April 1915, a hundred years before this book, Rupert Brooke was probably more admired and more widely read than any other young Englishman. W.B. Yeats had called him "the handsomest man in England." Beauty might be dismissed as merely the luck of birth, but it added another dimension to the soldier-poet – the quality of glamour. Not only that, but the fatal glamour of the hero who sacrifices himself for the lesser beings who live in his shadow. D.H. Lawrence would write of "the terrible glamour ... of Homer, and of all militarism," and Vera Brittain saw that glamour as the "real problem" for pacifists:

> The causes of war are always falsely represented; its honour is
> dishonest and its glory meretricious, but the challenge to spiritual
> endurance, the intense sharpening of all the senses, the vitalising
> consciousness of common peril for a common end, remain to
> allure ... The glamour may be the mere delirium of fever, which
> as soon as war is over dies out and shows itself for the will-o'-
> the-wisp that it is, but while it lasts no emotion known to man
> seems as yet to have quite the compelling power of this enlarged
> vitality.[1]

No young Englishman could have mattered more when, on Easter Sunday 1915, the Dean of St Paul's read out "The Soldier" from his pulpit. The opening line of the sonnet was "If I should die, think only this of me"; and within three weeks the poet was dead. Early reports said he had died of sunstroke, not far from Troy, as if the god Apollo had struck down his rival. First comes the myth, then the biographer – to despoil the corpse. Rupert was not killed by a god, or even by the enemy, but by a mosquito; and his beautiful exterior covered much ugliness within.

In 1987, the centennial of his birth, I started to uncover Rupert's inner life in *The Neo-Pagans*. The twenty-seven years between that book and *Fatal Glamour* correspond to the number of years that Rupert lived. Over such a span, times will change, and authors will change with them. *The Neo-Pagans* was a work of horizontal biography, focusing on relationships between a small group of friends from 1908 to 1912. I tried to do equal justice to all members of the group, not just to Brooke as their charismatic leader. In any case, the Brooke estate would not allow me to write a comprehensive and sequential biography (they had contracted with someone else for such a work, though he never delivered). In the aftermath of the 1960s, one of my interests was in the utopian ideals of young people who were trying, however fitfully, to build together an Edwardian counterculture. Today, a counterculture is nowhere in sight, and bohemia of any kind seems to have perished. In a world that seems even more threatening than it did in the summer of 1914, what lessons can we draw from the collapse of the European bourgeois order? Our focus necessarily shifts to the forces of disintegration in Britain, and in Europe generally, as the utopian dreams of Edwardian summer were blown away by war and nascent totalitarianism.

Historians approach the Great War with comprehensive ambitions to explain high politics, imperialism, arms races, mass movements, and the like. A biographer who tells the story of a single junior officer has far more modest aims. Still, a personal history has its own value, giving us an inward sense of how and why young England marched away in August 1914. Rupert Brooke (1887–1915) was a creator, but a wayward and difficult personality. He was a poet – in a war that, more than any other since the siege of Troy, has been defined by its poets. And his individual story gains a deeper significance as part of the collective tragedy of Britain's public school elite as infantry subalterns in the Great War. How much was particular to Rupert, how much typical of his class and generation?

Rupert left a huge and revealing mass of private correspondence, and a small body of poetry. George Orwell put his finger on the "Rupert

Brooke problem" when he wrote, "Considered as a poem 'Grantchester' is something worse than worthless, but as an illustration of what the thinking middle-class young of that period *felt* it is a valuable document."[2] But Orwell wrote in ignorance of the document's origins. We now know a great deal about Rupert's emotional history, and how the poem offered a coded solution to the crisis he had lived through in the previous six months. It is an intensely personal document, not just a bundle of public school clichés. Orwell did not look beyond the institutions in which Brooke's life was embedded, to the distinctiveness of his personal history (and Orwell himself was scarcely a "typical" Etonian!).

Orwell also recognised that popular art deserved respect just because it *was* popular, and that the qualities that made it popular were not always obvious. John Lewis-Stempel's *Six Weeks: The Short and Gallant Life of the British Officer in the First World War* has a footnote listing the soldier poets of the Great War. It runs to three and a half pages in double-column. Rupert's poems stood out, even though their sentiments and their form were entirely conventional. He was following in the footsteps of A.E. Housman, and why do lines like these enter into the canon?

> Into my heart an air that kills
> From yon far country blows.

It would be hard for a non-native speaker to grasp the condensed power of such a couplet, where almost all the effect comes not even from Housman's twelve simple words, but just from the order in which he says them. Rupert's voice was lush, rather than minimalist:

> Breathless, we flung us on the windy hill,
>   Laughed in the sun, and kissed the lovely grass.

This may be kitsch, but it found its audience – first because Rupert expressed common feelings, but also because of the words and rhythms in which he expressed them.

After Venus, Mars; and the two poems that set the tone for the early months of the war were Rupert's "The Soldier" and John McCrae's "In Flanders Fields." Both came to be seen as lies; the truth tellers would be Siegfried Sassoon, Wilfred Owen, and their comrades in disillusion. But this is too stark an opposition. The dark poets of 1916–18 were themselves formed by the establishment that had made the war. They were content to use traditional poetic forms, and many subalterns took Rupert's *1914 and Other Poems* into their dugouts at the Somme or Passchendaele. Robert Graves's war poems resembled Rupert's in everything except their content.

Whether to extol the war or to condemn it, almost the only poetic voice to be heard was that coming from the public school. Even at Rupert's centennial, the British system of elites persists, in ways unlike any other country. Whether on the Left or the Right, at Fettes or at Eton, political and cultural power still rests with the 7 percent of the population that is privately educated, and beyond that with the less than 1 percent from the ancient public schools and from Oxbridge. Rupert's battalion of the Royal Naval Division sailed for Gallipoli with about a thousand enlisted men and thirty officers. Of those thirty, seven were in the "Latin Club," who ate together and looked down on their colleagues. One of the seven, Johnnie Dodge, was an American whose prep school had been St Mark's. The other six were all from the nine Clarendon Commission schools: three from Eton, two from Rugby, one from Winchester.

Today, inevitably, there is in England an organisation whose aim is to heal the wounds of "Boarding School Survivors." But I do not judge the public school system (of which I am myself a "survivor") quite so harshly. It was the European system of rival states that was responsible for the Great War, not the schooling of the English upper-middle class. Lewis-Stempel's *Six Weeks* pays tribute to the spectacular bravery, generosity, and self-discipline of the English infantry subalterns, many of whom were not yet twenty-one years old, and for whom school was almost the only world they had known. As the voice of their doomed ideals, Brooke's war sonnets are not "worthless" in Orwell's sense, but have their place in a body of poetry unmatched by any of Britain's other wars. Max Egremont has reminded us that the war poets were not pacifists: they may have hated everything they experienced in the trenches, but still they fought.[3] Brian Bond has gone further in reconsidering the war's "literary myth," arguing that the war was "necessary and successful," and well fought by the British and Allied armies.[4] Bond's judgment implies that Brooke's war poems should not simply be written off as sentimental and misguided. If the war *was* a success, then the spirit revealed in the poems did much to make it so.

The Latin Club may have been an obnoxious little clique, poisonously arrogant and spouting ancient Greek over the dinner table. But integral to their pose was contempt for death. More than contempt, even: an eagerness for it, and five of the seven would be in their graves by 1918. Here, the biography of the individual Rupert Brooke contributes to the great question of why the European war began, and how it unfolded. Whether the initial spark was kindled by chance or by necessity, once the war was under way young men of all countries were desperate to take part in it. Michael Adams has gathered some of the evidence in *The Great Adventure: Male Desire and the Coming of World War I*. Rupert was speaking for innumerable other young men when he compared enlistment to taking the plunge, "like swimmers into cleanness leaping." Nothing less than war could wash away the sins of the previous years of civilian life.

Such sins, real or imaginary, formed part of what Christopher Clark has called a "crisis of masculinity."⁵ The positive side of this crisis was defined by Virginia Woolf as a specifically male propensity for rivalry, aggression, and militarism. But Rupert's trouble was more on the negative side: feelings of guilt and failure that could only be purged through comradeship and violence. Whatever the broad causes of male eagerness for war, the special value of Rupert's case is that we know more about his inner life before 1914 than just about any other Englishman. Endowed with the sublime egotism of a poet, Rupert could distill his feelings into a few memorable lines, or let them overflow into the hundreds of thousands of words of his intimate letters. These letters contain every conceivable mood: euphoria, nervous exhaustion, romantic idealisation, misogyny, socialist universalism, crude chauvinism. If Rupert had any kind of coherent self, it was assembled from radically incongruous parts.

That incongruity is particularly evident in Rupert's sexual fluidity, where bisexuality is only the beginning of his curious history. A beautiful woman would be left in no doubt about how she was valued, and what was expected of her. For a beautiful man, his looks were more likely to produce confusion, and even be felt as a stigma. A pretty boy was nice enough, but could there be a pretty man? This was a good part of Rupert's troubles, and the contrast between his career and Bloomsbury values is striking. Bloomsbury accepted the variability in people's dispositions, expressed in varying objects of desire and sexual acts.

Rupert had a continuous gay life, relatively consistent and satisfying, and rooted in public school homoeroticism. In his twenties, he embarked on a series of turbulent affairs with women. Only two of these affairs – in Tahiti, on the other side of the world – ran smoothly. For most women Rupert was a disastrous lover: unreliable, misogynist, without respect or empathy. For him, as for many young men like him, going to war was a welcome escape from heterosexual obligations. It becomes painfully clear from Rupert's letters that he was not afraid of death, but was afraid of marriage.

We may admire the relentless hedonism of Duncan Grant, or the rationality of Lytton Strachey, but Rupert's case is more intriguing because it was so erratic. By today's standards, he behaved shamefully in his relations with women. Part of the time, this behaviour was a deliberate revolt against the Bloomsbury code of relationships (which has become the dominant code for the Western middle class of today). In his early twenties, Rupert seemed to be pioneering a new and enlightened post-Victorian way of life. His neo-pagan and Fabian friends were "children of the sun," their eyes turned to a radiant future. Then came the crack-up of 1912, which gave birth to the nasty Rupert: blimpish, misogynist, and anti-Semitic. This can be seen as a reversion to public school orthodoxy, or as a psychic break, in which Rupert needed to repudiate parts of himself that he could no longer tolerate. Like a bar-stool drunk, he needed someone to quarrel with – Bloomsbury in this case – whether or not they wanted to quarrel with him. In 1915 they would mourn his death, despite his hateful campaign against them.

If Bloomsbury was ready to make its peace with Rupert, his biographers have not always been so forgiving. As we learn more about our subjects, do we end up liking them, or despising them? In *Jacob's Room*, Virginia Woolf tried to understand the young men of her class who sacrificed themselves in Flanders or Gallipoli. She had no sympathy for any crisis of masculinity that might be resolved by the war. Yet she was deeply curious about the separate, hidden lives of her male friends. After *Jacob's Room* she turned, in *Mrs Dalloway*, to the post-traumatic injuries of those who survived.[6]

We can say that Rupert's bad behaviour to women and foreigners was just a return to what was typical of his class. The fault then lies with the public school system, and Rupert can even be seen as a victim of it. Yet a biography is hardly worth writing without an assumption of its subject's personal accountability. In the Second World War there was a general system of occupation in France, but individual Frenchmen responded to German rule in radically different ways. Rupert made his own choices, and there is an immense body of evidence about why he made them. We are well placed to understand him, if not to pardon him. Further, the understanding can be applied on many different levels, from national attitudes towards Germany to ideas of mental illness that were applied to his 1912 breakdown. A biography should present its evidence to its readers for them to judge, rather than delivering an already determined verdict.

Evidence, however, needs to be summed up, into a consistent pattern of action and character. For Rupert, trying to reach that consistency turned out to be a dangerous task. Before 1911 he managed his emotional life by dividing it into separate compartments, keeping his various friends and lovers in the dark about what he was up to with others. His gay circle was shielded from his heterosexual partners (who were also kept ignorant of each other). Politics was another distinct sphere of action. In the background, always, was his formidable mother: at once the most important person in his life, and the one who knew least about his intimate affairs.

During 1911 Rupert could no longer keep intact the barriers between his different worlds, and the result was the emotional breakdown of the first half of 1912. This coincided with the wreck of the *Titanic* (15 April 1912), and happened for a similar reason: water began to spill over the top of the ship's watertight compartments, flooding from one to the next until the ship went down. Rupert recovered by cutting troublesome people out of his life, and by constructing a simpler and coarser identity. Thus stripped of the past – cleansed, as he saw it – he was happy to merge his fate with that of the Hood Battalion and to write to Ka Cox his own epitaph: "It's a good thing I die."

1

Rugby
August 1887–September 1906

The child may be father to the man, but most of the time the child's inner life is beyond a biographer's reach. We know the social class and the institution that Rupert Brooke was born into; we know something of his parents and their rather odd marriage. Rupert wrote letters and school exercises from an early age, but he was writing to satisfy someone else's requirements. For his whole life he would write compulsively yet hardly ever, it seems, straight from the heart. Like an actor, he would put on a mask – many masks – to hide his true face. As he pours out his soul in a flood of letters, some of them thousands of word long, something crucial is always held back; or else what he says to one doesn't fit with what he says to another.

One of the things that Rupert almost never wrote about was his childhood. He does mention a few things that happened when he was at school, including his clandestine love affairs. But we are never told how it felt to be small, what he cared about or feared, which grown-ups he loved and which he disliked. There seems to be a kind of defensive amnesia in this silence about his early years. So what might Rupert have been defending against? We know that the baby sister who came before him died, that his mother longed for another girl and resented Rupert when he came along instead. He was made aware that he was the wrong sex, and perhaps should not be there at all. He formed a lifelong habit of appeasing his mother, trying to satisfy whatever expectations she had for him, and giving her as much of his company as he could spare. At the same time, he had a secret life of rebellion against "The Ranee," as he called her – that is, the oriental despot who ruled over her husband and three sons at School Field house, Rugby School.[1]

Rupert's father, William Parker Brooke, was born in 1850. The son of a parson, he had taken a First in Classics at King's College, Cambridge, and been elected to a fellowship. But no one became rich as a fellow, so Brooke shortly left to teach for six years at Fettes, near Edinburgh. In 1879 he married Ruth Cotterill, who was a matron in one of the houses and the sister of a fellow teacher. She was more handsome than pretty, and was two years older than her husband (though he may not have known this). She could certainly take over the social duties that her shy, scholarly husband found hard to manage. But she was also domineering and fiercely moralistic, as one might expect of a clergyman's daughter and a niece of the bishop of Edinburgh. Parker Brooke, who was only five foot three, soon acquired a look of hiding behind his moustache; nor was it hard to see from whom he was hiding.

Fettes was a recently founded offshoot of Rugby, so it was a step up the ladder for Brooke to move to the parent school in 1880. Once established there, he never tried to rise further. He taught at Rugby for thirty years, gaining fame for such exploits as giving marks from zero downwards, or bringing his dog to class and making it sit in the wastepaper basket. He had a habit of nervously fiddling with keys in his trouser pocket while teaching. His pupils unkindly suspected him of fiddling with something else; they gave him the nickname of "Tooler," and "Ma Tooler" for his wife. True or not, the story went round that Mrs Brooke sent her husband out after dark to gather horse droppings for her garden.

The hunt for droppings was hardly necessary because public school masters were very well paid in Victorian times. The headmaster of Rugby earned nearly £3,000 per year in 1862; a senior housemaster about £1,600.[2] Parker Brooke also had some inherited capital, so he was comfortably off from the beginning of his career. In 1891 he became housemaster of School Field. This was a crucial promotion, since he could now pad out his salary with a handsome profit on the food and accommodation supplied to the fifty boys in his house. Mrs Brooke now became a combination of matron, lodging-house keeper, and substitute mother to the boys. She kept one sharp eye on their morals and the other, equally sharp, on the cost of their food.

Rupert was a product of Rugby School, in every sense of the word. His father had been there for seven years when Rupert was born on 3 August 1887. He was the second of his parents' three sons, after Richard and before Alfred. His first name came from the Cavalier general Prince Rupert, whom his father admired. His middle name, Chawner, came from one of his mother's ancestors who had been a fanatical Roundhead. The combination proved to be a good index of his divided soul – long hair on the outside, puritan disposition within. As Rupert grew up, Mrs Brooke was frightened by his delicate health. She was reluctant to let him get too far out of sight and when he was ten sent him to a prep school, Hillbrow, that was only a hundred yards down the road.

Hillbrow

Rupert started at Hillbrow in the autumn of 1897. His brother Richard was already a pupil there, and Alfred would follow in due course. Such schools were a Victorian invention – Hillbrow was founded in 1859 – designed to help the upper-middle class to consolidate their position in a changing social order. They took in boys at an earlier, more vulnerable age than the public schools, and had even greater influence in shaping their characters. Prep schools were good at getting boys ready for the battle of life, which satisfied the parents who paid through the nose for sending them there. But not every boy was pleased with his treatment and one of them, George Orwell, did more than anyone else to give them a bad name. He called them "those (on the whole) nasty little schools at which small boys are prepared for the public school entrance examination. Incidentally these schools with their money-grubbing proprietors and their staffs of underpaid hacks, are responsible for a lot of the harm that it is usual to blame on the public schools. A majority of middle-class boys have their minds permanently lamed by them before they are thirteen years old."[3]

Still, neither Orwell himself nor his schoolmate Cyril Connolly were permanently lamed by "Flip" and "Sambo," the husband and wife proprietors of St Cyprian's. At Hillbrow three of Rupert's near-contemporaries became notable writers or artists: James Strachey, Duncan Grant, and Robert Graves. Rupert was more of a conformist than those three, though he was a real poet and had no trouble thinking for himself. Nonetheless, the English prep school system was designed to "make men" of a particular kind, and with Rupert it largely succeeded.

In his critique of St Cyprian's, Orwell focused on money and the snobbery that went with it. The Northcote-Trevelyan Report of 1854 proposed that entry into the upper ranks of the civil service should be by competitive examination. To join the administrative elite (which was still very small) now required being stuffed with knowledge at a public school. That knowledge was primarily of Latin and classical Greek, starting from about the age of ten. Prep schools had to grind into their boys enough acquaintance with ancient languages to prepare them for the more intensive grinding when they continued to public school. This was a labour-intensive process for which the schools charged very high fees. When Orwell entered St Cyprian's in 1911, the fees were £180 per year, nearly twice the income of a skilled worker.[4] Parents accepted this as the price of getting their sons into a public school, and from there into universities and professions.

On a straightforward economic calculus, prep school fees were an investment that was expected to pay off in future income and social status. Northcote and Trevelyan had taken a wider view, though. They wanted to entrust Britain's future to a meritocratic elite, rather than to a corrupt aristocracy and its hangers-on. This went further than just requiring intelligence and administrative skill in the country's rulers. A consultant to the report was Benjamin Jowett, the great Platonist and future master of Balliol. His dream was to create something like a modern corps of guardians, as described in the *Republic*. Boarding schools would separate boys from their families to make them into a disciplined and unselfish ruling class. Cutting them off from female influence was part of the design (Jowett spent his entire adult life at Balliol, and never married).[5]

Like the guardians, prep and public school boys lived in something equivalent to barracks. They were under discipline every hour of the day; they lived in fear of their masters and older boys; they had drill sergeants to give them military values. They had to learn how to endure, without the physical or emotional comforts of home. Today, we have organisations like "Boarding School Survivors," who condemn the system as institutional child abuse, producing adults with lifelong post-traumatic damage. Therapist Nick Duffell has described a "strategic survival personality," the result of boarders "cutting off their feelings and constructing a defensively organised self that severely limits their later lives."[6]

Even if we agree with Duffell, we have to recognise two kinds of exceptions. Some boys, Rupert Brooke among them, believed that their school days were indeed the happiest days of their lives. Rupert told his beloved, Noel Olivier, that she should read St John Lucas's *The First Round* "if you want to know what boys feel like and are like."[7] The hero is much happier at school than when he is home with his overbearing father. Other boys become creative rebels, like Orwell or Graves, though they may still retain large parts of the public school character. And family life has its own kinds of damage, so that a child might find at school a refuge from worse things at home.

It remains moot who Rupert might have become if the public school system had not held him so firmly in its grip. That grip may have been loosened by his starting Hillbrow as a day boy. But by April 1901, the census records him as a boarder. Probably his parents wanted him to have some experience of boarding before he entered Rugby in the autumn of that year (though he would be living in their own house). It is possible that Rupert himself wanted to board because day boys, at most schools, were looked down on. By the age of thirteen, then, Rupert was entirely in the hands of Thomas Bainbridge Eden, headmaster of Hillbrow, and of his wife Horatia Katherine, who was the power behind the throne.

Who were the Edens, and what kind of distinctive atmosphere did they create at Hillbrow? Mr Eden was forty-one in 1897, when Rupert arrived at the school. He was an Oxford graduate who had gone to Rugby as a boy, and Hillbrow's first priority was to be a feeder school for its greater neighbour. Eden had been married for seven years to Katherine Gatty, who was eleven years older than him. They had no children. Their marriage was partly one of convenience, because a schoolmaster was greatly helped by having a wife to share his duties, especially if he aspired to be a head of house. The Eden marriage seems to have had a good deal in common with that of the Brookes. Both wives were the daughters of clergymen, and treated their younger husbands with condescension, verging on contempt. Eden was a magistrate, but it was his wife who wielded the gavel. Mr Eden and Mr Brooke even looked alike, with bristling moustaches under receding foreheads above and receding chins below.

James Strachey remembered Mrs Eden as "an embittered martinet who intimidated her husband and the four assistant masters quite as much as the boys."[8] Her sister Juliana Ewing was a successful writer of children's books, and her mother had founded *Aunt Judy's Magazine*, the first magazine for children. Katherine became the editor when her mother died, giving it up before she married Mr Eden. He was "apologetic and easy-going," according to Strachey. "Nothing that the boys could perpetrate was so vexing to Mrs Eden as her husband's mildness of temper."[9] Orwell portrayed Mrs Wilkes as a similar termagant in "Such, Such Were the Joys," though she could also be seductive with her favourites.

Hillbrow inflicted on Rupert the usual discomforts of drafty corridors and dubious food; but the emotional discomforts had a more lasting effect. Being bullied by Mrs Eden probably contributed to his later misogyny, and his conviction that if he married he would expect to be the absolute ruler of his household.[10] Yet he also absorbed the double standard that men were weak and willful, women the guardians of proper behaviour. His nickname at Hillbrow was "the Oyster"; he was a silent observer of the schoolboy world, but not a heretic or a rebel. He emerged from his shell enough to pass his exams with credit and excel on the playing field. When Rupert was thirteen, at the end of his Hillbrow career, he wrote in an album that his ambition was "to be top of the tree in everything," and that his idea of misery was "Ignorance, poverty, *obscurity*."[11] The twig was bent, and the tree would grow accordingly.

The great consolation of school life was friendship, all the more intense for the cutting off of family ties. Rupert's great chum for his first two years at Hillbrow was James Strachey, younger brother of Lytton. James left to go to St Paul's. He and Rupert were both clever, a bit out of the common run, and inclined to make fun of school routines. At this time Rupert was still chubby-faced and wore his hair cut straight across in a fringe. James summed him up as "friendly and amusing but as yet decidedly not glamorous."[12] Six years later, at Cambridge, things changed. Rupert had become startlingly good-looking; James fell abjectly in love with him, but had to settle for only friendship in return. They broke off irrevocably in 1912, when Rupert declared war on everyone and everything connected to Bloomsbury. Between 1905 and 1912, though, Rupert was closer to James than to anyone else. The deep structure of his character was to be a poser and a manipulator, without any firm sense of identity. James was the only person for whom he was willing to lay all his emotional cards on the table.

The intense bond between Rupert and James was really a design feature of the prep school system. Removing a boy from his family did not
remove his need for affection; it just displaced it onto others who were
suffering in the same way. Orwell claimed that at St Cyprian's he was
"in an almost sexless state, which is normal, or at least common, in boys
of that age."[13] This may have been the case if puberty did not begin until
age thirteen, just when boys were going on to a public school. Still, prep
school boys certainly had intense friendships that were precursors to a
later gay identification. At Hillbrow this was true of all four sensitive
and artistic boys with whom we are concerned: Brooke, Strachey, Grant,
and Graves. The first three all became actively, though not exclusively
gay as adults. Graves fell in love with other boys or young men, but felt
it wrong to give his love a physical expression. He believed that all-male
schooling was bound to have this effect: "In English preparatory and
public schools romance is necessarily homosexual. The opposite sex is
despised and treated as something obscene. Many boys never recover
from this perversion. For every one born homosexual, at least ten permanent pseudo-homosexuals are made by the public school system: nine
of these ten as honourably chaste and sentimental as I was."[14]

If sexuality remained latent for Rupert at Hillbrow, it was not so for
its headmaster, Mr Eden. Graves arrived at the school around the time
that Rupert was going on from Rugby to Cambridge. He learned that
"there was a secret about the headmaster which some of the older boys
shared – a somehow sinister secret."[15] Eden, it turned out, was in the
habit of fondling his favorite pupils when they were having their baths.
One day in 1906 or 1907, Eden "came into class beating his head with
his fists and moaning, 'Would to God I hadn't done it! Would to God I
hadn't done it!'"[16] He fled to Liverpool where, according to Duncan
Grant, Rupert "tracked him down; told him he must *not* be in this state
of mind; he must go back to the school, pack up quietly and leave in decent order. Rupert saved him."[17]

Why would Rupert, a second-year student at Cambridge, come forward to save Mr Eden from disgrace and possible arrest? If his secret
was known by the older boys, he must have been following his pedophile
inclinations for some years. He broke down in public, one assumes, because some boy told his parents, or another teacher, what had been going
on. Either Rupert wanted to show loyalty to his former teacher and family friend, or he did not see that Eden had done anything particularly

wrong. Had Rupert himself been one of Eden's targets? Whatever his motives, he did his bit to make sure that Eden's misdemeanors would be hushed up, rather than punished. By the 1911 census, Eden was living in West Hampstead with his wife and a servant, and describing himself as a "Retired Tutor." He lived to be eighty-eight, dying in 1944.

The Old School

Thomas Arnold was headmaster of Rugby School from 1828 to his death in 1842. When he came to Rugby it was not the most aristocratic or ancient or intellectually distinguished of the great public schools, but Arnold turned it into by far the most ideological one.[18] Largely because of Arnold, secondary schooling is a more divisive social issue in Britain than in any other country. Thanks to him, too, Cyril Connolly could become famous for his "Theory of Permanent Adolescence": "the greater part of the ruling class remains adolescent, school-minded, self-conscious, cowardly, sentimental, and in the last analysis homosexual."[19] For many middle-class Englishmen, Connolly argued, school is such an intense experience that everything that happens afterwards is an anticlimax.

Like the rest of Lytton Strachey's "Eminent Victorians," Thomas Arnold was a visionary, a gifted organiser, and a bit of a crank. As a young man he looked on his country and saw "a mass of evil a thousand times worse than all the idolatry of India."[20] The remedy for this terrible state was, to him, obvious. Anglicanism must become the living religion of everyone living in England. This was no small task, but in accepting the headmastership of Rugby, Arnold felt that he was tackling a manageable piece of it. A genuinely Christian school could be the model for a future Christian state, and the nursery for those who could build it. His first step was to clear the ground. The morals of Rugby were those of the country squires who sent their sons there; as Arnold saw it, no morals at all, mere paganism and disorder. "Evil being unavoidable," he proclaimed, "we are not a jail to keep it in, but a place of education where we must cast it out to prevent the taint from spreading." A storm of floggings and expulsions soon put Evil to flight. Now Arnold could set up his own ideals: "first religious and moral principle; secondly gentlemanly conduct; and thirdly intellectual ability."[21] He broke with public school tradition by making himself the school chaplain. Rugby would now be governed by a single, awesome head: king, prime minister, and acrchbishop of Canterbury rolled into one.

In 1835 Arnold's future biographer, A.P. Stanley, wrote an article for the *Rugby Magazine* called "School a Little World." A public school was "not only a place where boys are receiving knowledge from masters," he argued, "but a place also where they form a complete society among themselves – a society in its essential points similar, and therefore preparatory, to the society of men ... The schoolhouse, the chapel, and the playground, forming as they do one united group, become a tangible focus, in which the whole of our school existence is, as it were, symbolically consecrated."[22] School life would become a sacred drama, in which the boys' life became one anxious struggle after another: to pass the exam, to resist evil, to win the game.

Arnold deliberately narrowed the range of age and class in his school. Though ancient statutes required Rugby to educate a certain number of boys from the town, he found ways to keep out the sons of tradesmen and farmers. But he also discouraged the aristocracy from sending their sons, fearing that these boys would be too arrogant and dissipated to bend to his yoke. His students would be drilled to become the future governors, warriors, and thinkers of Britain. Girls, of course, would continue to be excluded, as they were from all the other Victorian public schools. In the old days, schoolboys could roam freely in the town, and some even kept whores. The reformed schools, following Arnold's example, cut off their students from almost all feminine influence. At home there were mothers, sisters, and domestic servants – all of them posing threats to a boy's "manliness." At school, only the housemaster's wife would give the boys any female affection or homely comfort.

Arnold's "little world" was actually far more single-minded, ideological, and ascetic than the world outside its gates. The main entrance to Rugby School – a little doorway set into a gate at the top of the town's bustling High Street – recalls the scriptural eye of the needle. After one passes through the School House quadrangle, the perspective opens out on "The Close," with its great sweep of rugby pitches. On them the ritual contests of public school life are still re-enacted in games of rugby and cricket. School sports in the Victorian era became even more codified and symbolic than the pursuits from which they derived: hunting and warfare. When history called, the step from playing fields to Flanders fields had been taken already in imagination.

If he had been no more than a beady-eyed autocrat, Arnold would never have had so wide an influence. But his nature also had its gentler side, when he turned to his pupils a face of warmth, understanding, and Christian love. This side of him appears in the worshipful portrait of "The Doctor" in Thomas Hughes's *Tom Brown's Schooldays*. A cynic might point out that successful dictators are good at displaying affection for small children and dogs. In any case, two different paths led from his work. One was the path of unthinking submission to the nation's cause. It inspired the "service classes" that ran the British Empire and it culminated in the mass sacrifice of the infantry subalterns of the Great War. The other way pushed the Victorian ethic of improvement to its utopian limit; it led to sexual reform, Fabian socialism, the "simple life," and other attempts to build the New Jerusalem in Britain. The straight road to Waterloo and the crooked road to Wigan Pier began, after all, from the same place – the playing fields of Eton.

School Field

When Rupert entered Rugby School he was assigned to School Field, his father's house. From having been a boarder at Hillbrow, he now went to school by staying at home, a peculiar and anxious situation. His mother probably was equally anxious, about his physical and moral health. She could also save the cost of his lodging in some other house. He was one of the fifty boys who lived at School Field, and one of the family; he had to conceal from his friends how he felt about his parents, and conceal from his parents what his friends felt about them. Leading two lives under the same roof, his personality developed along two separate lines. One Rupert was a British stereotype: a model student who also got into the rugby First XV and the cricket XI. He applied himself to the classics and kept up a facade of purity for his puritan mother. The other Rupert belonged to the upstairs dormitory, a world that seethed with contempt for his parents, and with erotic intrigue.

Rupert needed a safety valve from the stress of life under his parents' roof. There were two gay men who lived in Rugby, in part so that they could cultivate friendships with boys at the school. One was St John Lucas, a poet, novelist, and aesthete who was eight years older than Rupert. Their friendship was a gesture of revolt against public school philistinism, and it gave Rupert affection and approval that were not supplied by his parents. Lucas introduced him to Wilde, Dowson, and Baudelaire. Rupert duly produced poems with titles like "Lost Lilies" and an abortive novel whose hero, Chrysophase Tiberius Amaranth, sits in a "small pale green room" smoking opium-flavoured cigarettes. Another admirer of Rupert's was Arthur Eckersley, a playwright and journalist who lived in Rugby. He was twelve years older than Rupert, and would be remembered as "a lover of Youth," but "always reserving first place for his mother."[23] In the summer of 1907, he spent three weeks with Rupert at Bournemouth, coaching him after his mediocre results in first-year Cambridge exams.

From the age of sixteen until his death, Rupert was continually under the protection of an older man who encouraged his writing but also idolised him for his looks. In no case, so far as we can tell, did these relationships progress to any sexual intimacy. It would be trite to say that Rupert needed a substitute for his actual father, weak and defeated as he was. Perhaps he just liked being under an older man's wing in a quasi-domestic relationship, and we need look no further than that. Others have looked further, of course, and John Lehmann has made the case in detail that repressed homosexuality was at the root of Rupert's later emotional problems.[24] His case was more complex than that. Rupert's sexual identity emerged, like everyone's, from the family nexus. His domineering mother had wanted him to be a girl. After he reached puberty, she did her best to drive away any young women who seemed to threaten her hold over her beautiful boy. His father was too ineffectual to be an example of manliness for his sons. Rupert did become intimate with a series of older men – St John Lucas, Arthur Eckersley, Charles Sayle, Eddie Marsh – all of whom were gay or in the closet. But there is still no simple answer to the question "was Rupert gay?" Graves and Connolly believed that homosexuality at the public schools and Oxbridge was situational, the natural consequence of segregating young males with no access to women. This made it just a way station on the path to sexual maturity. Jacques Raverat told Virginia Woolf that homosexuality was quite natural up to the age of twenty, after which young men should leave it behind in order to marry and have children. An opposing view sees homosexuality as, for those who choose it, intrinsic to personal identity. It remains a foundation stone of the gay self, even if social pressure makes individuals conform to heterosexual norms.

Both kinds of arguments now need to be reconsidered, especially for the years leading up to 1914. Eve Kosofsky Sedgwick, Richard Dellamora, and others have shifted the focus from sexual behaviour to masculine identity. Public school homosexuality is now placed on a continuum extending from sodomy to ideal and intimate friendship. All such attachments served to consolidate homosocial power within the interlocking hierarchies of gender and class. Paradoxically, though, this power had a masochistic tinge, in the sense of resting on discipline and self-denial rather than on sensual fulfillment. Adrian Caesar argues that "the idealism inculcated by the English public schools, which had its basis in Christianity, gave rise to a code of 'manliness' immediately before the First World War which actively encouraged and rejoiced in pain."[25] Becoming a man meant learning to hold back your emotions; feelings were dangerous and were suitable only for those lesser beings, women.

In the nineteenth century, Sedgwick argues, there was no "association of a particular personal style with the genital activities now thought of as 'homosexual.'"[26] Her point is confirmed by Virginia Woolf, writing in 1925 about the younger generation of gay men: "I can't help finding it mildly foolish; though I have no particular reason. For one thing, all the young men tend to the pretty and ladylike, for some reason, at the moment. They paint and powder, which wasn't the style in our day at Cambridge."[27] Rupert Brooke greatly admired Oscar Wilde but never adopted any of his mannerisms (other than on paper). When he launched his vendetta against Bloomsbury, from 1912 on, he abused the Stracheys and their ilk as "eunuchs." He despised them for their lack of manly assertiveness and their ivory-tower intellectualising, not for any feminine affectations.

Studies of Bloomsbury and of the Cambridge Apostles have made us familiar with the terms "Higher Sodomy" and "Lower Sodomy" (though Strachey's biographer Michael Holroyd never specified what physical acts went with each). The Higher Sodomy was a sequel to what was called, in *Tom Brown at Oxford*, "sentimental friendship." At Rugby, Tom and East have deep affection for each other. They are the same age, study and play together, and protect weaker boys against bullies. They know about sex between boys but will have nothing to do with it, since there can be no "true manliness without purity." Tennyson celebrated his sentimental friendship with Hallam in *In Memoriam*. It might be expressed

through the conventions of heterosexual romantic love, or the pederasty
of classical Greece. But sentimental friendship was affectionate and idealistic rather than sexual, and it posed no obstacle to marriage and par-
enthood after leaving school or university.

Today, the enlightened view is that love, whether homo- or heterosexual, should be free to progress unhindered to mutual sexual fulfillment. Not so for Thomas Arnold. "None can pass through a large
school," he wrote, "without being pretty intimately acquainted with vice;
and few, alas! very few, without tasting too largely of that poisoned
bowl."[28] What Arnold calls vice is a predictable result of public schools
being gender-segregated total institutions. Hierarchy may be an instinctual need, part of our primate inheritance. Still, public schools made hierarchy a universal rule, and took it to extraordinary lengths. Every boy
in the school had a place on the ladder of status, marking them as superior to those below and inferior to those above. Their school career was
one long climb up the ladder; at the same time they had to engage in horizontal struggle in the classroom or playing field – against their peers,
against other houses, and against rival schools.

Everyone understood that hierarchy was founded on violence. When
you entered the school, you expected to be beaten; eventually, you would
gain the right to beat those below you. That was just the official violence; an unofficial realm started with bullying and might extend to torture, such as roasting a boy in front of a fire in *Tom Brown's Schooldays*.
The masters condemned bullying but in practice they condoned it because they upheld the code of silence whereby victims should never inform on their tormentors. Bullying had its uses, too: it hardened the boys,
teaching them the martial virtues that their country would need, once
they had left school.

Three of the four great European powers – Germany, France, Russia
– had conscription and large professional armies. The British officer
corps was tiny by Continental standards: before 1914, only about 170
candidates entered the Royal Military Academy at Sandhurst each year.
In time of war, mass expansion had to come from the public schools
where, in effect, every boy had acquired a military disposition by the
time he left school, along with some basic military training in the Cadet
Corps. The school culture made it a second nature to obey or to give orders, according to one's place on the ladder. And the system worked, producing the fantastic bravery and self-sacrifice of the amateur subalterns

in the Great War. Only two British officers were executed for desertion in 1914–18.[29] Unlike other armies, the first duty of a British officer was to look after the welfare of his men. His second was to lead from the front, so that officers died at twice the rate of the rank and file. Rupert made light of it, but he undertook the usual military apprenticeship in the Rugby Cadet Corps.

If the public schools deserve admiration for their war record, their sexual system is more problematic. For Alisdare Hickson, their besetting sin has been institutional homophobia – the complex web of rules and physical barriers directed against the "menace" of schoolboy homosexuality. Official discourse glorified "purity" and warned fiercely against "vice." Rupert's Rugby headmaster, Herbert James, allegedly told his boys that "If you touch it, it will fall off."[30] Promiscuous friendship was a danger: boys were not supposed to be friends with anyone outside their house, nor with any boys older or younger than themselves. But the danger could not, in practice, be controlled. Sexual hierarchy was stronger than all official attempts to deny it. *Tom Brown's Schooldays* describes the "small friend system," "the miserable little pretty white-handed, curly-headed boys, petted and pampered by some of the big fellows, who ... did all they could to spoil them for everything in this world and the next." The painter Simeon Solomon saw in this a paradise of beauty and love, presided over by an angel. Tom Brown will have none of it. Such boys, he says, are the "Worst sort we breed ... Thank goodness, no big fellow ever took to petting me."[31]

Some time after he arrived at Rugby School, when he was about fifteen or sixteen, Rupert's face lost its boyishness and people became conscious of him as an astonishingly handsome young man. This was not just an individual quality; he also stood out as an example of the ideal public school type. Rupert took advantage of his looks, naturally, but they also made him uneasy. Part of this may have been the fear, common in beautiful people, that they are only admired for their superficial gifts, or that they don't really deserve to be worshipped. More importantly, Rupert found it hard to respond when others felt affection for him. With women this might go further, stirring up in Rupert a positive disgust at the emotions some besotted woman might be sending his way.

There is no evidence of Rupert having been an older boy's pet, though he must have had admirers when he was a pretty boy just entering the school at fourteen. He had a sentimental friend in Hugh Russell-Smith, who was his own age, and at least three known passions for younger boys. The first was in the beginning of 1906, when Rupert was eighteen. Michael Sadler was a year younger and in another house. He set the ball rolling by telling the school photographer that he wanted to buy a photograph of Rupert. This required Rupert's permission, and he identified his admirer as a boy with "the form of a Greek God, the face of Hyacinthus, the mouth of Antinous, eyes like a sunset, a smile like dawn ... It appears that the madman worships me at a pale distance: which is embarrassing but purple."[32] Living in a purple style was very much Rupert's ambition at this point. The original Antinous was a Greek boy beloved by the Emperor Hadrian, who was thirty-five years older. Antinous drowned in the Nile when he was eighteen, and his beauty inspired many posthumous statues.

At first Rupert could do no more than make eyes at Sadler in Chapel, but in such affairs it was the image that counted. "It is my obvious duty," Rupert wrote, "to live the aesthetic life I preach, and break the laws I loathe." By the end of March the two boys were exchanging letters, with Rupert doing his utmost to put Pater and Wilde in the shade: "The Greek gods lived that you might be likened to them ... the fragrance of your face is myrrh and incense before the pale altar of Beauty." And so on. "How much I am in earnest," Rupert reported, " – or how much he is – I really can't say."[33] On the surface, Rupert was an entirely conventional and successful public school boy. His affair with Antinous was designed to prove that he was something more, a boy who was playing his part in a great myth: "I have discovered whither the Greek gods went, when they left Olympus ... They came to the English public schools. I have seen them often, young unconscious deities in flannel, running swiftly over the grass. Apollo is here, divinely cruel, and Dionysus, who maddens by his presence. Even Jove, lewd and bearded as of old, is not absent."[34]

In such letters, Rupert likes to go too far, and then be laughed at for his posturing. But so much effort goes into the joke that he no longer seems to know the difference between his showing off and his real feelings. Long before he met Sadler, he was writing poems about despair, doomed love, "red mournful Roses." He tried to get his beloved to respond in kind to his "odorous and jewelled phrases," but all he got from Sadler in return was "Sunday is very dull now that you are not in Chapel."[35] Antinous failed to live up to his name. Once the affair was over, it was immortalised in fashionably homoerotic love poems ("My only god ... dreams of men and men's desire"), seasoned with portentous hints of outlaw status ("I dared the old abysmal curse"). If Rupert was in love, he was also well aware of what being in love required of him: "You wonder how much of my affaire is true. So do I. (So, no doubt, does he!) It does not do to inquire too closely. It is now very pleasant. Some day perhaps we shall grow old and 'wise,' and forget. But now we are young, and he is very beautiful. And it is spring. Even if it were only a romantic comedy, a fiction, who cares? Youth is stranger than fiction."[36]

Probably the "affaire" went no further than smouldering glances and the occasional kiss. Rupert always had to watch out for his mother, as he would tell Ka Cox (two weeks after he had gone to bed with her for the first time), "'Katharine Cox seems,' she almost beamed, 'to go *everywhere.*' 'Oh, yes,' I agreed: and then we were fairly launched on you. I felt the red creep slowly up – Damn! It's just as it always was; even from the time when the holiday mention, at lunch, of the boy of the moment, in the House (with apologies, dear!) left me the level red of this blotting-paper, and crying with silent wrath."[37] There was no chance at the school of any obviously flamboyant carrying-on without Mrs Brooke seeing it or hearing about it. Rupert's secret life was mainly confined to letters, or an occasional country walk with his beloved.

The Sadler affair ended in July 1906. It must have been Sadler who broke it off, though they had to part in any case. Sadler was going to Oxford, Rupert to Cambridge. His heart was "slightly fractured, or at least strained," and Rupert could only write a poem imagining that they would meet again when both were old and grey:

Some day I shall rise and leave my friends
And seek you again through the world's far ends,
You whom I found so fair,
(Touch of your hands and smell of your hair!)
My only God in the days that were![38]

Rupert consoled himself by staying for ten days with the Russell-Smith boys at Brockenhurst, in the New Forest. "I forgot my weariness for a time," he told his classmate Geoffrey Keynes, "in assuming the part of cheerful imbecility. I played it so well that for a time I deceived myself too." His letter of thanks to Mrs Russell-Smith had a private joke: "I loved it all ... and especially one of the hammocks – the one further from the house. Please give my love to it – a delightful hammock!" It was delightful because, as Rupert told James Strachey, Denham Russell-Smith "had often taken me out to the hammock, after dinner, to lie entwined there."[39] Larking around in the forest and on the tennis court by day, snuggling in the hammock by night. Rupert and Denham had been fondling each other in the dorm at School Field for some time, perhaps going as far as mutual masturbation. But it was never a romantic affair like the one with Sadler, and, when he went to Brockenhurst, Rupert had already fallen in love again with another boy in his house, Edwin Charles Lascelles. Denham would not come back into Rupert's life, and his bed, until three years later.

That affair had begun in the spring of 1906. Lascelles was just sixteen, three years younger than Rupert, and had been at Rugby for two years. He had aristocratic connections, to the earls of Harewood, but he left Rugby early and made no great mark in later life. He got some small parts on the London stage from 1911 onwards, but never established himself as a professional actor.[40] During the war, Lascelles was commissioned in the Royal Army Service Corps, a relatively safe berth. Afterwards, he seems to have lived quietly on a private income, in a cottage at Drewsteignton, Devon. He never married, and when he died in 1950 most of his money went to his housekeeper and to the RSPCA. Rupert kept a photo of Lascelles in his room at Cambridge, and continued to see him in later years. He seems to have been more seriously in love with Lascelles than with either Michael Sadler or Denham Russell-Smith. This would be a reason for keeping very quiet about the affair, and none of their letters have survived. About Lascelles's looks we have only Rupert's praise of his "brunette radiance."[41] They were close for a few months in 1906, though in the autumn they could only see each other when Rupert came home from Cambridge. That was a time when he felt unsettled at King's and was nostalgic about leaving Rugby. But in January 1907 something went wrong, just about the time that Rupert's elder brother Dick died of pneumonia: "I came up [to Cambridge] on Thursday, partly to escape my Rugby School friends who were coming back that day, and whom I daren't face, and partly that I might be alone. Another thing has happened that hurts a great deal, too; but that affects only me so I suppose it doesn't matter."[42]

Most likely he had received a letter from Lascelles ending their relationship. When he spoke later of the "enormous period of youthful
Tragedy with which [he] started at Cambridge," he meant both the loss
of his schoolboy love for Lascelles and the struggle to make a place for
himself at King's after his "effortless superiority" at Rugby.[43] If the
"other thing" was breaking off with Lascelles, he was probably the inspiration for four of Rupert's poems, later in 1907: "My Song," "Failure," "Pine-Trees and the Sky: Evening," and "The Wayfarers." All of
them are laments for lost love, in which Rupert expresses himself more
directly than in the neo-decadent style of his earlier poems. "The Wayfarers" is dated June 1907, around the time that Lascelles left Rugby,
perhaps to travel:

> Is it the hour? We leave this resting-place
>   Made fair by one another for a while.
> Now, for a god-speed, one last mad embrace;
>   The long road then, unlit by your faint smile.

Virtually all Rupert's erotic feelings, until near the end of his second
year at Cambridge, were directed towards boys. All were younger than
him. This was not at all unusual for public school boys of his generation.
His three main love affairs at Rugby were sentimental and idealistic, with
only limited physical expression. The red line between the Higher and the
Lower Sodomy was anal penetration, and Rupert almost certainly did
not cross it. Still, he twice showed that he considered sexual coercion a
normal feature of school life, and that he would defend the strong against
the weak. Once was around 1907, when he came to the defence of Mr
Eden at Hillbrow. In 1909 he stepped up again to defend a Rugby master accused of buggery of a pupil.[44] Three years later, he told Virginia
Woolf about the rape of a ten-year-old boy by two fourteen-year-olds,
which he seemed to find highly amusing. These episodes show that Rupert was uncritically loyal to the public school code, in which the sexual
exploitation of weaker boys was taken for granted. If it became known,
it should if possible be covered up and smoothed over. Beating and bullying, similarly, were accepted as just part of the order of things; it would
be a worse crime to "sneak" about them. "Take your punishment and
never complain" continued to be the word when it came to the greater
horrors of the Western Front.

Rupert would only lose his equilibrium when dealing with something not provided for by public school training: emotional intimacy with a young woman. The only one he was at all close to when growing up was his cousin Erica Cotterill, who was six years older. They kept up a bantering correspondence over the years, but there was no romantic interest on either side.[45] The one woman Rupert did know intimately was his mother. He chafed against her moralistic regime, but could never break away from her. She posed no threat to his affairs with boys because he took good care that she would know nothing about them. He would be equally secretive about heterosexual affairs later on, but he was always ruled by his mother's ideas about how women should behave and could never meet any other woman on her own terms. In his gay relationships, he could either get what he wanted, or else carry on blithely when faced with disappointment. On the other side of the street, Rupert could never be comfortable with any woman he cared for (except perhaps with his Tahitian loves, Mamua and Taatamata). Worse than that: he could be utterly destructive towards them, without any remorse or insight as to why he was being so nasty. It may be that all public school boys were likely to have "difficulties with girls" later on, but with Rupert this disability was specially damaging, both to himself and to others. We can put part of the responsibility on Mrs Brooke, also. As a clergyman's daughter, a former matron, and the wife of a housemaster, she too belonged heart and soul to the public school system. Even for a sensitive boy, there was no place to hide. Those who tried to reject the system, or make fun of it – Graves, Waugh, Connolly, Orwell – still carried it with them all their lives. Rupert could be no exception.

For Christmas 1906 Rupert went home to Rugby from Cambridge for a month. While he was there, his brother Dick died of pneumonia, after only a week's illness. He was six years older than Rupert, and the two were not especially close. Dick was not as strong as Rupert, emotionally or physically, nor as brilliant. He had started a business career in London instead of going to university. But Parker Brooke took the death hard, and lost whatever authority he had kept within the family. Rupert now became both Mrs Brooke's favourite son and the "man of the family," the single focus of her ambition and her powerful will.

In April, Rupert went to Florence with his brother Alfred, who was now a pupil at Rugby too, and still living in their father's house. At their pension in Florence a fellow guest asked Rupert if he came from a public school, and after a minute's contemplation pronounced, "Rugby!"[46] Nothing abashed, Rupert went off to place flowers on the graves of W.S. Landor and A.H. Clough: both poets who had died at Florence, and both old boys of, yes, Rugby. "I have been happier at Rugby than I can find words to say," he would write later to Frances Darwin: "As I look back at five years there, I seem to see almost every hour golden and radiant, and always increasing in beauty as I grew more conscious: and I could not, and cannot, hope for or even imagine such happiness elsewhere. And then I found the last days of all this slipping by me, and with them the faces and places and life I loved, and I without power to stay them. I became for the first time conscious of transience, and parting, and a great many other things."[47]

There is no reason to doubt that this schoolboy happiness was indeed more real than almost all the emotions that Rupert experienced afterwards – more real because it was part of a more enclosed and less ambiguous world than anything he would know in later years. He experienced his first year at Cambridge as a second act to his time at Rugby, and in almost every way a disappointing one. One reason for the disappointment was that he continued his habit of dividing his life into separate compartments, each with its own set of friends. They saw that Rupert came and went, but about *where* he went they often were left in the dark. This policy worked for Rupert for at least four years after his arrival at Cambridge. In 1911 he finally tried to unify the different elements of his life, only to find that they were explosive when combined.

The next three chapters describe Rupert's parallel lives: his most crucial attempts at friendship and love in from 1906 to 1910; his political career; and his membership in the Apostles. My justification for this treatment of his Cambridge years is that Rupert at this time lived in compartments of his own choosing. One of them was closed off by the vow of secrecy he had taken when becoming an Apostle. The second compartment was his political life as a Young Fabian. This remained separate because most of his older friends in the Apostles were keen Liberals and scornful of his enthusiasm for socialism. One the other side, that of "friendship and love," most of his deeper emotional ties were not formed within the Fabian circle. From Chapter 5 onwards, all these interests will be merged in a single narrative of his life.

2

Cambridge: Friendship and Love
October 1906–May 1909

Justin and Jacques

Rupert Brooke went up to King's College to read classics because his father had done the same, because his uncle Alan Brooke was dean of the college, and because he had won a scholarship. Until a few years before, King's had been a college exclusively for Etonians, and it still kept an atmosphere of aristocratic leisure. But within a few days of his arrival at King's in October 1906, Rupert became friends with two young men who came from a different mould. Justin Brooke (no relation) was at Emmanuel College and sharing lodgings with a fellow student there, Jacques Raverat. Justin's father was a small grocer in Manchester who single-handedly built up his shop into one of the largest tea merchants in Britain: Brooke Bond. Arthur Brooke could well afford to send his four sons to public school, but, like many progressive Northern businessmen, he mistrusted the education provided for the sons of the gentry. However, he was open-minded enough to send three of his four boys to J.H. Badley's new progressive school in Sussex, Bedales. Justin Brooke arrived there in 1896, when he was eleven years old. After two years, his father transferred him to Abbotsholme, a more radical establishment. Three years after that, one of the headmaster Cecil Reddie's regular scandals erupted and Justin was returned to Bedales, where he became head boy in his last year.

Justin's life and character fell under the long shadow of his father. Arthur Brooke had the characteristic stubbornness and emotional incompetence of the Victorian self-made man. He forced Justin to give up his natural left-handedness when he was small. When Justin decided that he

wanted to become a schoolteacher, like Badley, his father scotched that
ambition too. Justin's two older brothers had gone directly from school
into the family firm; Justin, his father decided, could best serve the enterprise by qualifying as a lawyer. He duly went to Emmanuel in 1904 but
took a backhanded revenge on his father by devoting most of his time
and energy to the theatre. Through Justin, Rupert began a long but not
very fruitful involvement with the theatre too. His looks got him onto
the stage, but once there he didn't quite know what to do with himself.

Jacques Raverat's father Georges was also a successful businessman in
Le Havre, with much other property scattered around, including a Paris
apartment and two chateaux. He was a friend of the educationalist Edmond Demolins, who in 1897 had published *A quoi tient la superiorité
des Anglo-saxons?*[1] The Anglo-Saxons were a superior breed, he argued,
who had started by dominating the Celts and the Normans, and were
now on their way to dominating the entire planet. They were a thor-
oughbred race who deserved to rule over lesser breeds and mongrels.
Not only that, the English educational system produced well-rounded
individuals with energy and enterprise, whereas the French Lycée aimed
at nothing more than producing successful bureaucrats. Demolins went
to visit Cecil Reddie at Abbotsholme and J.H. Badley at Bedales, and
sent his son to the latter. Georges Raverat did the same for Jacques.
When Jacques was sixteen in 1901, he left Bedales to study mathematics at the University of Paris. But he was discontented there, and in 1906
he persuaded his father to send him to Cambridge.

Justin Brooke could hardly miss a new arrival at King's who was making a splash with his looks and neo-decadent style, and who had the same
name as his elder brother. Obviously, this Rupert Brooke and Jacques
should meet, since they were both poets (though Jacques destroyed his
verses without letting anybody see them). Jacques's first impression was
not favourable. Rupert struck him as an affected schoolboy aesthete.
After a while, he realised that this was how Rupert coped with so much
open-mouthed admiration of his good looks: "a childish beauty, unde-
fined and fluid, as if his mother's milk were still in his cheeks ... The fore-
head was very high and very pure, the chin and lips admirably moulded;
the eyes were small, grey-blue and already veiled, mysterious and secret.
His hair was too long, the colour of tarnished gold, and parted in the
middle; it kept falling in his face and he threw it back with a movement
of his head."[2]

Jacques, Justin, and Rupert were soon talking from breakfast to midnight of poetry, art, sex, suicide; laughing at "the ridiculous superstitions about God and Religion; the absurd prejudices of patriotism and decency; the grotesque encumbrances called parents."[3] On 23 November, Jacques's mother committed suicide and he returned to France. He came back to Emmanuel in January, and he and Rupert would become the closest of friends. Rupert and Justin were never as intimate, though Justin remained at Cambridge and brought Rupert into a long series of theatrical projects. Jacques and Justin also made Rupert aware of what Bedales stood for, as an altogether different kind of school from Rugby. This connection became a vital one two years later, when Noel Olivier became a student there.

Justin had been taught by Badley that the spoken word had more life in it than the written one. He was a star actor at Bedales, and soon became a mainstay of the Cambridge Amateur Dramatic Club, specialising in leading ladies since female students were forbidden to act alongside men. His neat, birdlike features and twenty-two-inch waist made him a natural ingénue. Not surprisingly, his looks appealed strongly to his own sex, though he chose not to return the interest. So far as Jacques was concerned, Justin did not return anyone's interest. Justin once admitted that he didn't understand what friendship was, and had never been sorry to say goodbye to anyone. He was, Jacques felt, "incapable of passion, or even of deep affection. Nonetheless, we were very good friends on these terms and even, strangely enough, quite intimate."[4]

For Justin's production of Aeschylus' *Eumenides* in November 1906, Rupert was cast as the Herald. All he had to do was stand downstage looking pretty and pretend to blow his trumpet at the right moment. Rupert tried to make a joke of the adulation he provoked in the audience, but he was all too serious when he confided to Geoffrey Keynes his plans for getting ahead in Cambridge society: "I shall be rather witty and rather clever and I shall spend my time pretending to admire what I think it humorous or impressive in me to admire. Even more than yourself I shall attempt to be 'all things to all men'; rather 'cultured' among the cultured, faintly athletic among athletes, a little blasphemous among blasphemers, slightly insincere to myself. However, there are advantages in being a hypocrite, aren't there?"[5]

Rupert's posing and playacting came from the strange circumstances under which he had grown up, and from his awareness that other people had become abnormally conscious of him. Because of his good looks he was flattered, sought out by both sexes, constantly noticed. Beauty meant being at other people's disposal, reflecting back to them whatever they wanted to see in him. He was forced into being secretive, even sly, because he was always juggling claims that had to be kept separate. Having dazzled some gathering, he would disappear down a rabbit hole and pop up at a different occasion. He ended up living "many subterranean lives," and taking a positive pleasure in being at the centre of a web of deceit.[6] Beauty also threatened Rupert's sexual identity: because his looks appealed equally to both sexes, he was left feeling confused and angry about roles that were imposed on him from without. Rupert's puritanical mother had deeply inhibited his sexual responses. By and large, he was not flirtatious. He held conventional ideas about sexual etiquette and would lash out against those whom he felt were pursuing him – especially if they were women, who seemed to him to be betraying their honour by taking the sexual initiative.

Andermatt

Jacques had been obliged to abandon his studies at Easter 1907. He would feel deathly ill for no good reason, then suddenly feel better. The doctors could not even decide whether it was his body or his mind that was sick. He had always been prickly and temperamental – a "Volatile Frog," Virginia Woolf would call him – but now his moods were more extreme and he often found it a strain to be in company. No one at all realised that he was already in the grip of a progressive and incurable disease. Jacques's father took him back to France to recuperate, and by December he seemed well enough to join Rupert and his younger brother, Alfred, for a winter sports holiday at Andermatt in the Bernese Oberland. But he suffered a "maniacal episode" on the train to Andermatt, and soon had to be removed from the hotel to a nearby sanatorium.[7] It is now recognised that acute hysteria in someone of Jacques's age, and with no history of mental illness, may signal the onset of multiple sclerosis. This was indeed his unhappy fate. But the disease was not diagnosed for another seven years, and in the meantime he was treated as if he was simply nervous and neurotic. Everyone sensed that he was ill; no one, least of all Jacques himself, could do much to help it.

Andermatt was part of the latest undergraduate craze: to spend Christmas skiing and tobogganing in the Alps. You could enjoy a fortnight's holiday – including train, hotel, and enormous meals – for about a pound a day. About half of Rupert's party were girls, many of them from the cloistered precincts of Newnham. At Cambridge it was forbidden for a male undergraduate even to go for a walk with a girl from Newnham or Girton. The skiers were strictly chaperoned, of course, by Mrs Leon, mother of the Newnhamite Marjorie Leon. Even so, Andermatt was a crucial step for Rupert out of the predominantly male world he had grown up in. Before going, he told his cousin Erica that the group would be "Mostly young, heady, strange, Females. I am terrified." When he got there he reported that they were not so terrible as he had feared: "Several are no duller to talk to than males."[8] Behind the facetiousness lay a revelation: of the appeal of mixed company, and of one young woman in particular, Brynhild Olivier. This was Rupert's introduction to the four Olivier sisters, who would play havoc with his feelings, and draw out his poetic talent, for at least the next five years. Without their influence he might have remained little more than a conventional public school boy and minor Apostle. In the company of the Oliviers, he became a changed man; though, to his cost, he never succeeded in changing them.

Bryn, as everyone called her, was not a Cambridge student. She was brought by her older sister Margery, a leader of the Cambridge Fabians. Margery had been put in charge of her three younger sisters (the other two were Daphne and Noel) when their father, Sir Sydney Olivier, left England to become governor general of Jamaica in April 1907 and took Lady Olivier with him. Bryn, just two months older than Rupert, had been named after the wise queen in William Morris's *Sigurd the Volsung*. Her parents had many ties with the Morris and Edward Carpenter circles, and Sir Sydney had been one of the first Fabians (he and his friend Sidney Webb signed up in 1885). The Oliviers were founding members of the "aristocracy of the left" that had developed around the Fabian Society. The Webbs and the Shaws were childless, but families like the Oliviers, the Blands, the Peases, and the Reeves had produced a clutch of progressively raised children who had grown up with the Society and were now young adults. The four Olivier sisters were all handsome and made an overwhelming impression when seen arriving as a party, even more when accompanied by their equally striking parents. Their cousin

Laurence would become the most handsome and eminent of them all, though in 1907 he had only just been born. Of the sisters, Bryn stood out as the true beauty, with her father's riveting good looks. "Most fetching," was one contemporary's verdict, "sweet, charming, gay. Very pale amber eyes."[9] Rupert had met someone who could snap up every glance in the room as effortlessly as himself.

The natural thing to do in the evenings, in those days, was to put on a play – and what could be better than *The Importance of Being Earnest*? As the obvious belles of the company, Rupert would be Algernon and Bryn, Cecily. To play the lover both in jest and in earnest was enough to sweep Rupert off his feet. "There is One! ... oh there is One," he told his cousin Erica, "aged twenty, very beautiful & nice & everything ... My pen is dragging at its bit to run away with me about her. I adore her, for a week."[10] It was characteristic of Rupert to wonder whether he was ex- periencing his first love for a woman, or just playing the part expected of him in a holiday romance. What kept the affair within bounds was Bryn's ability to play the game without any risk of losing her head. She already had enough admirers to know how to take their measure; also, she was shortly to go back to Jamaica with her parents, where she stayed for most of 1908. Even if Bryn had been more pliant, a real love affair was not thinkable at Andermatt. The young ladies still wore long skirts to go skiing. They were not expected, nor did they expect themselves, to go to bed with anyone before marriage. If they should break this rule, the current state of contraception put them desperately at risk of scandal.

Groups like the skiers at Andermatt had scarcely existed before the Edwardian years. In Victorian times, propriety, and lack of an inde- pendent income, made it almost impossible for such mixed groups of middle-class youths to go on extended outings together. When they first appeared, around the turn of the century, their members still believed that the period between adolescence and marriage should be a sexual moratorium. Love could more easily spread among a cluster of friends, instead of being saved for the narrower pleasures of the couple. The wheel of sexual choice had begun to spin, but all had agreed to wait a few years before cashing in their stake. Too much sexual commitment could be the enemy of friendship. Prolonged courtship created the group, and the end of courtship would eventually destroy it.

Noel

Four months after Andermatt, on 10 May 1908, the Cambridge Fabians gave a dinner in honour of Sir Sydney Olivier, who was on a brief visit home from Jamaica. It was a "socialist meal" of one course followed by fruit, served to twenty-five people in Ben Keeling's rooms. Three of Olivier's daughters were in Cambridge for the dinner in their father's honour. Rupert already knew Margery, but it was his first meeting with Daphne and Noel, who had come back to England with their parents after several months in Jamaica. Rupert found himself opposite Noel at dinner. She was barely fifteen, and her contribution to the dinner party was to look shy and break a coffee cup. Despite Noel's awkwardness – perhaps because of it – Rupert was immediately stricken. For Bryn he had felt infatuation; for her younger sister, he developed a more serious and sustained passion. It was his first heterosexual love, but it followed the pattern of what he had felt for Michael Sadler, Charles Lascelles, and Denham Russell-Smith. All were younger than Rupert, so that he could feel in control; all were emotionally evasive, so that the relationship would not easily develop into a physical expression that might then burn itself out.

David ("Bunny") Garnett saw Noel Olivier as a figure out of a George Meredith poem, like "Earth's Preference" (for the young over the old), "Daphne," or "The Woods of Westermain." Meredith's woods are full of dryads, mysterious girls who outrun the young men who seek them out. He lived at Box Hill, not far from the new forest suburb of Limpsfield Chart, in the Surrey downs. Sydney and Margaret Olivier had moved there with their daughters in 1895, into a converted double cottage called the Champions. Sir Sydney (as he became in 1907) was a man of commanding presence – handsome, athletic, and formidably intelligent. He had decided that the best way to put his Fabian principles into practice was to work within the Colonial Office for a more humane administration of the British Empire. His only weak point was his inability to put himself in the place of his less gifted fellows. "He was a law unto himself," Bernard Shaw observed, "and never dreamed of considering other people's feelings, nor could conceive their sensitiveness on points that were to him trivial."[11]

With no brothers to restrain them, the Olivier girls took their cue from their father's Olympian manner. "They were all aristocratic creatures,"

Garnett wrote of them. "Pride was the moving force of their lives; they felt contempt easily; pity did not come naturally, except for animals."[12] Their self-containment was reinforced by their parents' disdain for conventional schooling. The three older girls did not go to school at all, but were intermittently tutored at home. All of them spent much of their childhood roaming the woods for miles around.

A year after the Oliviers moved to Limpsfield, Edward and Constance Garnett followed, to build a house nearby at The Cearne, Crockham Hill. Their only child, Bunny, would have a playmate his own age, the three-year-old Noel, and Constance could translate her Russian novels in the peace of the country. Others were drawn to this nucleus of the Oliviers and Garnetts: political exiles from Russia like the Kropotkins and Stepniaks; Fabians like the Peases and Hobsons; literary visitors like Conrad, Ford Madox Ford, or D.H. Lawrence. Limpsfield was different from both the planned utopian community of Welwyn Garden City and the "beer and cricket" flavour of villages then being colonised by middle-class intellectuals. "There was no church within two miles," recalled Bunny Garnett, "no rookery, no immemorial elms, no ancient red brick or mellowed ashlar walls, no water, no fertile soil. Instead there was a great horizon, solitude, and the encompassing forest."[13] Leading such unbounded lives, the children there grew up contemptuous of established society. Rupert admired this freedom of spirit in the Olivier sisters, especially Noel, and tried to emulate it. But his own upbringing and temperament were far more constricted. In Neo-paganism, as it came to be called, there would always be an uneasy coexistence between the pastoral anarchy of Limpsfield and the pastoral reaction of Belloc; and between the new Bedales and the old Rugby.

When the Neo-pagans came together at Cambridge in 1908, they had no thought of any formal manifesto to found their group. They were friends of Rupert, and friends of each other, who had a common style of youthful unconventionality and overlapping links to Bedales, Fabianism, Cambridge, and the Simple Life. The central group would include Rupert, Justin Brooke, Jacques Raverat, Gwen and Frances Darwin, Ka Cox, and the Olivier sisters. Fringe members included Bunny Garnett, Geoffrey Keynes, Ethel, Sybil, and David Pye, Dudley Ward, Godwin Baynes, and Ferenc Békássy.

Apart from liking each other, they had various dislikes in common. They agreed that the social conventions of the previous century needed to be consciously trampled on. For some members of the group – Rupert in particular – this meant judiciously snubbing their parents. There were other negative definitions. Being Neo-pagan was something that Young Fabians did when they were not doing politics, or that the children of Fabians did as a way of not following in their parents' footsteps. They were keeping alive the ideals of H.G. Wells's *A Modern Utopia,* after the purging of its author and his ideas from the Fabian Society. They were the friends to whom Rupert turned when he wanted to keep James Strachey and the other Apostles at a distance, and in whom Justin Brooke found refuge from his father and Brooke Bond tea. Neo-paganism was, finally, the antidote to the creed of "John Rump," a retired public school housemaster who was the butt of one of Rupert's satirical poems. Rump ascends to heaven, with top hat and umbrella, and tells God that what *he* believes in is:

> Safety, regulations, paving-stones,
> Street-lamps, police, and bijou-residences
> Semi-detached. I stand for Sanity,
> Comfort, Content, Prosperity, top-hats,
> Alcohol, collars, meat.[14]

When Beatrice Webb called Amber Reeves "a dreadful little pagan" she had in mind the new feminism of cigarette-smoking and careers, free thought and free love. Neo-paganism was not nearly so radical or aggressive. It was, rather, the paganism of Diana and Juno: of free-thinking but chaste young women, who would live as comrades with both sexes, before entering a devoted and domestic marriage. They thought of themselves as an emancipated new generation, and flouted convention by consorting with young men unchaperoned. But they drew a sharp line at sexual freedom; there, they were as much the "gatekeepers" as their mothers before them. Paradoxically, it was this restraint that allowed the Neo-pagans to continue as a stable group of friends for several years. Rosamund Bland and Amber Reeves, two less inhibited Fabian daughters, both found themselves married in 1909. Given the current state of contraception, and of middle-class morality, any sexually active young woman became a loose cannon that had to be quickly tied down. For women, the cycle from licence to confinement was bound to be short.

Nonetheless, the Neo-pagan ideal of comradeship was bound to clash with the realities of sexual desire and possessiveness in young men and women alike. Was a young woman to be looked on as a soulmate or a bedmate? Was she to be an untouched nymph, a mistress, or a wife? The Victorians had firm answers to these questions, but the more thoughtful young Edwardians would not accept them. They were determined to make new rules, out of their own imagination and experience. But rules there still would be.

Comus

It seems right that Rupert and Noel's first shared activity, and the project that made the Neo-pagans into a group with Rupert as its leader, should be a production of Milton's *Comus* in July 1908. Here was a masque about a young virgin who loses herself in a forest, is accosted by a silver-tongued seducer, but is saved through the intervention of an Attendant Spirit – played by Rupert. The production was sponsored by Christ's College to celebrate the tercentenary of the birth of its former student and Cambridge's greatest poet. Justin and Rupert were enlisted as directors, but Justin also had finals to think about, so Rupert found himself both stage manager and playing the longest part.

Justin had begun a revival of Elizabethan drama at Cambridge the previous autumn, with a production of Marlowe's *Doctor Faustus* for the new Marlowe Dramatic Society. Justin wanted to do at Cambridge what his Headmaster Badley had already done at Bedales: to present Elizabethan verse as living, rhythmic speech (instead of stilted recitation), and to cast women in the female roles. Unfortunately, the fellows of Newnham were not yet willing to let their young ladies take part in such a dubious venture. Nonetheless, *Faustus* was performed on 11 and 12 November 1907. The general verdict was that it was odd but effective, despite having no music, scenery, or footlights. Rupert played one of the leads, Mephistophilis, though he made no great impression. In everyday life he was theatrical to a fault and could read poetry brilliantly to his friends, but on stage he tended to choke.

Because *Comus* was a masque rather than a play, and was being produced out of term, Justin and Rupert could cast their net more widely than previous student directors and even have women in the female roles. Francis Cornford, a young classics don from Trinity, played the seducer Comus; Jane Harrison recruited young ladies from Newnham, including Dorothy Lamb as Sabrina. Albert Rothenstein came from London to paint the scenery. Two cousins, Frances and Gwen Darwin, were given the job of designing the costumes. Neither of them was at Newnham, but as granddaughters of Charles Darwin they could claim deep roots in the Cambridge intellectual aristocracy. Frances's father, Francis, was an eminent botanist and a fellow of Christ's. She had inherited from her grandfather the prognathous jaw and vaguely simian features that inspired the famous Victorian cartoon of the ape blending into the man. Her looks were comely enough, though more striking than winsome. She was already sensitive, artistic, and a poet when Rupert met her, and her photographs suggest that she liked striking a pose almost as much as he did.

Frances was a year older than Rupert, but when the production of *Comus* began she had just returned to Cambridge after four years in limbo. Her mother's death, when Frances was seventeen, had caused a series of nervous breakdowns. She had been shuttled from one cure to another in Cannes, Switzerland, and England. In later life she would again suffer from bouts of depression, yet she had a base of stable common sense that her friends would often rely on in troubles that lay ahead.

Gwen Darwin's father, George, was another leading scientist, a professor of astronomy and fellow of Trinity. Like Frances, Gwen belonged to the first generation of academic children that appeared when dons were permitted to marry from 1878 on. Her girlhood, in the tight-knit and high-minded society of Victorian Cambridge, had not been easy; she was "fat and clumsy and plain" – and shy and bespectacled for good measure. But these awkward years had developed her gifts of sense and observation. In the year of *Comus* she was twenty-three – a year older than Frances – but only just emerging from her powerful family. She had wanted to be a painter since she was thirteen. Her parents had finally acknowledged that her talent for drawing was more than just a childish knack, and had agreed that she could go to London and enroll at the Slade.

Frances and Gwen drew in other young women, to help with the costumes, like Ka Cox and Sybil and Ethel Pye (neighbours of the Oliviers at Limpsfield), or just to clean brushes, like Noel.[15] But most of the power gravitated to Rupert, who became effectively the producer, director, and star. From Justin, Rupert had learned the actor's knack of making himself a centre of attention. His friends became his daily audience – an insidious bond, perhaps, but one that raised casual gatherings into occasions that lingered in memory. The pleasures of the group required also that each should care more for the ensemble than for any favourite partner. So Rupert was not entirely facetious in asking his collaborators on *Comus* to swear that none of them would get engaged to be married within six months of the masque's performance.[16] Having assembled a group of friends of which he was the unchallenged leader (unlike his subordinate role in the Apostles or the Fabians), Rupert wanted to steer them into the future with closed ranks.

Frances Darwin saw how Rupert's beauty made him into a symbol for his admirers. Noticing once that his blond locks were highlighted by the sun from a window above the stage, she captured the moment in a little poem:

> A young Apollo, golden-haired
> Stands dreaming on the verge of strife
> Magnificently unprepared
> For the long littleness of life.[17]

After Rupert's death the poem became merely sentimental, a cultural cliché of the Great War. But Frances had grasped the contradiction in Rupert's position: the golden boy of his tribe who could not live up to his pedestal, fatally undermined by the adulation he provoked. His long hair, casual dress, and schoolboy-hero manner were the target for every kind of gush and sentimentality. More than could be true of any beautiful young woman at that time, Cambridge made Rupert into a figure of sexual myth. But it could not have done so if he had not accepted the role. Frances describes how the girls taught him to hang his head upside down and shake out his hair; afterwards he could be seen "rumpling his fingers through the front and gazing in the glass with melancholy flower-like eyes. 'I can't get it right. Is it right now? Will my hair do now?'"[18]

For all Rupert's care, the actual performances of *Comus*, at the New Theatre on 10 and 11 July, fell short of a triumph. The literary world outside Cambridge was well represented. Thomas Hardy even came up from Dorset. Rupert was invited to breakfast with him, and summed him up memorably as "incredibly shrivelled and ordinary, and said faintly pessimistic things in a flat voice about the toast." Also present on the first night were Alfred Austin, the poet laureate; Robert Bridges, who left early; and Edmund Gosse, who, when someone congratulated him on having heard *Comus*, replied, "I have overheard it."[19] Lytton Strachey's review in the *Spectator* gave the fairest summing-up of what the production had achieved: "How infinitely rarely does one hear, in any theatre, the beauty that is blank verse! From this point of view, the performance at Cambridge was indeed memorable ... The existence of such a body of able and enthusiastic lovers of poetry and drama must be welcomed as at least an augury of a better state of things."[20]

The weakness of the Marlowe Society was that their productions had more poetry than drama. Rupert loved gorgeous language, but he had little sense of creating a character or working in an ensemble. There was still a gulf between the universities and the London stage. Few of the Marlovians became professional actors, and they were complete novices at presenting a natural interplay between men and women. The whole production was a kind of glorified charade, like the set-pieces of so many Edwardian parties. After the final performance, a cast party followed at Newnham Grange – Gwen Darwin's home on the river – where the actors remained in costume to mingle with their guests. Rupert's tunic was so short and tight he couldn't sit down; he could have danced, along with the rest, except that dancing was something he could never bring himself to do.

When the party ended, Mrs Brooke carried off her son for three months in Rugby (including a subdued twenty-first birthday on 3 August). She was disturbed by his seeming to be overtired and overexcited, by his cloudy academic prospects, since he had let his studies slip, and by the company he kept. The girls, especially, seemed ominously "fast." She could see the impact of Rupert's looks on his peers, and intended to keep him under her eye – not to say under her thumb – for as long as she could.

Making Pairs

Neo-paganism might have an image of breezy freedom and friendship, but it needed to make a place for love as well; and there could be the rub. Less than three months after *Comus*, the cast learned that Frances Darwin and Francis Cornford had broken their vow of loyalty to their friends and become engaged. The *éminence grise* of the affair had been Jane Harrison, a kind of honorary Neo-pagan who preached nude bathing and similar pastimes as tributes to the ancient Greeks. She had long been Francis Cornford's mentor, and recognised that his painful shyness might be thawed by the intense and emotionally vulnerable Frances. The match between Frances and Francis was of her making, and proved a credit to her insight.

The years when Frances might have been at university had been taken up with rest cures, or with home life under the watchful eye of her father. But she was content to be an academic wife and let others pursue more worldly ambitions. Her taste had always been for art and poetry, in any case, and marriage to Francis was no bar to becoming a poet. By marrying a well-established don who was twelve years older than her, she would put herself on the fringe of the Neo-pagans even before they were well launched. Having the security of domestic life, she was often cast into a maternal role by her friends, and missed out on most of the "soul-making" that lay ahead.

Jacques was another of the vulnerable ones, who needed a partner to help him face life. After he recovered from the acute phase of his Christmas 1907 breakdown, his father brought him from Switzerland to England in the hope of finding an effective treatment. When Rupert broke down four years later, he said that he and Jacques had gone mad for the same reason: the burden of too many years of sexual frustration.[21] If it is true, as doctors say, that nobody dies of pain, then perhaps nobody goes mad from chastity either. Nonetheless a remarkable number of the Neo-pagans, of both sexes, had nervous breakdowns in the years between puberty and marriage.

Jacques's problem was organic, of course, but he still had to cope with the same problems as his friends, no matter how ill he felt. If lack of sexual companionship was a burden, it can hardly have helped that the accepted treatment for nervous collapse was to keep the sufferer almost completely removed from society. Jacques was not allowed to see anyone for months at a time, except for a few old and trusted friends such as Justin or Geoffrey Lupton, another old Bedalian. He stayed for some time at Froxfield Green, near Bedales, where Geoffrey plied his trade of making archaic furniture and building Arts and Crafts houses.[22] Jacques wrote to Ka Cox that he would like a similar future for himself. Ka, meanwhile, was also to pursue the Simple Life in a cottage. Reading between the lines, it seems obvious that Jacques hoped to share it with her. If his letters to Ka often seem bombastic and grandiose, it may be partly due to the euphoria that is a common symptom in the early stages of MS. Often there are swings to the opposite pole, also, and when Jacques came up to Cambridge in May 1908 he was too weak and nervous to see either Ka or Rupert. After a week he collapsed again and was taken for treatment to Dr J.M. Bramwell, one of Britain's leading hypnotists: "Dr Bramwell is to cure me in a fortnight, simply by suggestion, a delightful process: I simply sit and say Prospero's speeches to myself or bits out of Lear whilst he just 'speaks' to the subliminal self. You soon get into a state not vastly different, I imagine, from the Buddhist Nirvana and your heart and soul are soon filled with an ineffable peace and quiet and silence hardly broken by his whisper. And in three days he has made me better than I had been for months."[23]

Jacques and his father took Bramwell with them for a long holiday at Finistere in Brittany. Jacques lay nude in the sun, read Housman, Henley, and Meredith, and let Bramwell operate on his subconscious. For all that, it was November before he could return to England, staying again with Geoffrey Lupton (who was now building a house near Bedales for the writer Edward Thomas, using traditional methods of carpentry and plastering). Jacques was still afraid to visit Cambridge, he told Ka, because it would be "like a return from the land of the dead to the land of the living … I should hardly know a soul and those I knew, they will have travelled so far from where we parted."[24] But after nearly two years of illness he still had no firm hope of even seeing Ka and his friends regularly, still less of settling down with any of them.

In his emotional life, Rupert found himself by the autumn of 1908 almost as nervous and frustrated as Jacques, though for different reasons. To fall in love with Noel Olivier on a couple of hours' acquaintance in May seemed easy and inevitable, but what sequel could there be? She was a fifteen-year-old schoolgirl, who was not even allowed to receive letters from admirers. The production of *Comus* cannot have allowed for more than a few snatched hours together, after which they did not see each other for months. Rupert spoke of himself as frantic, at the Fabian Summer School, with a "purulent ulcer of *hysterica passio*" – of loving Noel with no prospect of expressing it freely.[25]

Because he could not openly woo Noel, Rupert hit on the subterfuge of cultivating an intimacy with Margery Olivier, using their joint work for the Fabians as a pretext. From time to time, he hoped, Margery would bring him into contact with Noel. The scheme paid off in an invitation for Rupert to join Margery and Noel on another Christmas ski trip, to Klosters in Switzerland. The group of about thirty was, again, mostly from Cambridge. One of them, who became a new friend, was Godwin Baynes, a well-known Cambridge rowing blue who was now a medical student.

Rupert summed up the holiday as "Switzerland fair (I morose) Noel Olivier superb."[26] Noel celebrated her sixteenth birthday at Klosters on Christmas day. The time Rupert was able to spend with her confirmed his love, but nothing was settled about what it could lead to. Noel was still firmly virginal and virtuous – like almost all girls of her age and class – with no intention of having a real affair with Rupert. But it was not just sexual caution that kept their relationship unripe. Three and a half years later, Rupert told James Strachey, with deep bitterness, that Noel seemed remarkable when one was in love with her, and was very kind, but didn't have any real emotions.[27] He had persuaded himself, by then, that the whole Olivier family were "adamantine." They didn't respond to others because they simply didn't understand what others were feeling. Many of Noel's friends, and almost all her suitors, seemed to end up judging her in similar terms. Much of her surface coldness may have been because she was less self-confident than she looked. She had grown up in the shadow of three strong-minded elder sisters, and had convinced herself that her pretty face was offset by "an ugly little body."[28] Her skin broke out easily, and there was always the shadow of her overwhelmingly beautiful older sister Bryn. She did, in fact, feel passion; but she never yielded to it until she was entering middle age.

Rupert's problem was rather different. He didn't keep passion at arm's length, but he tended to have several passions at once. They conflicted with each other, and left him confused about what was flood and what was froth. Like Noel he was virginal and virtuous but finding it more and more oppressive to be so. One side of him that believed in virtue was nourished by his ideal passion for Noel; the other side wanted sensual fulfillment but devalued any woman who seemed ready to give it to him. The more lonely and dissatisfied he felt, the wider the split in his emotional makeup. And his mother was always there as the third point of any triangle he found himself in. He went directly to her from Klosters, playing the dutiful son, then quarrelled with her constantly as if to work off his resentment that it *was* a duty.

Preparing for the end of his undergraduate days at King's, in the spring of 1909, Rupert felt squeezed between unfulfilled desire and unappealing duty. He decided to take his Easter break in "the greenwood," as E.M. Forster would call it. The line of escape was to the southwest. Rupert's first two weeks were spent with Hugh Russell-Smith at Becky Falls, near Manaton on Dartmoor. He was supposed to be revising for his final exams, but he had decided to leave the classics behind as soon as possible. Instead, he read the Webbs' Minority Report on the Poor Law, and worked on a new design for living: "I am leading the healthy life. I rise early, twist myself about on a kind of pulley that is supposed to make my chest immense (but doesn't), eat no meat, wear very little, do not part my hair, take frequent cold baths, work ten hours a day, and rush madly about the mountains in flannels and rainstorms for hours. I am surprisingly cheerful about it – it is all part of my scheme of returning to nature."[29]

From Becky, Rupert went to the Lizard for four days, for G.E. Moore's Easter reading party. As he split hairs with the Apostles, Rupert was laying an elaborate plot to join a party of quite a different sort. Having got word that Margery and Noel Olivier were going to be in the New Forest, he persuaded Dudley Ward to find out where they would be and arrange to drop in on them "accidentally." The rendezvous was a discovery of Ben Keeling's: the hamlet of Bank, no more than a few houses set around a clearing deep in the forest. A superb cook called Mrs Primmer let out rooms in her cottage, which became a favourite with the Cambridge Fabians. Margery Olivier had arranged a Newnhamite reading party there, with her friends Evelyn Radford and Dorothy Osmaston. Noel would come down from Bedales to be under her older sister's watchful eye. For Rupert, the meeting with Noel was an enchantment, by which he could slough off his old self and start afresh. He shared his secret with Jacques:

> I was lost for four days – I went clean out of the knowledge of anyone in England but two or three – I turned, and turned, and

covered my trail; and for three-four days, I was, for the first time
in my life, a free man, and my own master! Oh! the joy of it!
Only three know, but you shall ... For I went dancing and leaping
through the New Forest, with £3 and a satchel full of books, talking to everyone I met, mocking and laughing at them, sleeping
and eating anywhere, singing to the birds, tumbling about in the
flowers, bathing in the rivers, and, in general, behaving naturally.
And all in England, at Eastertide! And so I walked and laughed
and met a many people and made a thousand songs – all very
good – and, in the end of the days, came to a Woman who was
more glorious than the Sun and stronger than the sea, and kinder
than the earth, who is a flower made out of fire, a star that laughs
all day, whose brain is clean and clear like a man's and her heart
is full of courage and kindness; and whom I love.

This is about as far as one can get from the languid aesthete of three
years before, but Rupert's new attitude was no less suspect. Suspect even
to himself, since he went on to assure his correspondent that he was "not
unlike the R.B. you used to find, as you say, learning Ernest Dowson by
heart."[30] What is he up to this time, one wonders: learning by heart to
be a Child of Nature? Rupert in the role of Pan is not altogether convincing, especially when he prances in constant fear of the Ranee, who
waits for him suspiciously in her boarding-house at Sidmouth – and expects him to arrive from the west rather than from the east, requiring
more subterfuge on Rupert's part.

What were the real emotions of those four days at Bank? Pictures
show us Rupert in boots and Norfolk jacket (made popular by George
Bernard Shaw), looking more hearty and less conscious of the camera
than usual. His hair is shorter, too – perhaps because he expects to confront the Ranee before long. Noel, in her Bedales tunic, looks down with
a shy smile; she is at the opposite end of the group from Rupert, with
Margery planted warily in the middle. In fact, things were not so quiet
as they look in the picture. The trouble, which would fester for years,
was that Rupert had succeeded too well in pretending an interest in
Margery. She had fallen in love with him, and Noel's presence must have
seemed an irritation and a stumbling block. Meanwhile, Noel was slipping away for soulful meetings with Rupert among the great trees that
surrounded their cottage.

On Rupert's side, there are two revealing poems inspired by the days at Bank. One is really his first breakthrough into serious and mature poetry: "Oh! Death will find me, long before I tire / Of watching you." The speaker, who has died before his beloved, finally sees her arrive in the underworld:

> Pass, light as ever, through the lightless host,
> Quietly ponder, start, and sway, and gleam –
> Most individual and bewildering ghost! –
> And turn, and toss your brown delightful head
> Amusedly, among the ancient Dead.

The beloved, whom he has never possessed in life, acknowledges his gaze, but does not respond to it. Her aloofness, we suspect, is just what makes her lovable. "The Voice" gives their relation a darker outcome. It begins at twilight, with the poet brooding on his love:

> Safe in the magic of my woods
> I lay, and watched the dying light.
> And there I waited breathlessly,
> Alone; and slowly the holy three,
> The three that I loved, together grew
> One, in the hour of knowing,
> Night, and the woods, and you –

But when the girl comes through the woods to join him, her "flat clear voice" breaks the spell:

> You came and quacked beside me in the wood.
> You said, "The view from here is very good!"
> You said, "It's nice to be alone a bit!"
> "How the days are drawing out!" you said.
> You said, "The sunset's pretty, isn't it?"
> By God! I wish – I wish that you were dead!

After lavishing sentiment on his absent beloved, the poet turns hysterical when the real person appears and fails to sense his mood. However euphoric Brooke may have been at Bank, his happiness seems to have rested on the lack of any real dialogue between himself and his love.

When the days of academic reckoning came in May, Rupert had not worked steadily at Greek or Latin for many months, and he cared more for picnics or sleeping out on the Backs than for examinations. Conceivably he was constructing another pose – the schoolboy who never swots but does brilliantly on the exam – and had worked secretly and hoped to do well. In any case, he only managed a Second. Frances Darwin (who was in the know) refrained from telling him that he almost got a Third. Surely there was something deliberate in Rupert's turning away from the classics. His father had won his First at King's, gained a fellowship there, and taught classics for a living. Rupert had to succeed in his own way, avoiding a mere repetition of his father's early triumphs – which had led only to his present eclipse at School Field. If this entailed a conspicuous failure to live up to high expectations, then so be it. In any case, Rupert had his own hopes, which by now had crystallised into the belief that he could be one of the English poets. When Hugh Dalton had come to visit him at Rugby the previous October, Rupert showed him the memorial in the school chapel to Arthur Hugh Clough, who had composed "Say Not the Struggle Naught Availeth" while dying of malaria in Florence. Rupert pointed to the bare wall beside it and said, "They are keeping that for *me*."[31] Was it just a joke, or was he already weighing the odds? Clough had died at forty-two; Rupert would be up on the wall in less than ten years – a portrait medallion from one of Sherrill Schell's overblown photographs. It would take an even more romantic death to put him there.

3

The Fabian Basis
October 1906–December 1910

Young Fabians

Rupert's vocation in life was as a writer and scholar. But his second great passion was for politics. That he was a committed man of the left did not fit comfortably with the legend that grew up after his death. A young hero who hated the upper classes could not be a hero for everybody, so it was best to keep quiet about his partisan activities. Also, the upper classes did not hate him; rather, they were making him one of their pets during the last two or three years of his life. One is left wondering how Rupert would have squared that circle, if he had lived.

Rupert was born a little Liberal, and might have been expected to remain one when he grew up. His mother was keenly interested in politics, and remained a hard-core Liberal all her life. When Rupert arrived at King's he was still keeping up a pose of world-weary decadence, in part as a gesture of opposition to his mother's do-gooding. But that did not lead to any action, beyond moping in one's room and writing gloomy poems. Soon he was looking for wider and more radical prospects. The Liberals had won a landslide victory in the February 1906 election, beginning eight years of sweeping social reforms. But standard electoral politics held little appeal for eager young intellectuals. They would be expected to study law or economics, gain some practical experience, and perhaps get a chance to run for Parliament in their late twenties. Hugh Dalton, a friend of Rupert's, ended up as the most successful politician of his generation at King's. He was defeated in four elections before becoming an MP in 1924, when he was thirty-seven. He first got into Cabinet when he was fifty-three. Another young Fabian, Clement Attlee, did

social work in the East End and qualified as a lawyer, before entering
Parliament at age thirty-nine. Virginia Woolf imagined that Rupert, if he
had lived, might have become prime minister; but he was never interested in doing the sorts of things that aspiring prime ministers were expected to do.

With a kindred spirit, Hugh Dalton, Rupert started a reading club
called "The Carbonari," inspired by the secret society of Italian revolu-
tionaries. Jacques Raverat made him an admirer of Hilaire Belloc, the
aggressively anglophile Frenchman who had become a British subject in
1902 and had been elected to Parliament in 1906 as a Radical Liberal.
In June of 1907 Belloc came to speak at Cambridge. By the end of the
evening he was too drunk to go home unaided, and Rupert volunteered
to shepherd him to his bed.

Belloc sided with the working class and the Irish, but was too eccentric
and egotistical to march in step with the rising socialist tendency. In
alliance with G.K. Chesterton he broke away from the Fabian socialists
to promote "Distributism," a neo-medieval alternative to modern capitalism. His ideal, as Rupert saw it, was to go back to the merry days
before the Reformation when every Englishman had a cottage, a field,
and all the beer he could drink.[1] Such heartiness and love of the English
countryside strongly appealed to Rupert. But there was also a bullying
and suspicious side to Belloc's nature, including a rabid streak of anti-
Semitism. Raverat embraced this prejudice, and passed it on to Rupert.
From then on, anti-Semitic slurs were freely sprinkled in his letters,
usually harping on the Jews as rootless, intellectually destructive outsiders. He and Jacques imagined that the traditional English way of life,
based on the field and the village, was threatened by urban plutocrats of
mongrel origin. Belloc himself went much further, wanting actually to
revive the Middle Ages and restore the supremacy of Rome. He was a
belligerently orthodox Catholic, an anti-Dreyfusard, and an enemy of
female suffrage (lecturing to an Extension class, he pointed to his women
students and said, "These are not the kind of women we want to make
our wives").[2] The Catholicism was too much for Rupert to swallow, but
the anti-Semitism and anti-feminism he adopted as incongruous elements
in his socialistic beliefs. At this stage, such dislikes were perhaps only
two of many other affectations. After his nervous breakdown in 1912,
however, they took on a more obsessive and sinister tone as cornerstones
for the aggressive philistinism of his last three years.

Belloc's campaign for "Distributism" was really a one-man band, which meant that by late 1907 a leftist student at Cambridge was almost bound to gravitate to the "scientific" socialism of the Fabian Society. George Bernard Shaw, H.G. Wells, and Beatrice and Sidney Webb had been putting up an intellectual fireworks display that more than doubled the size of the Society, though it still had only about two thousand members.[3] Ben Keeling, a Trinity undergraduate and fiery revolutionary, set up a branch of the Young Fabians at Cambridge. He promoted a speech by the militant trade unionist Keir Hardie. When a mob of rugger-playing hearties vowed to prevent it, Keeling foiled them by deploying two counterfeit Hardies, rigged out with beards and red ties. In his room he had a large poster of the workers of the world striding ahead with clenched fists, over the slogan "Forward the Day is Breaking." The only actual workers that the undergraduate socialists knew were their bed-makers, who would give them advance warning of raids by the hearties. Nonetheless, revolution was in the air and the Cambridge students were eagerly debating how it would come and what part they would play in it.

At first Rupert would put only one foot into the socialist camp, signing on as a Fabian associate rather than a full member. His uncle Clement Cotterill, a disciple of William Morris, had just published a pamphlet whose title put Fabianism in a nutshell: *Human Justice for Those at the Bottom from Those at the Top*. Rupert told Cotterill that he hoped to convert the Cambridge Fabians to "a more human view of things ... Of course they're really sincere, energetic, useful people, and they do a lot of good work. But, as I've said, they seem rather hard ... They sometimes seem to take it for granted that all rich men, and all Conservatives (and most ordinary Liberals) are heartless villains."[4] To go even as far as this set Rupert on a different course from his two closest friends, Jacques Raverat and Justin Brooke. Both were the sons of rich men and expected to inherit a comfortable patrimony. Jacques remained a folk-revolutionary of the Belloc type, while Justin steered clear of politics.

A crucial difference between the Fabians and Belloc lay in their attitude to the crusade for women's suffrage. Belloc was a patriarchal chauvinist, whereas the Fabians were coming round to equal rights. Their constitution was called "The Basis," to which full members had to give formal consent. After much internal debate they passed an amendment to the Basis, in January 1907, calling for "equal citizenship of men and women." The Fabian Society became the first place at Cambridge where male undergraduates and the women of Newnham and Girton Colleges could meet on equal terms. In 1906 Edith Moggridge was actually elected president of the Society, though Girton refused her permission to take up the post. When Rupert joined and got on to the steering committee, the Newnhamite Ka Cox had just become treasurer. She was the daughter of Henry Fisher Cox, a Fabian who also had enough business sense to become a prosperous stockbroker. His first wife died young, leaving three daughters: Hester, Katharine, and Margaret. Henry then remarried and had two more daughters before dying suddenly in 1905, when Ka was eighteen. Ka and her two grown-up sisters were left financially independent. She had a cottage near her father's old estate in Woking, and shared her sister Hester's flat in Westminster when she was in London. She was in the unusual position, for a young woman of her class, of being relatively free to live and travel – and even to love – as she pleased.

Ka had gone to a feeder school for Newnham, St Felix's in Southwold. It had been founded by Margaret Gardiner as "a school where girls are treated like sensible creatures."[5] One of Ka's friends there was a Jewish girl, Marjorie Leon, who came with her to Newnham (and who was one of the skiers at Andermatt in Christmas 1907). Ka was not conventionally pretty, but she had a sweet nature and a fresh, clear-skinned look that appealed to many of her fellow students. "She was an aesthete," one of them recorded, "– wore loose, diaphanous clothes with Peter Pan collars (not stiff high ones with bones sticking into the neck like ours) and had silver baubles in her hair ... At nineteen she was a miracle of poise, maturity and charm." Male undergraduates were equally susceptible to Ka's appeal. They felt that she would accept and nurture them, soothing the trials of their young manhood. Rupert once called her "a Cushion, or a floor."[6] Her troubles would begin when she discovered needs and wants of her own.

At Andermatt, Rupert had been much impressed that his party were "nearly all Socialists, and ... all great personal friends of H.G. Wells."[7] Since 1903 Wells had chosen the Fabian Society as his vehicle for bringing about a new Britain. Originally founded to study and debate social questions, the Society had plenty of intellectual firepower, directed by Sidney and Beatrice Webb, Sydney Olivier, and George Bernard Shaw.[8] Wells wanted to turn it into a disciplined vanguard – not just contemplating social change, but provoking and guiding it. For two years now, he had been trying to make the Society the instrument for a root-and-branch transformation of British life. He had been successfully boxed in by the old guard on the Fabian executive: the Webbs, Bernard Shaw, Hubert Bland, and Edward Pease. But Wells had made more head-way with several of the old guard's wives and children, who were attracted by his feminism, his eagerness to transform private as well as public life, and his sheer bounciness. He was the roguish uncle, always ready for a spree. As the children of his Fabian friends went to university Wells tried to recruit them, and at the same time to get a taste of under-graduate pleasures that had been denied him in his own hard-pressed student days at the Normal School of Science in South Kensington.

In February 1908 Wells gave a lecture to the Cambridge Young Fabi-ans. Afterwards, he agreed to discuss "the family" – which meant his new and dangerous ideas on sex – with a group of students and dons in Rupert's rooms at King's. Rupert was by now a firm Wellsian, and he soon moved to become a full member of the Fabians by assenting to the Basis. This committed him to the abolition of private property, rent, and interest (though by constitutional means rather than violent revolution). Wells had given Rupert two incentives to take the plunge and become a full-blooded socialist. There was, first, the wonderful painlessness of being a Wellsian revolutionary. "Socialism may arrive after all," Wells suggested, "not by a social convulsion, but by ... a revolution as orderly and quiet as the procession of the equinoxes." The leader of this stately march would be the "Constructive Socialist," who undertakes "what-ever lies, in his power towards *the enrichment of the Socialist idea*. He has to give whatever gifts he has as artist, as writer, as maker of any sort to increasing and refining the conception of civilized life." The cynic might observe that this would allow Rupert to go on doing what he was doing already, but with a good social conscience. Ingenuous as always, Wells had just informed the *Labour Leader* that he didn't want people to live in slums on a pound a week, so why should he live that way him-self? "I am ready to go on working for [socialism]," he announced, "hav-ing just as good a time and just as many pleasant things as I can."[9]

An opposite sort of appeal lay in the disciplined half of Wells's split personality. He had started out as a scientist, and believed that social re-form should be tackled in the same spirit of inquiry. What tipped the balance for Rupert to sign the Basis was reading *New Worlds for Old*, where Wells argued that "In place of disorderly individual effort, each man doing what he pleases, the Socialist wants organised effort and a plan."[10] But who would be in charge of the plan? Wells saw no problem: the planners should be superior individuals who had both conscience to be shocked by poverty and ignorance, and intellect to create a better social order. In *A Modern Utopia* he had imagined a new kind of ruling class, the high-minded and ascetic "Samurai." Rupert read it when it first appeared in the *Fortnightly Review* in 1904–05, and started to think along Wellsian lines. Unlike the existing British aristocracy, the Samurai would be an intellectual elite, living modestly and abstaining from alcohol and tobacco. They would be recruited from young men and women whose revolutionary ardour had not yet been blunted by the cares of everyday life. Samurai training would include a period of sexual experimentation, which pointed to the "hidden agenda" that Wells was trying to insinuate into old-guard Fabianism: "The majority of those who become *samurai* do so between twenty-seven and thirty-five. And, between seventeen and thirty, the Utopians have their dealings with love, and the play and excitement of love is a chief interest in life. Much freedom of act is allowed them so that their wills may grow freely. For the most part they end mated, and love gives place to some special and more enduring interest, though, indeed, there is love between older men and fresh girls, and between youths and maturer women." Once a year the Samurai were required to spend a week alone in the wilderness, in order "to secure a certain stoutness of heart and body in the members of the order, which otherwise might have lain open to too many timorous, merely abstemious, men and women."[11]

This enticing curriculum was a reversal of Wells's own experience: he had practised self-denial in his youth, by hard necessity, and was now revelling in a promiscuous middle age. His Samurai rulers would work intensely and keep the lower orders under strict scientific control, but in their private lives they would be moral adventurers and a law unto themselves. Wells himself did not aspire to be a muscular Samurai mountaineer. His need for adventure was centred on the pursuit of "fresh girls," as he ambiguously called them. It was splendid that his friend Sydney Olivier should become a Samurai governor of Jamaica, improving the lot of the "subject races." But Wells needed something closer to centre stage. He liked invitations from the society hostess Lady Desborough, or making thousands of pounds on his popular novels, or chasing the daughters of his Fabian colleagues. He was so made, furthermore, that part of the enjoyment of these actions was to ensure that everyone could see what he was up to. His recklessness ensured that he would before long be in hot water, both with the outraged right and the puritanical left.

On 10 May 1908 the Cambridge Fabians gave their dinner at Trinity in honour of Sir Sydney Olivier. Two guests came in late, and had to sit on a window sill: Olivier's old friend H.G. Wells, and a bright-eyed Newnham student called Amber Reeves. Amber was the daughter of a leading Fabian couple, Maud and William Pember Reeves. Her father was soon to be appointed director of the Webbs' new foundation, the London School of Economics, and Amber herself had served as treasurer of the Cambridge Young Fabians. Wells was in hot water at the time with the Fabian executive. He had written a letter supporting the Liberal candidate, Winston Churchill, in a Manchester by-election, even though there was also a socialist in the running.[12] At the Fabian annual meeting on 22 April, he had tried to defend his letter, then walked off the platform in a huff.

The row over the Churchill letter was only the visible tip of a bitter quarrel between Wells and the Fabian old guard that had been seething for three years. Publicly, Wells had annoyed them by pressing the Society to support children's allowances, as a means of undermining the "masculine proprietorship" of women. Privately, he enraged them by drawing their wives towards feminist ideas, and their daughters towards sexual emancipation – in the form of going to bed with *him*. In 1905 he had a brief affair with Rosamund Bland, the nineteen-year-old daughter of Hubert Bland. Wells claimed that he was not especially attracted by Rosamund's plump and brown-eyed charms, but wanted to save her from her father's incestuous advances.

In the spring of 1908 he was involved, more deeply this time, with Amber Reeves. She was the same age as Rupert, not quite so good-looking but an equally magnetic personality. Amber was precocious sexually, as well as intellectually. After some months of friendship with Wells, she took advantage of his visit to Cambridge for the Olivier dinner to tell him that she was in love. When he asked her "with whom?" she threw herself into his arms. Wells was not one to miss an opportunity, and they went to bed without more ado. What gave this passionate encounter an extra spice was that it took place in Amber's room at Newnham, to which Wells had been admitted on the claim that he was an old friend of the family. Both of them were exactly the sort of people who would enjoy being, in all likelihood, the first couple to use a Newnham room for such a purpose. However, their embrace had to be incomplete because H.G. had failed to stop at a chemist first. Having agreed to meet again soon in Soho, for a more leisurely encounter, they made it to Trinity in time for dinner. One wonders what excuse they gave for being late.[13]

Wells's extramarital caperings were part of his campaign for putting "New Women" in the vanguard of social reform. This points to a contrast between two of the couples at the Olivier dinner. H.G. Wells and Amber saw Fabianism as going hand in hand with sexual experimentation. Rupert and Noel were embarking on a conventionally chaste and idealistic relationship. Rupert did not expect his passion for socialism to spill over into his romantic life. That would still belong to the ancien régime.

Fabian Summers

In August 1908 Rupert went to the Fabian Summer School at Llanbedr, near Harlech on the Welsh coast. The first one had been organised the year before by Charlotte and George Bernard Shaw. For thirty-five shillings a week Fabians were offered board, lodging, outings, and lectures on marriage or socialism by G.B.S.:

> some hundred members of both sexes and all ages living in 3
> Houses and camping out roundabout there, listening to lectures
> in the morning, and bathing and rock-climbing in the afternoon,
> discussing in the evening – food almost vegetarian and clothes of
> the most unconventional – ladies in "Gyms" and men in any de-
> scription of flannels ... Mixed up with these university men and
> girls, were some score of elementary teachers and minor civil ser-
> vants – some of the new pension officers – , the whole making a
> most varied little world, living in intimate companionship one
> with the other.[14]

It is easy to laugh at the vegetarian food, the Swedish drill in the morning, and the dress code: tunics for the ladies, knee-breeches for the men, sensible shoes for both. But the crankishness was incidental to building a classless community, dedicated to a brighter future for Britain. The Fabian Summer School's values owed a good deal to Edward Carpenter's Millthorpe. Unlike Millthorpe, however, it had no erotic agenda and no connection with the long rhythms of country life. It was a temporary encampment, designed to energize its participants and then send them back to the front lines of social reform in the cities.

Beatrice and Sidney Webb decided to attend in person for four days in 1908. Beatrice, who was staying at Leominster before going to the Summer School, issued a blanket invitation to any Fabians heading for Llanbedr to stay the night. Rupert and James Strachey duly turned up, accompanied by Ben Keeling, Dudley Ward, Hugh Dalton, Arthur Waley, and Gerald Shove.[15] Ward, a new friend of Rupert's, was reading economics at St John's. His manner was shy, bumbling but likeable, his appearance humdrum, his politics vigorously Fabian. Although Rupert became very fond of him, Ward never quite stood out; he was always "dear old Dudley," making himself useful somewhere in the background. Beatrice, however, was favourably impressed by him, and still more by Dalton: "one of the most astute and thoughtful of our younger members – by nature an ecclesiastic – a sort of lay Jesuit – preparing for political life."[16]

The Webbs were at this time much concerned with eugenics and the virtues of the "highly regulated races" who had sex well under control, like the Japanese and the Germans.[17] They hoped that the Young Fabians could be made into a kind of socialist Jesuit order, with Beatrice and Sidney standing in the place of the pope. "There are some," Beatrice had noted in her diary, "who wish to reach a socialist state by the assertion of economic equality – they desire to force the property-owners to yield to the non-property owners. I prefer to have the forward movement based on the obligation of each individual to serve the state, in return getting maintenance." What this really meant was that a disciplined elite of civil servants would regulate the lives of everyone else. The Webbs found an impressive precedent for this in the Salvation Army, who were setting up rural colonies for the destitute: "They represent in part a true 'Samurai' class ... If the State undertakes the drainage system the Salvationists are quite the best agency to deal wisely with some of the products of this drainage system ... Their spirit of persistent work, their extraordinary vitality – even their curious combination of revivalist religion, with the technique of a very superior and reformed 'Variety Artist' exactly suits the helpless, hopeless, will-less man, a prey to sexual impulses, to recover his virility and faculty for regular life and regularwork."[18]

For the Webbs, the main purpose of the Summer School was to provide strict training for future political leaders. It was not to be a holiday camp or an experiment in living. Unfortunately for them, many of the students went there in search of novelty, or simply a good time. The young university men and women took a malicious pleasure in shocking their straitlaced elders and flouting the rigid rules of chaperonage. By the fourth school, in 1910, Beatrice's dissatisfaction was focused on the Cambridge "clique" of Brooke, Dalton, James Strachey, Clifford Allen, and William Foss: "They are inclined to go away rather more critical and supercilious than they came ... 'They won't come, unless they know who they are going to meet,' sums up Rupert Brooke ... They don't want to learn, they don't think they have anything to learn ... The egotism of the young university man is colossal."[19] It was quite true that they skipped lectures and generally ignored the school rules. But James's main reason for going was the hope of getting his mattress next to Rupert's, in the stable where the young men slept. Rupert provided Lytton Strachey with titillating reports of fun and games after lights-out: "Daddy [Dalton] was a schoolboy in dormitory; and conceived a light lust for James – who, I thought, was quite dignified about it. He would start up suddenly behind him and tickle him gently under the armpits, making strange sibilant cluckings with his mouth meanwhile. And when James was in bed Daddy stood over him, waving an *immense* steaming penis in his face and chuckling softly. Poor James was nearly sick."[20]

One suspects that such campy outbursts helped to keep the Newn-hamites away from the Summer School. Ka Cox, for one, refused to go even when urged by Rupert; perhaps she did not care to compete for his attention when he was constantly shadowed by James. Beatrice Webb certainly sniffed out something distasteful in the Cambridge Fabians and Apostles, though she was apparently unaware of their submerged gay life:

[Bertrand Russell] is a bit of an "A" – Artist, Anarchist and Aristocrat, and in spite of his acquired puritanism, is apt to be swept away by primitive instincts ... I am sorry now that Bertie went to Cambridge – there is a pernicious set presided over by Lowes

Dickinson, which makes a sort of ideal of anarchic ways in sexual questions – we have, for a long time, been aware of its bad influence on our young Fabians. The intellectual star is the metaphysical George Moore with his *Principia Ethica* – a book they all talk of as "The Truth"! I never can see anything in it, except a metaphysical justification for doing what you like and what other people disapprove of! So far as *I* can understand the philosophy it is a denial both of the scientific method and of religion – as a rule, that is the net result on the minds of young men – it seems to disintegrate their intellects and their characters.[21]

But there was more to Rupert's position than Apostolic metaphysics or "primitive instincts." He was not the kind of person to sit quietly while, for example, the actor-manager Harley Granville-Barker argued that under socialism "all women will have dresses of the same material and wear them for the same length of time."[22] Still inspired by the myth of the Golden Age, Rupert was a utopian and a humanist who shrank from the juiceless planned societies of Shaw and the Webbs. His only socialist poem, "Second Best," ended with a vision of post-revolutionary brotherhood, a joyous celebration by the Children of the Sun:

Yet, behind the night,
Waits for the great unborn, somewhere afar,
Some white tremendous daybreak. And the light,
Returning, shall give back the golden hours,
Ocean a windless level, Earth a lawn
Spacious and full of sunlit dancing-places,
And laughter, and music, and, among the flowers,
The gay child-hearts of men, and the child-faces,
O heart, in the great dawn!

For the Apostles, such a vision would be too vague and lush; the Webbs would have made the same criticism, if for different reasons. Rupert's brave new world was neither a coterie nor a technocracy, but a place where personal life was made radiant. It was inspired by William Morris, by Wells, and by Campanella's vision of a "City of the Sun." It was not enough for Rupert to be just a Fabian (especially now that Wells was on his way out), or an Apostle, or even both in turn. He was reaching for an integrated vision that would make the world a better place, and himself more complete. The conflict between the "great dawn" and old-fashioned monogamous love had yet to declare itself.

A Caravan Tour

In spite of his cool reception by the Webbs, Rupert went to two more Summer Schools, in 1909 and 1910. In July of the latter year he did more, renting a caravan to travel through Hampshire and Dorset with Dudley Ward, making speeches for reform of the Poor Law. A Commission on the Poor Law had reported in February 1909. Its majority had argued for piecemeal reform, but Beatrice Webb had written a Minority Report saying that the whole system needed to be overthrown. To fight for her views in the political arena, she and Sidney formed the National Committee for the Prevention of Destitution. There was a tinge of absurdity in Rupert and Dudley going from one village green to another, haranguing the yokels, even if they were part of a well-organised campaign with thousands of supporters. Nonetheless, the campaign failed, for reasons that struck at the root of the Fabian idea. Since the time of Dickens, the Poor Law and its Boards of Guardians had been a stink in the nostrils of enlightened opinion. The system of relief was a typical British muddle, a haphazard combination of state and private charity, of workhouse and "outdoor" (i.e., home) relief. Everything rested on the principle of deterrence. The infirm, aged, or unemployed should be given enough support to keep them alive, but at a level well below that of the poorest employed workers.

Sorting out ancient British muddles was meat and drink to the Webbs. They wanted to replace the local Boards of Guardians with a national system of boards to provide health care, pensions, and relief. But the central issue was what to do with the able-bodied unemployed, and here the Webbs could not break with deterrence. They viewed poverty as a social disease that needed to be quarantined, then treated. Whether the poor wanted to be treated was irrelevant. The state should operate like the Salvation Army, indoctrinating the people it helped and dividing them into grades. "It is essential," Sidney Webb wrote, "that the [unemployed] should be always moving up *or* down, by promotion or degradation."[23]

Meanwhile the Liberal chancellor of the exchequer, Lloyd George, was incubating a comprehensive scheme of state unemployment insurance. For Beatrice, this had "the fatal defect that the state got nothing for its money – that the persons felt they had a right to the allowance whatever their conduct ... That is, of course, under the present conditions of human will, sheer madness, whatever it may be in good times to come."[24] Rupert signed up for the Webbs' campaign, but in fact his views on unemployment relief sounded more like Lloyd George:

> When we are in trouble or danger from other people, we throw ourselves on the State in the shape of the policeman or the law court. This "loss of independence" does not weaken the character; it leaves men free to use their energies more profitably. For a working-man to spend his time in unaided, individual encounters with thieves, disease, and the devil of unemployment, certainly may (if he is always victorious) foster and widen his sense of personal responsibility and self-reliance, but it is still more certainly a *ridiculous and sentimental waste of time and trouble* ... It is not possible, as Society is organised, for every man to get work.[25]

Rupert's and Dudley's decision to tour the southern countryside, rather than the industrial North, showed their roots as Simple Lifers and devotees of Olde England. Their choice of a caravan followed the example of the gypsy artist Augustus John rather than the Webbs, who insisted on bourgeois amenities and efficient working conditions. There was no reason, except nostalgia, to travel by horsepower instead of by train or bicycle. Starting near Winchester, Rupert and Dudley went southwest through the New Forest as far as Corfe and then came back, speaking on village greens and street corners as they went. At Wareham it came on to rain and their cat was run over by a car, so they retreated to a hotel for beds and a lobster tea. No doubt the rustics of Wessex were bemused to be told about poverty by two fresh-faced young men from Cambridge, but it took determination and moral courage to stick at it for twelve days, and few of Rupert's other friends would have been able or willing to do as much in a good cause.

Jacques Raverat, for example, was taken along to a Fabian dinner by Dudley Ward and Margery Olivier and detested everything about it: "What beasts! What swine they are! Long before midnight Keeling and

[R.H.] Mottram and three or four others were as drunk as lords and much more loathsome. It would be difficult to imagine any sight more revolting, more pitiably mean, tawdry, contemptible and joyless ... I went home, treading on air, never before so conscious of the bestiality of men, and my immeasurable pride." Nonetheless, Jacques spent a week canvassing in Walworth for the Liberal candidate in the January 1910 general election, and was surprised to find how well he could do it. "The enthusiasm was quite spurious," he told Ka Cox, "and I'm afraid I haven't any political sense after all: I remain quite impartial and aloof, really, thinking how foolish all this turmoil and how vain, and how much misspent these energies. I think my democratic principles are purely intellectual; and my instincts – well, the less said about *them* the better."[26] Jacques's instincts, and Justin's too, were shaped by having rich fathers. They wanted to claim their independence, but by way of bohemia rather than political activism. Ka Cox spent much of her life on good causes, but mostly in a more traditionally feminine style of nurture, nursing the sick or aiding refugees during the war. Of the Olivier sisters, only Margery showed much political sense. Having been brought up on Fabianism from the nursery, they looked elsewhere to find their adult identities.

Even Rupert had little relish for the political process itself. Working in the second 1910 election, he complained about the conflict he felt in being both a Fabian and a disciple of G.E. Moore: "It is not true that anger against injustice and wickedness and tyrannies is a good state of mind, 'noble'. Oh, perhaps it is with some, if they're fine. But I guess with most, as with me, it's a dirty mean choky emotion. I HATE the upper classes."[27] Keeling was at this time the manager of one of the new Labour Exchanges, at Leeds. He had found the workaday world a letdown after Cambridge, and Rupert had to lecture him on his "pessimism":

I suddenly feel the extraordinary value and importance of everybody I meet, and almost everything I see ... That is, when the mood is on me. I roam about places – yesterday I did it even in Birmingham! – and sit in trains and see the essential glory and beauty of all the people I meet. I can watch a dirty middle-aged tradesman in a railway-carriage for hours, and love every dirty greasy sulky wrinkle in his weak chin and every button on his spotted unclean waistcoat. I know their states of mind are bad.

But I'm so much occupied with their being there at all, that I don't have time to think of that.[28]

These moments of euphoria would have been viewed with suspicion by the Apostles, who held that a good state of mind was less valuable when it was experienced by an inferior person. At a gathering in January 1909 "Sheppard delivered an indictment on poor Rupert for admiring Mr. Wells and thinking truth beauty, beauty truth. Norton and Lytton took up the attack and even James and Gerald … stabbed him in the back. Finally Lytton, enraged at Rupert's defences, thoroughly lost his temper and delivered a violent personal attack."[29] Nonetheless, by using "states of mind" as a touchstone, Rupert was defining politics much more widely than the Webbs would have done. "Every action," he wrote, "which leads on the whole to good, is *'frightfully'* important … It is not a question of either getting to Utopia in the year 2,000 or not. There'll be so much good then, and so much evil. And we can affect it."[30] The key word here was "Every." Why shouldn't private life contribute as much good, in the long run, as organising transport to the polls in a general election? A single-minded political commitment would require submission to large and menacing powers: first the Webbs, and behind them what Rupert called "Modern Industry." Rupert had no intention of going to live in the gritty world of factories and workhouses. The North of England would remain for him what it was for most people of his kind: what you passed through on your way to the Lake District or the Highlands.

Rupert devoted a great deal of youthful energy to politics, but very much on his own terms. Did Virginia Woolf make any sense, then, when she imagined that Rupert, if he had lived, might have become prime minister? One war veteran did become the youngest member of Parliament in the December 1918 election, at the age of twenty-two. He had served in the trenches, and was handsome, aristocratic, and a spellbinding orator. This was Oswald Mosley, elected as a Conservative in Harrow. He soon became a Fabian and from 1924 made his career in the Labour Party. Dissatisfied with Labour's failure to cope with unemployment, Mosley left to found the neo-fascist New Party in 1931. His model was Mussolini, another veteran of the trenches and former socialist.

Might Rupert have followed Mosley's path rather than, say, Hugh Dalton's? In 1913 he had seen New Zealand's model welfare state, and realised that it was still a far from ideal society. He held to his Fabian views, but when he returned to England much of his social life was spent with aristocrats and Liberal politicians. The foundation stones of Rupert's political identity had become militarism, nationalism, anti-feminism, and anti-Semitism. Fascism, whether of the Italian or German variety, has been called "the socialism of the soldier."[31] Mosley was not able to rally a mass following in Britain, but lack of popularity has rarely given pause to political fanatics. If Rupert had joined the British Union of Fascists in 1934, it would have been quite consistent with his views in 1914. But what he might have become, or how Britain might have changed if it had not lost the generation of 1914–18, no one now can say.

4

Apostles, and Others
October 1906–October 1909

Brothers

At Andermatt, Christmas 1907, Brynhild Olivier had introduced Rupert to the pleasures of flirting with a woman. Before that his only objects of desire had been boys, and "giggling females" were to be avoided if possible.[1] For the remaining seven years of his life, Rupert was almost always in love or in lust with a woman, sometimes with several at once. Yet what happened to him at Andermatt was not a classic conversion experience, where someone discards an old self and is reborn as an entirely different person. Rupert continued to feel desire for men, and to respond when they showed desire for him. When Jacques Raverat and Gwen Darwin got married, he commented that "Gwen's the only woman in England, and Jacques almost the only man, I've never lusted for."[2] He did not feel obliged to choose between an exclusively gay or straight identity. It would be presumptuous for a biographer to choose for him, by saying that he was "really" or "fundamentally" one or the other.

Rupert may have had a fluid sense of gender, but straight and gay desires played out in two quite different social arenas, each with its own rules. Relations with well-brought-up English girls were governed by strict propriety, and by the constant fear of an undesired pregnancy. The gay world, on the other hand, was clandestine and anarchic, with few inhibitions about asking for sex, or agreeing to it. If Rupert remained coy and rejected most of the men who desired him, it was because he did not have an anarchic temperament. The letters he exchanged with James Strachey spoke freely about gay intrigues and sentiments, yet Rupert always denied the sexual union that James longed for so abjectly. Still,

Rupert was entirely at home in the gay world of Cambridge; he required only that it be kept hidden from the realm of respectable heterosexuality.

One of Rupert's gay inclinations was his need to be taken under the wing of an admiring older man. When he arrived at King's in October 1906 his rooms were across the hall from a famous local character, the snobbish aesthete and Apostle Oscar Browning. Dismissed from Eton on suspicion of moral turpitude, Browning had returned to be a fellow of King's, where he had been an undergraduate. But his fin-de-siècle affectations were too much for Rupert to take, so instead he found a replacement for St John Lucas in Charles Sayle, who wrote Uranian poems and novels and worked at the university library.[3] Sayle had gone to Rugby, where he had had a sentimental friendship with J.H. Badley (the future headmaster of Bedales). He went on to Oxford, but was sent down for some kind of sexual misconduct. Small, fussy, and spinsterish, his nickname was "Aunt Snayle." Bertrand Russell called him "a well known ass." Now forty-two, he had a little house at 8 Trumpington Street where he entertained a stream of students and fell tremulously in love with the prettiest ones. "I do not know if these undergraduates love me," he wrote in his diary, "but I know that they love me to love them!"[4] He was also a pedophile, swooning over working-class boys whom he called "Angels of Earth."

During his first two years at Cambridge, Rupert was a constant visitor to Sayle's house, sometimes staying overnight. Geoffrey Keynes and the climber George Mallory were often there with him. Their intimacy was of a kind that has long vanished, and today it appears both touching and preposterous. As with St John Lucas, Rupert was drawn to an older man who could give him domestic tenderness and sympathy. He must have known that Sayle was infatuated with him, but almost certainly there was no sexual contact between them. In later years Rupert kept quiet about the friendship with Sayle, realising how pathetic his way of life might appear to an outsider. Sayle had no such second thoughts. "I do not know in what language to moderate my appreciation of this great man," he wrote in his diary, "great in his ideals, great in his imagination, great in his charm. The world will learn to know him later on. It has been mine to know him now."[5] Before dismissing this as mere gush, we should remember that it was exactly how most of Britain would judge Rupert in his posthumous heyday.

An invitation to Trumpington Street was not hard to come by. The "Cambridge Conversazione Society" or "The Apostles" was far more exclusive, but in both cases long blond hair and a pretty face made it easier to gain admission. When Rupert was infatuated at school with Michael Sadler or Charlie Lascelles, he was older than them and the one who set the terms of the relationship. With the Society, Rupert was in the junior position. He was now the object of desire, and had to decide if he wanted to satisfy the passion that he aroused in older or less physically attractive men. He set a pattern of toying with his suitors' emotions but never responding with equal love or desire. The one who most persistently and most vainly desired him was his Hillbrow schoolmate James Strachey. James had not gone on to Rugby but to St Paul's School in London, first as a boarder and then as a day boy. He renewed a correspondence with Rupert in the summer of 1905, when James was preparing to enter Trinity College. They were the same age, but James went to university a year before Rupert. In September Rupert accepted an invitation to visit the Strachey family at a house they had rented, Great Oakley Hall, near Kettering. "I wasn't particularly impressed," Lytton reported to J.M. Keynes. "His appearance is pleasant – mainly, I think, owing to youth … He's damned literary, rather too serious and conscientious, and devoid of finesse." Duncan Grant was given a more positive account: "He has rather nice – but you know –yellow-ochre-ish hair, and a healthy young complexion. I took him out for a walk round the Park this morning, and he talked about Poetry and Public Schools as decently as could be expected."[6] When Rupert went to King's in December to write his scholarship exams he travelled with Geoffrey Keynes and stayed at the Keynes home on Harvey Road. He met J.T. Sheppard, already a fellow of King's and an Apostle, and the mathematician H.T.J. (Harry) Norton, who was at Trinity, and would be elected to the Society in January.

Rupert's debut in gay Cambridge aroused a curious mixture of rivalry and cooperation in those who pursued him. It was accepted by Lytton and other Apostles that James was most in love with Rupert, and therefore entitled to lobby the Society for his beloved's admission. But anyone in their little circle could also try their luck with the new beauty, and keep everyone else informed about progress. As soon as Rupert arrived at Cambridge in October 1906, Harry Norton put in his bid. "Of course the pose is pretty bad, damnably bad," he reported to Lytton, "And Mr

Sadler is responsible for much ... But on the other hand; he is quite, yes quite, unintelligent. Of course he is hopelessly wrong-headed; but he is willing and anxious to learn." Willing to learn, yes, but not to go to bed with Harry: "He also thought one shouldn't commit sodomy 'since in physical things we should obey the dictates of Nature.' And when I burst into tears and asked who Nature was, he replied 'Well, Evolution or God.'" Norton had to be satisfied with ogling Rupert's appearance in *The Eumenides* in November: "Conjecture is already rife as to the state of his legs."[7]

The production of Aeschylus' *Eumenides* was directed by Justin Brooke. Rupert unfortunately suffered from stage fright, so Justin cast him as the Herald. All he had to do was stand downstage in a short skirt, look interesting, and say nothing. Eddie Marsh, private secretary to the young cabinet minister Winston Churchill, experienced the coup de foudre at his first sight of Rupert's "radiant, youthful figure." A.C. Benson, an older fellow of Magdalen, made a note in his diary: "A herald made a pretty figure, spoilt by a glassy stare." James Strachey, now at Trinity and able to renew his acquaintance with Rupert, left a note after the performance telling him how beautiful he looked. For his first year and a half at Cambridge, Rupert found himself in the role of the young and pretty boys that he had admired during his last two years at Rugby. If the role had come to him from outside, he was nonetheless happy to accept it. In a single evening he had become Cambridge's pin-up of the year, and he threw himself full tilt into the role of the gay and handsome ingénue. Even the eminent Newnham classicist Jane Harrison was drawn into the game, with a wry reference in a lecture to Rupert's *bon mot* that "Nobody over thirty is worth talking to." So easily infatuating others, Rupert was in danger of becoming fatuous himself.

When James made him a declaration of love after the performance of the *Eumenides*, Rupert made it clear that he wanted nothing more than friendship – and probably not even that unless James could control his infatuation. But James went on pursuing him, getting as close as he dared, and then retreating when Rupert turned skittish. He followed Rupert into the Fabians, abandoning his former conservatism without a pang. But in the company of political enthusiasts like Ben Keeling, or of emancipated New Women like Ka Cox or Margery Olivier, James was bound to look pallid and peripheral. What use was it to be loyal and intelligent when you had the personality and status of a schoolboy swot? If he wanted to shine in Rupert's eyes, he would have to get him on to his own ground and in a more intimate setting. The ideal way – the only way – to do this was to promote Rupert's election to the Apostles, of whom James had been a member since February of 1906.

The Society was founded in 1820 as an exclusive and idealistic circle of male friends. They referred to each other as "brothers," and signed their letters "Yours fraternally." Several Apostles of the 1880s and 1890s, such as Eddie Marsh, G.L. Dickinson, J. McT. E. McTaggart, and G.E. Moore, were romantically drawn to their own sex, but they were shy of giving their feelings a physical expression, and might even have denied that they had such feelings at all. From 1901 to the beginning of the war, however, a majority of those elected were actively gay, and among these Lytton Strachey and John Maynard Keynes were most influential in setting the Society's tone. Under their regime, talk about philosophy and the good life was combined with compulsive flirtation. Gradually, the "brothers" divided into two distinct types. Some – Lytton and James Strachey, Keynes, J.T. Sheppard – were intellectually and sexually on the prowl, often as a way of making up for feelings of physical inferiority. To be both clever and ugly was their uneasy fate. Then there were those whose ticket of entry was their boyish good looks and the passion they had inspired in someone from the first group: people like Arthur Hobhouse, Cecil Taylor, and Brooke himself. Whatever intellectual gifts they had, these were not the main reason they had been elected. Within a few years, the Society had been reorganised around the sexual couple.

Rupert became an Apostle on 25 January 1908. He owed his election mainly to James, who had to overcome heavy opposition from unnamed quarters. Three years earlier, Lytton Strachey and Keynes had pushed through the election of another yellow-haired public school hero, the Etonian Arthur Hobhouse. He had turned out to be a grave disappointment to them, both sexually and intellectually.[8] His sponsors probably feared that Rupert would be a pea from the same pod, but finally gave in to James's pleadings. Rupert held his own as an Apostle, however. For the Easter vacation of 1908 he was asked to join G.E. Moore's reading party at Market Lavington, on the edge of Salisbury Plain. Since he scarcely knew Moore, this was a notable endorsement from the man whose *Principia Ethica* had made him the unchallenged intellectual leader of the Society. Being invited to one of Moore's reading parties was the entry into an inner circle that included most of the Apostles who became members of "Bloomsbury."

Reading parties were an old public school and Oxbridge tradition, and Rupert had already been on a few with his school friends. But the gathering at Market Lavington was in a different league altogether. Besides Moore there were Keynes, the poet Bob Trevelyan, the barrister C.P. Sanger, the economist Ralph Hawtrey, the critic Desmond Mac-Carthy, and Lytton and James Strachey. For someone who had scraped through his preliminary classics exams with a shaky second the previous May, Rupert might seem to be in over his head. But his looks, good humour, and native wit pulled him through. "Rupert Brooke – isn't it a romantic name?" Lytton told Virginia Woolf, "– with pink cheeks and bright yellow hair – it sounds horrible, but it wasn't ... I laughed enormously, and whenever I began to feel dull I could look at the yellow hair and pink cheeks of Rupert."[9]

In fact, Rupert's animal spirits were badly needed by the group at the Green Dragon Inn. Moore's philosophy fitted in cosily with the aesthetic interests of a few congenial souls, but it counted for very little in the world beyond Trinity and King's. Many of the Apostles gathered at Market Lavington had been struggling with arrested development, spinsterism, hypochondria, and inanition. In the egregious Saxon Sydney-Turner these traits had been raised to the level of a vocation, and James Strachey was an equally sad case. He was "a creature, not a man," in Gwen Raverat's eyes, "and pitiable for all his brains. He would sit curled up on the sofa looking like a cat that is afraid of wetting its feet."[10] "Excessive paleness is what I think worries me most," Lytton had once confided to Leonard Woolf. "The Taupe [E.M. Forster] ... saw this about me, and feeling that he himself verged upon the washed-out, shuddered."[11] One measure of the "paleness" of the 1908 reading party was that everyone there, except MacCarthy, either married late or not at all.

Rupert's history with the Apostles was largely a continuation of the public school culture that had formed his personality at Rugby. He had everything he needed to succeed in that world, but this also meant that there was little pressure on him to change his emotional habits, or to absorb the challenge of new and different experiences. Social life with his "brothers" was comfortable, and comforting. It was also sterile, in providing no sustenance for Rupert's truest vocation, as a poet. Instead, he could only imitate, somewhat feebly, the vocabulary and the moral system imposed by G.E. Moore.

In becoming an Apostle, Brooke was also committing himself to having two separate sets of friends at Cambridge. One set would follow the Bedalian style of country living, theatricals, and an easy mingling of men and women. The other was exclusively male and devoted to gossip and philosophical speculation; it was also clandestine, which made it hard for Rupert's other friends to understand why he spent so much time with people they mistrusted, and why he disappeared every Saturday night during term. He had to divide his loyalties, and cunningly keep one life separate from the other. Though he became a loyal "brother," he would never give himself wholeheartedly to the Society. He didn't mind catering to the Society's obsessive interest in the subject of "copulation" (as they called it). But Rupert flatly refused to become the lover of James, or of any other "brother" (with one possible exception).[12] On the other hand, he never minded being pursued by older Apostles, whereas women who pursued him were bound to be treated badly.

In April 1909 Rupert went to another of Moore's reading parties, at the Lizard, in Cornwall. It was freakishly warm, and Rupert spent the days swimming in the surf and lying on the beach to dry. His new pose of being a child of nature put James Strachey under a severe strain. "This afternoon," he reported to Lytton, "for the first time in my life, I saw Rupert naked. Can't we imagine what you'ld say on such an occasion? ... But I'm simply inadequate of course. So I say nothing, except that I didn't have an erection – which was fortunate?, as I was naked too. I thought him – if you'ld like to have a pendant – 'absolutely beautiful.'"[13] Once again, James plucked up courage to invite Rupert to his bed (as he had done intermittently since 1906), and once again he was bluntly refused. Rupert preferred to spend his nights in trying to beat off Moore's relentless attacks on Fabianism. Moore was notoriously gifted and persistent at deflating other people's enthusiasms. He did not deflate Rupert, but his ascendancy over the Apostles at this time meant that Rupert would have to look elsewhere for friends who would share his political beliefs.

The Dance of the Sheets

Rupert moved to Grantchester in July 1909, and his friends came to frolic with him in the river and under the apple boughs. But by October the light was fading and he began to suffer from lonely nights. A few months before, James Strachey had given up on the hope of Rupert going to bed with him, or with any other young man. "I found out something about him," James told Duncan Grant, "which *did* make me despair. He's a *real* womaniser. And there can be no doubt that he *hates* the physical part of my feelings *instinctively* ... just as I should hate to be touched by a woman."[14] James, however, was only half right. Rupert wanted to lose his virginity, but not through a surrender to some older, predatory Apostle. Nor, whatever his "womanising" instincts, could he expect Noel or any other young woman he knew to surrender to him. His solution was to invite Denham Russell-Smith to come and stay, for the weekend of 30 October. Rupert had been closer friends with Denham's older brother Hugh, but found Denham more physically appealing. He was two years younger than Rupert, which fitted Rupert's pattern of being attracted to younger boys. If he was going to be initiated into sex, it would not be by an act of submission. It was not until his nervous breakdown, three and a half years later, that Rupert told the story of that weekend to James Strachey. It was probably the most revealing letter he ever wrote:

> How things shelve back! History takes you to January 1912 –
> Archaeology to the end of 1910 – Anthropology to, perhaps, the
> autumn of 1909. –
>   The autumn of 1909! We had hugged & kissed & strained,
> Denham & I, on and off for years – ever since that quiet evening
> I rubbed him, in the dark, speechlessly, in the smaller of the two
> small dorms. An abortive affair, as I told you. But in the summer
> holidays of 1906 and 1907 he had often taken me out to the
> hammock, after dinner, to lie entwined there. – He had vaguely
> hoped, I fancy, – – – But I lay always thinking Charlie [Lascelles].
>   Denham was though, to my taste, attractive. So honestly and
> friendlily lascivious. Charm, not beauty, was his *forte*. He was not
> unlike Ka, in the allurement of vitality and of physical magic. –

oh, but Ka has beauty too. – He was lustful, immoral, affectionate, and delightful. As romance faded in me, I began, all unac-
knowledgedly, to cherish a hope – – – But I was never in the
slightest degree in love with him.

In the early autumn of 1909, then, I was glad to get him to
come and stay with me, at the Orchard. I came back late that
Saturday night. Nothing was formulated in my mind. I found him
asleep in front of the fire, at 1.45. I took him up to his bed, – he
was very like a child when he was sleepy – and lay down on it.
We hugged, and my fingers wandered a little. His skin was always
very smooth. I had, I remember, a vast erection. He dropped off
to sleep in my arms. I stole away to my own room: and lay in bed
thinking – my head full of tiredness and my mouth of the taste of
tea and whales, as usual.[15] I decided, almost quite consciously,
I *would* put the thing through next night. You see, I didn't at all
know how he would take it. But I wanted to have some fun, and,
still more, to see what it was *like,* and to do away with the shame
(as I thought it was) of being a virgin. At length, I thought, I shall
know something of all that James and Norton and Maynard and
Lytton know and hold over me.

Of course, I *said* nothing.

Next evening, we talked long in front of the sitting room fire.
My head was on his knees, after a bit. We discussed sodomy. He
said he, finally, thought it *was* wrong … We got undressed there,
as it was warm. Flesh is exciting, in firelight. You must remember
that *openly* we were nothing to each other – less even than in
1906. About what one is with Bunny (who so resembles Denham). Oh, quite distant!

Again we went up to his room. He got into bed. I sat on it and
talked. Then I lay on it. Then we put the light out and talked in
the dark. I complained of the cold: and so got under the eider-
down. My brain was, I remember, almost all through, absolutely
calm and indifferent, observing progress, and mapping out the
next step. Of course, I had planned the general scheme beforehand.

I was still cold. He wasn't. "Of course not, you're in bed!"
"Well then, you get right in, too." – I made him ask me – oh!

without difficulty! I got right in. Our arms were round each other. "An adventure!" I kept thinking: and was horribly detached.

We stirred and pressed. The tides seemed to wax. At the right moment I, as planned, said "come into my room, it's better there...." I suppose he knew what I meant. Anyhow he followed me. In that large bed it was cold; we clung together. Intentions became plain; but still nothing was said. I broke away a second, as the dance began, to slip my pyjamas. His was the woman's part throughout. I had to make him take his off – do it for him. Then it was purely body to body – my first, you know!

I was still a little frightened of his, at any too sudden step, bolting; and he, I suppose, was shy. We kissed very little, as far as I can remember, face to face. And I only rarely handled his penis. Mine he touched once with his fingers; and that made me shiver so much that I think he was frightened. But with alternate stirrings, and still pressures, we mounted. My right hand got hold of the left half of his bottom, clutched it, and pressed his body into me. The smell of sweat began to be noticeable. At length we took to rolling to and fro over each other, in the excitement. Quite calm things, I remember, were passing through my brain "The Elizabethan joke 'The Dance of the Sheets' has, then, something in it." "I hope his erection is all right" – – – and so on. I thought of him entirely in the third person. At length the waves grew more terrific: my control of the situation was over; I treated him with the utmost violence, to which he more quietly, but incessantly, responded. Half under him and half over, I came off. I *think* he came off at the same time, but of that I have never been sure. A silent moment: and then he slipped away to his room, carrying his pyjamas. We wished each other "Goodnight." It was between 4 and 5 in the morning. I lit a candle after he had gone. There was a dreadful mess on the bed. I wiped it as clear as I could, and left the place exposed in the air, to dry. I sat on the lower part of the bed, a blanket round me, and stared at the wall, and thought. I thought of innumerable things, that this was all; that the boasted jump from virginity to Knowledge seemed a very tiny affair, after all; that I hoped Denham, for whom I felt great tenderness, was sleeping. My thoughts went backward and forward. I unexcitedly reviewed my whole life, and indeed the whole universe. I was tired, and rather pleased with myself, and a little bleak. About six it was grayly daylight; I blew the candle out and slept till 8. At 8 Denham had to bicycle in to breakfast with Mr Benians, before catching his train. I bicycled with him, and turned off at the corner of – , is it Grange Road? – . We said scarcely anything to each other. I felt sad at the thought he was perhaps hurt and angry, and wouldn't ever want to see me again. – He did, of course, and was exactly as ever. Only we never re-ferred to it. But that night I looked with some awe at the room – fifty yards away to the West from the bed I'm writing in – in which I Began; in which I "copulated with" Denham; and I felt a curious private tie with Denham himself.

So you'll understand it was – not with a *shock*, for I'm far too dead for that, but with a sort of dreary wonder and dizzy discom-fort – that I heard Mr Benians inform me, after we'd greeted, that Denham died at one o'clock on Wednesday morning, – just twenty four hours ago now.[16]

The impact of Russell-Smith's early death belongs to the story of 1912. In 1909 his role was to give Rupert an escape from his sexual impasse. That he was not in love with Denham made it easier to seize the passing opportunity. For someone of Rupert's class, homosexuality opened a much easier and earlier path to sexual satisfaction. He may have felt "great tenderness" for Denham, but his main object was clearly "the boasted jump from virginity to Knowledge." Having taken the jump, his interest in Denham soon dwindled. There is no suggestion that Rupert felt for his sexual partner anything like the deep passion that James Strachey had long cherished for *him;* nor did his one-night stand with Denham make any difference to his love for Noel or to his determination to marry her. Rupert now knew about "all that James and Norton and Maynard and Lytton know and hold over me"; but he made no move to join their circle as a sexual partner. It took him three years to even tell anyone else about Denham.

It was part of Denham's attraction that he was unknown to Rupert's regular friends. The affair exacerbated his self-division, between the "dirtiness" of copulation and the "purity" of romantic love. "I thought of him entirely in the third person" and "[I] was horribly detached" sum up the relation between Rupert and his lover. And his secretiveness was stronger than ever, since he could hardly have discussed his escapade with any of his still virginal woman friends – least of all Noel. It is possible, also, that he might have had a few more passing encounters with men of a similar kind. Three months after Denham's visit, Rupert was propositioned by a Romanian physicist he met in Munich. To James, Rupert made a joke of this. He described how the Romanian fell to his knees in front of him and groped at his fly, until they were inconveniently interrupted.[17] But Rupert agreed to go and stay with his new friend in Bucharest, except that a former teacher fell ill in Florence and he had to go there instead. On the other hand, it could be argued that Rupert's experience with Denham had the paradoxical result of making him more eager and enterprising in seeking a female partner with whom he could enjoy "the dance of the sheets."

5

Grantchester
June–December 1909

In a Grove

As Rupert digested his mediocre exam results, he had a retreat already
planned at Grantchester, three miles upstream on the Cam. He claimed
that he left Cambridge because he was "passionately enamoured of solitude."[1] But anyone who really wanted to be a hermit should not choose
a picturesque spot within an hour's stroll from scores of acquaintances.
Before he moved there in June 1909, Grantchester was already one of
Rupert's favourite places, for tea in the famous orchard or bathing in
Byron's Pool, a secluded stretch of the river a few hundred yards from
the village. Nor could he really be alone when living as a lodger with the
Stevensons, who ran the teahouse. Their honey came from bees kept by
the Neeves at the Old Vicarage nearby. Rupert would always be a lodger
with someone, and there is no record of his ever cooking a meal in his life.

Rupert's exile made him even more of a Cambridge celebrity and the
village became the backdrop for his performance as a student Simple
Lifer:

I work at Shakespere [sic], read, write all day, and now and then
wander in the woods or by the river. I bathe every morning and
sometimes by moonlight, have all my meals (chiefly fruit) brought
to me out of doors, and am as happy as the day's long. I am
chiefly sorry for all you people in the world. Every now and then
dull bald spectacled people from Cambridge come out and take
tea here. I mock them and pour the cream down their necks or
roll them in the rose-beds or push them in the river, and they hate
me and go away.[2]

Later, when he had briefly dropped his mask, he would admit to James Strachey that "Solitude is my one unbearable fear."[3] Like many magnetic personalities he was at his best with enough people to count as an audience, and became ill at ease as the number dwindled. His new image – the elfin vegetarian socialist, roaming barefoot through the meadows and leaping naked into the river – was a guaranteed star turn. His friends flocked to see and imitate it. Rupert had created a new student style, which caused him and his followers to be nicknamed "the dew-dabblers." In 1911 Virginia Woolf would give them a more durable name, the "Neo-pagans."

In the summer of 1908 Rupert had started calling himself "a wild rough elementalist. Walt Whitman is nothing to me."[4] If Whitman was Neo-paganism's spiritual grandfather, its godfather was Edward Carpenter, with his gospel of nudity, sunbathing, and sandals. In *Civilisation: Its Cause and Cure*, Carpenter had predicted the coming of a new and glorious post-Christian man:

> The meaning of the old religions will come back to him. On the
> high tops once more gathering he will celebrate with naked
> dances the glory of the human form and the great processions of
> the stars, or greet the bright horn of the young moon which now
> after a hundred centuries comes back laden with such wondrous
> associations – all the yearnings and the dreams and the wonder-
> ment of the generations of mankind – the worship of Astarte and
> of Diana, of Isis or the Virgin Mary; once more in sacred groves
> will he reunite the passion and the delight of human love with his
> deepest feelings of the sanctity and beauty of Nature; or in the
> open, standing uncovered to the Sun, will adore the emblem of
> the everlasting splendour which shines within.[5]

Unlike the Oliviers, Rupert had not grown up with any special closeness to nature. Everything he did in his days at Grantchester was done to make a point, including his report in a letter to Noel:

> I wander about bare foot and almost naked, surveying Nature
> with a calm eye. I do not pretend to understand Nature, but I
> get on very well with her, in a neighbourly way. I go on with my
> books, and she goes on with her hens and storms and things,
> and we're both very tolerant. Occasionally we have tea together.

> I don't know the names of things ... but I get on very well by
> addressing all flowers "Hello, Buttercup!" and all animals
> "Puss! Puss!"⁶

This was typical of the gratingly facetious style of Rupert's letters to Noel
and she, also typically, quickly brought him down to earth: "no doubt
you have a tremendous capacity for enjoyment, only I wish you wouldnt
talk about Nature in that foolish and innocent tone of voice – you call it
making jokes, and I suppose you think it's nice; but I dont like it a bit –
I've told you why lots of times."⁷ Noel had spent half her childhood in
the woods, and they were her first school. She cared deeply about nature, and wanted to know as much as possible about it. Rupert knew
only that Grantchester required a pose, which he was only too eager to
provide. Unfortunately for him, he had fallen in love with someone who
had no appreciation – or tolerance – for poses of any kind.

Jacques Raverat was one of Rupert's first visitors in June. Instead of
the mannered decadence of Rupert's first year at Cambridge, Jacques
now found him a creature of sunshine and fresh air: "he had given up tobacco and any kind of alcohol, he lived on vegetables and fruits and
dressed in a dishevelled style that showed off his beauty very effectively.
He was well aware of it, and relished the romantic and Byronic impression given by his long hair and open-necked shirt." In the morning
Jacques and Rupert bathed in Byron's Pool before setting off to London
to see Shaw's banned play, *The Shewing-up of Blanco Posnet*.⁸

Apart from the carefree image, what would Rupert live on, and what
would he live for? There was no chance of his getting a fellowship in
classics, but he persuaded his father to continue supporting him while he
switched his studies to English literature, which was gaining recognition
as a university subject.⁹ He started by writing an essay on Shakespeare
for the Oldham Prize, which he would win early in 1910. This paid £66
in two installments, more than many workers would make in a year. The
next step would be to write a dissertation on Elizabethan drama, and
submit it for a fellowship at King's. This was a feasible plan, though it
would take Rupert three and a half years to succeed at it. Meanwhile, he
was developing as a critic and writer of reviews, work that would not
have come his way if he had remained in classics. He had been winning
a steady flow of guineas in the poetry competitions of the *Westminster
Gazette*. More significantly, Ford Madox Ford published four of his

poems in the July *English Review*, and paid him £3 for them.[10] Rupert's real plan, he told A.F. Scholefield, was not to be a fellow of King's or a lecturer in Leeds: "I am going to be a bloody POET."[11] Specifically, he wanted to write traditional lyric poetry, but inspired by the philosophy of G.E. Moore: "The man who does not know that the human ear finds metre very beautiful, and that the most lovely effects have been got by the combination of words, metre, and ideas, is a fool. The object of literature is to evoke certain very valuable states of mind. They can best be (it is surprisingly observed) got by poetry, that is by metre, words, and ideas, much more often than by prose. Certain of them poetry alone can produce."[12]

The poetic lifestyle was displayed in two riverside picnics Rupert organised at Overcote, outside Cambridge. The picnickers included Justin Brooke, who drove everyone in his new Opel 10/18 car (the first intrusion of the motor age), Gwen and Margaret Darwin, Ka Cox, Dorothy Lamb, Geoffrey Keynes, and Donald Robertson.[13] Activities included boating (in the newly popular Canadian canoes), wrestling, riding horses bareback, plaiting daisy chains, swimming in the nude (men and women separately), and falling in the river. Rupert crowned the day by reading Herrick's great ode to the pleasures of May:

Come, let us go, while we are in our prime,
And take the harmless folly of the time!
We shall grow old apace, and die
Before we know our liberty.

Rupert was now in his prime, and happy to be admired for it. Henry James was invited by Geoffrey Keynes and Charles Sayle to sample a round of Cambridge pleasures, from breakfasting with Maynard Keynes to going down the river with Rupert. Standing on the punt in his white open-necked shirt and flannels, Rupert did what he called his "fresh, boyish stunt" to killing effect. James was susceptible to pretty young men, even while keeping an acute sense of what prettiness was worth. "He reappears to me," James wrote in his later tribute, "as with his felicities all most promptly divinable, in that splendid setting of the river at the 'backs.'"[14] Does "promptly" carry a hint that Rupert's felicities were too blatantly on the surface, too readily trotted out for a famous visitor? James was too downy a bird, surely, to swallow Rupert's myth whole. He even entertained the idea that Rupert was a "spoiled child of history." But at the news of his death in the Aegean, he wept.

After James, John. The swarthy bohemian Augustus John turned up in July to pitch his camp at Grantchester. Thirty-one years old and already famous, John had been commissioned to paint a portrait of Jane Harrison at Newnham. If Rupert was flirting with the Simple Life, John had flung himself into it head over heels. Obsessed with the threatened extinction of the gypsy way of life, he decided to become a gypsy himself, leaving his Chelsea home to travel with an entourage of "six horses, two vans, one cart, six children, Arthur [a groom], a stray boy 'for washing up,' a broken-down wagon, Dorelia [Dorothy McNeil] and her younger sister Edie."[15] The children, all boys, were by his wife Ida and his mistress Dorelia. John had lived with the two women in a ménage à trois until Ida died in childbirth two years before.

Another of John's mistresses, Lady Ottoline Morrell, came to sample his gypsy-style lodgings, but retreated to her home in London after one night. Rupert was delighted to hang around John's encampment and romp with his pack of children (and also with the five-year-old Gregory Bateson, another resident of Grantchester). Nonetheless, he did not copy either John's riotous dress (gypsy hat and sandals) or riotous sex life. Inspired by Whitman and Meredith, John posed as "a robust pagan with a creed that personified Nature as a mother."[16] Indeed, he got so deeply into his pose that it effectively ceased to be one, whereas Rupert's wildness and roughness were mostly on paper. He was never able to provide himself with one wife, let alone John's long train of wives and mistresses. Nor was he able to support himself on his own talent, as John already did. Though he affected to be free as a bird, Rupert at Grantchester did nothing that truly endangered his academic prospects.

Learning From Bedales

After their meeting at Bank in April 1909, Rupert had gone back to Cambridge, and Noel to Bedales. As soon as his exams were over, Rupert started intriguing to visit Noel at her school. He needed help from Jacques Raverat, who was living nearby with his schoolmate Geoffrey Lupton. Jacques's mental and physical problems had ended his career at Cambridge, but he was able to visit Florence in March 1909, and in discovering the Old Masters he also found a vocation for himself, as an artist.

Noel was reluctant to have outsiders turn up in front of her school-mates, and particularly to deal with Rupert's manic advances, whether by letter or in person. They managed only a brief and awkward encounter while walking outside the school. By now Noel was a dedicated Bedalian, and the clash of values between Rugby and Bedales would be central to the remaining six years of their relationship. Yet Bedales had grown out of Rugby, if only by reaction; and Rupert's attraction to the Bedales spirit revealed his own dissatisfaction with the world in which he had grown up. If the Fabians gave him the hope of making a new world through political reform, Bedales offered a more personal solution, by joining in a new way of life.

The Victorian public schools and universities were total institutions. They would not have liked to admit it, but they still had much in common with the monasteries from which they had sprung. Total institutions have a way of begetting their own most ferocious adversaries: Luther the spoiled monk, Stalin the spoiled seminarian. One such adversary, though a much gentler one, was Edward Carpenter. In 1880 Carpenter decided to turn his back on the system that had formed him. He had become a clerical fellow of Trinity Hall, Cambridge, in 1867, when he was twenty-three.[17] After six years of teaching, Carpenter found himself becoming disillusioned in turn, though more with the academic than with the spiritual world: "I had come to feel that the so-called intellectual life of the University was ... a fraud and a weariness. These everlasting discussions of theories which never came anywhere near actual life, this cheap philosophising and ornamental cleverness, this endless book-learning, and the queer cynicism and boredom underlying – all impressed me with a sense of utter emptiness. The prospect of spending the rest of my life in that atmosphere terrified me." Carpenter decided to renounce both his fellowship and Holy Orders. Soon, he had a vision of what he should do instead: "it suddenly flashed upon me, with a vibration through my whole body, that I would and must somehow go and make my life with the mass of the people and the manual workers."[18]

For the next seven years, Carpenter travelled the Midlands as a university extension lecturer, but by the end of this period he was close to a nervous breakdown, tormented by unfulfilled homosexual desires. Finally, he took Whitman's advice: "The great thing for one to do when he is used up, is to go out to nature – throw yourself in her arms – submit to her destinies." In the summer of 1880 he moved from Sheffield to the hamlet of Totley, where he lived with a scythe maker named Albert Fearnehough. His companion had a wife and two children, but he seems to have satisfied Carpenter's sexual needs as well.

In 1883 Carpenter published his first major book, *Towards Democracy*, and set up a utopian community at Millthorpe, on the edge of the Derbyshire moors. Attracting a stream of curious visitors, Carpenter made his home into a potent centre of propaganda. Like Arnold's Rugby, Millthorpe was the work of a dominant, single-minded, magnetic personality. Its ideal was summed up in the phrase the "Simple Life." Carpenter supported himself by growing vegetables and by writing; he proclaimed his comradeship with manual workers; he dressed in tweeds and homemade sandals (he called shoes "leather coffins"); he sunbathed, swam nude in the river at the end of his garden, and denounced the evils of the town and the factory. His remedy for Britain's ills was socialism, rural self-sufficiency, and sexual reform. The Millthorpe colony fascinated middle-class young men who suffered from the classic late-Victorian anxieties: worries over sexual identity, dissatisfaction with politics, or simple "neurasthenia." That Carpenter had found the courage to leave Cambridge made him an oracle for those who remained there, such as Goldsworthy Lowes Dickinson and E.M. Forster, and for the many other intellectuals who were fretted by modernity.

Carpenter had left the educational system in disgust; Cecil Reddie did so too, but then went back to try and renew it. Reddie came from the Anglo-Scottish middle class and went to school at Fettes, where Parker Brooke would have been one of his teachers. In 1885 he returned to Fettes to teach, and soon became a thorn in the side of his headmaster. Reddie was an eager socialist and member of the Fellowship of the New Life – the utopian society from which the Fabian Society was born. After only two years at Fettes, Reddie moved on to Clifton College, another satellite of Rugby. Here, he lasted only a year. He could not take orders from a superior and he loudly disagreed with every existing plan of education, especially in the public schools:

> Listen to the four maxims of a great English school perpetually
> dinned into the boy's ears. Be industrious; that is, try and get
> above your comrades. Be self-restrained; cork up your feelings

and be cold, formal, and "moral." Be modest; that is, be prudish and affected, be "gentlemanly" instead of natural and healthy. Be pure; that is, conquer and kill one lust ... but never a word against lust of money, lust of power, lust of comfort.

These are the "moral" maxims of an immense school; but, as one boy, starved on these husks, said: "But, oh, sir, affection is foreign to the whole spirit of this place."[19]

Close to a breakdown, Reddie fled to Carpenter's Millthorpe for refuge. As he recovered, Reddie decided that he should go out and found a school of his own. Carpenter's father had died a few years before, leaving him £6,000; he contributed funds, and Reddie started Abbotsholme School in 1889. Its ideal was "the nurturing and disciplining of the young child so that it might come to live the life of true freedom; to be a law unto itself, and a beneficent power in the world."[20]

Unfortunately, Reddie was an autocrat and a crank as well as an idealist, and he kept Abbotsholme in a perpetual uproar. His personal style was completely at odds with his principles. He took it for granted that he should have absolute rule, not just over the boys, but over the staff too. Abbotsholme, he said, was like a battleship, and he was the captain on the bridge. Everyone in the school had to wear a Simple Life uniform of his own design: a Norfolk suit of grey tweed with big pockets and knee breeches. The regime of cold baths and manual labour was too much for the thirteen-year-old Lytton Strachey, who was sent home after a few months. Justin Brooke was another dropout.

Racked by desertions and mutinies, the "battleship" could not steer a straight course and Reddie suffered a series of nervous breakdowns. He could not recognise his own lust for power, nor his pederastic instincts. Between the ages of eleven and eighteen, he believed, schoolboys should go to a single-sex school, with only bachelor masters. "Worship of the male type," he wrote, "is the natural hero-worship of adolescence; and comradeship is the natural outlet for the affections among normal boys during this period ... The greatest crime against youth is the crime of accelerating puberty."[21]

When Reddie was at last forced to retire, in the 1920s, there were only three boys left in the school. It was J.H. Badley who made progressive education work. The son of a country doctor, he arrived at Rugby in 1880 at the same time as a new master: Parker Brooke. Superficially, Badley seemed to bend to the public school yoke. He became both the top pupil in classics and a member of the First XV at rugby. His ambition was to return to Rugby as a master. But at Cambridge he became a Simple Lifer, influenced by such friends as Roger Fry, Goldsworthy Lowes Dickinson, and Carpenter himself. When Reddie founded Abbotsholme, Badley signed on as one of the first teachers. After three years, however, he broke with Reddie. He wanted two things that were anathema to his headmaster: to make Abbotsholme co-educational, and to marry. "My greatest friend at Cambridge," he recalled, "came of a rather well-known feminist family – Garrett Anderson – and he converted me to co-education as being the right thing to be done. Eventually I married his sister, who was of course still more keen, and who insisted if we had a school it must have boys and girls together."[22]

Like almost everyone who features in this biography, Badley had "a bit of capital" to back up his ideals. He found a country house called Bedales near Haywards Heath, Sussex, and opened his own school in 1893. For the first five years, it was a school for boys only, since Badley had his hands full without the added stigma of sexual mixing. "Old Bedales," as it came to be called, held faithfully to Carpenter's ideals. Here is what impressed one ten-year-old boy on his first day there: "Mr. Powell, the second master ... wore clothes unlike other men's, a pale blue tweed suit with leather at the cuffs, grey stockings and a red tie, and on his feet were very large homemade leather sandals. Everything in his house was very clean; the walls were whitewashed with few pictures; there was plain oak furniture and bare boards. After the evening meal, Mr. Powell went into the kitchen to help his wife wash up."[23]

The atmosphere of the school was spartan. The boys (and later the girls) had a large tub under their beds; they began the day by filling it with cold water and jumping in. They were driven on long cross country runs; they froze in winter and were hungry year round; they bullied each other and were beaten, though not so regularly or savagely as at more conventional schools. But Bedales found its supporters among the bohemian fringe of the upper-middle class and grew steadily. In 1900 it moved from Sussex to newly built quarters on a farm at Steep, near Petersfield, where it remains and flourishes.

Like many things at Bedales, the students' work on the land combined idealism and practicality. Badley certainly believed that nature was the best of teachers, but he also thought that there was more to be done than sit around in it. At harvest time, Bedalians put in a full day in the fields.

The rest of the year they studied in the morning and worked with their hands in the afternoon. The emphasis on country pursuits gave Bedales some reputation among the Continental landed aristocracy, such as the Békássys of Hungary who sent all six of their children there. Nearly a fifth of the early Bedalians were foreigners, recruited by Badley to avoid the imperialist chauvinism of the established public schools.

Backed up by his wife, Badley took on the other kind of chauvinism in 1898, when four girls entered the school. "We dubbed [them] 'beastly shes,'" recalled Peter Grant Watson, "and set about to make their lives as intolerable as possible."[24] It was a typical Bedales paradox, however, that when Watson fell in love with one of the girls it was now his own life that was made intolerable, with one of the younger masters leading the hue and cry. When he was fifteen, Jacques Raverat was taken aside for a lecture by the captain of the school. "The Chief (as Badley was called) doesn't like stupid and obscene jokes about women," he was told. "It's not something to joke about – and also there's nothing funny about something perfectly natural ... Sooner or later you're bound to know what women are like. I myself have bathed with naked girls."[25]

Seen through French eyes, Badley's ideas on sex were at once touching and absurd, and so were the female teachers that he dutifully hired: "The mistresses were almost always advanced women, feminists, socialists, Tolstoyans, etc. They dressed according to their theories: sandals, hygienic Jaeger fabrics, dresses without waists or shape called Gibbahs ... usually in a deliquescent green, thought to be artistic; no corsets, naturally – not hygienic – the hair drawn into flat *bandeaux;* in a word, everything needed to make women as unattractive as possible."[26]

Carrying all this ideological baggage, how did Badley succeed as well as he did? Unlike Reddie, he was no raving crank, and he was a highly gifted and devoted teacher. He had to keep up the appearance of a reputable, fee-paying school for the middle class. There would be self-expression without anarchy, nudity without fornication. Badley's vaguely leftist ideals owed more to William Morris than to Marx. He wanted his pupils to appreciate arts and crafts, physical labour, and country life. In the early years, little was done to prepare Bedalians for competitive examinations. Instead of stringing his students up for the battle of life, Badley taught them the arts of peace, leisure, domesticity.

At Bedales, the symbolic space of the public school was turned inside out. The buildings had no mock fortifications, nor did they enclose their playing fields. Instead, they opened on the woods and meadows where the students would learn to cultivate the land, but could also roam at will. Badley's personality dominated his school as much as Arnold's had dominated Rugby; but one cannot imagine Arnold shovelling out the school's earth-closets for a waiting line of boys with wheelbarrows. There were cooking and sewing classes at Bedales but only for boys, since Badley thought that they were the ones who needed lessons. For the patriarchal mystique of Rugby, Bedales substituted an ideal of rational comradeship between the sexes. Badley retired in 1935, though he went on living at the school; he died in 1967, at the age of 101. As with Thomas Arnold, his students never forgot him and they carried his influence throughout their lives.

Rules For Camp

In late July 1909 Rupert joined an outing organised by the young and enterprising Bunny Garnett. Bunny found an ideal spot to camp on the River Eden near Penshurst, a short ride from his country home at The Cearne and the Olivier house at Limpsfield. After a week he was joined there by Godwin Baynes, the herculean medical student who had been on the last Christmas excursion to Klosters. Godwin was "openhearted, warm, affectionate and generous," Garnett recalled. "Having escaped from a strict nonconformist upbringing at home, with prayers muttered into the seats of chairs before breakfast, he had become an enthusiastic neo-pagan."[27] Instead of hymns in the parlour, he now sang Wagner arias as he strode along the ridges of Snowdon. Bryn, Noel, and Daphne Olivier arrived next, with their neighbour Dorothy Osmaston; then Harold Hobson (an engineer friend of Bunny's) and Walter Layton – soon to be engaged to Dorothy. Finally, Rupert and Dudley Ward turned up – by the same "coincidence" that had brought them to Bank at Easter. But this time Margery was not there to keep a jealous eye on his walks with Noel. A story of Bunny's catches the true Olivier style – panache or blind arrogance, depending on one's prejudices:

> On Sunday morning the rustics of Penshurst came down and leant in a line upon the parapet of the bridge, staring into the pool in which we were to bathe.
> "Come on," said Daphne. "They're not going to stop us."

Nor did they. We bathed, ignoring them, and Noel, not to be put off from her high dives, picked her way along the parapet between the rows of wrists and elbows, politely asked for standing-room in the middle, and made a perfect dive into the pool. With florid expressionless face, the nearest labourer shook his black Sunday coat-sleeve free of the drops which had fallen from her heel.[28]

Camping out was just coming into style. It was more adventurous than the traditional reading parties for undergraduates, and more likely to include women (often, it must be said, because they understood the mysteries of cooking and washing up). At Bedales camping was actually part of the curriculum and Old Bedalians were reunited at an annual camp, invariably attended by "The Chief." He would welcome the Boy Scout movement, founded by Baden-Powell in 1908 to prepare British youth for colonial life and, when necessary, for colonial warfare. Scouting, Badley argued, "satisfies ... the universal craving for adventure and for open-air life which is particularly strong in the 'Red Indian' phase of growth; a phase through which children normally pass in their recapitulation of the social and economic development of mankind just as they have passed, before birth, through a recapitulation of organic evolution."[29] Instead of a cadet corps with uniforms and drill, Bedales had a scout corps, whose training was modelled on the Boer commandos. The open field was more appealing than the parade ground, but students did not go there just to dabble in the dew. Like everything else at Bedales, camping had plenty of rules:

> The Camp is always pitched near a bathing-place, for Bedalians, like fish, cannot live long out of water ... The Camp itself consists of four tents – the cook tent, one sleeping tent for the girls, and two for the boys. Bedding of straw, bracken, or heather is provided, and each camper brings with him three blankets, one of which is sewn up into a sleeping-bag. Pillows most of us scorn; the most hardened do without, the others roll up their clothes, and thus make a good substitute.
>
> Every other day, at least, is spent in a good tramp across the country – ten or fifteen miles at first to get into training, but this may be increased to twenty, or even twenty-five, later on ... We

take sandwiches with us for lunch, thus avoiding an elaborate midday meal, and on the longer walks find tea on the way, arriving back at Camp in time for a bathe and supper. Then we adjourn to the neighbouring farmhouse (whence we get our bread, butter, eggs, and milk) and for the rest of the evening sit lazily, while the Chief and another take turn and turn about in reading aloud some novel. After a strenuous day of walk, a slack day in Camp usually follows, with plenty of bathing and perhaps a short walk in the afternoon to get up an appetite for supper. Too many slack days, however, should be discouraged, as they mean extra work for the cook, and anyway we don't come to Camp to slack.[30]

At Penshurst, Noel showed her Bedalian spirit by joining the men to bathe nude in the river – under cover of darkness, but using a bicycle lamp to show them where to dive. "There is much to be said," Badley proclaimed, "for the practice, where possible, of nudism as a means of mental as well as of bodily health ... Under right conditions, amongst friends and at camp for instance, it is perfectly possible and, I believe, all to the good. But I have never wished to make it the rule for all, as there are some whom it makes unwholesomely sex-conscious."[31] There would be mixed nude bathing in the junior school (to age twelve or thirteen); then boys separately in the nude, girls with their choice of nudity or a costume; at mixed events all wore costumes. At an Old Bedalian weekend, Noel once scandalised Badley by diving nude off the high board in sight of everyone. He insisted on bathing suits after that. Badley was trying to carry water on both shoulders, even if the side of restraint outweighed that of liberation. Neo-paganism had similar contradictions. There was the cult of the body beautiful and scorn for social conventions; but there was also a strict, self-imposed chastity before marriage. It was an unstable mixture of impulses, and for some an explosive one.

Bunny Garnett saw Rupert for the first time at the Penshurst camp: "His complexion, his skin, his eyes and hair were perfect. He was tall and well built, loosely put together, with a careless animal grace and a face made for smiling and teasing and sudden laughter. As he ate in the firelight I watched him, at once delighted by him and afraid that his friendliness might be a mask. What might not lie below it?"[32] Rupert's poem "Jealousy" shows one emotion that lay below. A girl whom the poet once admired for her coolness and wisdom is now "Gazing with silly sickness" on a fool, whose "empty grace ... strong legs and arms ... rosy face" suggest Godwin Baynes. Godwin did propose to Bryn a couple of months after the camp and, if they are models for the two lovers, the poet cast a morbid eye on their affection. He imagines them married: the husband's strength running to fat, love sinking into habit, until the last act:

> And you, that loved young life and clean, must tend
> A foul sick fumbling dribbling body and old,
> When his rare lips hang flabby and can't hold
> Slobber, and you're enduring that worst thing,
> Senility's queasy furtive love-making.
> That's how I'll see your man and you?
> But you
> – Oh, when *that* time comes, you'll be dirty too!

Rupert started with a pastiche of seventeenth-century satire, but soon his own preoccupations took over. For him, "dirtiness" was moral rather than physical, and was caused by sexual experience. His Neo-paganism was a willful, sometimes desperate attempt to escape from his engrained puritanism. The Olivier girls, raised by free-thinking parents, were more instinctually pagan than he could ever be. A further reason for his confusion was Noel's strategic control over her own emotions. She had had several chances to be with Rupert in 1908–09: at the dinner for her father, during the production of *Comus*, at Bank in the New Forest, and at the Penshurst camp. Rupert had no hesitation about feeling and expressing his love; but at Bedales the rule was that tender emotions were best kept hidden. A school friend reminded her of this, four years later: "I sometimes fear I am still capable of that absurd sensation, i.e. a pash ... My dear, pashes are vain and silly (tho' I don't for one moment say 'unreal') things I have come to the conclusion."[33] It was not until three years after their first meeting that Noel was ready to admit to Rupert the "pash" she had felt for him from the very beginning:

> I thought: there is Rupert in Germany, very wise and clever ...
> and he is very beautiful, everyone who sees him loves him; when I
> first saw him cracking nuts in Ben Keeling's rooms with Margery,
> I fell in love with him, as I had fallen in love with other people

before, only this time it seemed final – as it had, indeed, every time – I got excited when people talked of him and spent every day waiting and expecting to see him and felt wondrous proud when he talked to me or took any notice. When he talked for a long time on the river I got more and more in love and said so to myself when he was there ... At camp at Penshurst I was driven silly with love and it was perhaps at that time that I felt it most strongly.[34]

Rupert often blamed Margery Olivier for keeping Noel away from him, but it was just as much that Noel kept herself away for fear of being at the mercy of her emotions. Her elusiveness, paradoxically, provided fuel for Rupert's passion; perhaps, on some level, she saw an advantage in this. But if Noel had been more open about her feelings, Rupert might have been less frantic in his attempts to break into her citadel.

Rendezvous in 1933

Going to Cambridge had not made Rupert free of his gloomy parental home. He was still regularly summoned back to Rugby for weeks of seclusion, while his mother anxiously watched him for signs of illness or strain. Later in that summer of 1909, he decided to break the tedium of family life by bringing his friends to his family. He persuaded his parents to rent a large Victorian vicarage at Clevedon, on the Severn estuary, and there they awaited the invasion. The Ranee, however, was already on her guard. At Rugby she had met a young lady who knew the Oliviers. "My, yes!" the Person shrilled, "the Oliviers! they'd do anything, those girls!"[35] It was shocking enough that the Oliviers roamed around Britain unchaperoned, but what really frightened Mrs Brooke, most likely, was the risk of an imprudent early marriage that could torpedo the career of her favourite son.

For the first two weeks at Clevedon there were few visitors, and Rupert was ill. "My only way of keeping in touch with 'life,'" he told Dudley Ward, "is playing tennis barefoot. It's not so effective as living in a tent and a river with three Oliviers: but it annoys the family ... The family atmosphere is too paralysing." Then the guests started to arrive in packs and the family, which meant the Ranee was even more annoyed.

Most irritating was Bryn, with her complete disregard of drawing-room convention. "It's such a responsibility taking Bryn about," Margery had written to Rupert. "People always fall in love with her." Not the Ranee, however. "I prefer Miss Cox," she told Gwen Darwin, "her wrists are very thick and I don't like the expression of her mouth, but she's a sensible girl. I can't understand what you all see in these Oliviers; they are pretty, I suppose, but not at all clever; they're shocking flirts and their manners are disgraceful."[36]

The failure at Clevedon underlined the homelessness of the Neopagans. Ka's parents were dead, the Oliviers' parents mostly in Jamaica, Jacques's father in France. There were advantages, however, to being orphans. In lodgings, still more in a tent or a river, they could live by their own rules. Gwen Darwin, whose parents were alive and highly respectable, was not allowed to go on these frolics unless she could convince them that a suitable chaperone would be there too. "Sometimes I think that every one ought to be killed off at 40," she had written to her cousin Frances, "when I see what a misery all parents are to their children."[37]

Another solution to the problem of parents was to make sure that when you got older you would be nothing like them. Walking on the cliffs at Portishead, Rupert, Margery, Bryn, Dudley, and Bill Hubback hit on a scheme to bring this about. The poet John Davidson had recently drowned himself in Cornwall at the age of fifty. The year before, in *The Testament of John Davidson,* he had glorified the life of the road as the only antidote to age and death:

I felt the time had come to find a grave:
  I knew it in my heart my days were done.
I took my staff in hand; I took the road,
And wandered out to seek my last abode.
        Hearts of gold and hearts of lead
          Sing it yet in sun and rain,
        'Heel and toe from dawn to dusk,
          Round the world and home again.'

What if Davidson had only faked suicide? they wondered. Perhaps he was now enjoying a secret life, after casting off all his responsibilities: "The idea, the splendour of this escape back into youth, fascinated us.

We imagined a number of young people, splendidly young together, vow-ing to *live* such an idea, parting to do their 'work in the world' for a time and then, twenty years later, meeting on some windy road, one prear-ranged spring morning, reborn to find and make a new world together, vanishing from the knowledge of men and things they knew before, resurgent in sun and rain."[38] The walkers made a solemn pact to meet for breakfast at Basel station on 1 May 1933. Turning their backs on England, they would start a new life, "fishing for tunnies off Sicily or ex-ploring Constantinople or roaring with laughter in some Spanish inn." Jacques was invited in November; Godwin Baynes, Ka, and a few others would also get the call. "The great essential thing is the Organised Chance of Living Again," Rupert told Jacques, instead of becoming "a greying literary hack, mumbling along in some London suburb, middle aged, tied with more and more ties, busier and busier, fussier and fussier ... the world will fade to us, fade, grow tasteless, habitual, dull."[39] It is unclear why 1 May 1933 was the target date, except that by then they would all be twice their present age, and Mayday was a festival of springtime and youth. They could hardly have foreseen that by the appointed day Rupert and Jacques would be dead, Margery insane, the others tied to duties that would make the gathering unthinkable. What really mattered, anyway, was the vision as it first came to them, for Rupert's long letter of invitation to Jacques is the closest thing to a "Neo-pagan manifesto."

Their great aim was to throw off the natural accumulations of age: houses, jobs, spouses, children. One was not made old just by living long but by accepting a place in society without protest. To avoid being like your parents, you had only to get rid of everything your parents had got. "We'll be children seventy-years, instead of seven," Rupert vowed in con-clusion. "We'll *live* Romance, not *talk* of it. We'll show the grey unbe-lieving age, we'll teach the whole damn World, that there's a better Heaven than the pale serene Anglican windless harmonium-buzzing Eter-nity of the Christians, a Heaven in Time, now and for ever, ending for each, staying for all, a Heaven of Laughter and Bodies and Flowers and Love and People and Sun and Wind, in the only place we know or care for, ON EARTH."[40]

But instead of "living romance," Rupert meekly went home to Rugby after Clevedon. For three weeks his mother subjected him to "nightly anti-Olivier lectures" (which meant attacks on Bryn, whom the Ranee wrongly suspected of being Rupert's favourite Olivier). Meanwhile, Margery Olivier attacked him from the other side. Rupert had evaded Margery's vigilance by turning up unannounced at Bank and for the Penshurst camp. But Margery made sure that Noel did not come to Clevedon, and made it clear to Rupert that his attentions to her were not welcome. After he went home, Margery followed up with a long letter that kept him up all night with anxiety. Rupert would only do harm to himself and Noel, Margery argued, if he declared his love outright and tried to draw her sister into a premature commitment:

> Love, for a woman, she said, destroyed everything else. It filled her whole life, stopped her developing, absorbed her. "You'll see what I mean if you look at women who married young," she grimly adds. "No woman should marry before 26 or 27" (why *then?* if it kills them). And later "if you bring this great, terrible, all absorbing thing into Noel's life now it will stop her intellectual development," etc. It's a bloody thing, isn't it? The Logical outcome is that one must only marry the quite poor, unimportant, people, who don't matter being spoilt. The dream of any combined and increased splendour of the splendid you, or the splendid I with the splendid X – that's gone. We can't marry X. At the best we can, if we try to marry X, marry her corpse.[41]

Despite Rupert's fulminations, he was probably being given good advice – even if it was tinged with Margery's self-interest. Of the four sisters she was the most committed to intellectual and political causes; she was also the only one without a train of lovesick men. She was trying to be a New Woman and she wanted the same for Noel, a free space in which to work out her destiny. But it was naive to speak of Noel's or Bryn's destiny without accepting that their beauty was inevitably part of it. Nor did Margery admit how much she wanted to keep Rupert away from Noel in order to have more of him for herself.

In laying claim to Noel, Rupert also had his own inner divisions to contend with. One side of him longed for marriage, to move from fitful immaturity to love and sexual fulfilment. But the other side loved Noel precisely because he imagined her as a nymph who would vanish into a thicket if pursued. This Rupert, in his poems, harped on the physical and mental unsavouriness of old age. "Menelaus and Helen," for example, fills in what Homer left untold:

He does not tell you how white Helen bears
Child on legitimate child, becomes a scold,
Haggard with virtue. Menelaus bold
    Waxed garrulous, and sacked a hundred Troys
    'Twixt noon and supper. And her golden voice
Got shrill as he grew deafer. And both were old.

Often he wonders why on earth he went
    Troyward, or why poor Paris ever came.
Oft she weeps, gummy-eyed and impotent;
    Her dry shanks twitch at Paris' mumbled name.
So Menelaus nagged; and Helen cried;
And Paris slept on by Scamander side.

The poem reveals Rupert's fear of actually sharing a life with any of the young women he might love. By the time he sailed to the modern wars of Troy at Gallipoli he was consciously acting the poem out, preferring a warrior's early death to the long anticlimax – as he feared it – of married life.

To back up her views, Margery simply left Noel immured at Bedales, refusing to bring her out for any occasion where she might meet Rupert. He was unable to see her at all for five months after Penshurst. As autumn closed in at Grantchester, he began to suffer from fits of loneliness and depression. He had barely scraped through his exams, he was cut off from the girl he loved, he had struck so many attitudes that he no longer knew who he really was, and he was mired in sexual frustration that seemed likely to drag on indefinitely. All of this contributed to his seduction of Denham Russell-Smith in October, as a compensation for his failure with Noel.

"The Charm" shows how Noel fed Rupert's imagination but not his need for everyday love or companionship:

In darkness the loud sea makes moan;
And earth is shaken, and all evils creep

About her ways.
>   Oh now to know you sleep!
> Out of the whirling blinding moil, alone,
> Out of the slow grim fight,
> One thought to wing – to you, asleep,
> In some cool room that's open to the night,
> Lying half-forward, breathing quietly,
> One white hand on the white
> Unrumpled sheet, and the ever-moving hair   .
> Quiet and still at length!

Rupert wrote this within a month of his adventure with Russell-Smith, which should perhaps be included among the evils that creep around the world at night. Certainly the "unrumpled sheet" on which the beloved lies contrasts with the "dreadful mess" on the bed of lust. Rupert's sexual initiation, instead of giving him a more realistic vision of Noel, led him to make her even more of a wax figure, unconscious of desire.

Going to Town

The Clevedon vision of escaping over the hills was a reaction to the opposite kind of shift that the Neo-pagans now had to make, from student life to a serious vocation. Rupert could live poetically at Grantchester, but most of them would have to make their way in London, and their outings would now be holidays from the work that held them in the capital. From 1909, London began to replace Cambridge as a centre for their shared lives. Even Rupert needed a pied-à-terre there, so he joined his father's National Liberal Club. As clubs went, it was cheap and politically progressive. At one visit or another, he must have bumped into a fellow contributor to the *Westminster Gazette* called Raymond Chandler, a year younger than himself. They both wanted to be poets, but Chandler soon gave it up. His success, unlike Rupert's, would come late, and be achieved by cynicism rather than sentiment.

Gwen Darwin had been chafing at home for years. She did not have enough to do, her health was uncertain, and she felt smothered by an extended family that was almost an institution in Cambridge. She wished she had been born a man so that she could follow her interests without interference. In the autumn of 1908 her parents finally let her study art at the Slade School in Chelsea. She would live with her uncle William, but to be an apprentice artist in the anonymity of London was to her a liberation and a joy. Justin had come at the same time, to be articled to a firm of solicitors as preparation for joining his father's company.[42]

Jacques Raverat came to London in November, renting rooms in Chelsea. He was taken on as an apprentice at the Ashendene Press, where his project was to typeset Blake's *Marriage of Heaven and Hell*. In the afternoons he studied drawing at the Central School of Art; after Christmas he transferred to the Slade, which brought him into daily contact with Gwen.

Ka had decided to spend a fourth year at Newnham, but her social work projects often brought her to London, and the flat in Westminster that she shared with Hester became a centre for her Neo-pagan friends. Gwen Darwin, having escaped from her own dominating family, was especially charmed by Ka's way of life – a home without parents:

> Ka's flat was a pleasant place. It seemed to belong to her alone, for Hester was always out at some gaiety or other. There we lolled in chairs, and sat and lay on the floor, and smoked and talked; talked easily, openly, intimately, while Ka treated us all like children, with indulgent affection.
>
> There was always tea for us, or coffee in the evening, and we used to put the light out and sit with the fire light flickering on the walls and casting odd shadows on the ceiling ... I used to lie on the sofa, while Justin perched like a bird on the end; Ka sat with her white hands on her lap, and Margaret would be on the floor by the hearth, leaning her tired head against the chimney. And sometimes Brynhild would drift in like a gentle fragrance; or Noel with her bag of books, to tease Justin until they came to blows in childish horseplay. And Geoffrey would talk big and tell wild stories, to be laughed at after he had gone; and James would come in out of the rain like a distressed cat, to look at Rupert with adoring eyes. And then rather early, Margaret would say she must go or Aunt Emily would be frightened; and one by one we would drift off to affairs of our own, until only one or two of us were left alone with Ka, talking, talking till late at night.

And – I don't know what the others felt – but to my mind,
always hidden among the shadows behind our backs, was Death –
Death waiting to catch us who were so young and full of hope;
Death, ready to snap us up before our work was done – Death,
barely hidden, waiting to destroy all our youth and beauty
and grace.[43]

After a frenetic social round in London – including an appearance at
the Slade Arts Ball in a recycled version of his *Comus* costume – Rupert
left for his third Christmas in Switzerland, this time at Lenzerheide.
Margery Olivier organised the party; she included Daphne but not Noel
or Bryn. Ka and Justin begged off also, though Jacques came, to make up
for his awkward exit at Andermatt. Rupert blamed Noel for failing to
appear. He was in rather a surly mood for the holiday and, as it turned
out, there would be no more Christmases in Switzerland for the Neo-
pagans. Four months after the plan for their reunion at Basel, here they
were in Switzerland and already far from unanimous in spirit or commitment. The forces that would eventually drive them apart were starting to work, for those who had eyes to see them.

6

Ten to Three
January–September 1910

Death of a Schoolmaster

On the way back from Lenzerheide, Rupert fell ill with inflammation of his mouth and throat. He blamed it on some bad honey he had eaten in Basel. Soon after he had to deal with something more serious – the collapse of Parker Brooke's health. "He has been unable to see more than men as trees walking," Rupert told Dudley Ward. "He's a very pessimistic man, given to brooding, and without much inside to fall back on – in the way of thought. It has been bad to see him tottering about the House, or sitting thinking and brooding over the future for hour on hour, never speaking, and always in pain."[1] Parker Brooke had been in decline since his son Richard's death three years before, but now he had suffered a stroke. Two weeks later a second stroke carried him off, at fifty-nine. After his early brilliance at school and university, he had slowly dwindled into hen-pecked mediocrity. His career helped to create Rupert's almost pathological fear of age.

After the funeral, Rugby agreed that Rupert should come from Grantchester to run School Field until April. This continued his father's salary and profits, and gave his mother time to find a new home. The Fabian Society, of which Rupert was now president, was entrusted to Hugh Dalton and a rising young student politician, Clifford Allen.[2] Rupert had fifty-three boys to look after (though not to teach) for two months. It was the only time in his life that he held down a regular job, apart from his seven months in the Royal Naval Division at the end of his life. He rated himself "an efficient schoolmaster, tired and high-voiced and snappish" – and not afraid of discipline. Giving a flogging was an "extraordinary sensation," he told James Strachey. The boy he flogged "had broken his furniture to small pieces with a coal-hammer. But I had no consciously sexual emotions. I cried a little after he had gone."[3]

Taking over his father's job closed the circle of Rupert's upbringing. He had been born in a house near Rugby School, and now he had become a master there. The worst thing about it, he found, was the company of the other masters. He wrote an exasperated poem to Dudley about his eagerness to escape, but one passage showed how much affection he still had for schooldays – or rather, for schoolboys:

> They do not know the Light.
> They stink. They are no good. And yet ... in spite
> Of the thousand devils that freeze their narrowing views
> (Christ, and gentility, and self-abuse)
> They are young, direct, and animal. In their eyes
> Spite of the dirt, stodge, wrappings, flits and flies
> A certain dim nobility. ... So I love ...
>   each line
> Of the fine limbs and faces; love, in fine,
> (O unisexualist!) with half a heart,
> Some fifty boys, together, and apart,
> Half-serious and half-sentimentally.

By unisexualist, Rupert seems to have meant someone who combined male and female qualities. Or did he just mean one who loved his own sex? In either case, Rupert's attraction to young males was inseparable from the world of public school, where he had triumphed on the rugby field and first fallen in love.

As he wound up as house master, Rupert also helped his mother to retire from School Field. She chose to live a quarter of a mile away in a large semi-detached house at 24 Bilton Road, separated from the traffic only by an exiguous front yard. "It's the first time I have ever lived at a number," Rupert reported. "I've always been at a house with a name, before. The difference is extraordinary."[4] The difference was that Mrs Brooke had slipped down a rung or two within the middle class, and the kind of hospitality she could offer Rupert's friends was correspondingly reduced. The contrast between his home and such places as the Oliviers' house in the woods at Limpsfield, still more the Raverat château at Prunoy, was now much wider. Rupert had become one of the least well-off in his circle of friends.

Lack of grandeur might have been made up by charm, but 24 Bilton Road had only pretentiousness and gloom. In a misguided attempt to create privacy, its architect had put the entrances of each semi-detached around the side, in a dark little porch with columns; the stuccoed facade had a sinister blankness, as if the inhabitants had been bricked up inside. With Alfred now at Cambridge, Mrs Brooke would live mostly alone. When her sons visited, they would enter a sealed environment. Rarely, now, would Rupert's disturbing young friends, with their breezy manners and unsound beliefs, cross the threshold. The memories of schoolboy prowess that Rupert enjoyed when he visited School Field were gone. Bilton Road was a constant reminder that his family was in decline.

Parker Brooke's death consolidated the Ranee's emotional hold on Rupert. The death itself did not move him deeply, or not visibly so at least. It was part of the Neo-pagan creed to claim that they and their parents belonged to utterly different worlds. For Rupert, however, no real separation was possible. When he visited his mother, he slipped into his father's vacant role. He bowed to her moral authority, even as he chafed under the yoke and looked forward eagerly to the time of release. But always, before long, he would be drawn back. In any case, he could not afford an open break. Parker Brooke had built up a capital of at least £15,000, all of which he left to his wife. This would yield an income of about £600 per year.[5] Instead of passing on a share to her sons, thus making them financially independent, she promised Rupert an allowance of £150 per year, paid quarterly. She did pay it for the rest of his life, though it was never increased. She also provided for his younger brother Alfred, now a freshman at Cambridge. Rupert had just enough to live on, and could get some further earnings from freelance writing and winning academic prizes (in 1913 he would gain a second income as a fellow of King's). He might make £40 or £50 per year from literary earnings, but his whole way of life remained precarious when his mother could cut him off at any time. He could have achieved independence by taking a job, to be sure, except that the only thing he was qualified for was schoolmastering, and he had just learned how intolerable that was. So a silver cord kept him tied to his mother. He could never make himself a permanent home anywhere else during the five years of life that remained –

as if to do so would be disloyal to the woman who followed his affairs, with anxious love and reproof, from Bilton Road.

Folly and Evasion

From late 1909 onwards, Rupert wrote a series of poems complaining about Noel's failure to live up to their trysts earlier in the year, in the New Forest and at Penshurst. In "The Hill," the most romantically appealing of these poems, the beloved turns away on a momentary impulse:

> Breathless, we flung us on the windy hill,
> Laughed in the sun, and kissed the lovely grass.
> "We are Earth's best, that learnt her lesson here.
> Life is our cry. We have kept the faith!" we said;
> "We shall go down with unreluctant tread
> Rose-crowned into the darkness!" ... Proud we were,
> And laughed, that had such brave true things to say.
> – And then you suddenly cried, and turned away.

"Desertion" says little more about her reason for slipping apart:

> Was it something heard,
> Or a sudden cry, that meekly and without a word
> You broke the faith, and strangely, weakly, slipped apart?
> You gave in – you, the proud of heart, unbowed of heart!
> Was this, friend, the end of all that we could do?

Rupert's long separation from Noel had ended when he wangled an invitation to the annual Shakespeare play at Bedales. He went down on 18 December 1909 with Jacques. We do not know what passed between Noel and Rupert, but he was bitterly disappointed by the meeting. Margery managed to keep Noel from joining Rupert at Lenzerheide after Christmas, and may not have been above trying to turn her against Rupert by passing on gossip about him. Perhaps Margery saw Rupert flirting with Bryn at the riotous Slade Arts Ball; perhaps Margery, there or in Switzerland, decided that Rupert was flirting with herself. Whatever the provocation, or the interference by Margery, Noel clearly felt that

Rupert was too ardent and needed to be cooled off. Rupert had been trying to write shorter and less florid letters, perhaps in the hope that this
might make Noel more willing to open up to him. He always found it
difficult to write a sincere letter, he told her, because of his "folly and
evasion and cowardice." Noel trumped him by saying that, when it came
to letters, "evasion and cowardice succeed very well."[6] At this point,
whether in letters or in love, evasion alone was Noel's weapon of choice.

Bunny Garnett had been infatuated with Noel since the age of about
four, and regularly tried to breach her defences. In a letter of April 1910
she tried to explain herself. Bunny's father, meeting her on the train from
London to Oxted, had told her that all the Oliviers were afraid of emotional commitment, of "giving themselves away" to another person. That
was not quite it, Noel said; in fact, she *had* fallen in love, and more than
once (she surely had Rupert in mind in saying this). But for her, youth
meant that one had such passions while knowing, at the same time, that
they wouldn't last. Therefore, one wasn't touched to the quick or deeply
threatened by them; and the whole charm of being young, for her, was
precisely in recognising that one's feelings weren't permanent.[7]

It is not clear whether Noel offered this as an explanation or an
excuse. She was secretive to a high degree – not from any fondness for
intrigue, like Rupert, but because she was just "close" by nature. Mary
Newbery and Noel liked each other well enough when they were at
Bedales to share a bath regularly, but Noel never said anything about
her love affairs. Men who were attracted to Noel found her maddeningly
impervious and invulnerable. They could scarcely appreciate how she
limited her spontaneity in order to protect her youthful freedom of
action. Indeed, Noel found that after years of holding back her emotions
they did not appear on cue when she decided that she was ready to
commit herself at last. She did not truly fall in love until she was nearly
forty, and then she did so with all the risk and abjection that she had so
carefully steered away from in her teens.

During the winter of 1909–10 Rupert saw Noel only once, and he felt
that she was deliberately hiding from him. Trapped in his schoolmastering at Rugby, he longed to see her as soon as he was released in April.
What he got instead was an offhand note: "you don't climb at Easter, so
good-bye for some time."[8] He tried to intercept her train at Birmingham
when she passed through on her way to Wales, but missed her and was
left standing like a fool on the platform. All he could do was fall back on

the Society and go to Lulworth Cove for a week with James and Lytton Strachey. Lytton was nursing a frustrated desire for George Mallory, the most recent athletic beauty to catch his eye. With Rupert pining for Noel they got on better than before, and would remain good friends until the upheavals of 1912.

The Oliviers, and several other Neo-pagans, were keen Morris dancers and rock climbers. Although he had been capped for both rugby and cricket at school, Rupert would neither dance nor climb. He feared, probably, the different kinds of exposure that went with these pastimes. At Bethesda, near Snowdon, Noel joined Bryn, Jacques, Godwin Baynes, Rosalind Thornycroft, Bill Hubback, Eva Spielman, Mary Newbery, and H.A. (Hugh) Popham – a Cambridge diving champion who struck Ka Cox as "an odd silent lonely sort of party."[9] This was Jacques's first opportunity to get to know Noel well, and his description of her suggests what Rupert was up against:

> She was fairly short, but very strong and well set on her feet. Much later a rejected lover could say that she looked just like a chest of drawers and, to be malicious, the comparison had just enough truth in it to be funny. She had an admirable head, admirably set on her handsome round neck, brown hair, flat complexion, the face very regular and unexpressive, even a bit hard. But it was lit up as if by the beam of a lighthouse when she turned her large grey eyes to you. One could hardly bear their gaze without feeling a kind of instant dizziness, like an electric shock. They seemed full of all the innocence in the world, and of all the experience also; they seemed to promise infinite happiness and wonderful love for whoever could win her ... But one would be quite wrong. Like her sisters, she had been raised according to the most modern and advanced principles, in almost complete liberty. They had picked up a few practical ideas about life, and above all an emancipated and determined appearance. But their parents, overly intellectual, had not given them the breathable milieu that they needed in order to develop. One sensed that they all lacked something ...You didn't have to know [her] for very long to see that her great beauty, and her excessively perfect health, were matched by only a good average, practical intelligence, little sensitivity, no tenderness, no imagination.[10]

Summer of 1910

That spring, Rupert tried hard to beat down his love for Noel, since she was so firmly and painfully resistant to his ardour. "There's a stage where one believes she's a 'great creative genius,'" he told James Strachey two years later. "It's rather a nice one. It lasted 22 months with me. Conversation with her breaks it down in the end."[11] Conversation, at least, was more possible once the summer got under way. In late January 1910 Margery and Daphne had gone to see their parents in Jamaica, not returning until early October. With only Bryn to watch over her, Noel became more accessible physically, if not emotionally. At the end of April, Rupert went down to Limpsfield with Jacques for four days. They walked cross-country to Toy's Hill with Noel, Bryn, and Ethel Pye, savouring the first bluebells in the spring woods and the smell of the wet earth. In the pub where they had tea, there was a canary which, it was decided, looked exactly like Jacques.

Bryn came up to Cambridge soon after and the high summer of Neo-paganism came into full swing. This was the golden age of mass breakfasts under the apple blossoms in the orchard at Grantchester: the women still primly attired in shirt-waist blouses and skirts, the men in ties – except for Rupert in his open-necked blue shirt (matching his eyes), orchestrating the day's amusements. A punt was moored at the foot of his garden, for long excursions up and down the river. Inviting Bunny to visit, Brooke promised him "apple-blossom now, later ... roses bathing and all manner of rustic delight, cheeses, and fruit."[12]

This friendly invitation had some guile mixed in. Bunny was nice enough, but he was barely out of school. His major attraction was knowing the Oliviers so well. Encouraged by Rupert, he set up a cruise on the Norfolk Broads for five days at the end of June. Their companions would be Godwin Baynes, now the medical officer of health for Hampstead; Bryn; and an old family friend called Dr Rogers to serve as chaperone. Bunny shared a cabin on the wherry *Reindeer* with Rupert, and found him "simple, sincere and intimate, with a certain lazy warmth."[13] Rupert had plenty of warmth, to be sure, but not much simplicity. In his dissatisfaction with Noel, Rupert was again finding Bryn very appealing. The long days on the water showed off her gaiety, and her supple figure, to advantage. One sister for lust and liking, one for love; he pondered this riddle as he sat on the deck writing a long essay for the Harness Prize (which he won) on the English puritans. Inspired by his Neo-pagan company, Rupert jeered merrily at the absurdities of the puritan mind. He had not yet realised how much puritanism there was in himself, and how violently it was due to erupt.

Three weeks later, after much scheming, Rupert managed to see Noel briefly at Bedales. He had made contact with the writer Edward Thomas, who lived in his Geoffrey Lupton house at Wick Green. His wife Helen was teaching part-time at the school. Noel could come to have tea with him, though she had to be accompanied by another girl and have a pass signed personally by the headmaster.[14] A fortnight later they were together again at Bucklers Hard, on the Beaulieu River in Hampshire. It had been a shipyard in the eighteenth century, building warships with timber from the New Forest. Bryn and Dudley Ward had scouted the place after the cruise on the Broads. They found hay fields, a splendid landing-stage from which you could dive, and two rows of old brick cottages with a grassy street between them. It was then a remote clearing surrounded by woods, far from the over-built mecca for trippers that it is today.

The Beaulieu camp was carefully organised in proper Bedalian style. There was a large cook tent, borrowed from the school, and a small lugger rented for the two weeks they were there. Most of the days were spent either in or on the river. Rupert and Dudley came from their Fabian caravan tour to join Ka Cox, Godwin Baynes, Jacques, Noel, and Bryn. An outer circle included Harold Hobson, Hugh Popham, Bill Hubback and Eva Spielman (now engaged to each other), Sybil and Ethel Pye, and their younger brother David. One quiet evening – it may have been on his twenty-third birthday, 3 August – Brooke went aside with Noel to gather wood and asked her to marry him. They had known each other for over two years, but she was still only seventeen. Her response was a half measure: to accept Rupert's proposal, while not allowing him to tell anyone of her decision.[15] But it was obvious that something was up between them, and Jacques's vignette suggests how it may have appeared to the other campers: "she accepted the homage of his devotion with a calm, indifferent, detached air, as if it were something quite natural. No doubt she was flattered by his attentions, for she cannot have failed to see something of [Rupert's] beauty and charm; also, she saw how he was sought out, admired, showered with adulation on every side. But he did not inspire respect in her; she found him too young, too chimerical, too absurd."[16] What Jacques saw was only part of the truth. Six months later, Noel gave Rupert her own understanding of what had happened at Beaulieu:

> He bowed his head and said the truth about what he felt; I understood and was sorry and I loved his head so I kissed it and then he and history made me believe that I was a lover as well as he.
>   I'm not, Rupert. I'm affectionate, reverent, anything you like but not that. And so I get worried and sorry when you look devoted and I don't mind about Ka or German Duchesses at all, and I never feel jealous; only affraid of your loving me too much.[17]

Yet Noel ended her letter by telling Rupert she would always love him. What she meant, presumably, was that she could love, but could not be a lover in the sense of wanting deep commitment and physical closeness.

What about feelings of sexual desire? In all the thousands of words exchanged between Rupert and Noel, this is the great unspoken question. It seems to have been taken for granted by the Olivier sisters, as by most young women of their class, that it was both the safest and the most moral thing to remain a virgin until marriage. Noel almost certainly followed the rule, according to a letter that her friend Mary Newbery sent her in 1914: "Well, I have done it, taken the plunge. But we always considered, once in love, what is marriage, it just follows. But does it? I love him, and he loves me – but I have not settled that I want to marry him … You are quite right to have hung back – Just wait till it really happens and you won't hesitate for an instant."[18]

When it came to sex, the tribal customs of Bedales were paradoxical, reflecting the peculiar beliefs and magnetic personality of The Chief. Badley managed to convince his students that it was weak and silly to fall in love with anyone. Justin Brooke, for example, was handsome, charming, and ready to strip off at a moment's notice. But during Neo-pagan times it all led to nothing: "Until I was twenty-seven, I avoided things with a puritanical and somewhat cowardly dexterity. I was a boy in every way. Then one day a person whom I shall never cease to honour and be grateful to, insisted on kissing me. I was surprised, rather shocked and intensely disappointed about it all. But the lady persevered: made me realise things and then when I began to make love to her sufficiently obliquity left me, so that all was well."[19]

An engagement that was kept secret, and set no date for the wedding, was hardly a real engagement at all. Neither Rupert nor Noel had a clear understanding of how far they were bound to each other. Nor were they any more free to spend time alone together. They could at least be in touch for another fortnight, when they moved on from Beaulieu to work on an encore performance of Marlowe's *Faustus*. It was staged on 17 August for a group of visiting German students. Women could join the cast this time because it was not an official university production. Justin Brooke, who returned from tramping around California and British Columbia at the beginning of July, was immediately recruited to direct the play. He cast Francis Cornford as Faustus, Jacques as Mephistophilis, and Rupert as the Chorus. There were appropriate supporting roles for various other Neo-pagans. Bryn made a dazzling Helen in a low-cut robe with powdered gold in her hair. She didn't have to speak, just make the audience believe in "the face that launched a thousand ships." The only thing she had to rehearse, she joked, was how to walk like a lady. Ethel Pye embodied the Deadly Sin of Lechery – perhaps her extreme admiration for Rupert had been noticed? – and Ka was Gluttony. Noel was a humble understudy to Envy.

Again, the play itself seemed secondary to the preparing and celebrating of it. Bryn, Noel, and the Pye sisters stayed at the Old Vicarage, a stone's throw from Rupert's lodgings at The Orchard. Sometimes they came home from rehearsals by water, Rupert skillfully guiding the canoe along the dark and winding river. Their diversions, when they stayed home, were swimming and reading aloud. Whatever Rupert's stiffness onstage, he was a magnetic reader in company. He needed a sympathetic audience to loosen his tongue, and he had a shrewd eye for setting, like reading *Paradise Lost* high up in a chestnut tree with Noel and Sybil. In the evenings it might be *Antony and Cleopatra* or Meredith's *Modern Love*, over at the Old Vicarage:

> Our sitting room was small and low, with a lamp slung from the ceiling, and a narrow door opening straight onto the dark garden. On quiet nights, when watery sounds and scents drifted up from the river, this room half suggested the cabin of a ship. Rupert sat with his book at a table just below the lamp, the open door and dark sky behind him; and the lamplight falling so directly on his head would vividly mark the outline and proportions of forehead,

cheek and chin; so that in trying afterwards to realise just what lent them, apart from all expression, so complete and unusual a dignity, and charm, I find it is to this moment my mind turns.[20]

Sybil was in love with Rupert, of course, and saw him through hungry and uncritical eyes. Jacques's view of those days of rehearsal was much less sentimental:

> He read Noel his poems – poor Rupert – and others too – Donne, Milton, Yeats, Swinburne – in his slow, slightly affected voice; she listened politely but a little bored and often, I think, completely mystified; she would have understood Chinese poems as easily. I still remember seeing him, when he was painting some piece of scenery, touch the tip of her nose caressingly with his brush, as she came over to watch; she seemed to find this joke much more to her taste than serious readings or conversations. It was, it must be said, more suited to her age. In all, she felt for him only a certain affection, tinged with a little disdain. But Rupert did not take it too hard. He was completely given over to his adoration of her; bitterness – along with desire – had not yet entered into his heart.[21]

To break the tension there was always Byron's Pool, where, Rupert teasingly told Lytton, "It wouldn't stiffen you even at all to hear of what it was the rosiest chatteringest delirium for me to do – bathing naked by moonlight with the ladies. For I, of course, am with Jane [Harrison] in these matters."[22] Sybil Pye remembers him coming from the river and hanging upside down from a poplar tree to dry his long hair, a pose that reminded her of a Blake woodcut. Rupert was playing the game of "to the pure all things are pure" with his entourage of four comely young women. They *were* pure, so far as we can tell; but Noel was naturally without shame, whereas Rupert was consciously trying to deny his puritan heritage. And at what point would the game become earnest, when they all had to make their sexual choices, and live with them? Gwen Darwin expressed the longing of many of them that their maturity should never arrive:

> I wish one of us could write a "Ballade des beaux jours a Grantchester." I can't bear to think of all these young beautiful

people getting old and tired and stiff in the joints. I don't believe
there is anything compensating in age and experience – We are at
our very best and most livingest now – from now on the edge will
go off our longings and the fierceness off our feelings and we shall
no more swim in the Cam – and we shan't mind much ... If one
of those afternoons could be written down just as it was exactly
it would be a poem – But I suppose perhaps a thoroughly *lived*
poem can't be written – only a partially lived one. O it is intolerable, this waste of beauty – its all there and nobody sees it but
us and we can't express it – We are none of us great enough to
express a thing so simple and large as last Thursday afternoon.
I don't believe in getting old. I hate it, I hate it –²³

A Chateau in Burgundy

After *Faustus*, Jacques Raverat returned to France to join in another attempt to build a new form of life. A family friend called Paul Desjardins,
professor of literature at Sèvres, had bought an ancient Cistercian abbey
at Pontigny, near Auxerre. He restored it, and in August 1910 held the
first of a series of intellectual assemblies there. The aim of Pontigny, as
Jacques understood it, was to become "the stronghold of European *Culture* against all barbarian invasions: americans, utilitarians, fanatics and
all other materialistic incarnations of Evil; and it is to combine a revival
of craftsmanship and scholarship working as it were hand in hand."²⁴ In
the event, Pontigny became a successful talking shop for French and
British intellectuals in the 1920s and 1930s. Andre Gide was its most
prominent supporter. More inspiring for Jacques was a gathering of
his English friends at his family home at Prunoy, on the northern fringe
of Burgundy. Frances and Francis Cornford were invited to come in
September, along with Bryn, Noel, and Ka. Rupert asked Ka if he should
try to escape from Bilton Road and come himself, to harmonize the clash
of sensibilities:

It will be splendid for both parties – and for everyone else – if
Brynnoel and France/is love each other. But that sort of joining-up
is made easier by an extra person who knows and loves both lots
and has a calmer, more intriguing and farseeing mind than the

romantic dreamer Jacques. So that I felt, though they of course *would* join, Francis' brooding and Frances' energy and Brynnoel's shyness and partly affected stupidity might *just* possibly make it less complete and happy than it would be under the benign encouragement of one so wise and so competent in *both* the languages and natures as (I was perfectly confident!) myself ... (No, I'm not pretending, even to myself, that I imagine you hadn't thought of it just as much as I; having seen, as you did, for instance, the frightened gleaming silence of Bryn and Noel at Faustus' time – in company.)[25]

In part, Rupert just wanted to bridge a cultural gap. Francis Cornford was a thirty-six-year-old don with a brilliant book on Thucydides, Frances an offshoot of the Cambridge aristocracy even if she had not herself gone to university. Bryn, on the other hand, had never sought an intellectual career; at this time she was trying her hand at making jewelry, with frequent interruptions for country outings or going to London theatres. Noel was aiming at medical school rather than university. One can see how both sisters might have been intimidated by the bantering intellectual style of Cambridge, and also how they might hold on defensively to their own powers of beauty, vigour, and tribal solidarity.

What had been overlooked in all this anxious anticipation was the effect of the place where they were to gather. Probably his English friends joked about Jacques's château, imagining it as an oversized country house; when they arrived, they would find a combination of domestic charm and grandeur. Georges Raverat, its first bourgeois proprietor, had bought the Château de Vienne in 1901 from the impoverished Comte de Goyon. It had been built between 1710 and 1725 by the Lalive family, favourites of Louis XIV, after they had razed the medieval château that stood on the site. Used mainly in the summer for hunting, the château was not built for warmth, but for light. The main block had great windows that gave a clear view right through the building. There were scores of rooms of all shapes and sizes, towers with conical roofs, huge chimneys for the wood-burning stoves in the cellars, stables, a walled kitchen-garden, and some seven hundred acres of woods and tenant farms. Best of all, for these particular guests, was the sweeping park behind the house that led to a large and secluded artificial lake.

Jacques went for long walks with Bryn and found her "more marvellous than ever ... radiant and wild rose like." With his romantic sensibility, he dreamed of some charm to preserve the friendships he had enjoyed since his recovery in 1909. When he had seen Justin off to America nine months earlier, they were already planning a ceremony for his return:

> On midsummer day, at night, we'll make a solemn sacrifice again to the Gods of perpetual youth, to close the cycle and celebrate most worthily his deliverance and birth. I am pondering over the ritual even now: there must be fire; and water, clear spring water poured at sunrise out of a cup of virgin crystal; and wreaths of dog roses and honeysuckle; and there should be a bird in a cage to set free at dawn and a fair prayer to sing as we dance hand in hand round the leaping fire.

After Ka left Prunoy, the rest of them took up the idea of composing a Neo-pagan rite:

> We had some fair days even after you went – for all that I was a little sad. And we invented fires, after bathing, between tea and suppertime. I wish we had thought of that before. We talked a great deal of the urgency of some kind of ritual, mystery, initiation, symbolism and we planned a great litany of the four elements. But I doubt whether it will ever come to anything. As Francis says, we are all much too rational and self-conscious – all except Frances perhaps, that child.[26]

Francis Cornford was steeped in Cambridge anthropology and well able to design a modern ritual for his friends. Nonetheless, they were right to doubt their power to be real, rather than Neo-pagans. Their best hope lay in poetry, that attenuated modern substitute for living myth. In poems like "Dining-room Tea" and "Grantchester" Rupert would come as close as any of them did to settling their quarrel with time and change.

The immediate quarrel for Rupert, though, was with Noel. Nominally, he had to pay tribute to the Ranee by spending the rest of August and all September at Bilton Road, and working on his Elizabethans. But he was anxious to slip away for a couple of clandestine meetings with Noel, as a way of confirming the pledge that they had made to each other at Beaulieu River. After *Faustus* she went to stay at Walberswick, Suffolk, with Mary Newbery. Rupert wanted to meet her somewhere nearby, which she flatly refused to do. Then he wanted to turn up at Prunoy, and met with the same refusal. Once Noel had admitted her love for him, Rupert felt that she should be with him whenever possible, by hook or by crook. Noel had a very different prospect. She knew that if she presented Rupert as her fiancé she would bring down on herself a storm of disapproval, starting with her family, but also including people like Badley, who would never allow one of his pupils to be formally engaged, especially one who was still only sixteen. "If we cant meet without schemes," Noel told Rupert, "I would rather, by far, not see you for half a year."[27] Apart from these social difficulties, she felt that having made her promise of love to Rupert, he should now wait quietly and calmly for the time, some years ahead, when they could get married. Knowing that she loved him should make him patient; whereas for Rupert it made him impatient to build a shared life. In that sense, exchanging vows in the woods at Beaulieu left them as much at odds as they had been before.

7

Couples
October 1910–May 1911

Changing Partners

During 1910 several young men in Rupert's circle were becoming frustrated and impatient. How long could the young women they loved go on hinting that they would embrace sensuality some day – but not yet? Either their love had to be followed through to its logical consummation or they would pursue sex outside the group, as Rupert had already done surreptitiously with Denham Russell-Smith.

Towards the end of June, Jacques Raverat went walking with Ka Cox in the Lake District. Somewhere near Ullswater, love, as he put it, sat down between them like a "rude, unbidden guest." In fact, this was the natural result of an intimacy that had already lasted three years. But their relations had always been lopsided. Although he was two years older than Ka, Jacques felt her to be more mature, more wise and good than himself. His ill health made him long to be mothered and protected. "Think of me but as a wild and wayward child," he wrote to her, "and sometimes lay your cool hand on my head." Yet in reaction against his own loneliness and dependency he had often denounced love, seeing it as a snare that had humbled too many of his friends. "To love and yet to be *perfectly free*," he wrote her, "is not that an ideal?"[1]

In Gwen Raverat's novel, Ka is asked why she won't agree to marry Jacques. "He doesn't seem enough of a person somehow," she replies, "he's such a baby. He doesn't seem worth marrying." Jacques was full of grandiose plans, but he was also pathetically nervous and fragile, with sores along his wrists.[2] He kept pouring out his heart to Ka; for whatever reason, she would only return him friendship for love. Her years at Newnham were now over, and she was living either with her sister Hester in London or at her own cottage in Woking. She wanted a vocation, but had no financial need for one, and no firm idea of what it should be. Meanwhile, she was active in Fabian causes and lecturing at Morley College for working men and women. Jacques proposed to Ka again several times during the autumn. She would neither accept him, nor send him away.

Rupert, meanwhile, was very much in the same boat. After *Faustus,* in August, Noel again told him that he was too disturbing and made herself unavailable. Two months later she granted him one of those hurried and semi-clandestine meetings at Edward Thomas's house. It was becoming clear that in agreeing to be "engaged" to him at Bucklers Hard she had actually committed herself to very little. In several poems of this time, Rupert imagined his love for Noel as no more than a death-in-life.[3]

Godwin Baynes was another one trapped in the Olivier orbit through unrequited love for Bryn. He was twenty-eight in 1910, and already launched on his medical career. Bryn was fond of him, but not fond enough to commit herself to marriage. Baynes was not willing to be put off indefinitely, so when climbing in Wales at Easter 1910 he proposed to one of Bryn's cousins, Rosalind Thornycroft. She accepted him, though it would take them another three years before actually marrying.[4] The engagement may have contributed to Bryn's unsettled feelings during the year. She had never gone to school, much less university and it seemed time to find herself a vocation, now that she was twenty-three and with no immediate prospect of marriage. She had done some painting, and an art jeweller named Wilson agreed to take her as a live-in apprentice. Bryn worked with him for some months at Platt, in Kent. But the close work caused problems with her eyes, and the summer's excursions kept calling her away from her workbench.

Bryn's mother was always trying to keep her daughters by her in Jamaica, and Bryn agreed that when Margery and Daphne came back to England in October she would take their place. Before leaving, unhappy with the empty months that stretched ahead, she unburdened herself to Hugh Popham. Hugh jumped to the conclusion that she was in love with him – as, he confessed, he already was with her. Her response to Hugh was designed to cut off his hopes, yet one senses that she was sincere in speaking of her own unhappiness and confusion: "You made a person who was very fond of you and who had during the last few days gone through too many excitements and emotions for her nerves to be quite steady absolutely unbearably sorry for you too. Perhaps you did not know I could mind things ... I meant once, quite a long time ago, to warn you against myself – but it seemed altogether too silly and impossibly presumptuous ... you must not make me hate myself any more."[5] Perhaps she did not know herself what her trouble was, but it was not going to be resolved by someone who was two years younger than herself and still an undergraduate. Although Bryn was beginning to think that marriage and having children was the best thing for her to do, she did not see Hugh as a credible husband. When she came back from Jamaica after six months she refused his invitation to May Week and generally avoided his company. But Hugh would bide his time, and at last carry off the prize.

At the end of November, Rupert formed his own plan to break out of his impasse. He had already decided to spend the spring term in Germany. Before he went, he would go for a quiet holiday and settle things calmly with Noel. Margery and Daphne were going to the Alps with Hugh Popham, so Noel would be at a loose end for her Christmas break from Bedales. She would have to be chaperoned, of course, but Ka agreed to come and watch over her, and Jacques would be company for Rupert. The holiday would start the day after Christmas, at Lulworth Cove. "You'll have to arrange about Noel," Rupert told Ka, "– unless you think she'd be a nuisance, and the conversation *too* much above her head. You'd be responsible (to Margery!) that that very delicate young flower keeps her pale innocence, and her simple trust in God unshaken by the world-worn scepticism of Jacques and me. You *appear* (which is the point) equal to *that* responsibility."[6]

Noel agreed to come to Lulworth, but with the caveat that "Margery knows best." Then, on 22 December, she wrote to tell Rupert that she was going to Switzerland with Margery and Daphne instead. She claimed that she had made the decision herself, but Jacques went down to Limpsfield, and reported that Noel was "oppressed with a sense of responsibility to that woman her mother."[7] If Noel went on holiday with two young men, might not Ka's presence make things look, if anything, worse? But Rupert believed this was just a pretext. Once again, Noel was using a conventional excuse to avoid an honest encounter with him. "What hurts," he told Ka, "is thinking her wicked. I do, you see. Not very judicially, but I do. And what's to be done if you think a person you know so well is wicked? I don't see what I'm ever to do about Margery."[8]

Ever since Margery had flatly told Rupert to call off his stubborn pursuit of Noel he had made her the villain of the affair, for wantonly cramping her youngest sister's emotional life. But Margery had been in Jamaica from January to October, and Rupert should have realised that it made little sense to make her responsible for Noel's continued evasiveness. It was plain now, anyway, that Noel had been pulling her own strings all the time. "I find I've been a devil to Margery," Rupert confessed to Ka, "as well as in every other way. She says she never interfered (after a momentary impulse). Noel agrees. Ecco! Where am I? ... I *am* a beast, after all. Worse than ever. But apologising to Margery is a little thing; finding oneself in a mere Chaos of disconnexions is the horror."[9] As he planned his holiday with Ka and Jacques, Rupert must have felt that his relations with Noel had reached, after two and a half years, a complete dead end.

* * * *

Lulworth village was a single row of cottages, tucked cosily between the downs and the sea. From it you could sally out for strenuous walks along the cliffs around the miniature harbour. In those days before rural bus services Lulworth was well off the beaten track. Its remoteness and its layout (a bit like an ocean liner) made for an intense emotional atmosphere – as if the visitors had sailed away from their everyday life. After three raucous Christmases in Switzerland the party at Lulworth was there to take stock, rather than to celebrate. Gwen had wanted to come, but her family frowned on her going away without a married woman as chaperone. So there were only four arriving at Churchfield House on Boxing Day: Rupert, Jacques, Ka, and Justin. By day they rambled and picnicked up on the downs; in the evening they read *Prometheus Unbound* aloud. Justin was, as usual, the observer and the sympathetic ear, but between the other three the atmosphere was tense. They were each shifting their emotional investment. Jacques again asked Ka to marry him, and was again given the half-serious answer: "You're too much of a baby."[10] Rupert was broody and went for long walks alone. He wrote to Bryn in Jamaica, telling her that it was time to seize opportunities and stop worrying about what people might say.

In her novel, Gwen Raverat shows the tip of the iceberg emerging, when Rupert and Jacques return to Ka's flat after the journey from Lulworth:

They sat like mummies on the sofa while she lit the fire. Jacques thought there was something terribly feminine about her heavy form, as she squatted on the hearth, puffing with round cheeks; something eternally servile and domestic, utilitarian. "She's a good woman," said Jacques to Rupert. "A good squaw," said Rupert. These were almost the only words that were said ... The fire and the tea melted them a little, but they would not talk; and directly afterwards Rupert said: "Come on Jacques," and with a couple of gloomy goodbyes they left. In the street Rupert's arm came through Jacques'. "I like men," he said.[11]

At Lulworth, Rupert had turned towards Ka in reaction against Noel. Noel held aloof and always denied, whereas Ka served and accepted. But her acceptance stirred up crosscurrents of emotion in Rupert: a mixture of desire, contempt, repulsion, and the wish to reaffirm male comradeship against the world of women. Under all of these was a powerful sense of guilt for his own lack of integrity. "I'm red and sick with anger at myself," he told Ka after Lulworth, "for my devilry and degradation and stupidity ... I was mean and selfish, and you're, I think, of the most clear and most splendid people in the world."[12] He was falling in love with Ka, but doing so in a way that was bound to cause trouble for her, for himself, and for Noel.

Faschingsbraut

With all the festivities of 1910, Rupert had lagged far behind schedule with his fellowship thesis for King's on the Elizabethan dramatists. By September he had decided that he would have to submit it a year late, at the end of 1911. Four months of study in Germany were supposed to make him into an expert philologist, but his real reason for going was to escape the frustrations of his personal life in England and sort out his conflicting emotions about Noel and Ka. Yet, on the night that he left for Munich, he invited both of them to supper, which left all three of them tongue-tied and embarrassed.

From the beginning of 1911 to the outbreak of war in August 1914, Rupert would spend almost half his time out of England. There were better chances of sexual freedom across the Channel; not coincidentally, the further from England was also the further from the surveillance of his mother. He went down to Limpsfield early in January for a couple of days, to try and clear the air with Margery and Noel before he left. "I shall be glad," he told Ka, "to be in Germany, at peace. Rest means being where no one knows you."[13] The stay in Germany was meant to disentangle him from his undergraduate follies, and launch him into a more sober adulthood and career. In the event, the outcome was more the reverse. During his year and a half at the Orchard, Rupert had come as close as he ever would to having a stable home, a single beloved, a cohesive group of friends, and even a coherent personality. When he left for Munich on 9 January 1911 he had four years and a few months left to live, and was heading towards a series of emotional crises that would last until his death.

To study in Germany was a natural move for any aspiring academic, but to go to Munich showed the particular Germany that attracted Rupert. The academic centre of the country was Heidelberg and the political one Berlin. Munich promised a warmer and softer life than either: as D.H. Lawrence put it, on his first visit a year and a half later, "a lovely town, all artists, pictures galore." The artists lived mostly in Schwabing, the headquarters of German bohemianism.[14] The country branch of Schwabing was Ascona, where writers, psychiatrists, dancers, and *naturmenschen* lived on a mountain and tested the very limits of civilised life.[15] By going to Munich, Rupert was looking for sensual adventure rather than mere academic improvement (in fact, he did no serious studying while he was there). Adventure he found; but he recoiled from the experience and left Munich without having accepted the spirit of the city. While he was in Munich, the painter Sophie Benz killed herself with poison supplied by her lover, the mad psychiatrist Otto Gross. English Neo-paganism was like a children's party when put beside what was happening in Schwabing and Ascona. But bohemian life in Munich left Rupert hesitant and uneasy, and his return a year later was largely an attempt to redeem the disappointment of his first visit.

In 1908 the kaiser had dismissed Hugo von Tschudi, director of the National Gallery in Berlin, for being too sympathetic to modern art. Tschudi left for the friendlier climate of Bavaria, where in 1909 he became general director of the state museums. He stood as friend and patron to the avant-garde artists of Munich, who organised themselves first as the

Neue Kunstlervereinigung Munchen, later as the Blaue Reiter group. Their
leading spirit was the Russian émigré Wassily Kandinsky, allied with
Franz Marc, Hans Arp, Paul Klee, and the musician Arnold Schonberg.
Somewhere on the fringes of bohemia, at once sympathetic and ironic,
was Thomas Mann. At the time of Rupert's stay he was writing his own
meditation on paganism, beauty, and transience, *Death in Venice*. In September 1910, just before the London Post-Impressionist show, Kandinsky's group put on a show in Munich with works by Braque, Picasso,
Rouault, Derain, Vlaminck, and Van Dongen. As in London, these paintings set off a furore. "Either the majority of the members and guests of
the Association are incurably insane," said one newspaper, "or they are
shameless bluffers who are not unfamiliar with the age's demand for sensation, and who are capitalizing on it."[16]
Into this crucible of modernism drifted Rupert, armed with a few
scraps of German and a passion for the drawings of Augustus John:

> I move among the Munchen P[ost] I[mpressionist]s. They got up
> an exhibition of their French masters here last year; and go pil-
> grimages to all the places where Van Gogh went dotty or cut his
> ears off or did any of the other climactic actions of his life. They
> are young and beetle browed and serious. Every now and then
> they paint something – often a house, a simple square bordered
> by four very thick black lines. The square is then coloured blue or
> green. That is all. Then they go on talking … It is all very queer
> and important.[17]

This report was for Jacques, so that he could compare the artist's life in
Munich with the Slade. The aim of Rupert's account, it seems fair to say,
was to render the "queer and important" familiar and unimportant:
Cambridge looking down its nose at the Continental avant-garde. After
Munich, Rupert would be equally unimpressed by Vienna. In time, his
most famous poem would take insularity to its logical extreme by vow-
ing to turn a foreign field into British soil.
    Insularity was reinforced, in Rupert's case, by the fear and self-doubt
that threatened him whenever he was left to his own devices. When
asked what experiences he was having, he said he had come to Munich
"*exactly* to escape 'experiences.' I'd been having too damned many! …

'Experiences' – one stays in England for *that*."¹⁸ Was he just going
through the motions of foreign travel from a sense of duty, like the rev-
ellers who filled the streets for Fasching, the carnival of Lent? Rupert
was left with his eternal fear of losing himself in spontaneous action. The
worm of self-consciousness had turned his affair with Denham Russell-
Smith from an experience into an experiment; now, when opportunity
with a woman came his way, he would find himself in a similar plight.

On the "Bacchus-fest" night of Fasching at the end of February, everyone roamed around dressed, as scantily as possible, like ancient Greeks.
Each man was looking for his *Faschingsbraut* – his carnival bride for a
day, or a week. "I found," Rupert told Jacques, "a round damp young
sculptress, a little like Lord Rosebery to look on. We curled passionate
limbs round each other in a perfunctory manner and lay in a corner, sip-
ping each other and beer in polite alternation." The evening progressed
well along Dionysian lines, but when it came to the crunch both Rupert
and the sculptress found that they were "conscious, sensible intellectuals" rather than devotees of Bacchus.¹⁹ The girl went home with her
mother and Rupert slunk back to his lodgings at dawn, naked, cold, frustrated, and ridiculous.

Elisabeth van Rysselberghe was a more serious proposition. Rupert
met her briefly around the beginning of February, probably through the
painter Frau van Ewald, who had taken him under her wing. Unlike most
of the other young ladies that he met in Munich, Elisabeth spoke fluent
English. Three years younger than Rupert, she was the daughter of the
leading Belgian Neo-Impressionist painter Theo van Rysselberghe. The
Flemish poet Emile Verhaeren was her godfather. She was visiting
Munich with her mother Maria, a writer who travelled widely and was
an intimate of Andre Gide's literary circle. At the beginning of March,
Elisabeth came back to Munich by herself, giving Rupert a chance to
"snatch the opportunity" of an affair, as he had told Bryn he was now
determined to do. Elisabeth was an ardent and impulsive soul who had
fallen head over heels in love with Rupert. She was dark-skinned, with
large sad eyes and aquiline features – a bit like Noel in appearance,
though Elisabeth's looks were more strong than pretty. She was attracted
to men who were weaker than herself, with a feminine side to their nature. One sees a lot in common between her and Ka, qualities of devotion and integrity that would reassure Rupert – but also, unfortunately,

make him skittish. Here was a free-spirited young woman, alone with him in a foreign city, making it plain that she was in love with him. All he had to do, it seemed, was plunge into the waves of passion.

In his sonnet "Lust" Rupert tells how he "starved" for Elisabeth, how "the enormous wheels of will / Drove [him] cold-eyed" in her pursuit. But when she actually responds to his desire, he pulls up short of his goal:

> Love wakens love! I felt your hot wrist shiver,
> And suddenly the mad victory I planned
> Flashed real, in your burning bending head
> My conqueror's blood was cool as a deep river
> In shadow; and my heart beneath your hand
> Quieter than a dead man on a bed.

One suspects that it was not the heart, but another organ that failed him. Soon Rupert was complaining to Ka that he was "in a state of collapse – from disease and Elisabeth. She is a Rat."[20]

When it came to sex Rupert could always talk a good game, but he had trouble finishing in front of the net. Recoiling from his difficulties with Elisabeth, he went off to Vienna to stay with Ernst Goldschmidt, a Cambridge friend. Ernst was from a wealthy Jewish family; he got out in the 1930s and became a leading antiquarian book dealer in London. As with Rupert's other Jewish friends – Arthur Schloss, Albert Rothenstein, and Leonard Woolf – Ernst enjoyed his company, but would not have done so if he had known what Rupert was saying behind his back.

Elisabeth wrote to Rupert in Vienna, agreeing to spend a couple of days with him at Venice, later in April. Would he desire her, there, she asked wistfully? Of course he would, Rupert vowed, in the middle of a roundabout disquisition on the dangers of pregnancy. Elisabeth promptly wrote back to tell him that she was not prepared to "give herself" to him in Venice. He told her that she should expect to take "Life," and the sooner the better – "Life" meaning a brief affair, with a clear understanding that there would be no strings afterwards. Rupert was bitter at the lesson he had just learned, that honesty about one's intentions was not the best policy when dealing with romantic young ladies. "I can't help believing (am I right?)," he told her, "that if we'd met in Venice, that *there*, touching your hands, looking into your eyes, I could have made you understand, and agree. But I preferred to be honest. And so perhaps one of the best things in my life, or yours, is lost – for a time – through a desire for honesty!"[21]

Rupert now had to go to the aid of his old classics master, Bob White-law, who had been taken ill in Florence. Before going, he returned to Munich for a melodramatic settling of accounts with Elisabeth. Having fled from the emotional complications of England, Rupert found himself fleeing the worse complications he had stirred up in Germany:

> The parting with Elisabeth was most painful. I felt an awful snake. Especially when she said she would kill herself, and I felt frightened of the police. She's quite come round, and apologised for her telegram; and, it appears, we're to have a week at Mar-seilles in August. I am very bitter with myself, and frightened of England ... The maid-servant suddenly brought two students to see the room, and found her with her hair down weeping, at full length, on that *plateau* of a sofa, and me in great pain on one leg in the middle of the room, saying "Yes ... yes ... yes ..." But, anyhow, do assure me that one *ought* to tell the truth: and that it's not honest to want to be raped.[22]

Elisabeth, Rupert felt, wanted to be promised eternal love and then swept off her feet; whereas he wanted her to copulate with him on fixed terms, having first carefully read the directions that came with the syringe. Both of them were by now thoroughly confused, guilty, and unsatisfied. But Elisabeth would soon rally and make another attempt to win his love.

Rupert went to a string of Ibsen plays in Munich, of which *John Gabriel Borkman* made by far the strongest impression on him. Mrs Borkman is an ice queen who wants to make her son, Erhardt, as deathly as she is. Erhardt mopes around the house complaining, "Ich muss leben, Mutter! Ich muss leben!" Finally, he escapes to the south with Mrs Wilton, a divorced woman seven years older than himself. Rupert iden-tified with Erhardt, though he could not order his own affairs so deci-sively. He had not joined the vanguard of Schwabing, figures like Ludwig Klages, Fanny zu Reventlow, and Otto Gross who had declared war on bourgeois convention. But when he heard from Gwen Darwin about her tangled relations with Jacques and Ka, he affected the Ibsenite stance that we can always seize our Fate by the neck: "You said you'd all three

felt, that week, as if you were in the hands of some external power, rush-
ing you on. External Power? What? God? The Life-Force? Oh, my Gwen,
be clean, be clean! It is a monstrosity. There is no power. Things happen:
and we pick our way among them. That is all. If only you'd been at
Camp last year, you'd have learnt that one can sail eight points *into* the
wind. To be certain of it is the beginning and end of good behaviour."[23]
What did Rupert's nautical metaphor mean? Apparently that the Neo-
pagans were free to ignore convention, and that telling the truth about
one's emotions was guaranteed to keep any love affair on a steady course.
But since that camp Rupert had done more drifting than sailing, whatever he claimed to Gwen.

Clearly, however, that drift was carrying him away from Noel and towards Ka. Rupert told her to make a clean break with both Jacques and
Gwen – good advice, perhaps, but not quite disinterested: "Why are you
sad? … Lust. But that's absurd. You'd never have gratified that anyway
… Even if, as I'll grant, a sort of lustjealousy may plague you (an infinitely pale reflection of part of that plagues me every time I hear of anyone getting married!), that doesn't come to much. Tragedy – much pain
– doesn't come from that, for any creature." The heaviest blows to Ka
were her wounded vanity, and the fear of losing both Jacques and
Gwen as friends. Rupert, however, told her to cheer the engaged couple
on: "Jacques and Gwen are in love and are going to marry. That is very
fine … It is a risky business, as they're both so dotty. I hope Gwen won't
hurt her wood-cuts with babies, or Jacques get domesticated. It's very
splendid. They'll be in love for a couple of years. I hope they'll do it more
gracefully than most."[24] His agenda, as soon as he got back to England,
was clear: to catch Ka on the rebound, and succeed with her where he
had failed with Elisabeth.

One definite result of going to Germany was to harden Rupert's politics. The Jewish milieu of Vienna in which Goldschmidt lived provoked
some nasty racial sneers in Rupert's letters, but he found the Aryans even
more repellent: "I have sampled and sought out German culture. It has
changed all my political views. I am wildly in favour of nineteen new
Dreadnoughts. German culture must never, never, prevail. The Germans
are nice, and well-meaning, and they try; but they are SOFT. Oh! They
ARE soft. The only good things (outside music perhaps) are the writings
of Jews who live in Vienna."[25] This bulletin went to Eddie Marsh, now
private secretary to Winston Churchill at the Admiralty. Rupert was not

just unveiling his own visceral chauvinism, he was trying to get it high on his country's agenda. The naval rivalry between Britain and Germany had been getting more intense for some years, coinciding with a rash of small colonial wars and crises on the periphery of Europe. Rupert came back from Munich convinced that Britain should keep Germany in check, and fight her if necessary. Along with his anti-Semitism, this nascent imperialism exposed the shallow roots of his professed Fabian beliefs. He, and all Europe with him, was now only a short step away from the catastrophes of 1914; a step that was fatally easy to take when no one realised what 1914 would come to stand for.

A Wedding Has Been Arranged

Part of Rupert's confusion lay in having made an implicit declaration of love to Ka, heedless of her long and intimate involvement with Jacques. But while he was in Germany that relation quickly unravelled. At the same time as she dampened Jacques's ardour, Ka had kept hinting that he might be more warmly received by Gwen, who was probably her closest friend. Gwen was now twenty-five, the same age as Jacques, and had been with him at the Slade for a year. Next to someone like Bryn she might seem plump and plain, but she had wit, a keen eye for character, and a real, if small-scale, artistic talent. This last gift was the strongest bond between her and Jacques. Both were exhilarated by the great Post-Impressionist Exhibition in London during November, and both had an almost fanatical devotion to their artistic work. They knew what they wanted, and they wanted the same thing. In the right circumstances, it could be enough to kindle love between them.

Whatever emotional difficulties he may have had, Jacques was not a self-divided puritan like Rupert. He considered it long overdue that he should have a regular sexual fulfillment, and fiercely denounced the chastity of middle-class girls – especially English ones. Jacques was not really the rampant immoralist he claimed to be, but he did know that sexual convention was putting him under an unbearable strain. "I wish you could once see right into me," he wrote to Ka after one confrontation, "you would know that I am not wise, but most feeble, most fond and foolish, lustful, vain, ambitious, cruel – my only grace, love ... And between these two I am torn and buffeted: my love and my desire: my wild and passionate desire to try and *make you* love me; and the fear I have that you *should* love me; because I love you and because I know myself so vile a thing."[26]

After Lulworth, Jacques apparently decided to go from push to shove. In Gwen's novel, he bluntly tells Ka that it is time she "had him," with or without marriage:

> "But supposing I had a baby?" said Ka, "I mustn't harm you, you know."
>
> "Why on earth should it harm me?" said Jacques, "... It's *you* it would be supposed to harm ... of course we could be married before it was born if you wanted to."
>
> "I don't know that I do want to," said Ka.
>
> "As you please," said Jacques exasperated, "that's your business. I'll provide for the child if there is one. Or if you want to be *prudent*" (with a sneer at the word) "we won't have one. We can take precautions; though I should like to have a son ... Only for God's sake make up your mind."[27]

Ka's response was to say she *would* have him – but not yet. To Jacques this meant that she was playing a game, like a hen running from a cock. It was his cue, he realised, to sweep her off her feet: "But his anger rose steadily: why couldn't she confess what she wanted? What a liar she was. Well, if she could be obstinate, he could be obstinate too. No, he would not take her as she wanted 'so that she can say afterwards she couldn't help it'; not though he died with the effort to restrain himself."[28] In the novel, Jacques flings Ka back into her chair, storms out, and takes the night train to Paris. After ten days of debauchery, he comes back "knowing women." He snubs Ka when he sees her, tells Gwen what he has done and asks her to marry him. She goes off to Ka, who tells her that she fell in love for the first time at Lulworth – but with Rupert: "One night when the others were all out, I was sitting by the fire with him. And suddenly I found I was shaking all over and I wanted to take his hand. And he was shaking too ... But, you see, Gwen, he really loves Noel. So he can't care for me like that." Ka cannot decide whether or not she wants Jacques, while Gwen admits she loves him without reserve. Next day they are engaged, while Ka dithers. In the evening Jacques comes to her, and tells her, "it seems simpler to marry Gwen ... She's got bones in her mind. We understand each other. It's rather like marrying yourself in a way; but it's all right. Anyhow it's settled."²⁹

All this, or something very like it, happened in January and February 1911, while Rupert was out of play in Munich. Soon Jacques's and Gwen's engagement was announced, to the general approval of their friends. By April, however, Virginia Woolf was regaling her sister Vanessa with stories of how Jacques's emotions were wilder than ever:

> [Jacques] says now that he is in love with them both; and asks Ka
> to be his mistress, and Gwen to satisfy his mind. Gwen is made
> very jealous; Ka evidently cares a good deal for Jacques.
>
> Obviously (in my view) J. is very much in love with K: and not
> much, if at all, with Gwen. Ought they to break off the engage-
> ment? J. has doubts, occasionally; Ka sometimes thinks she could
> marry him; Gwen alternately grows desperate, and then, accept-
> ing J's advanced views, suggests that Ka shall live with them, and
> bear children, while she paints.³⁰

As Virginia saw it, Jacques had "muddied their minds with talk of the un-chastity of chastity." He was certainly bombarding Ka with immoralist orations: "Chastity is criminal. Particularly in women. The more I think of it, the worse I think it. It's much worse than prostitution and equiva-lent to murder, suicide, abortion or self abuse. A society where it is not only tolerated but encouraged is rotten, rotten, rotten."³¹

It was Gwen, the most mature and sensible of the three, who called them to order. For a while she was ready to give up Jacques, or even to share him with Ka, but at last she gave her rival her marching papers:

> I would never have consented to marry Jacques, if I had thought
> you loved him like that. I now think that it is possible you will
> find you do, when you face up to things. Which *you must do* Ka.
> But now I think things have changed and I think Jacques loves me
> more than he does you (I hate being so brutal). If either you or J.
> have the *least* doubt of this, I absolutely refuse to go any further
> in the matter.

But if things are as I think, I am sure that for *your own sake* all such relations must stop between you and Jacques; and that it will be better if you don't see Jacques at all for a longish time.

Jacques chimed in with a recantation of his polygamous hopes:

The truth – it's hard – is that since the beginning of this year, I've not really wanted you except "in the common way of lust – and friendship." The difficulty was that no one knew – not yourself even – what you felt about me. It seemed that as I ceased to *need* you, you began to need me. And I was afraid of being cruel and truthful – so much so that I sometimes deceived myself. Now I am *sure* that I am in love with Gwen and not with you. You see I'm very honest and brutal about it.[32]

With these ungracious farewells, the door was firmly shut in Ka's face. Jacques had been reading *Les liaisons dangereuses,* and trying to follow its example of sexual sophistication. But the Neo-pagans were, at heart, nothing like the jaded aristocrats of Laclos. Although Gwen had started with a weak hand, she had known what she wanted and managed to get it. The marriage was set for early June, followed by a month-long painting honeymoon at – Churchfield House, Lulworth! For the rest of the summer they would go to France. Their "Moment of Transfiguration" – as Rupert sardonically called it, borrowing Jane Harrison's phrase – would now be a strictly private affair, with Ka written out of the script. Both Rupert and Ka had started the year with failed love affairs; and both were now free to turn to each other.

8

Combined Operations
January–December 1911

Virginia Gives It a Name

What might be called a collective affair between Bloomsbury and the Neo-pagans began near the end of January 1911, when Virginia Stephen (soon Woolf) met Ka Cox at Bertrand Russell's house near Oxford. Like many individual affairs, this one started in excitement and mutual admiration; began to conflict with rival commitments after a few months; and ended a year or so later in crisis and a good measure of rudeness and dislike. Later some friendship survived, and after both sides had suffered their share of death and disaster the affair reached its final stage: nostalgia. But why should relations between these two groups follow such an erratic course? Superficially alike, Bloomsbury and the Neo-pagans had crucial differences of style, beliefs, and morals. They might still have made peace with each other, but Rupert's vagaries in 1911, and his truculent philistinism in 1912, opened a breach that had become an abyss by the time of his death three years later.

In March 1910 Rupert was sorting through drawers at School Field, getting ready to move out after his father's death. He came across "two old photographs, 1893 perhaps, of me, Dick, Adrian Virginia Vanessa Toby Leslie – – – all very sporting and odd. Virginia and Vanessa are incredibly old in it: a little gawky: Virginia very fat faced."[1] This would be the Brookes and the Stephens playing cricket on the sands at St Ives, when Rupert was six and Virginia eleven. When he was ten, Rupert met Duncan Grant and James Strachey at Hillbrow School; at fourteen, Geoffrey Keynes joined him at School Field. After James fell in love with him and got him into the Society, Rupert knew all that went on in

Bloomsbury. But Bloomsbury, he took care, knew much less of what went on with him. "He lived a kind of double life," Jacques recalled, "he had two sets of friends that he was not interested in bringing together; for a long time, he even tried to keep them apart. Was this because of his natural love of mystery, from fear of too great an incompatibility and mutual disdain, or did he fear a rapprochement at his own expense – that both sides might be exposed to a dangerous influence?"[2]

Why did the wall between the two groups break down in 1911? In the first instance, because Virginia took a fancy to Ka, just after Rupert had gone off to Germany for four months. They met through their mutual friend Ray Costelloe, a Newnham student and niece of Bertrand Russell's wife Alys.[3] Having missed going to Cambridge herself, Virginia was intrigued by the new generation of women students. She found Ka, who was five years her junior, "a bright, intelligent, nice creature; who has, she says, very few emotions." Soon they were firm friends. Virginia was in an unhappy state: "To be 29 and unmarried – to be a failure – childless – insane too, no writer."[4] She compared her gloomy isolation with Ka's Cambridge career, her vigorous hikes, her political work with the Fabians. These young people had a style of their own, Virginia decided, and deserved a nickname: the "Neo-pagans."

Neo-paganism had been current since the 1880s, as a label pinned on the Pre-Raphaelites. A few years before Virginia picked up the idea, Edward Carpenter had been lecturing on Neo-paganism as a modern ideal. In April 1911 Rupert heard from James Strachey that "Virginia had become a ... what is it? 'Neo-Pagan'? ... Lord! Lord!"[5] James had stayed with Virginia in the middle of March, so we can assume that she began using the term around then – and that Rupert greeted it with surprise and derision. Nevertheless, it stuck, though without spreading beyond Bloomsbury and environs. It was a private joke; but also something more, especially for Virginia.

When she first imagined Ka, Rupert, and their friends as Neo-pagans, Virginia did so almost wistfully. They were only a few years younger than her own generation, but they seemed to have a much firmer hold on the strings of life. The Bloomsbury style of exclusive other-worldliness could easily be seen as a form of invalidism: physical with Lytton and James Strachey, social with E.M. Forster and Saxon Sydney-Turner, psychological with Virginia. Except for the Bells and the MacCarthys, Bloomsbury seemed unable even to have children. Virginia and Lytton were brilliant in conversation, but slow and uncertain writers. Around 1911 they often wondered if they could ever bring a substantial work to completion.

Can Neo-paganism be dismissed as just a passing fancy of Virginia's, and of Bloomsbury in general? It is true that if one judges the Neo-pagans as a significant and fashionable group of youthful pioneers, their joint activities tended to fizzle out after 1912, when Rupert abdicated as their leader. But they continued to play an important role in Virginia's imagination. She used elements of Ka's pre-war life for her portrait of the politically idealistic Mary Datchet in *Night and Day*. After that, *Jacob's Room* was an elegy for Rupert as much as for her brother Thoby. It was also her attempt to come to terms with how Rupert's generation of young men had embraced the World War.[6] In personal relations, close ties persisted between Virginia and Noel Olivier, Ka and Jacques Raverat; and there would be a decades-long affair between Noel and James Strachey.

Virginia saw the Neo-pagans as capable of a clean start, free from the Victorian gloom and debility that had shadowed the youth of herself and her friends. They also stood for a move from town to country. 1910 had been for Virginia a year of nervous breakdowns and long rest-cures away from London. She found these retreats so agreeable that she decided, at the end of the year, to rent a modest house at Firle, Sussex. "Another side of life reveals itself in the country," she explained to Clive Bell, "which I can't help thinking of amazing interest. It is precisely as though one clapped on a solid half-globe to one's London life, and had hitherto always walked on a strip of pavement."[7] Perhaps she could recapture some of the glory of her childhood summers in Cornwall, rudely interrupted when her mother died in 1895.

Such were the overtones of her plan to go on holiday to France with Ka, in April: "I mean to throw myself into youth, sunshine, nature, primitive art. Cakes with sugar on the top, love, lust, paganism, general bawdiness, for a fortnight at least; – and not write a line." Behind the high spirits, we sense that Virginia found Ka very appealing physically. This is not to say that "general bawdiness" would mean a real affair with her. Virginia's passions – for Madge Vaughan and Violet Dickinson – had been unconsummated, girlish crushes. But she gave Ka a pet name, "Bruin," that suggested the mixture of affection and sexual interest she felt for her.[8]

The trip to France fell through when Virginia had to rush to Turkey to help her sister Vanessa, victim of a miscarriage in a remote village. But Virginia's plan was clearly to take up the Neo-pagans, and to sound them out. She expected to renew her acquaintance with Rupert when he returned from Munich. Meanwhile, she invited Jacques in March to stay at Firle for a weekend. They too became friends – though each found the other somewhat intimidating – and Jacques urged her to make the step from country house to living in a tent, at the Neo-pagan camp in August.

Looking back at this time, Virginia spoke of Jacques as an "adorable" young man. Bertrand Russell was less impressed:

> I went to Grantchester ... to tea with Jacques Raverat who is to marry Gwen Darwin. He has immense charm, but like all people who have superficial and obvious charm, I think he is weak and has no firm purpose. He is staying with Rupert Brooke whom I dislike. I find there Keynes and Miss Olivier (daughter of Jamaica Olivier) and Olwyn Ward, daughter of Prof. James Ward. Young people now-a-days are odd – Xtian names and great familiarity, rendered easy by a complete freedom from passion on the side of the men.[9]

Russell was in the throes of separating from his wife, Alys, in order to pursue his affair with Ottoline Morrell. Perhaps he was annoyed by the offhand way the male and female Neo-pagans treated each other, and he certainly loathed Rupert's breezy, schoolboy-hero manner. But Jacques's engagement had scarcely been settled so casually as Russell imagined. After staying with Virginia at Firle, Jacques had gone off for a walking tour in Cornwall with Dudley Ward, to make up his mind about his love triangle with Ka and Gwen. Virginia at this point knew only about his engagement to Gwen, which struck her as too self-consciously lusty. Jacques "is quite red, quite unshaven, hatless," she told Clive, "with only one book – Rabelais; in two months, he says, ... That I take to mean, bed with Gwen. It is portentous; I think the dots give the feeling rather well. How malicious we are about them! But I suppose they have their own brand of malice." Soon afterwards, Ka took her out on the downs and confided the whole story. No doubt Virginia showed concern and sympathy, though to her sister she gave an acid survey of the future of

Neo-paganism: "cynically considering the infantile natures of all concerned, I predict nothing serious. Ka will marry a Brooke next year, I expect. J will always be a Volatile Frog. Gwen will bear children, and paint pictures; clearly though, J. and K. would be the proper match ... I'm sure J. will always be susceptible; and as Gwen will grow stout, he will roam widely."[10] By involving herself with the loves of Ka, Jacques, and Gwen, Virginia was serving two of her own interests. First, she loved intrigue for its own sake; then, she was trying out at second hand the possibilities of heterosexual love for herself. Until now, she had been interested mainly in her own sex, and her male friends had been largely gay. But she was nearly thirty, and becoming reconciled to the idea that the sensible thing for her to do was to marry. The Neo-pagans were to her an intriguing new society, in which young men and women mingled freely and tried out a series of sentimental attachments before settling down. She hoped to be both entertained and guided by observing them.

Diplomatic Overtures

Rupert arrived back from Florence early in May. The immediate task he faced was to write his fellowship dissertation on John Webster and Elizabethan drama. He had less than eight months to do it, and this time he could not hope to get through by skimping and bluffing – as he had done too often before in his academic career. For the balance of the year, he had to stay in England and try to put work before pleasure.

At Grantchester, he began by moving house. The Stevensons, his landlords at the Orchard, had had enough of the free and easy ways of Rupert and his friends. Bare feet were apparently the last straw, and when Dudley Ward came to stay at the Orchard with two German girls, Rupert warned him that they would have to keep their boots on at all times.[11] Fortunately, Mrs Neeve at the Old Vicarage next door was willing to give Rupert room and board, including the famous honey from her husband's bees. The house was a bit decrepit but had a pleasant garden, and was so close to the river that its sounds and smells filled the three rooms where Rupert lived. He described it to Elisabeth van Rysselberghe as one of the loveliest but also one of the unhealthiest houses one could imagine. It was infested with fleas and woodlice, against which Mrs Neeve waged ineffectual war with a yellow powder. Not surprisingly,

Rupert took to sleeping out on the lawn. The birds woke him up at 2:30 a.m.; he would curse them, and finally get back to sleep, and wake with his hair wet with dew.

Jacques and Gwen married in Cambridge on 7 June 1911. There was a dinner a week before at Gwen's house, where Rupert met Monsieur Raverat and renewed his acquaintance with Virginia. He was not having a happy return to Grantchester, after Jacques had asked him if he and Noel were in love. "I *think you* aren't," he continued "and I *know she* isn't." Rupert needed Noel to give Jacques the lie, but got this instead: "If Jacques had asked me that question I shouldn't have had the determination to answer anything but a frank 'no!' because I dont believe we are ... You seem to *want* us to be in love so much; why do you? I dont want to do what Jacques and Gwen do and I dont want their emotions, I know quite well what they are like, they destroy all one's judgement and turn one into an ape."[12] That left Rupert feeling like a dog tied up outside the house. "I'd a bad touch," he reported to Ka, "of that disease you too'll have known. The ignoblest jealousy mixed with loneliness to make me flog my pillow with an umbrella till I was exhausted, when I was shut into my lonely room to read myself to sleep, and they went roaming off to tell each other truths ... But we might convalesce together." He was not jealous of Jacques's possession of Gwen, since on the sexual plane she was never anything more to Rupert than "a square-headed woman who cuts wood."[13] His jealousy was of the married state itself, mixed with fear of losing his closest male friend, and the first one to marry.

This fear turned out to be largely justified. Gwen and Jacques were married equally to each other and to art; from now on, friends would play a lesser role in their lives. Rupert, full of romantic idealism, did not think of marriage as a partnership based on a common interest. But Gwen had taken warning from the way her cousin Eily's artistic ambitions had been swallowed up by marriage: "You know all the artists in the world feel like that when they're married – except for J. and me. Particularly the women. For they are quite clean cut in 1/2. There never was anything in the world like us before – except Mr and Mrs Browning only for some reason my fiance does not like me to say this." Before her engagement Gwen believed that she valued her work more than people, but with Jacques she discovered the power of her "dreadful feminine craving for someone to love and pity."[14] The solution, once she was married to him, was for both of them to submerge themselves in work and cut themselves off from the overcharged emotional atmosphere that Ka had created. It may seem unkind to note that Gwen suffered as the "Plain Jane" of the group and that she may have had a residue of hurt feelings over this status. Certainly she was frank enough about the jealousy and exclusiveness she felt towards Jacques, once she had won him.

Ka thus had no rival claims when Rupert, once installed at Grantchester, began sending her plaintive letters asking her to visit and hinting that he was falling in love with her. But she must have been uneasily aware that when he got back from Munich he was somehow too busy to join her in Yorkshire for a walking tour. Instead, he made the rounds of his friends and went down to Limpsfield when Bryn returned from Jamaica, with Sir Sydney, on 14 May. She had written to Rupert affectionately from the boat and mentioned that it was time she got married – a hint that deserved investigation, presumably. Having been shut out by Jacques and Gwen, Ka needed sympathy and trustworthiness from Rupert. What she got instead was an all-too-Apostolic frankness about his confused emotions. When Geoffrey Keynes asked for a portrait Duncan Grant had painted of her, Rupert lectured her on the Neo-pagan code: "Oh, come. The group of people we're part of may be awfully honest and genteel and chaste and self-controlled and nice – but at least we're far enough ahead for that. We don't copulate without marriage, but we *do* meet in cafes, talk on buses, go unchaperoned walks, stay with each other, give each other books, without marriage. Can't we even have each other's pictures?" That seemed to draw the lines clearly enough; as did Rupert's vow that he wanted to be "*damned* intimate" with Ka. But she would have done well to heed the warning that went with it: "I'll try to cut off all the outside, and tell you truths. Have I ever seemed to you honest? That was when I got one layer away. There are nineteen to come – and when they're off what?"[15]

Noel, meanwhile, was not being altogether firm in her position. Having told Rupert to accept that she didn't love him, she went to stay in Oxford with her parents and started reeling him back in: "I shall be dangerously affectionate at times; so please, if you come, be stern with me, because I should hate to find myself drifting into a relationship that I can not maintain with you; last summer was glorious at the time, and now I love it for that; but it was sometimes so dreadful … that I feel I shall never want to do quite the same again." She signed the letter "Love from

Noel." Rupert duly went up to Oxford, at the end of July, but nothing dangerous followed. He tried again a few days later: they were both going to the Neo-pagan camp in Devon later in August, and Rupert proposed that they meet secretly three days before and walk together cross country to the camp. Noel swatted him away: "That idea won't do; you must wait until I'm 21."[16]

Meanwhile Elisabeth van Rysselberghe had turned up in England in July, and she would be twenty-one in three months. Rupert arranged to meet her in the Italian Room at the National Gallery, and said he was glad to see her, but in fact he would be glad only if a spell of cohabitation could be arranged. He told Ka later that he felt a "horrible mixture of lust and dislike" for Elisabeth at this time.[17] She was staying, unhappily, with the family of a clergyman at Teddington. Rupert told her to go and engage rooms at a nearby town, after which he would join her; then he said he was tired and confused and didn't really know what he wanted. It was simple enough, in fact: he wanted to hide her from his other friends, to go away with her for a week of passion when he could find the time, and then be free to move on. Elisabeth loved him, but would not have him on those terms. They met occasionally and secretly until the autumn, when Elisabeth went back to Paris.

Rupert's best chance of getting a committed lover now lay with Ka. The idealistic side of his nature remained faithful to Noel, however awkward it might be actually to carry on any connection with her. From Ka he wanted sensuality, when he was feeling lustful, or somewhere to lay his head, when his strenuous and complex activities brought him to the point of nervous collapse. Since Ka was above all someone who needed to be needed, they were in a way well matched. But neither their friends, nor society at large, nor their own consciences, would allow them to be peaceably together on any such terms.

Still, forming a couple was very much on the program that summer. "I am thinking a good deal, at intervals, about marriage," Virginia Stephen informed Vanessa in August.[18] Similar impulses were at work among some of the Bloomsbury men. The Society was at a low ebb in 1911, and its members inclined to seek new horizons. After James Strachey moved to London to work on the *Spectator* in 1909, only three of the younger Apostles were left at Cambridge: Rupert, H.T.J. Norton, and Gerald Shove. From Shove's election in January 1909 nearly two years passed without the election of a new member. There was an uneasy balance between Fabians and Liberals, and between those who were gay and those who were not. Bill Hubback, Frankie Birrell, and others were looked over, but none aroused general enthusiasm. In November 1910 J.T. Sheppard, Rupert's former tutor at King's, pushed through the election of his "special friend" Cecil Taylor. It was a blatant case of sexual favouritism, like the election of Hobhouse five years before, and had no better result. Taylor's main claim to fame was the unfortunate one of having three balls. There was a tendency in the Society to jeer at him behind his back; he was nicknamed "the squitter-squatter," and Rupert never took him seriously. It would be fifteen months before the next election.[19] Though Rupert still attended on Saturday nights and read several papers, the Society at this period claimed only a modest share of his interest and energy.

For two years after he joined the Society, Rupert had deliberately kept Apostles and Neo-pagans apart. The Neo-pagans knew little or nothing about the Apostles. They could see why James constantly hung around Rupert, but why did Rupert tolerate him? James had a nervous dislike of women; he was sensitive about his ailments and his physical awkwardness, but could be cuttingly sarcastic to people who threatened him. "He felt for our group, and perhaps especially for Ka, a kind of jealousy," wrote Jacques. "He had the face of a baby and the expression of an old man; he seemed to take no pleasure or interest in material life or the physical world, and to exist only in the realms of pure intellect."[20] But jealousy is also a bond. Two quite different groups of friends wanted to claim Rupert. In the long run they were bound to find a way to share him – and to discover, in the process, other things they had in common.

To Rupert's divided and compulsively secretive nature, such a merger was deeply threatening. "He did everything he could to hold off a rapprochement," recalled Jacques. "He may have been right, but despite all his efforts he couldn't prevent it. Finally James, whom he could not keep away, made the treaty of union between these two milieux, which had become too curious about each other, but which were deeply incompatible. The results were sometimes comic; but the rapprochement led Rupert into an ordeal that was sufficiently cruel and tragic to justify fully the instinctive fear he had of it."[21] A good index of relations between the two groups was the connection between James and Noel. James first became interested in her because she was loved by the person he loved.

This was a pattern with him: he had told Rupert in February that he had "flirt[ed] half heartedly with Michael [Sadler] and Alfred" – Rupert's former beloved and his brother.[22] In Rupert's room there was a picture of Noel; in James's a picture of Rupert. If James could get close to Noel, the triangle would be completed and he would be less of a yearning hanger-on in Rupert's life. After putting him off for two years, Rupert arranged for James to meet Bryn and Noel while they were staying at the Old Vicarage during the production of *Faustus,* in the summer of 1910. But James for some reason failed to keep the appointment. "Bryn was especially eager," Rupert told him. "And I'd very carefully brought Noel up to the point at which she could and must meet an Apostle. So there's a year or so lost for *her* education. And even you might have Widened a little." If he did not actually meet them, James had discovered by going to the play how attractive the Neo-pagan ladies could be: "The beauty of the evening was of course Bryn as Helen of Troy – though chorus [Rupert] was also admired in some quarters ... I had the pleasure of seeing Noel Olivier in the audience. She certainly looks intelligent as well as beautiful. I expect you'll hear more of her before you die."[23]

Lytton did not get to know Noel and Bryn until three years later, when he shared a holiday cottage with them in Scotland. "Noel is of course more interesting," he then observed, "but difficult to make out: very youthful, incredibly firm of flesh, agreeably bouncing and cheerful – and with some sort of prestige. I don't quite know what. I suppose somehow of character: as for the intellects, I couldn't see much trace of *them*."[24] Firmness of flesh seems to have been James's fancy, for two weeks after seeing Noel he was struck at the Fabian Summer School by another "delightful Bedalian ... an absolute boy."[25] This was Alix Sargant-Florence, the only girl to play cricket for the boys' First XI. "Very handsome, built like one of the Medici tombs," was Mary Newbery's memory of her. Ten years later she would become James's wife.

It took until the summer of 1911 for the fences between the Neo-pagans and Bloomsbury to come down altogether. Rupert kept shuttling between London, Grantchester, Rugby, and Limpsfield, often with two or more Oliviers in tow. Diaghilev's Russian Ballet, in its first astounding London season, was a magnet for him and for them all. After one performance, Lytton claimed that "the audience for it contained everyone I knew in Europe."[26] At the end of July, Rupert was going to *Scheherazade* for the third time. James had sent him a note asking if he could meet Noel there, to see if she was as amazing as he imagined. Rupert did better: he invited James to dine with Margery and Noel before the performance at one of his favourite haunts, Eustace Miles's vegetarian restaurant. James was as far removed from the Bedales type as one can imagine, and Noel gave short shrift to his finicky intellectualism. Nonetheless, a friendship was launched that would have great consequences for all three of them.

Having given the Neo-pagans a name, Bloomsbury now drew them into its androgynous embrace. Duncan Grant came to Grantchester to paint; Lytton took lodgings in Cambridge for June; and a troop of friends came up for the end-of-term festivities. James Strachey reported to Rupert that Maynard Keynes had buggered Justin in the middle of one garden party, to the embarrassment of the Neo-pagan onlookers. Translated from Apostolic hyperbole, this meant that Keynes had tried to fondle Justin – whom he fancied as a "faun or creature of the wood" – and was sent off empty-handed.[27] In fact, the sexual currents were flowing in the opposite direction. Their revels with the Neo-pagans showed how the "Bloomsbuggers," as Virginia called them, were being converted to the pleasures of mixed company. Many of them would marry, in due course – or at least, like Duncan Grant and Lytton Strachey, set up house with a woman. And Virginia decided that it would be an interesting experiment to stay with Rupert for five days at the Old Vicarage.

Virginia had kept an eye on Rupert's career through her friends in the Apostles and in spring 1909 they had become casual friends, going to Ottoline Morrell's for tea and meeting at James Strachey's rooms in Cambridge. On the latter occasion, however, Virginia decided that Rupert's silence meant disapproval of her presence, and the friendship languished until her interest in Ka revived it.[28] Whenever Virginia went to Cambridge she became sensitive to the complacencies of male society there, and their instinctual closing of ranks against female intrusion. At Grantchester she felt herself to be on safer ground. She went there in mid-August to see how Rupert's version of "Life in the Country" might compare with her own, also to see how much of his charm might rub off on her at close quarters. Not too close, we may be sure – they slept on opposite sides of the Old Vicarage – though both might relish spreading some whiffs of scandal among the curious onlookers. Mostly they ran a joint literary workshop: Rupert with his thesis and forthcoming collection of poems, Virginia at her endless revisions of her first novel, *The Voyage Out*. The climax of the visit, if legend be true, came when he got her to bathe naked at Byron's Pool and showed off his party trick – jumping in and emerging with an instant erection.[29] Virginia, who prided herself on knowledge of earth closets and "the female inside," presumably took it in her stride. More nymph than maenad, she was not to be bowled over by Brooke's caperings. Perhaps, like many beauties, they were also relatively immune to each other.

When Virginia left, Rupert came with her for a short visit to Firle. They made their way through London despite a railway strike at Victoria – where Rupert, Virginia reported, "tried to work up some Socialist enthusiasm." Whether it was in Virginia, the passengers, the workers, or Rupert himself is left unclear. Some skepticism about Neo-pagan politics is surely apparent, and also in Virginia's further comment that "He does not eat meat, except when he stays here, and lives very cheaply."[30] Rupert did boast at this time that he dressed himself on three pounds a year; this may not have been too far off the mark, since when not naked he was at least barefoot, and most of his eye-catching open-necked shirts were made by Ka. His role as the Noble Savage of the Cam was relished as much by Virginia as it was by him – so long as the good humour of it lasted.

The Banks of the Teign

During Virginia's visit to Grantchester, Rupert was already planning a more ambitious venture. This was to be "Bloomsbury under Canvas," a joint camp with the Neo-pagans. Jacques had first proposed this to Virginia in April; since then Maynard Keynes had met the Oliviers (through Mary Berenson) and other new links had been made. "The company going to Camp," Rupert told Maynard, "is quite select and possible company for such delicate blooms as Virginia and Duncan; and Bryn is white with desire that they should come."[31]

The chosen spot was Clifford Bridge at the edge of Dartmoor, where a long meadow bordered the River Teign as it ran through wooded hills. Earlier in August the Old Bedalian camp had been set up there, and Justin Brooke arranged for the Neo-pagans to take over their gear on 24

August. Lytton was installed beforehand at nearby Manaton, where Rupert had discovered an attractive guesthouse in a rocky valley. At Becky House, Lytton could work on his first book – *Landmarks in French Literature* – and walk on the moors with a series of Apostolic visitors: G.E. Moore, Gerald Shove, and Leonard Woolf (who had just returned from five years in Ceylon).

The company provided for Bloomsbury included the Olivier sisters (except Margery), Justin, Geoffrey Keynes, and an old Bedalian named Paulie Montague. Paulie was a devotee of Elizabethan music who made his own instruments – both very Bedalian hobbies. He joined the Royal Flying Corps and was killed on the Macedonian front in October 1917. Maitland Radford also turned up, and made Bryn nervous by falling in love with her. The surviving photographs show the Neo-pagans all dressed for the part, while Gerald Shove lies on the ground in a suit and a trilby hat. He lasted only one night, though this was enough time, according to Ka, for him to fall in love with Bryn too.

Hovering at the fringes were James Strachey and Maynard, both more at home in the drawing room than with a canoe or sleeping bag. James turned up late and spent a miserable night under a bush, wrapped in a blanket. For a confirmed hypochondriac this was pretty game, but he went back to the comforts of Becky House after being lampooned by Rupert:

In the late evening he was out of place
And utterly irrelevant at dawn.

Lytton wisely stayed away altogether, pointing out to Rupert that the ground was rather an awkward shape for sitting on.

Maynard, however, more than held his own. "Camp life suits me very well," he told his father. "The hard ground, a morning bathe, the absence of flesh food, and no chairs, don't make one nearly so ill as one would suppose." With his usual competence he passed the threefold ordeal that made one an honorary Neo-pagan: "sleeping on the ground, waking at dawn, and swimming in a river."[32] Virginia, too, did nobly. Ka brought her down two days after the camp had begun. On her first evening she walked eight miles from the station with Ka, found no one there on arrival, and ate rotten blackberry pudding by mistake in the dark. A picture shows her sitting on the ground with Rupert, Noel, and Maitland Radford in front of a five-barred gate. Her hair is tied in the approved Neo-pagan gypsy scarf and her expression is, reasonably enough, quizzical.

Virginia must surely have been amused by the Neo-pagan cult of nudity. Someone at Clifford Bridge tried to immortalise the occasion by taking nude photographs of the campers. Maynard Keynes had taken such pictures of Duncan Grant when they were on holiday in Greece the year before, and he had told Duncan that "when I'm at Burford everyone who stays with me will be forced to have their photographs taken naked."[33] Whether Keynes was the one with a camera at Clifford Bridge is not known; the photographs are not now to be found.

The camp lasted for eighteen days, and, by the end, nerves were strung tight. Bryn, who was in charge of cooking and finances, took a dislike to Justin. "Poor old Bryn, what are we to do with her?" Rupert asked Ka; but he didn't know what to do with himself either. Finally, he lost his temper and went off by himself, and lay out all night, crying, on a hill by Drewsteignton. Ka had left by then, so it must have been Noel who drove him to fury and despair, as she so often did. He went from Clifford Bridge to stay five days with James and Lytton at Becky to get over it. They roamed the moors laughing and arguing – Lytton, with his knickerbockers and tam-o'-shanter looking like "a mechanical Scotch Christ on a walking-tour."[34]

When the camp was just beginning, Rupert was already musing on how to save it from "devouring time." On the day Virginia and Ka arrived, the others had walked over to Crediton to see Paulie Montague's parents. During the camp Rupert wrote "Dining-Room Tea" about that visit. The poem is a tribute both to Noel and to the whole group that formed the setting for Rupert's love. One might keep an individual friend for life, but these gatherings of ten or twelve were like a moment in the play of a fountain: a combination of people, place, and emotion that was lit up for a moment, then gone forever:

> they and we
> Flung all the dancing moments by
> With jest and glitter. Lip and eye
> Flashed on the glory, shone and cried,
> Improvident, unmemoried;
> And fitfully and like a flame
> The light of laughter went and came.

> Proud in their careless transience moved
> The changing faces that I loved.

Then the poet seizes on a single face in the crowd – surely Noel's – and the flow is arrested:

> Till suddenly, and otherwhence,
> I looked upon your innocence.
> For lifted clear and still and strange
> From the dark woven flow of change
> Under a vast and starless sky
> I saw the immortal moment lie.
> I saw the stillness and the light,
> And you, august, immortal, white,
> Holy and strange; and every glint
> Posture and jest and thought and tint
> Freed from the mask of transiency.

The lover, the beloved, and Time are the eternal triangle of lyric poetry. What is typical about Rupert's love poems, though, is the lack of understanding between the poet and his beloved. The woman gives him a glimpse of transfiguration, but never knows that she has given it:

> How could I cloud, or how distress,
> The heaven of your unconsciousness?
> The eternal holiness of you,
> The timeless end, you never knew.

While the laughter plays around the table, the poet goes "a million miles away" – then comes back to this single summer evening in Devon.

His beloved's unconsciousness was an old story with Rupert by now, and had become a self-serving myth that did little justice to Noel's sense of her own personality and interests. What saves "Dining-Room Tea" is how the poet makes the beloved's unconsciousness stand for that of the whole group. In their spontaneous joy, they are unaware of the party's aesthetic value. Only the poet, from his position of detachment, can see it and capture it. Virginia Woolf would make a similar event, Mrs Ramsay's dinner party, the centrepiece of *To the Lighthouse*. But there the radiant moment is kindled by Mrs Ramsay's labours as hostess and mother. The success of that party comes from her nurturing; Rupert, in his, is either carried along with the others' joy or stands above it with a superior vision.

To the Lighthouse epitomised Bloomsbury's struggle against transience and loss. They remained a group for so long because they had such solid foundations of tolerance and mutual affection. The Neo-pagans, on the other hand, were facing disintegration after only a few years together. Part of their fragility as a group derived from a simple inferiority of character and talent, compared with Bloomsbury. In the long run, they had less to build on. But sexual dynamics had a part in it too. Most members of Bloomsbury were either gay or married late. In their twenties they were relatively promiscuous. These love affairs caused turmoil and jealousy but when they burned out friendship reasserted itself, and was often strengthened by the ordeal. The Neo-pagans, despite being younger, suffered more from the legacy of Victorianism. So long as their young ladies, at least, did not "copulate before marriage," they were all caught between the millstones of chastity before marriage, monogamous domesticity after it. Their sexual choices weighed more heavily, because they were thought to be "once and for all"; and, under the pressure of those choices, the vision of unity in "Dining-Room Tea" would quickly fade.

Working in Fitzrovia

Returning to London from Dartmoor, Rupert learned that Dudley Ward was engaged to Annemarie von der Planitz. Their engagement, coming three months after Jacques's marriage, seemed to Rupert another nail in the coffin of his youth. "Luckily it's not very definite," he told Ka. "Dudley won't give up his freedom for some years yet. But I'd so idolized him … I felt so awfully lonely."[35] Dudley was too stiff and sober and reticent to count as a true Neo-pagan, but Rupert found his conventionality reassuring. Once married, which he was within months rather than years, Dudley became for Rupert a trusted refuge in times of trouble.

Having met the engaged couple, Rupert congratulated them on not appearing *too* engaged: "You live in the present; like me (an Infantile Paralytic) and Mr George Meredith (now, alas! dead)."[36] But calling himself an Infantile Paralytic was rather too good a joke at his own expense.

Was he really, like Peter Pan, a "boy who would not grow up"? And was he using Noel's unattainability as an excuse to avoid following his friends into marriage and maturity? If so, an obvious cure was at hand. For three years he had kept up both his soulful love of Noel and his twilight affairs with Denham, Elisabeth, or Ka. Why not combine soul and sense at last, by turning wholeheartedly to Ka? After his nervous breakdown, he blamed himself to Ka for failing to make that, or any other choice, during 1911:

> For a year you loved me, and I loved Noel and you – Oh I was a youthful fool, and I wronged you, I see, both of you, a great deal. I plead innocence and youth. But I *did* love, both of you, – with a growing uneasiness that if I gave either all I could give I'd scarcely be worthy, but that as it *was* – I was a beast to both. I loved you a great deal; more as the year went on, I think – Once or twice I felt your kindness and loveliness creeping over me, and loyalty to Noel made me kick. And in the autumn occasionally I was tired and cross and worried about Noel, and a little dead to you.[37]

Through the summer and autumn of 1911 the word "tired" becomes more and more frequent in Rupert's letters. Certainly he was trying to cram a great deal of research and writing into six months. But the underlying cause of his fatigue, and eventually of his collapse, was his inability to choose between Noel and Ka. Instead of resolving the dilemma he tried to ignore its pressure. "I'm determined to live like a motor-car," he told Ka, "or a needle, or Mr Bennett, or a planetary system, or whatever else is always at the keenest and wildest pitch of activity ... I am not tired! I am as lively as God, and working like an engine."[38] His manic side drove him to pack each day with activity, but he was living beyond his emotional means, and the bill would soon fall due.

Early in October Rupert decided that he would start spending weekdays in London and returning to Grantchester at weekends. The ostensible reason was that he needed to use the British Museum Library for his thesis, but he was probably finding the Old Vicarage lonely now that the fine weather was past, and he wanted to be closer to Ka. At Grantchester he was too well known to have any regular intimacy with an unmarried young lady, whereas in London the main hazard would be running the gauntlet of Bloomsbury gossip:

If you only knew what James said Virginia said So and So said ...
But your repper, my dear, is going. Oh, among the quite Advanced. I, it is thought, am rather beastly; you rather pitiable.
    All the worst things drive them on. The furtive craving to inter-
fere in the other people's lusts, the fear of unusual events, and
the rest. The mother and the clergyman are at one in these kind
hearts ... Is there no SIGN to give them, that each minute is final,
and each heart alone?[39]

This was really a message in code to Ka: that Rupert didn't want her to
be afraid of having an affair, but also that he didn't want to be manoeu-
vred into marrying her. Bloomsbury, of course, had little to do with the
values of mothers or clergymen, and was just coming up with its own
remarkable designs for living. Virginia had been sharing rooms with her
brother Adrian at 29 Fitzroy Square; the lease ended in November 1911
and she decided to set up a communal household at 38 Brunswick Square.
Besides herself and Adrian, there would be quarters for Maynard Keynes,
Duncan Grant, and Leonard Woolf on the top floor. It looked much more
improper than it really was, but friends and relatives were shocked, while
Vanessa helpfully pointed out that it was just across the road from the
Foundling Hospital.
    Ka's friendship with Virginia was making her a part of this milieu. Its
sexual heresies, along with her failed affair with Jacques and Rupert's
solicitings, threw Ka's morals into confusion. The rules of Neo-pagan sex
were that the women should appear fast but remain chaste, while the men
should practise chastity within the Neo-pagan circle and, if they could
manage it, enjoy a surreptitious licence outside. By proposing that he
and Ka should have an affair, Rupert was radically changing the game as
it had been played up to now. His opening gambit was to settle, around
12 October, in the studio at 21 Fitzroy Square that was shared by
Maynard Keynes and Duncan Grant. Grant was away, and Keynes lived
mostly at Cambridge. Rupert complained to Jacques that his quarters
were "inconceivably ... disgusting," but they were handy to the British
Museum, and allowed him to be alone with Ka whenever he wished.
Whatever his professed beliefs or his commitment to Noel, he had now
strung himself up to try and make Ka his mistress.
    Rupert's impatience may even have led him into another brief gay af-
fair as soon as he arrived in London. In her memoir *Old Bloomsbury*,

Virginia Woolf recalls an exchange with her sister: "'Norton tells me,' Vanessa would say, 'that James is in utter despair. Rupert has been twice to bed with Hobhouse' and I would cap her stories with some equally thrilling piece of gossip; about a divine undergraduate with a head like a Greek God – but alas his teeth were bad – called George Mallory."[40] Describing his affair with Denham Russell-Smith, Rupert says that he had never gone to bed with anyone before then (October 1909); the height of the Mallory boom was around May of the same year. Either the story about Rupert and Hobhouse was exaggerated, or it happened later. Hobhouse, once beloved by Maynard Keynes and Lytton, had faded from the Bloomsbury scene by 1909, but he was still an Apostle, and the discussions about electing new brothers in the autumn of 1911 could have drawn him back into his old orbit.

A letter from Maynard to James Strachey in October of that year might refer to James's hurt feelings about an affair between Rupert and Hobhouse:

> Yes, I should certainly suppose "nothing," but then that's not
> your theory of life. Nor after the night before does it seem to me
> that last night was really so very unexpected. And wouldn't it,
> if there had been so much as that going on on *both* sides, have
> come to a more palpable longitudinal head before midnight? It
> seems to me that you've now learnt to sit more firmly, but are
> not much nearer standing at the end of it. However, we'll see,
> I suppose. Isn't, perhaps, Covent Garden with Bryn almost out
> of the propriety?[41]

The reference could also be to James finding Rupert and Ka in a compromising position at Fitzroy Square, but James had never been really jealous of Rupert's "womanising" – up to now at least.

Noel was making her own contribution to Rupert's discomfort. She was now living with her parents in St John's Wood and beginning her medical studies. They could meet casually for the ballet or theatre, but proximity did not work any better for them than distance. Keeping quiet about his developing intimacy with Ka, Rupert bombarded Noel with long, half-hysterical letters, fuelled by sleeplessness and anxiety about his fellowship dissertation. The letters can be summed up in one quote:

"I love you more than anyone ever will. Damn you!"[42] Noel did her best to calm him, but on 15 December they went for a long walk on the Embankment and agreed that they should stay apart for some time. Rupert had to accept that Noel could not or would not yield to his demands.

Who was to blame for their failure over the past three and a half years? "Have you worked out, by the way," Rupert asked, "just *when* the Surrey and St John's Wood upper middle classes will permit you and me to go a walk together?"[43] He was still fuming about Noel's refusal to walk cross-country with him before Clifford's Bridge. One obvious response from Noel might be: "When we are married." Yet that was the one trump that Rupert would die without laying down. It was not a question of being "snug and safe and respectable," Noel fired back; she was breaking it off because they couldn't be together without ending in fury and mutual disappointment. All they could do was stay apart "until you love less, or I love more, or until we're both stronger and can bear anything."[44]

Before this, Rupert had moved from 21 Fitzroy Square, after only a month. It was horribly dirty, there were fleas, and he was under the eye of Virginia and Adrian at Number 29. Ka had found him rooms nearby at 76 Charlotte Street, and there they began a *demi-vierge* kind of affair that left both of them unhappy and unsettled:

And then we had those nights – – – I had such lust for your fine body, far more *(you never* understood!) than for Noel. I had passion for you, – and, as you know, other things, other ways of love, (I knew you – , *Ka*, – so deeply) as well. I was foolish and wicked, indeed. First, that I didn't chuck everything, turn wholly to you, marry you, if you would. Then, I was a fool … I'd baby ideas about "honour" "giving you a fair choice" "not being underhand" "men (!) and women (!) being equal" – – – I wanted you to fuck. You wouldn't, "didn't like preventives." And I respected you! … felt guilty and angry with myself when lust made me treat you "unfairly"!

I was getting ill and stupid … I was an object for pity – even love; not, of course, lust. You gave me strength, comfort, rest – for a bit. I threw all my affairs – all the mess Noel and I had made – onto you.[45]

When Rupert said that his friends didn't copulate before marriage, he might have added that they hardly knew how to do it. They were in a muddle over contraception for a start, but they were also stuck with the belief that premarital sex was only an overture to the real thing. Although they expected their marriages to be more sensual and companionable than their parents' had been, marriage was still a tremendous rite of passage, with the wife as the high priestess of its mystery. To draw back the veil casually or prematurely would arouse deep guilt. On the other hand, they assumed that the sexual act, by itself, would grant them maturity and strength of will. So long as his relation with Ka remained unconsummated, Rupert could hope that, once it was, his emotional confusion would be resolved. He did not foresee how upset he would be when she *did* respond to his sexual needs; and even more, when she responded to someone else's.

In the middle of these intrigues, Rupert's *Poems* were published by Sidgwick & Jackson, on 4 December. The volume was divided into two sections: the first decadent and implicitly gay, the second, after he met Noel, soulful and Neo-pagan. But Noel refused the dedication – partly, perhaps, because she suspected how deeply Rupert was now involved with Ka. Few of the poems had been written during 1911, but as soon as his thesis was done Rupert wanted to get back to his vocation – to be, he believed, "a great poet and dramatist." The significant fruits of the past year were two longer poems: "Dining-Room Tea" and "The Fish" (an impressive fantasy on what it might be like to be alive, but not human). Only five hundred copies were issued, but it was enough to gain recognition for Rupert as a young poet to be reckoned with.

He had decided to go back to Munich in the New Year: ostensibly to perfect his German, but mainly because Ka had promised to meet him there, far from Bloomsbury gossip. Before going, though, he wanted a New Year's holiday like the one he had enjoyed the year before, with Ka, Jacques, and Justin. He had planned that holiday himself, on the principle of "four or six or so a good number. Too many, or too vaguely composed, won't do."[46] This year he was working up to sixteen hours a day on his thesis, so Ka would make the arrangements. Her ideas, however, were different from his. She decided to repeat, at Lulworth, last August's camp. Neo-pagans (including the Oliviers) would mingle with Bloomsbury, some new faces would be blended in, and no longer could the party be counted on one hand. One of the new faces was the painter Henry

Lamb, whom Ka had met at a party and found "fascinating." Another could be called the last of the Neo-pagans, Ferenc Békássy.

"Feri" was still only eighteen, three months younger than Noel and a year younger than David Garnett. His parents belonged to the Hungarian landed aristocracy and lived in a romantic castle at Zsennye, near the Austrian border. They sent all six of their children to Bedales, probably because brothers and sisters could be together there and because of the school's emphasis on country pursuits. Mary Newbery remembered him at Bedales as gentle, sweet and shy – but not good-looking because of a weak chin. Though he had fallen in love with Noel at school, when he arrived at King's in October 1911 he soon got into the swim of gay Cambridge. Rich, intellectually adventurous and a poet, he at once caught Maynard's eye. Even with such a patron, he must have had unusual charm to be elected an Apostle only three months after his arrival. He was the first foreigner and the first Bedalian to join the Society. His brilliant debut indicates how popular Neo-paganism was with Bloomsbury at this point. Békássy soon became a frequent guest at 38 Brunswick Square, and Keynes would visit him in Hungary in the summer of 1912.

However, Békássy was an outsider's idea of a Neo-pagan rather than an established member of the group. Rupert did not like him very much, and not just because he was a rival for Noel's affection. When Békássy was made an Apostle in January, Rupert, who was in France, felt that he had been deliberately left in the dark. "The machinery for not having births till I was out of the way was a bit clumsy," he complained to James. "The gloom of Cannes is a trifle lightened for me by the reflection that *gott sei dank* I've done with all that." Unfortunately, Rupert's letter crossed one from James, containing a campy account of Békássy's successful debut at his first Saturday night meeting. Feri had shown great intelligence, James reported, and had also filled Keynes and Gerald Shove with such lust that they wanted to take him right on the ritual hearthrug.[47] Rupert quickly snubbed his enthusiasm for Feri, but by then it was a bit late for James to retract, and say that the Society had taken a wrong turn in electing him.

Rupert's real problem with Békássy, one would guess, was that the younger man's game was too close to his own. Békássy was a precocious poet of real talent, in both English and Hungarian. His fate was to become the Rupert Brooke of Hungary, killed on the Eastern Front two months after Rupert's death. He was also enthusiastically bisexual though, in the

Bedales way, he probably stopped short of actually going to bed with anyone. He loved Noel, but he also aroused lust in the Society, and himself loved a kind of doppelganger for Rupert named Frank Bliss. Bliss entered King's at the same time as Békássy; he came from Rugby and he read classics. He was elected to the Society in November 1912, jointly with Wittgenstein, and was killed in France in 1916. But even James Strachey came to feel that Békássy went over the score when it came to multiple relations: "'Feri' was here on Monday and talked to me for 5 hours. He came out like so many people – fairly confessed that he was 'in love' with (only guess) cette eternelle Noel. 'It runs on parallel lines' so he informed me 'with my feelings towards Bliss.' O God – if there is such a thing as blasphemy. I felt like Rupert almost inclined for the dagger."[48] Békássy may have been included in the Lulworth party on Noel's recommendation. Then Rupert, in the wake of his heart-to-heart with Noel on the Embankment, announced to Maynard that there would be "no Oliviers."

With the party set, Rupert sent off his thesis, slept for twenty-four hours in an armchair, and spent ten days with his mother. He started a poem on the state he had drifted into in the course of the past year:

All night I went between a dream and a dream
As one walking between two fires ...
The soul, like a thin smoke, is spread
Crying upon the air.[49]

One thing he had not taken into account was that Ka might also be torn between rival loves, and might inflict on him what he had inflicted on her and Noel. At Lulworth, he was about to discover that the knife can cut two ways.

9

Hungry Hands
December 1911–January 1912

Lulworth, 1911–1912

Rupert's break with Noel on 15 December was not just a predictable failure of first love. For three and a half years he had set his emotional compass by Noel's standard of female purity and self-control. As Ka stepped in to take her place, the polarity of Rupert's desire was reversed. Now he had to exert restraint on the frightening aggressiveness of female desire. His sonnet "The Descent" blames Ka for having pulled him down into the underworld of sex:

> Because you called, I left the mountain height, ...
> And from my radiant uplands chose the blind
> Nooks of your lost perpetual twilight.
>
> For there your white and hungry hands were gleaming,
> Your troublous mouth. And there we found desire ...
> There we found love in little hidden places,
> Lost human love between the mist and mire.[1]

At the end of 1911, those hungry hands had thrown Rupert into panic and indecision. His first instinct with sex was to keep it a secret, as he could do with Elisabeth van Rysselberghe and Denham Russell-Smith; but Ka was connected to everyone he knew, and their intimacy was bound to be known. When she embraced Rupert in his room on Charlotte Street, the touch of that warm and desiring body threatened to shatter his whole complex system of evasions and separations. To possess her would break the taboo that had allowed the Neo-pagans to see each other's nakedness, but never to seize and enjoy it. And with Ka there was a deeper threat: that she might turn into the sexual mother, a woman whose nurturing embrace concealed a predatory lust. As he came to know his old friend in this newly sensual way, Rupert both desired and feared consummation. When Frances Cornford said that Ka had "a frightening amount of sex," she was thinking of the danger to Ka herself, but Rupert was probably more frightened than anyone by the prospect of a real affair with her.[2] Then Ka, through impatience or mere whim, suddenly turned to another man who seemed more capable of meeting her own eagerness to lose her virginity.

Rupert, with his rigid sense of sexual honour, was still a Victorian at heart. Henry Lamb was a modern, ruthless, and mischievous seducer. Four years older than Rupert, he was the son of a professor of mathematics and a younger brother to the Trinity don Walter Lamb. His sister Dorothy taught at Bedales. He had nearly qualified as a doctor when, in 1905, he decided to throw up his career and turn artist. In 1907 he married Nina ("Euphemia") Forrest, also an art student. They went to Paris to live near Augustus and Dorelia John, which soon did for their marriage. Dorelia took a fancy to Henry, and Augustus to Euphemia. When the dust settled, Henry was left with a life-long attachment to Dorelia, while Euphemia struck out on a lively career as an erotic free-lancer. Henry continued to take his cue from John, affecting gypsy ways, sudden changes of address, louche habits. Physically, however, he was a very different type. John was swarthy and boisterous, Henry was blond, slender, elusive, and prickly. In his own way he was as handsome as Rupert, and his chiselled features and "evil goat's eyes" appealed forcibly to women.[3]

In the autumn of 1911, somewhere near Fitzroy Square, those eyes fell on Ka Cox. One of the things Henry had taken over from John was an affair with Lady Ottoline Morrell. She fixed Henry up in a studio next to her country house at Peppard, near Henley. But Ottoline was ten years older and a demanding patroness, encumbered with a husband and also, from the spring of 1911, an infatuation with Bertrand Russell. For Henry, Ka represented a target of opportunity. She enjoyed a private income, had vaguely artistic tastes, and had a reputation as a soft pillow to lie on. John was rich, and actually liked living in caravans; Henry was hard up, was used to bourgeois comforts, and had few scruples about accepting favours from his friends or mistresses. He was also feeling the nervous strain of his *vie de bohème,* and was seeing the same hypnotist who had treated Jacques Raverat a few years earlier, Dr Bramwell. Marriage to Ka was more appealing than trying to scratch out a living in Chelsea. Even Lytton Strachey, weary of his makeshift life, had half-seriously thought of marrying a "soothing woman" like Ka.[4] Lytton was not really serious about marrying her, but he rather liked the idea that Henry might. For the past year he had been desperately in love with Henry, but he knew that such a confirmed "womaniser" would not respond to his physical needs. All he could hope for was Henry's company in society, or for long stays together at country hotels. In return Lytton would entertain him with scurrilous wit, pay his bills, and accommodate his love affairs. He had to be careful, however, that Henry did not take up with the kind of woman who might try to cut Lytton out. Ka had no establishment of her own, and was accepted in Bloomsbury because she was both likeable and biddable. She could not expect to remove Henry from his usual orbit, and she was soon too besotted by him to object to his whims, or his friends.

Why should Ka have fallen so hard for Henry, just when her affair with Rupert was coming to a head? In Rupert's view, it was his "baby ideas about honour" and his weak nerves that made Ka vulnerable:

> Someone more capable of getting hold of women than me, slightly experienced in bringing them to heel, who didn't fool about with ideas of trust or "fair treatment," appeared.
>
> You'd met the creature at some party. I have your account: "Very unpleasant" you wrote "but fascinating." "Fascinating"!!! I dimly wondered … and passed on.
>
> The swine, one gathers, was looking round. He was tiring of his other women, or they of him. Perhaps he thought there'd be a cheaper and pleasanter way of combining fucking with an income than Ottoline. And his "friends" had come to the conclusion he might be settled with somebody for a bit. He cast dimly round. Virgins are easy game. Marjorie Strachey, I understand, was the first woman he met. What was her answer? Ka, was the second: an obviously finer object for lust, and more controllable. He marked you down.[5]

Rupert took it for granted that Henry had exploited Ka's lust and in-experience. But no external pressure was needed to make her pursue him. In those heady days following the Post-Impressionist Exhibition, Henry enjoyed the glamour of being a talented artist. He was a bohemian city mouse after the country mice of Cambridge – those earnest but often droopy undergraduates who were Ka's friends before she moved to Lon-don. While Rupert floundered emotionally after being rejected by Noel, Henry had years of erotic experience. He knew what he wanted, and how to get it. Outshone by Bryn and Noel, cut out by Gwen, Ka now had two dashing young men in pursuit of her. Who could blame her for rel-ishing her power?

Early in December Ka had invited Henry to join the party at Lulworth, and confided to Justin that she planned to flirt with him when he came. Rupert had gone to stay for a week in Eastbourne with his mother, to put the finishing touches on his thesis. Ka came to visit him there on 9 December, with the "madness in her mind" of her infatuation with Henry.[6] Rupert took the news of her outside interest badly. When he left for Lulworth on Thursday, 28 December he was still dazed and upset by it, as well as exhausted by work. Once at Churchfield House, he found that the Neo-pagans in the party Ka had arranged were heavily out-gunned by Bloomsbury. Gwen and Jacques had come no closer than Studland, fifteen miles off, so that only Justin and Ka were left of the old crowd. The three Oliviers had been replaced by three Stracheys: James, Marjorie, and Lytton. Feri Békássy also came, and Maynard Keynes after a few days. Then, in what seemed a major shift of allegiance, Ka an-nounced that when Leonard Woolf returned to Ceylon in May she would move into his room at Bloomsbury's HQ, the communal house at 38 Brunswick Square.[7]

Rupert had expected a soothing week in the company of Ka and a few trusted friends. Instead, he had a houseful of Stracheys. Then, to fill the cup, Lytton drove a carriage to Wool Station on Saturday and returned with Henry Lamb, who had been spending Christmas with Augustus John near Corfe. Lytton and Henry stayed together at the Lulworth Cove Inn, but took their meals with the main party at Churchfield House, which now seethed with intrigues and flirtations. Marjorie Strachey took a shine to Justin, whom she called "Duckie," while Lytton "would grope [Henry] under the table at meal-times in view of all the ladies."[8] Lytton's original plan, according to Rupert, had been to stay with Henry at Corfe and entice Ka to join them. Now Rupert gave them another opening by falling ill, on New Year's Eve:

> The creature slimed down to Lulworth; knowing about women, knowing he could possibly get you if he got a few hours alone with you (his knowledge turned out to be justified.)
>
> I was ill. Influenza (or poison in the house) frustrated me that Sunday. I was in the depths, leaning utterly on you. Oh my God! how kind and wonderful you were then; the one thing in the world I had.[9]

But Ka also found time to disappear for a long tête-à-tête with Henry. Later, Rupert told James Strachey that Henry "nearly seduced" Ka, which meant, presumably, that she drew back short of the final act.[10] But when she came back to Churchfield House, she told Rupert flatly that she was in love with his rival. Henry, she pointed out, was four years older than she (Rupert was a few months younger), and had the same first name as her father, who had died when she was eighteen. Rupert, sick and distraught, cast off his endless vacillation between Ka and Noel and asked Ka to marry him at once. She calmly refused. She intended to go on seeing Henry, she said, and hoped, indeed, to marry *him*.

Two prominent traits in Henry's character were a love of mischief and a dislike of being pinned down. Having played the spoiler between Ka and Rupert, he promptly slipped away. He had a running joke with Lytton about paying tribute to "the Obelisk," which was Henry's penis (as opposed to the rest of him). Back in London, he reported that "L'Obelisque m'aneantie, mais je finirais par l'asservir ... I may write if I recover but it's clear that a visit to the fillettes must be made first."[11]

Lytton had decided that Henry's propensity for rows and intrigues was taking both of them into dangerous waters. Henry's best bet was to get a rich and complaisant mistress, so even if Ka wanted to marry *him*, he would be foolish to marry *her*:

> I can't believe that you're a well-assorted couple – can you? If she was really your wife, with a home and children, it would mean a great change in your way of living, a lessening of independence – among other things a much dimmer relationship with Ottoline. This might be worth while – probably would be – if she was an

eminent creature, who'ld give you a great deal; but I don't think she is that. There seems no touch of inspiration in her; it's as if she was made somehow or other on rather a small scale.[12]

In any case, Henry was still formally married to Euphemia. Despite her rich and strange love life, some quirk of loyalty, or malice, made her refuse to give him a divorce. And Rupert and Ka did seem "to fit together so naturally – even the Garden-Cityishness." By this Lytton meant their Neo-paganism, projected into the future – a domesticated Simple Life in one of the new mock-rural satellite towns. Henry relished the mockery; he dubbed Rupert "The Cauliflower," and asked Lytton to arrange the match. "As the Garden City is quite near," he suggested, "wouldn't I be able to give them a wedding present of great permanence? Then we'ld all be quits."[13]

Lytton, however, was rapidly trimming his sails. It was one thing to indulge Henry's whims, another to have Ka become a fixture in his own inner circle, even as a mistress:

> I've now seen her fairly often and on an intimate footing, and I
> can hardly believe that she's suited to the post. I don't see what
> either of you could really get out of it except the pleasures of
> the obelisk. With you even these would very likely not last long,
> while with her they'ld probably become more and more of a
> necessity, and also be mixed up with all sorts of romantic desires
> which I don't think you'ld ever satisfy. If this is true it would
> be worth while making an effort to put things on a merely
> affectionate basis, wouldn't it? I think there's quite a chance
> that everything might blow over, and that she might even sink
> into Rupert's arms. Can you manage this?[14]

To achieve such a happy ending, Ka and Rupert had to be brought down to earth and reconciled to each other. Ka had wanted to follow Henry to London, but Lytton convinced her to stay and minister to Rupert instead. "Rupert is besieging her," Lytton told Henry, "I gather with tears and desperation – and sinking down in the intervals pale and shattered."[15] By 5 January the Lulworth party had been reshuffled to prop up its invalid member. It now consisted of Rupert, Ka, and four other Apostles – Lytton, Maynard, Gerald Shove, and Harry Norton. Gwen and Jacques at Studland were also called on for support, Rupert walking twenty miles along the coast to see them. Everything suggests that Rupert, in his distress, was looked after in a thoughtful and sympathetic way by his friends. There may have been some feeling, also, that the Society should take Rupert's part against Henry, the outsider. But in spite of everyone's care, Rupert kept sliding downhill. He was having a major nervous breakdown, which had been building up, he felt, for at least six months: "I had six days in the most horrible state you can think. I couldn't eat or sleep or do anything but torture myself. It was the most ghastly pain imaginable, worse than any physical pain, dragging on, unending – Everything seemed to go. If I thought I had to go through that again, I should shoot myself. It was madness – I can't describe it ... I wasn't I."[16]

When it became plain that he needed professional help, Gwen and Jacques were the ones who took him in charge. After a difficult journey, they delivered him to Dr Maurice Craig in Harley Street.

Nerve Exhaustion

Rupert's mental state in early 1912 is not easily defined. The former guardians of his reputation, Sir Geoffrey Keynes and Christopher Hassall, felt that he was too disturbed to be held responsible for his actions during this period. This is a defensible view; what is less defensible is their withholding of much of the evidence for a fair judgment of Rupert's condition. His letters at this time are sprinkled with crude attacks on those he blamed for his suffering. These were the usual suspects: women, gays, and Jews. They were not, of course, to blame; nonetheless, for his apologists, such passages proved that he was mentally unbalanced and "not himself." They therefore suppressed almost all of them. By this reasoning, anyone could be absolved from their darker impulses. Throughout 1912 Rupert's letters show him to be overwrought but able to write coherently about his troubled emotions.[17] Why suppress only those passages that show him in a bad light? One might just as well argue that the nasty parts show the "real" Rupert – the golden boy with the rotten core – and write off his charm and affection as mere hypocrisy. Rupert himself, in giving directions for his papers if he died in battle, said "let them know the poor truths."[18] It still seems the best rule for this, or any other biography.

What, then, was wrong with Rupert? Why should a lover's quarrel with Ka push him over the brink into an acute manic-depressive condition that lasted for six months or more?[19] It is surely crucial that Rupert's obsessive jealousy of Henry Lamb included an equally obsessive hatred of Lytton Strachey:

> If I can still, at moments, hate you [Ka] for having, in pitiful sight
> of a flirtation, invited that creature to Lulworth, and then left the
> rest of us, to go out walks and out for meals with him; how do
> you think I hate Lytton, who hadn't even your excuse of igno-
> rance and helplessness, for having worked to get the man down
> there, and having seen the whole thing being engineered from
> the beginning, – and obligingly acquiesced in it as one of the
> creature's whims? You told me – in the first flush of your young
> romance – of the whole picture – Lytton "hovering" (your word)
> with a fond paternal anxiousness in the background, eyeing the
> two young loves at their sport: – it was the filthiest filthiest part
> of the most unbearably sickening disgusting blinding nightmare –
> and then one shrieks with the unceasing pain that it was *true*.[20]

Rupert harped on two things about Lytton: his homosexuality and his love of insinuating himself into other people's emotions. Despite his own participation in the gay milieu, Rupert could not bear the idea of its escaping its bounds and mingling itself with heterosexual love – the school dormitory invading the family bedroom. He remained trapped in the double life, and double standard, that had guided him since childhood. His peculiar upbringing had made him abnormally sly and secretive; these qualities clashed with Lytton's open-minded and rational – perhaps too rational – approach to sex. Both men had been accustomed to orchestrate the emotions of their friends, but they did so in very different styles, until the merger of Bloomsbury and Neo-paganism made them into rival masters of ceremonies.

In his own eyes, Lytton was a kind of scientist of personal relations, doing battle with the remnants of Victorian prudery and hypocrisy in the cause of a new era of sentiment. Since Henry would not physically respond to him, he chose to advance his beloved's other sexual interests. Lytton saw this as a sensible compromise in which he settled for the biggest share in Henry's life that he could get. Rupert saw it as pimping. Perhaps he saw it as something worse and believed that Henry, like Julius Caesar, was Lytton's "wife" at the same time as he tried to be Ka's "husband."[21] That Rupert had his own bisexual history seems to have been exactly what made the Lulworth affair unbearable to him.

In the months leading up to Lulworth, Rupert had been struggling to complete his thesis, and simple exhaustion certainly contributed to his breakdown. Much of this work had been straightforward enough, setting out the social background to Elizabethan plays and doing technical analysis of plays with mixed authorship. But Rupert's own dilemmas broke through in his identification with the moral chaos of Jacobean tragedy: "The world called Webster is a peculiar one. It is inhabited by people driven, like animals, and perhaps like men, only by their instincts, but more blindly and ruinously ... A play of Webster's is full of the feverish and ghastly turmoil of a nest of maggots. Maggots are what the inhabitants of this universe most suggest and resemble ... Human beings are writhing grubs in an immense night. And the night is without stars or moon." Characters in the plays are ignorant of their own motives, Rupert notes, "like people in real life."[22] Where, then, might salvation be found? Could the woman's world provide a cure for his own moral confusion? Women were innately pure, but also innately weak and corruptible. In November, he had started to address Noel in his letters as "child." This became a nervous tic, frequent in his letters to various women until his death. Women had to be protected from people like Henry and Lytton, whom Rupert hated because he knew how close, in some ways, he had been to them. Henry, the great seducer, embodied a style of masculine predatoriness that Rupert both despised and envied. "All the women of that circle have been treated so well – too well – by the men they know," observed Dudley Ward, "that they're peculiarly at the mercy of the other sort of man when he comes along."[23] Perhaps so; but it was also true that Henry and Lytton drove Rupert into madness by acting out, without compunction, his own hidden or unacknowledged desires. His mother and Noel had shown him how women should be treated; but so might Webster's Flamineo:

Women are caught as you take tortoises;
She must be turned on her back.[24]

Dr Maurice Craig was one of Britain's leading psychiatrists. He was consulted by Leonard Woolf over Virginia's breakdowns, and treated many other intellectuals (as well as the future Edward VIII). His book *Nerve Exhaustion* sets out his approach to people like Rupert. "It is hyper-sensitivity," he writes, "which occasions in varying degrees the ultimate collapse of the nervous system ... Rapid and intensive work increases the hyper-sensitivity of the nervous system, and if this is already in an overstrung condition, the risks are obvious ... Sexual indulgence, whether by masturbation or intercourse, is a very important factor in the production of nerve exhaustion symptoms." That is how Craig saw Rupert, and presumably how Rupert saw himself when prompted by the great specialist. He also developed another of Craig's symptoms: "the writing of libellous postcards and letters."[25]

Craig's treatment had three parts: complete rest, weight gain, and 325 mg of potassium bromide each day:

My nerve specialist's treatment is successful and in a way pleasant, *aber etwas langweilig.* I have to eat as much as I can get down, with all sorts of extra patent foods and pills, milk and stout. I have to have breakfast in bed about 10 every day, go to bed early, never take any exercise, walk never more than two miles, and do no kind of brain-work.

After a few weeks of it one feels like Oldham or a sleepy version of the master of Magdalene.[26]

The bromide was supposed to reduce nervous excitement and suppress sexual desire, though Rupert reported that it seemed to have the opposite effect. It is no longer prescribed as a sedative, and at the time it often exacerbated the nervous symptoms that it was supposed to relieve.

After one or two sessions in Harley Street, Craig's patients would be packed off to the country to follow a regime of absolute tedium, either in the care of a relative or in a nursing home if they threatened violence. Mrs Brooke happened to be in Cannes for an extended holiday, so Rupert was sent there for his cure. It was not out-and-out quackery: the drugs did no real harm, while tranquility and good food helped many patients to feel better. Craig noted that most patients would recover after four to six months of seclusion. But there was no psychotherapy in any modern understanding of the term.

The strangest feature of "stuffing," as it was called, was the obsession with the patient's weight as an index of his or her mental state. Everyone was put on the same regime of inactivity and a fattening diet, regardless of the nature of their distress, and the cure was measured by how many pounds the patient gained each week. Thirty pounds in two months was the usual target. Rupert gained seven and a half pounds in the first twelve days of treatment, then another seven more gradually. When Virginia Woolf broke down after her marriage she was "stuffed" by Sir Henry Head. She weighed 119 pounds in September 1913 and 179 pounds fifteen months later. The mythology of Leonard Woolf sitting devotedly by her for hours at a time, spoon in hand and begging her to eat, appears in a different light when one takes into account "stuffing" as the standard – in a sense, the only – treatment for mental illness.[27] If patients tried to talk about their troubles, it would be taken as a morbid sign. Instead of responding to their feelings, the doctor would try to get them repressed again as soon as possible. If Rupert's letters to Ka seem obsessive and wild, we must remember that she was the only real therapist he had. Since she was also the main cause of his trouble, he alternately attacked her and cast himself on her mercy, which put her, also, under an almost unbearable strain.

On 9 January 1912 Ka took Rupert to Victoria and put him on the train to Cannes. She would stay in London for a week, then go directly to Munich; Rupert would join her there as soon as he was fit to travel. Elisabeth van Rysselberghe met Rupert at the Gare du Nord and looked after him for two nights and a day at her parents' villa, before sending him on to his mother in Cannes. "I find myself so unmoved and kindly with her," he reassured Ka, "Don't mind my being here a day. I'm not loving Elizabeth." What he now wanted, he said, was "to turn altogether to you and forget everything but you, and lose myself in you, and give and take everything – for a time. Afterwards – doesn't matter."[28] In other words, they should agree to ignore their other commitments – for just so long as their affair lasted. Moved by guilt and concern for Rupert's collapse, Ka accepted his dubious terms.

She had no intention, however, of staying away from Henry. She wrote to him from Lulworth, asking to meet for dinner in London on 7 January. In the week before she left for Munich she pursued Henry shamelessly, deeply offending Ottoline Morrell (who had taken on Bertrand Russell, but was still clinging to Henry). Having been declared surplus to requirements by Jacques and Gwen a year earlier, Ka was not willing to sacrifice herself on the altar of Rupert's jealousy. She would give him all the help she could, but neither would she give up Henry. This would not be made clear to him, however, until they met face to face.

Rupert, meanwhile, was being stuffed in Cannes, and consoling himself that he had at last cleared a path into the future:

> I'm certainer than ever that I'm, possibly, opening new Heavens, like a boy sliding open the door into a big room; trembling between wonder and certainty. ... I know now how beastly I was both to you and to Noel; and that one must choose – choose, being human – one thing at a time.
>
> I couldn't give to either of two such people what I ought, which is "all." Now I've got a sort of peace, I think; because I shall be able.[29]

During the three weeks of their separation he wrote to her daily, some of the letters thousands of words long. His mother was kept in the dark, though she realised her son was upset over something, and suspected Bryn of being responsible! In choosing Ka for his confidante and compulsively spilling out his troubles to her, he was making his own attempt at Dr Freud's new "talking cure":

> The pleasure of telling you about things is so extraordinarily great. What does it mean? Keeping telling you everything would, it seems, make such a wonderful and golden background for everything else between us. I've such a longing to get out of myself, my tight and dirty self – to put it all out in the sun, the fat sun. And it's so hard to tell the truth, to give oneself wholly away, even to you. So one wants to chatter and pour everything out ... and then perhaps truth may slip out with it ... I've never told anyone anything, hardly. "Secretive."

Rupert believed that his breakdown was caused not by overwork – the standard Victorian explanation for mental illness in men – but by sexual frustration: "I've been half-mad, alone. Oh, it's all mixed up with this chastity, and everything's a whirl, and still I'm mad and tiny and frightened … Jacques, being Jacques, went mad for half a year. I, being tougher and slower, defied chastity a bit longer, and then, naturally, would take it worse … It'll be a curious comment on civilization or women or something if I do go."[30]

His sexual experience was indeed scanty for a man of twenty-four, consisting mainly of one night with Denham Russell-Smith and a half-baked affair with Elisabeth van Rysselberghe. Ka's refusal of a complete sexual relation at the end of 1911 had brought matters to a crisis: to be kept on tenterhooks by her was evidently more nerve-racking than to be kept firmly at arm's length by Noel. Since chastity had pushed him over the brink, it made sense to Rupert that physical possession of Ka would restore him to health. He kept telling her that his vacillations between her and Noel, lust and love, were now over; he wanted only her "deep breasts" and other charms:

> It's funny, I still think, your idea that one doesn't – or that I didn't
> – love you physically, very strongly. When I felt last year, my
> whole conduct was wronging you, it wasn't, you know, that! It
> was that it'd come over me that I perhaps only loved you physi-
> cally and very much as a friend, – that I'd still to "only connect"
> lust and an immense comradeship. But I didn't imagine I hadn't
> *those*, you know! It's *possibly* true that mere prettiness and cham-
> pagne stir the penis most. But physical passion includes the penis
> but is more, it's hands and thighs and mouth that are shaken by it
> as well. And that's stirred by different things: strong beauty and
> passion and – undefined things.[31]

Having lost Noel, loving and possessing Ka might restore his sanity and achieve his manhood. But somehow he still couldn't envision a mature and mutually committed life with her – only a few months of wandering around the Continent, after which they would go their separate ways. To a well-brought-up young lady like Ka, this cannot have looked reassuring. Henry was married already, while Brooke was proposing a good deal less than marriage. If she accepted his offer, her future prospects would be seriously dimmed. Rupert, thanks to the double standard, had much less to fear from a romantic liaison. None-theless, Ka bravely set off for Munich, with Justin Brooke for company, on 16 January. She had convinced herself that she owed it to Rupert to be his mistress – and that she owed it to herself to end her "extraordinarily randy condition of virginity."[32] In the city of three thousand artists, safe from the prying eyes that surrounded her in England, she would take the plunge into bohemia.

10

To Germany with Love
January–April 1912

Coming Together

On the night of 30 January 1912, Rupert and Ka both set off by train. In the morning they would meet at Verona, halfway between Cannes and Munich. Rupert had set his heart on meeting in Italy. From Verona, he fantasised, they might slip away to Venice and be lost to the world for months. But, when they met, it was more as patient and nurse than as lovers. Ka realised at once that Rupert was too weak to travel. She took him back to Munich the next day and installed him in the same rooms he had in Schwabing the year before, at Ohmstrasse 3. There, his landlady took over the task of fattening him up with Ovaltine and bromides. Ka was staying elsewhere with friends of Rupert, the Kanoldts. The two of them did not have much chance to be alone, especially when Hugh Popham turned up and accompanied them on their daily outings.

After a week Ka and Rupert went to stay overnight at Salzburg, but they still held off from the final act. At last, on 17 February, they left for a weekend at the Starnbergersee, twenty miles south of Munich. On the train, Ka confessed to Rupert that just before she left for Germany she had spent the weekend at a country house where Henry was a fellow guest. The news sent Rupert into a frenzy of jealousy and humiliation, since his whole relationship with Ka rested on the assumption that she had renounced her interest in Henry. But he was at least moved to claim her fully for himself.

As lovers, they must have been painfully awkward and uncertain – if not quite as bad as J. Alfred Prufrock (T.S. Eliot had finished the poem eight months before, while staying at a Pension near Schwabing).[1] Ka had gritted her teeth and "equipped herself" for the deed, presumably with the "irrigator" that James Strachey had earlier described to Rupert when he had hoped to go to Venice with Elisabeth van Rysselberghe: "The more recommended kind is a glass (or metal) cylinder with a hole in its bottom out which the tube leads, and ends in a kind of tap ... You hang the cylinder – with the liquid – on a nail in the wall, and all you have to do is to turn the tap at the bottom of the tube, and the liquid rushes out. The enema is far the most popular instrument – and is generally effective. But it is essential to use it immediately after you've emitted." There could hardly be any more messy and humiliating method of contraception, especially in a rented room with no bathroom attached. An alternative was Henry Lamb's method, "withdrawal before emission. But *that* requires an iron nerve – and if it fails –."[2]

Coping with the irrigator, and with the ghostly presence of Henry, cannot have made for a carefree night of love. Still, they had together crossed over a threshold, as Rupert recalled a month later:

> I'm pitiful seeing the useless wasted spoilt old maids who creep
> down this road: and the young maids with their dirty suppressed
> decomposing virginity: and then I'm proud at them "Ka is not
> like you, and won't be. She knows." ... I remember the softness
> of your body: and your breasts and your thighs and your cunt. I
> remember you all naked lying to receive me; wonderful in beauty.
> I remember the agony and joy of it all: that pleasure's like a sea
> that drowns you wave by wave. I've the strength of an army, now.
> And I love you, in all the ways of love ... I feel myself standing up
> proud and strong and erect & naked in front of you, with all my
> sex bursting into flame. I feel you under me and hear your low
> cries – You, Ka, you. Nothing else means anything.[3]

The sexual thrill was not enough, though, for them to cast off every previous commitment. Three months later, D.H. Lawrence and Frieda Weekley would arrive a few kilometres away, at Icking, to live together as man and wife. Frieda had run away from her husband in Nottingham, and they expected never to live in England again. But the predominant concern for Rupert and Ka was, what would their families and friends think? What would their landlady think? What would *everybody* think? And the sexual act itself was so hedged about with taboos that it created as much tension when enjoyed as it did when denied. Even its essentials remained, to Rupert, something of a mystery:

> The important thing, I want to be quite clear about, is, about women "coming off." What it means, objectively – What happens. And also, what *you* feel when it happens. Have you (I'd like to hear when there's infinite leisure) analysed, with the help of that second night, the interior feelings you were yet dim about the first night (at Starnberg.)? And can you discover by poking about among your married acquaintances? … It's only that I want to get clear – perhaps it's a further physical thing we've to explore.[4]

But everything was done in a hurry, and only four days after the weekend at Starnberg they were on their way back to England. Ka could not manage the strain of being both Rupert's lover and his nurse, while tacitly keeping a place open in her heart for Henry. She wrote to James Strachey that she was miserable and unsure of what to do with Rupert. He had to be fed and cosseted like a fractious child, but one with an adult capacity to wound and disturb. Rupert was also writing to James, telling him that he was leaning with all his weight on Ka. "It is infinitely wicked," he confessed, "but I'm beyond morals. I really rather believe she's pulled me through. She is stupid enough for me to be lazy and silly enough for me to impose on her."[5] To help Rupert feel better, Ka had to listen to endless diatribes about her filthy behaviour with Henry. When Dudley Ward came from Berlin to visit them, he calmed Rupert down and lightened Ka's burden. The most sensible plan, Ka felt, was to share the task of propping up Rupert between herself, Dudley and Mrs Brooke.

They left Munich on 21 February; when they arrived at Victoria the next day Ka returned to her sister's flat, while Rupert went on to Rugby. Now the understanding was that Rupert would spend two months recuperating in England. In May he and Ka would stay together again in Berlin, where Dudley could be counted on for support. Each would be under the care of their families while in England – especially Rupert, who was too feeble to look after himself at Grantchester and would have to be sequestered at Bilton Road. His mother got on his nerves, but she would protect him from others who would get on his nerves more, and from the dangerously exciting social life he had led for the past year.

Rupert now developed a new obsession: that Ka was as exhausted as he was, and should therefore submit to a similar invalid regime. When she moved to 38 Brunswick Square on 1 March, she should not "look after Adrian Duncan Maynard Woolf Sidney-Turner or any other inhabitant." In the event, she stayed with her sister – perhaps because Virginia had suffered another nervous breakdown in February, or else because Rupert had objected so fiercely to her moving into Bloomsbury. For he had now appointed himself the guardian of her every move:

Ka, you've once given yourself to me: and that means more than you think. It means so very importantly that you're not your own mistress. And that, far more truly and dangerously than if I had you under lock and key – and with my "physical superiority." It means that you're not as free to do anything as you were. It means you mayn't hurt yourself, because it hurts me, like Hell. It means you mayn't make mistakes, because I pay. It means you mayn't foolishly and unthinkingly get tired and ill and miserable: because you make me tired and ill and miserable.[6]

Rupert's real concern upset him too much to be stated in plain terms. He was terrified that Ka might drift back into Henry's orbit and, now that she had given herself to one, give herself to another. But if women were so weak that they required constant male supervision, it followed that *any* man could make them do what he wanted; and most of the time Rupert could not be physically present to make sure of Ka. Having defined her as will-less and faithless, he had to live with the nightmare of what might happen to her in the moral quagmire of London.

Ka, whether out of a desire to be honest or a streak of malice towards Rupert, promptly reported that she had spoken to Henry at a social gathering. "I wish to God you'd cut the man's throat," he fired back. "See very little of the man, for God's sake. And don't be more of a bloody fool than Nature made you." Her contacts with Lytton Strachey aroused an even deeper, and more complex, fury. "I'm glad Lytton has been having a bad time," he fumed. "Next time you have one of your benignant lunches with him you can make it clear to him I loathe him – if there's any chance of that giving him any pain." Yet Rupert's most devoted male companion in these difficult months was James Strachey, now that Jacques was married and Dudley settled in Berlin. Stuck at Bilton Road with the

Ranee, Rupert needed James's weekend visits, but knew that anything he said to him was likely to go straight to Brunswick Square and environs. "I can't 'talk' to James," he told Ka. "I suppose he knows little, and misunderstands ... And I feel, rather wrongly, suddenly – that he's a Strachey – a brother, anyhow, of Lytton Strachey. He loves you: but it may be it's only his love for you that matters to him, not you. You know how the Stracheys feel? James *is* better than the rest. But one can't tell."[7]

Whether or not James was better, he was unshakably loyal. "God damn you," Rupert wrote to him before one of his visits, "God bum roast castrate bugger and tear the bowels out of everyone ... You'd better give it up; wash your bloody hands. I'm not sane."[8] James came anyway, as he always would until he was beaten off. Writing Virginia a letter of sympathy about *her* breakdown, Rupert regaled her with a piece of Rugby scandal:

> Church circles are agitated by what happened at Holy Trinity
> three Sundays ago. In the afternoon there is first a Choral service,
> then a children's service, then a Service for Men Only. Two four-
> teen-year-old choir boys arranged a plan during the Choral Serv-
> ice. At the end they skipped round and watched the children
> enter. They picked out the one whose looks pleased them best,
> a youth of 10. They waited in seclusion till the end of the Chil-
> dren's service. They pounced on their victim, as he came out, took
> him, each by a hand, and led him to the vestry. There, while the
> Service for Men Only proceeded, they removed the lower parts
> of his clothing and buggered him, turn by turn. His protestations
> were drowned by the Organ pealing out whatever hymns are
> most suitable to men only. Subsequently they let him go. He has
> been in bed ever since with a rupture. They were arrested and
> flung, presumably, into a Reformatory. He may live.[9]

In telling Virginia this, was Rupert mad, or just bad? Probably he was unaware that she had been sexually abused as a child by her half-brothers, and had a continuing phobia about being molested. Nonetheless, to write in this vein to someone in her condition was insensitive at best, sadistic at worst.

Noel seemed to be the one person towards whom he still had a conscience. "I see how beastly I was to you all the autumn," he wrote, "I'm ashamed of myself … I can't tell you all I want to, yet; because it isn't mine to tell – till it's finished with."[10] Her answer was simply that they had to wait and see how they would feel when they met, some months ahead. Her life, meanwhile, was not standing still. Now nineteen, and living a much less cloistered life as a London medical student, men were lining up to woo her. She was corresponding with Feri Békássy at King's, was being treated to tea and Wagner by James Strachey, and Adrian Stephen was also putting in his bid. All this attention she treated rather offhandedly; her real dedication was to her studies, which she pursued with her typical single-mindedness. From time to time, she heard about Rupert's illness but treated the news with a mixture of wariness and suspicion that it was just another pose. In the Olivier household, he commented sarcastically, it was "not done, or thought of" to get upset about his kind of misfortune.

Ka was overflowing with sympathy, but having her come to Bilton Road posed dangers of its own. If she and Mrs Brooke disliked each other, Rupert would be torn between them. If they liked each other too well, it would raise the spectre of an official engagement and marriage. He got Ka invited, after much hesitation; then he told his mother she had been at Munich, and another storm broke. It took all Rupert's dramatic skill to convince the Ranee that Ka was only a casual acquaintance whom he had met in Munich by chance. Meanwhile, he was regaling Ka with boasts of the "ferocious tempestuous ocean of lust" that he had in store for her. Somehow, though, it was not tempestuous enough to make him defy his mother and marry Ka. And when she came, the first time they had seen each other in a month, he could only lash out at her for her past misdeeds. Once she had left, he collapsed and cried himself to sleep. "Everything's gone from me –" he lamented, "love for Noel, writing, everything – is swept away." The only thing he had left was Ka's renewed promise to be with him in Berlin in May. But, back in London, Henry fell off his horse and Ka volunteered to apply fomentations to his wounds every morning. Once again, Rupert began to bombard her with letters that swung back and forth between indignation and despair. Yet going to bed with Ka had got him fantasising about Bryn, the most beautiful and sexually appealing woman he knew. He wrote to James that they should "abduct Bryn for Sunday to the Metropole at Brighton – and go shares."[11]

By the end of March, Rupert was finding life at Bilton Road unbearable. "Mention *nothing* connected with my life," he told Geoffrey

Keynes before he came to visit, "no names, nothing, for the Lord's sake. Relations between the Ranee and me are peculiar. And one must be very cautious."[12] He learned that he had failed to get his fellowship, though it was hinted that if he applied again his chances were good. Dr Craig had forbidden him mental work, but writing seemed to be the only occupation open to him. His thesis could be resubmitted without much revision, so he had no further need to grind away in libraries. If he stayed at home, his mother would prevent him doing anything, and would keep most of his friends away as well.

It was time for a break out, clearly; but Rupert was not really fit to be about on his own. He would need continuous help from his friends – for example, Jacques and Gwen: "I can't sleep. I'm leaving this Hell. I've got to defer the Deluge a month or two yet. I'm going – I don't know where – with J. Strachey for the weekend ... I'm entirely depraved and extremely unpleasant – but can I sleep in your Studio? .. I'm much less bother than last time."[13] Where he really wanted to go, it was becoming evident, was back to Noel. He told Ka that his love for Noel was "gone ... swept away," but Ka must have known him better than he knew himself. She could see that the woman who had not yielded to Rupert would always stand higher in his heart than the one who had:

> I shall see her once – I'm so ashamed (she's, you'll understand,
> *good, fine, wonderful)* – before I leave England. And then, you
> see, I may not see her for years, or ever, again ... I'm sick with a
> sort of fear, of seeing Noel. She – you don't know what she stands
> for – stood for to me – Do you I wonder understand about love,
> Ka? – it's rather a holy thing – I shall say (for a certain amount
> I *must* tell her) "I've taken away my love from you, Noel. I've
> given all my love to Ka. And she –" Perhaps Noel'll ask "what's
> she done with it?" (as one asks after a dog one sold last month) –
> I daren't look at her.[14]

Coming Apart

Rupert fled from his mother's house on Thursday, 28 March. He had dinner in London with James and Bryn, then went on to spend the night at Jacques's and Gwen's studio flat in Baron's Court. Rupert had decided that it was time to take them into his confidence, and get them to share his obsession about Ka's flirtation with Henry: "I can't bear that I should go about knowing some things alone. Jacques and Gwen and Justin – I feel I *must* tell them the horror, the filthy filthy truth. It's unbearable, suffering alone. I want to see their pain – ... And you – you'd see their faces – or be able to talk to them – people who *love you* – about things. Now, you see, it's so twisted. I'm the only decent person in 1912 you know – everyone else is in 1911."[15] The next night Ka came to see them, and after she left Rupert told Jacques and Gwen the story of Lulworth and its aftermath. He told them, too, that he and Ka were going to Germany in a month as man and wife, and that he wanted to marry Ka but she wouldn't have him. Having got this off his chest, he left the next morning for a long weekend at Rye with James. What Rupert did not say, however, was that he and Ka had slept together at Munich. Jacques solemnly advised him that they would both see things more clearly when they were no longer virgins. Jacques and Gwen were inclined to see the whole affair as a bad case of premarital jitters, with one partner emotionally faithful and the other wavering. The reality, of course, was far more complex – and put Rupert in a much worse light.

As soon as Rupert was out of the way, Ka came over for a tête-à-tête with Gwen. Jacques claimed to be too ill to see her, but was in fact too angry. They both felt that Ka, after the fiasco of her broken romance with Jacques, had gone against the grain of her nature by plumping for female independence, free love, and the company of degenerate intellectuals. Gwen, especially, was now taking an unashamedly conventional line:

> I think there's been too much nonsense about these Stracheys. Treating them as equals and all that. It's sentimental and encourages them. They *are* parasites you know, all of them ... I for one am a clean Christian and they disgust me.
>
> You seem to me to have absolutely no fineness of instinct about a certain goodness (there's no other word) which is essential. You have forgotten God. You think in your arrogance that you can manage your own life – But there is a humility more important than any intelligence. You have not the mind to govern your instincts – you are terribly muddled by education and talk ...

PS Why do all these people think that you are only good enough for a mistress and not to be married? You *are* you *are;* and to be loved all your life ... Jacques says Rupert has wanted nothing in the world but to *marry* you, for ever so long.[16]

Becoming a married woman had made Gwen much more outspoken – in fact, downright aggressive. Her stock of ideas was relatively small, but she made up for this by the ferocity with which she proclaimed them. She prescribed for Ka what had worked for herself: marriage, and large doses of hard work. Ka, in her state of willful self-assertion, was a loose cannon, dangerous to all her friends, and especially dangerous to Gwen, since who knew when she might again throw herself at Jacques? As a Darwin, Gwen demanded of Ka earnestness and sober commitment; as Jacques's wife, she condoned libertinism in the man but was appalled by it in the woman.

Jacques was less overbearing, but just as emotionally grievous. In the name of their love – which he claimed still continued – he asked Ka to reconsider her whole course of action since they broke up. Rupert truly loved her, Jacques believed, despite his current state of muddle and hysteria; but Ka's love for Henry was "not convincing, not inevitable." Going to Germany was a dangerous half-measure. To escape disaster, they must take a single, bold stroke: "If I were Rupert I'd not have you for a month, for a mistress. It's but a sop to your conscience. It should be all or nothing. You give him all except the one thing he wants, which is your love ... I think it's cowardly these reservations. Marry him first even if you must leave him afterwards one day. But these back-doors – that's not facing life."[17]

Both Gwen and Jacques were now unshakably convinced that their two friends belonged together. Years later, they were still waiting for Rupert to return and claim Ka's heart. When he died, much of the tragedy for them was that this reconciliation was now impossible. They kept making excuses for Rupert's erratic passions. In any case, they felt that only Ka could give him the ballast he needed. They viewed Bloomsbury as a rival and in many ways an enemy camp. Ka was too impressionable, anyway, to run in that company. She was not an intellectual nor sophisticated enough to treat sex as a game, as Gwen explained to Frances Cornford:

It was [Ka's] first going to Rupert at Munich that shocked me –
not her going if she had admitted it was for love – but her going
and saying "I don't love you – I nearly hate you, I love H.L., I
came out of pity"; she did it out of a mixture of real and unad-
mitted love for R. and a sort of false intellectual vanity and desire
for self abasement.

Rupert loved her then – if she had been honest then – if she
had married him (then or within a month or 2 afterwards) – he
would have loved and respected her always. It's an intellectual
vanity – her actions have been instinctive all through – her words
were simply rubbish. In this matter all through she has been simply pushed and driven by her sex. It was that pure and simple
with H.L.[18]

The Raverats' judgment of Ka may not have been fair, but what mattered was that she herself was coming to agree with it. Her wide-eyed devotion was bound to irritate anyone so restless and cynical as Henry. He
was starting to complain about her to his intimates and she must have
sensed his dissatisfaction. Ka was becoming more receptive to Rupert's
protestations of love, and more inclined to believe that marriage would
pull them out of their emotional swamp. Unfortunately, any real move
towards marriage was guaranteed to make Rupert shy away from her,
though neither she nor the Raverats understood this feature of his emotional makeup.

No sooner had Rupert gone off to Rye with James than he again
started to play the ardent and repentant lover:

There are two newly-married couples. The husbands have both
retired, just now (9.0). How it brings the old days back, eh.
    Have they got Irrigators? Are they using Oatine? The dears! ...
I feel mentally better for being beastly to you. I'm loving you extraordinarily ... Oh my God, I *want* you so tonight. Your nakedness and beauty – your mouth and breasts and cunt. – Shall I turn
in a frenzy and rape James in the night? I'd burn you like a fire if
I could get hold of you.[19]

Next day came more of the same, coupled with the demand that "You'd
better marry me before we leave England." But Ka was asked to reply

"chez Noel" at Limpsfield. "I'd like to get rid of that woman," Rupert
told her, "before I came into you. I'll crawl in for comfort – the old game!
I'm sick about Noel. I, even I, find my theories true – she gets hold of one
– oh, I know what I'm doing, it's all right!"[20]

Caught in his eternal balancing act, Rupert decided to see Ka in London on Monday afternoon before taking the train to Limpsfield that
night. In the meantime, however, she had been exposed to the full blast
of Gwen's and Jacques's disapproval. Seeing Rupert again was more than
she could face. She begged off the rendezvous, saying she was too tired,
and would stay at her sister's rather than go down to her cottage in Woking. On the train that was taking him to see Noel and Bryn, Rupert
erupted again:

> Are you wanting to make me wild before I see Noel, lest should
> be too nice to her? or do you want to get rid of me by killing me
> – can't you do it quicker easier ways?
>
> I'm going to do the hardest and one of the worst things ever
> done tomorrow. A thing you hardly understand. And all the time
> I, the filthied blasphemous I, will be agonizing about you.
>
> Wire that all's right, that you're in Woking.
>
> Gwen Jacques and a thousand more yourself me decency love
> honour good fineness cleanness truth – : you'd sacrifice them on
> your lust – and such lust – I'm frantic. I shall see you thank God
> or I'll kill myself – on Wednesday.[21]

Rupert was speaking in code because he could not bear to speak directly. When he forbade Ka to tire herself, what he meant was that she
must stay away from London, and particularly from those parts of it
where she might encounter Henry. His own "blasphemy" lay in re-
nouncing the chaste Noel for the fallen Ka. At Limpsfield he was struck
by how supportive and calm Noel was, given his unexplained neglect of
her over the past several months. Having stayed an extra day at Limpsfield, Rupert turned up at Woking on Thursday, 4 April for a much less
happy meeting. The passionate scenes he had imagined at Rye fizzled out
as soon as they were face to face. "I'm going to leave Ka alone," Rupert
reported to Jacques, "till she's rested and ready for Germany. I found
her (I came yesterday) pretty bad. To rest, as far as she will, is the best
thing for her: (and for me). She sees – anyhow – what other people

think."[22] What other people thought, evidently, was that Ka and Rupert should marry; and Rupert told Jacques that he had set himself a deadline to do just that by 10 May, the day before Dudley Ward and Annemarie von der Planitz were due to wed.

Revolver Practice

In the week after he left Bilton Road at the end of March Rupert saw all of his closest friends, decided that he and Ka should get married, and hinted in almost every letter he wrote that he planned to kill himself – and perhaps others. That would mean a Mayerling scenario, where in 1889 Grand Duke Rudolf of Austria had killed his mistress, Marie Vetsera, and then himself. Behind these wild words was a new crisis: Rupert was afraid that Ka was pregnant. When James gave him directions for contraception the previous April, in Munich, he had told him (wrongly, of course) that the safest time for intercourse was halfway between periods. Rupert's consummation with Ka was probably delayed accordingly, until 17 February 1912, when they had been in Munich for two weeks. Her period was due at the end of the month, and by the middle of March Rupert was trying to reassure her: "Do I see you've been fretting over the non appearance of your month, *allerschuhteruste?* I suppose it was my fault, upsetting your damn inside. But I sort of think you've been half-fearing we'd mismanaged the machine, and that your well-known fecundity had been set off." From Rye, on 30 March, Rupert noted that she must be "at, or nearly at" her period – presumably the second one due after they had gone to bed.[23] Then, the letters say nothing more. But there is no reason to doubt Cathleen Nesbitt's report: that Ka had a "still-born" child, and Rupert felt very guilty about it.[24] She might have got pregnant when she was with Rupert near Berlin at the end of May but February seems more consistent with the surviving evidence. After Ka went to stay with Virginia Stephen at the end of April, Virginia wrote to her: "I've heard about every household between this and Newhaven now, and I regret to say that the proportion of illegitimate children is quite amazing ... So you see, gossip is not confined to the Ap ... les [Apostles] and their satellites."[25] This might suggest that Ka had confided in Virginia about her pregnancy.

If he had the threat of becoming a father hanging over him, one can understand better why Rupert's actions, in his remaining two weeks in

England, were so frantic. He could not go back to Ka, and would not go back to his mother. Luckily, the faithful James stepped in once again. After the weekend at Rye (where they rang Henry James's doorbell, without reply), James took him back to Mrs Primmer's at Bank. She was "the best cook in England," Rupert said, which would help his "stuffing" cure. But his main reason for going must have been to revive memories of his secret rendezvous with Noel and Margery, three years before. That was Easter 1909; now he had come back to spend Easter in the forest again. The contrast between past and present, however, made him flatly suicidal. "It is thought by those who know me best (viz, myself)," he wrote, "that I shall die. Nor do I greatly want to live."[26]

Two months later, Rupert told James that he had decided "on April xth" to buy a revolver, but had found that in England it was not easy to get one. Under the Pistols Act of 1903, to purchase a handgun a licence was required, but they could be provided at a Post Office. It was an offence to sell a handgun to someone of "unsound mind," and perhaps Rupert gave that impression.[27] He might have made his vain search in Brockenhurst, after putting James on the London train on Tuesday the 9th. He was all alone, and had no idea of where he might go next. He had asked Bryn to come and look after him, but she was off climbing in Wales with the Hubbacks and Hugh Popham. What better way to die, after all, than to shoot himself in some glade where he had walked on a spring morning with Noel, in the days of his innocence three years before?

Lacking the necessary weapon, however, he had to go on living for a while. The next morning, a letter came from Bryn and he went off to Brockenhurst again, waiting several hours for her train. On arrival, she found that Rupert had made no explanation to Mrs Primmer about a single young lady coming to join him. But no objections were made, so they had four days in the forest together. On the rebound from killing himself – on the rebound from everything that had happened in the past year – Rupert now fell in love with Bryn. "For three whole months," he told her later, "I'd been infinitely wretched and ill, wretcheder than I'd thought possible. And then for a few days it all dropped completely away, and – oh! how lovely Bank was! – I suppose I should *never* be able to make you see what beauty is to me, – physical beauty – , just even the *seeing* it, in spite of all the hungers that come."[28] Bryn threw Rupert into a rapture by showing up in the nick of time, and by giving him kindly affection. It is unlikely that this included anything more than a sisterly kiss or a few melting looks. Rupert wanted to make love to *her*, certainly, but he was too shy to make his feelings or desires clear, and Bryn surely would not have yielded to them anyway. She cared for Rupert, and felt responsible for him when she was with him. But she was thinking more and more about marriage, and Rupert was obviously too shattered to make a proper husband for anyone.

Why had they never made a couple in better days? More glamorous than Ka, more accessible than Noel, Bryn would seem to be a perfect match for Rupert. At the beginning, they were perhaps too alike to make a pair: too sought-after for their looks, too backward in finding their own path in life. And Bryn had no academic pretensions, so that Rupert compulsively sneered, behind her back, at her lack of brains. When he fell in love with Noel, Bryn may have been mildly jealous; but she and Noel were basically a close and loyal pair, and Bryn never wanted to cut her sisters out. Rupert, however, saw Bryn as a last-minute saviour from his troubles, and he was clearly not restrained by the consideration that his honour was already engaged – and over-engaged – to Ka and Noel.

Rupert and Bryn left the forest together on Sunday the 14th for London, where they had tea with Virginia Stephen at Brunswick Square. She reported to Ka that Rupert was "slightly Byronic" (deadly modifier!) and that Bryn "has a glass eye – one can imagine her wiping it bright in the morning with a duster."[29] The eye was not literally glass, of course, but the image catches Bryn's shiny facade. After tea, Rupert and Bryn went down to Limpsfield to spend a few more days together. Since Noel was there too, his penchant for playing a double game around the dinner table must have been satisfied to the full.

On Thursday, his last day at Limpsfield, Rupert got a letter from Ka saying that she no longer wanted to go to Germany with him. His letters had become fewer and more distant, he was spending all his time with the Oliviers, and there was no indication that his moods had settled down. Unfortunately, Ka's refusal made them all the worse:

I wonder why you want me to kill you now rather than later.
Isn't it rather insolent of you, when I've rather resolutely gone away to get well *for* Germany, to make the beginnings of my success an excuse for trying to shirk Germany? ...
"Not the right and only thing" "not absolutely free" ... "it

may bring the most awful misery" are your funny little reservations and irrelevancies ...

My dear, you don't seem to recognise where we are. I suppose it's because you have had no pain worth calling pain. You twixt sentimentality and weakness – *I* don't know – played with mud. It raised a storm, that – you were startled – in the end tossed *you* a bit. At that you shrink in "quietness" and "peace," hastily, and demand a four month's respite. Things may have blown over by then. Oh Child, it won't do. You *must* realise that we're *en route*. You can't back out because you're tired or a little bruised.[30]

The most Rupert would concede was that they might have a week or two of celibacy when they first met in Berlin. Before they could thrash it out, a Hardyesque chain of errors intervened: one of Rupert's letters arrived at Woking after Ka had left for London, another was confiscated by her sister Hester. When Rupert came to London on Thursday evening, ready to confront her, he found no message at his club, while Ka thought he was cutting her because of her misgivings about Germany. On Friday she spotted him on a passing bus and they met later in Trafalgar Square, where Ka "collapsed and had to lean behind a lion, against Lord Nelson's pediment, till the crying was over. I think she thought I'd suddenly decided not to bother about her at all: and it brought her round with a jerk."[31] She had been bullied, against her better judgment, into going on a trip that she feared would end disastrously for her – which it did.

While Rupert was pressing Ka to go to Germany, the Oliviers and James were pressing him to stay at home. Ignorant of the real reason, they could not understand why he was setting off for an indefinite stay in the Prussian capital. Noel told James that she and her sisters felt a racial distrust of Germany. They feared to meet a fat and loud-voiced Rupert when he came back. They got him to miss his train on Friday and go to Harry Lauder instead. Bryn, who had left the party, weighed in with a "lovely hurried note in pencil, saying I must stop in England, on principle, because it was my Duty as an English Poet." After such an appeal, what could Rupert do but propose to her?

I, at 1.30 in the morning, and very drunk, wrote a *very* long letter, which said "My dearest, your letter would – if aught could – have saved me from making a hole in the water. *Not*, heart, because of the *general* grounds for living you advance, but (ah God), because your lips (I'm trembling) are like a rosebud, and they curve distractingly. I love you so ..."

Oh, I was young and mad.[32]

This was how Rupert described the letter to James, but the letter he wrote was nothing like a proposal. "Your letter was incredibly nice to get," he actually replied to Bryn. "If anything could have turned me North instead of South East, it would. But I'm going. It's the will of God." He was drunk enough to get the bearings of Limpsfield and Berlin reversed, and to end with endearments – though not so fulsome as the ones he invented for James:

Your letter (by the way, you *must* not address me as "R.": it's disgusting) was full of Brynnisms – I suppose you wouldn't notice it. I wept over it a little, quietly, in one of these black, shiny armchairs, this afternoon. I kiss you for it.
Rupert
I'm glad you're so beautiful.[33]

It is small wonder that Rupert's goodbye to Ka the next day, Saturday, 20 April, was "shy and hurried." Ka's dealings with him over the past fortnight had brought her to the end of her tether, and she went straight to Asheham afterwards for a rest in the country with Virginia. There she found another guest, Leonard Woolf. He had proposed to Virginia early in January, and had been told that she would have to know him better before giving him an answer. Now they were coming to the point, and it says much for Ka's nature that Virginia welcomed her company while making the most important decision of her life. On the 25th, Leonard sent in his resignation from the Colonial Service. Six days later, Virginia sent Leonard a cautious but encouraging statement of her feelings, and by the end of May they were engaged. Ka had thus seen two of her friends working out their future together with steadiness and mutual respect, despite a problematic sexual relation and Virginia's nervous fragility.[34] It would be hard for Ka not to take this as a cue. Could she not, like Leonard, bring Rupert to grasp his destiny, through her powers of understanding and devotion? Both love and conscience now proposed to her that this would be her task in Berlin.

11

The Funeral of Youth
May–August 1912

Syphilis of the Soul

For two weeks Rupert waited for Ka at a Pension in Berlin. While there he received a letter from Noel (now lost) that asked him to apply some judgment and moderation to his relations with Ka. That was not how he had seen it, during the week of crisis in April. "Either I won," he told Noel (that is, made Ka completely submissive to him), "or I lost and killed everybody." That was why he needed a revolver, which he now had acquired in Berlin. And he needed the psychological hardness to go with it:

> You see, it's no good going into it either weak or good. Either puts one into the power of the other side. And it's fatal to be in the power of that sort of woman. I know this sounds beastly to you, you little fool. But there it is. I tell you, I've done with the other business – the nobility and suffering business. It's not good for one, and I haven't got enough decency left to try it. Also, it's damned bad tactics ... She's deserved a lot more than she has suffered and will suffer. If she's lost, the more broken up and spoilt she is, the better.
>
> Ka's done the most evil things in the world ... Think of the filthiest image you can for the fouling of the best things by the worst. Ka is doing that. For the sake of all those things, and for the sake of the Ka I used to know, and for the sake of the good love there was between us, I'd not care if I saw Ka *dying* of some torture I could inflict on her, slowly.[1]

Noel, reasonably enough, wanted to know precisely what terrible crimes Ka had committed, but Rupert always evaded that question. The measure of Ka's crimes was simply how he felt about them. This was not exactly madness; rather, it was a conviction that his emotions were the only reality that mattered. And what he felt was "buyer's remorse" on a grand scale: the venom he directed at Ka was in inverse proportion to his lust when he was looking forward to possessing her. No doubt his hatred was fuelled by misogyny, and by a specific disgust with the female body and female ways of showing desire. His night of sex with Denham Russell-Smith had not led to any morning-after shame or remorse. Nor did he have any such feelings towards Noel; rather, his letter changed tone halfway through, from vitriol against Ka to sentimental reminiscing about days of glory with Noel.

Having got that off his chest, for the moment at least, Rupert still looked forward to the sexual delights he would enjoy once Ka arrived. Each day he went out to explore the countryside, looking for a pleasant village where he and Ka could lodge as man and wife. Around 8 May she arrived, livelier and happier than Rupert expected, and no longer infatuated with Henry Lamb. What she had wanted was to live with Henry as his mistress; what he wanted was to take her to bed occasionally, and borrow a few pounds as needed. Rupert was still convinced, though, that Henry would get his hands on Ka again if she tried to live on her own in London. Nor was he as pleased as he should have been to hear that she had really been in love with *him* the whole time. He had insisted on this second stay in Germany because he hoped to cure his jealousy of Ka by getting complete sexual possession of her. But once he had removed her from her dangerous acquaintances, she lay heavy on his hands. He was too conscious of the other hands she had passed through. He didn't really like or trust Ka any more, he told Dudley. "Noel is the finest thing I've ever seen in the world; and Ka – isn't."[2]

Rupert and Ka set off for the Feldberg Lakes north of Berlin on 20 May, already aware of how badly their affair had gone wrong. At the Pension in Berlin they had not been able to stay together, but in the country they would present themselves as "Herr und Frau Brooke." After a few days in Neu Strelitz they moved to Feldberg, on a lake where they could rent a boat. In a later sketch, he gave a glimpse of those days: "he saw quite clearly an April morning on a lake south of Berlin, the grey water slipping past his little boat, and a peasant-woman, suddenly revealed against

apple-blossom, hanging up blue and scarlet garments to dry in the sun."³
The trip lasted about two weeks and was cut short when Ka learned that
her sister Margaret's engagement had been broken. Ka hurried back to
England to console her, while Rupert returned to Berlin.

In July, when he had returned to Grantchester for a few weeks, Rupert
summed up the Berlin trip in a bitter little poem called "Travel":

'Twas when I was in Neu Strelitz
I broke my heart in little bits.
So while I sat in the Muritz train
I glued the bits together again.
But when I got to Amerhold,
I felt the glue would never hold.
And now that I'm home to Barton Hill,
I know once broken is broken still.

The "second honeymoon" of Neu Strelitz had turned into another fiasco. Rupert had fantasised hotly for three months about the sexual rap-
tures they were going to enjoy, but when it came to the point he was
either impotent or indifferent. Both he and Ka were ill, and the weather
was gloomy. But the basic trouble was that he felt emotionally dead.
Now that Ka had renounced Henry, and cared only for Rupert, he simply could not respond to her. When he was jealous of her, he seethed
with lust, anger, and self-contempt; once she was secure, the "duty" of
loving her made all his passions suddenly drain away.

To put the icing on the cake, Rupert finally got a reply to his parting
letter to Bryn, after forty days. It wasn't "a" letter, he told James, it was
"the" letter, an absolute smack in the face:

Refused – oh, Lord. There are some people (including all women)
one should never propose to by letter.
   "Dear Rupert," it begins. So *that's* something. "R" is dropped.
The words are well-formed. The letters go stiffly up and down.
Not much give and take about *her*, a graphologist would murmur
… The whole page gives the impression of a thoroughly superior
housemaid.
   I'd, of course, in the lonely evenings – oh, you know how
one *does* it – been wistfully murmuring "Banque" to myself.

A hundred times *Highland Waters* sounded vaguely from beyond
the balcony. A hundred times great beeches shadowily obscured
the great yellow stove. A hundred times I felt – oh, but that, I
remember, is a secret.

But she – oh, it had all passed from her, like water from a
duck's back, or facts from a philosopher. Bank was past, was
nothing ... "I must say that Berlin, just now, seems like a fussy,
exhausting irrelevance." – But earlier than that she's – oh, so
painstakingly, so deliberately, – drawn, with precision, the lines,
all lines. Did I ever tell you women were vague, sloppy? Not at
all, James: not at all. Clear as Euclid. She sizes up and dismisses
my letter to her. The emotional one. "All things considered, disingenuous was, I thought, the word for it." So that's at an end ...

Oh, there are pieces of playfulness in it, which I've not quoted.
Oh James: I think that Life's *just* too beastly to bear. Too utterly
foul.

But it's the irresistible, false, fondness of the whole that pins
me shrieking down.[4]

Ever since their first flirtation at Andermatt in 1907 Bryn had dealt with
Rupert as neatly and firmly as she had the rest of her impetuous suitors.
Her watchword in all these affairs was simple: to preserve her self-
control. At Bank, she had told Rupert how she had fallen hopelessly in
love when she was nineteen. Whenever she saw the man the room swam
and she almost fainted with passion. Her response was to hide herself
away until she had "cauterised" her love; for nothing was worth the
humiliation of being at someone else's mercy.[5] Now that she was twenty-
five, years of living by rule had given her a glossy and almost impene-
trable shell. Rupert's histrionics had small chance of cracking it; and no
chance at all when in fact he hadn't proposed to Bryn, only let slip a few
drunken hints about his feelings for her.

If Ka conceived while at Munich she would have been three months
pregnant by now. When she went back to England from Berlin the immediate crisis was apparently over, which suggests that she miscarried
either while Rupert was in Berlin by himself, or soon after she arrived
in Germany. Perhaps it happened at Neu Strelitz, where she was ill with
some unexplained ailment. That she had an abortion in April or May is

possible; but there is no evidence, and she would not have found it easy to arrange one. Whatever happened, it seems clear that Rupert was "off the hook" by the beginning of June. When Ka had to go back and comfort her sister, she and Rupert agreed to think things over separately and decide their future in two or three months' time. But the relationship was doomed, for his sexual interest in her was over.

Once Ka had gone Rupert was left in Berlin, staying with the newly-wed Dudley and Annemarie, and contemplating the wreckage of his life. He had wooed three women and won none; he had failed to get his fellowship; he had nowhere to go and nothing to do. Sex was the principal cause of his nervous breakdown; he could neither deal with his own desires nor tolerate other people's. He told Hugh Popham, who had got a job in the British Museum, that his ambition was to sneak in and spend the night embracing a female mummy; he had heard that most had died of syphilis, but hoped to find a clean one. A schoolboy joke, perhaps, but his reaction to Virginia's engagement to Leonard Woolf cannot have amused anyone but himself: "*I thought* the little man'ld get her. Directly he began saying he was the only man who'd had a woman she knew, and telling tales about prostitutes – oh, you should have seen the love-light dance and dawn in her eyes! *That* gets 'em. To him that hath shall be given: from him that hath not shall be taken away even that which he hath. Even that which he *hath*, James: one by one. Two, two for the lily-white balls: clothed all in hair, oh!"[6]

Rupert had always had a tendency to sexual hysteria, but loving Noel, so clear and firm by nature, had helped to keep it in check. When Ka came over to Berlin, she told Rupert that over the past few months James Strachey had fallen in love with Noel. For Rupert, this was the last straw. He did not fear that James would have much success: he was too neurasthenic, Rupert felt, and too obviously gay. But Noel was no longer a cloistered schoolgirl. She was following Ka into Bloomsbury, and wasn't nature bound to take its course?

> It's on the whole better to be in love with her than with most
> women; because she is much harder and rather honester than
> they. She's a very ordinary person underneath the pink-brown
> mist, you know. And she's just a female: so she may let you down
> any moment. As she's unusually unemotional and stony, and as

she's backed up by her adamantine family with that loony-man at the head, she *may* be fairly safe … But I expect, really, she won't fall in love with anybody for at least two years. After that there'll come a day when she'll suddenly feel a sort of collapse and sliding in her womb, and incomprehensible longings. It's when the ova suddenly begin popping out like peas. Then she'll just be ripe for anybody. But not for you, dear boy. Some rather small and very shiny man, probably syphilitic, and certainly a Jew. She'll crawl up to him, *will* Noel, – to Albert Rothenstein, or Mr Foss (if she has *very* good taste), or Mr Picciotto, or (if he's joined us) Mr Applegate – and ask him to have her. And no doubt he will. I need hardly ask you to visualise it.[7]

Looking across to London from Berlin, Rupert saw a society in which every fence was down. Lytton Strachey had ingratiated himself with Henry Lamb by playing the pandar between him and Ka. Rupert's younger brother, Alfred, was having an affair with Hilton Young.[8] Virginia, with whom Rupert had bathed naked at Grantchester, was now giving herself to a Jew. And James, along with other gay friends of Rupert's, was finding that he could love women as well as men. Rupert's own desires were so various and contradictory that they had to be rigidly segregated. He hated and feared Bloomsbury because it took a positive relish in bringing together impulses that he believed should never be allowed to meet. All of this lay behind his outburst to Jacques Raverat when Noel went to Virginia's for a weekend: "I suppose she's got too much sense – and she's got you and other wise people – to get spoilt in any way by the subtle degradation of the collective atmosphere of the people in those regions – people I find pleasant and remarkable as individuals."[9]

Much of Rupert's turmoil also came from guilt over his compulsive nastiness towards Noel. He had given her, he admitted, "evil and wrong in return for fineness … I had been so wicked towards Noel; and that filled me with self-hatred and excess of feeling seeking some outlet."[10] But, if he felt such remorse, why did he go on jeering at her? Because she was a woman and therefore, he believed, bound to be corrupted sooner or later; whereas a man like James could be relied on, at least for understanding and loyalty. For the moment, this even included acceptance of James's courtship of Noel:

What *I* say is, Fair play and no favours, and let the best man win! ...

My dear, you're male and you understand things: and even I want somebody like that I can exchange a sort of love with. After all, *I* have got and probably shall get only good things from my relationship to you: and it'd be rather *too* mad of me, wouldn't it, to sacrifice that for an off chance at a cunt? I'd rather have a brother than a penisholder any day. As long as I stay sanc I know that.[11]

James's infatuation with Rupert had ripened into nearly six years of faithful service and admiration. Some women, like Ka and Bryn, had let Rupert down; the rest of them would eventually, simply by virtue of being female. "I am touched also to tears for them," he told James, "because they never *quite* know what's up. Women aren't quite animals, alas! They have twilight souls, like a cat behind a hedge. What can one do?"[12] So Rupert still wanted to count James as an ally. He *did* advise him to give up pursuing "holes" and go back to balls (so long as they weren't Rupert's), though he knew James was probably too hopelessly romantic to do so. For all that, a break would not be long in coming.

What was Rupert to do now? He thought of becoming a journalist, like Dudley Ward, or just wandering on to Denmark or Sweden. But England still held unfinished business. Ka had to be given an answer in August; perhaps Noel or Bryn might yet have an answer for him. He wrote to tell Bryn that he felt as if he had just woken up with a headache after being asleep for six months, and hinted even more strongly that it was time for them to have a real affair. Though he tried to make her feel ashamed of her motto, which was "hold on tight to nurse," he was playing a cautious hand himself. He told her nothing about what he was up to with Ka, or what commitments he had made to Noel. Bryn's calling him "disingenuous" had stuck in his throat, but all it meant was that she knew how many secrets, and how much calculation, lay behind his facade of boyish impulsiveness. To get through to her he would have had to drop his mask, and that was the one thing he feared to do. He had opened his heart more to Ka than anyone, and she was already paying the price for knowing too much about him.

The next step was finally settled by a fit of homesickness for the land, if not the people, of England. He went down to Cologne to meet James at a giant exhibition of modern painting and while there he read *The Four Men*, a rhapsody in the Merrie Englande vein about Hilaire Belloc's beloved Sussex:

> He does not die that can bequeath
> Some influence to the land he knows,
> Or dares, persistent, interwreath
> Love permanent with the wild hedgerows.

It was all very Neo-pagan, complete with Belloc's animus against the late-coming Jews. The theme stuck in Rupert's mind, and two years later was reshaped into his most famous sonnet. But Sussex was never his county. When he went wandering outside Berlin, looking for a place where he could stay with Ka, it had only made him nostalgic for the country round Grantchester, which he had not seen for almost five months. In town he often whiled away the time at the Cafe des Westens on the Kurfurstendam, writing letters or scribbling in his notebook.[13] The cafe was full of long-haired intellectuals, artists and their models, socialists and *Naturmenschen* (the German equivalent of Simple Lifers) in sandals. Some of them were "*temperamentvoll* German Jews," including the poet Else Lasker-Schuler. She was there every day, lingering for hours over a single cup of coffee, and no doubt noticing the young Englishman who was also there to kill time. In this festival of Bohemia, Rupert scribbled a poem that rejected everything he saw around him. He first called it "Home," then "The Sentimental Exile," and finally "The Old Vicarage, Grantchester."

Mindful of what Bryn called his duty as an English poet, Rupert scorned the orderly German landscape in favour of England's "unofficial rose" – and its virtuous rustics. He only wished that his own morals had been as pure:

> In Grantchester their skins are white;
> They bathe by day, they bathe by night;
> The women there do all they ought;
> The men observe the Rules of Thought.
> They love the Good; they worship Truth;
> They laugh uproariously in youth;

(And when they get to feeling old,
They up and shoot themselves, I'm told).

It was not from feeling old that Rupert had wanted to shoot himself, but because *his* women had *not* been doing what they ought. Although the last lines of the poem may be read today as mere "camp," for him they were a strangled plea that the river and meadows might swallow his – and Ka's – sexual guilt:

And laughs the immortal river still
Under the mill, under the mill?
Say, is there Beauty yet to find?
And Certainty? and Quiet kind?
Deep meadows yet, for to forget
The lies, and truths, and pain? ... Oh! yet
Stands the Church clock at ten to three?
And is there honey still for tea?

"Considered as a poem," Orwell would write, "'Grantchester' is something worse than worthless ... an enormous gush of 'country' sentiment."[14] But how could Orwell call it "valuable" at the same time? Because, for him, poetry was a young person's game. It revealed their deepest feelings – and their deepest illusions – before experience forced them to know the world as it really was.

Still, Orwell's ideas about popular poetry are too narrowly sociological. "Grantchester" may be a long string of clichés about the sentiments of Oxbridge graduates in 1912, but only a few poems succeed in capturing such historical moments. The poems that get into the popular canon do so on their qualities of style, rather than just a lowest common denominator of feeling. A "gush," in Orwell's terms, just spills over higgledy-piggledy; but "Grantchester" has its own rhythm, diction, and narrative order. It is not mere chance that so many of Rupert's lines live on in the folk memory. Nor was Rupert merely dishing out commonplaces about English rivers, church clocks, and the rest. The miniature utopia of "Grantchester" arose from its contradictions: the seedy café in the middle of Berlin where it was written, the neurotic disaster of Rupert's love affair with Ka. Rupert was not just writing memorable verses on eternal lyric themes, as might be said of his mentor Housman, or even Thomas Hardy. Rupert was a personal poet, rather than a philosophical one, and his poems reflected his confused reaction to the Edwardian social and sexual transition. His gift was to combine, in memorable words, the sweet and the sour.

It was never plausible, though, that Rupert might recover his innocence by returning to the great good place where the clock had stopped. In fact, he had become too restless to be able to live at Grantchester for any length of time again. It was lost to him, honey and all, long before the Great War put it out of everyone's reach, embalmed in the last Edwardian summers. Nonetheless, it was to Grantchester that Rupert now decided to go: the place where he had been just before everything went wrong. "I haven't bathed since November," he joked. "There's a lot to wash off." Perhaps he could find a herb at the bottom of Byron's Pool that could heal his "syphilis of the soul."[15] He wanted desperately to recover his innocence – and to punish those who had taken it from him. On 25 June he boarded the ferry, with James, from the Hook of Holland. This got them back in time for the Society's annual dinner in London on 26 June. Rupert got drunk and maudlin with affection for his "brothers" – except for Lytton, who sat across from him at table – and alarmed E.M. Forster by weeping when he spoke to Bryn on the telephone. The Society, for its part, informally decided to take Rupert under its wing for the summer. He stayed with Eddie Marsh in London, then went to a weekend house party at Gerald Shove's; later there would be a visit to Roger Fry and a holiday with Maynard Keynes. Rupert had also become friendly with Leonard Woolf since his return from Ceylon a year earlier – a man who both saw Rupert clearly, and saw through him:

His looks were stunning – it is the only appropriate adjective. When I first saw him, I thought to myself: "That is exactly what Adonis must have looked like in the eyes of Aphrodite" ... It was the sexual dream face not only for every goddess, but for every sea-girl wreathed with seaweed red and brown and, alas, for all the damp souls of housemaids sprouting despondently at area gates.

Rupert had immense charm when he wanted to be charming, and he was inclined to exploit his charm so that he seemed to be

sometimes too much the professional charmer. He had a very
pronounced streak of hardness, even cruelty, in his character.[16]

Did Leonard realise that Rupert felt no such warmth or interest towards
him? He only saw one thing: that Leonard was a Jew.

Gerald Shove lived with his mother Bertha, a young widow, in a
Thames-side house near Goring. The group of Apostles was carefully
chosen to avoid upsetting Rupert. Harry Norton, Goldie Dickinson,
Eddie Marsh, and J.T. Sheppard were all friends of Lytton, but other
than that they had no connection with the storms of the last six months.
The atmosphere was not androgynous, as in Bloomsbury, but exclusively
gay – which Rupert clearly felt more comfortable with. He was in better
spirits by the time he met Bryn in London for lunch at Gustave's, then
went down for a few days to Limpsfield. Noel was there with Sir Sydney,
who had been much impressed by Bryn's reading of "The Old Vicarage,
Grantchester" over the Sunday breakfast table. But Noel and Bryn gave
Rupert sympathy only in carefully measured doses. Noel told James that
Rupert was at a loose end because he couldn't go on pretending to be ill.
By now, Noel mainly dealt with Rupert's tirades by ignoring them. She
did tell Rupert that his need to divide people into sheep and goats resembled her sister Margery's behaviour: "[She's] got your way of looking at people on the brain; all that about the hards and softs (ridiculous!)
unfortunately she carries it even further than you."[17] Since Margery was
becoming violent and descending into chronic schizophrenia this was not
a good omen.

Rupert wandered on to the Old Vicarage. But when he got there it
was not term-time, and he still had a nervous horror of being left alone.
Few of his friends were on call: the Raverats had gone to France, Ka
was spending her days weeping in the country. Bunny Garnett was off
to Munich to study botany and meet a young protégé of his father's,
D.H. Lawrence, who had just eloped with his English professor's wife.[18]
That left only Frances Cornford to rely on, and Rupert always found
it depressing to be with married friends after a few days. Frances was
overburdened with Neo-pagan casualties. As she comforted Rupert in
person, she also had to cope with pathetic letters from Ka. Justin Brooke
was on hand too, suffering from nervous exhaustion and colitis. Though
he was still nominally in articles he could not actually bring himself to

do anything. Rupert, who was two years younger, felt that Justin had simply failed to grow up. Nonetheless, he spilled out to him the story of his affair with Ka, and was given a lecture on how badly he had behaved. After that he tried to avoid seeing Justin at the Cornfords. "But I saw the 'Rupert is so frighteningly sensitive' look coming into F's eyes," he told Ka, "and she started pawing me. So I gave in, lest worse should happen. I don't mind, if he doesn't. Also I don't much mind him at Maynard's. It'll at least brighten up that rather dreary party. – Unless the females get nervy about him again."[19]

On the evening of 10 July, a few days after arriving at Grantchester, Rupert went to visit E.A. Benians, a history fellow at St John's College. He learnt that Denham Russell-Smith had died at the age of twenty-three. He wrote at once his long, confessional letter to James, about his affair with Denham three years before. There was a hidden motive, one suspects, in his regaling James with such a vivid account of how he had seduced Denham. He wanted to remind James of how firmly gay his life had been, and of how much he had been in love with Rupert. For James, he knew, was now shuttling between London and Limpsfield to pay court to Noel. He was thinking of going to Canada with Justin, Rupert told James; and then what would happen to Noel?

Noel stays in London, among all you people: a virgin of 19 with all the bright little ideas about the identity of the sexes that we've all had and that you have ... You know, with friends like you and your Bloomsbury acquaintances, she'll go through the same process as Ka. With Virginia buttering her up in order to get her for Adrian, with you, with all the rest, she'll soon be as independent as any man – like Ka. Then any dirty little man could get hold of her – not you, my little friend, for she knows you too well, – but anybody she doesn't know ...

This is an instance, chosen because though you don't love Noel, it may be true that you want to bugger her: so it may appeal to you.[20]

The next day he heard that Henry Lamb had quarrelled with Ottoline, and had met Ka. Rupert claimed to be past caring that she was "crawling in among those people again," but he treated Ka to a tirade about Ottoline and Lamb wallowing in slime together. Another outburst was triggered by the news that Leonard Woolf now knew about the Lulworth debacle. "They're a nice set, your friends," Rupert fumed, "(and mine – or once mine.) How did it come? Did the noble Lytton find it too good a story to resist? Or is it James? I suppose the Jew'll have to tell his wife. And she could never resist a good joke. So it's no good trying to do anything –."[21]

If Bloomsbury was so corrupt, why was Rupert still hanging around them for news and company? Jacques, for one, thought it was high time that both Rupert and Ka made a clean break. They should live in the country, he told them, away from homosexuals and real and pseudo-Jews (by which he meant the Stracheys). He hated Jews, Jacques went on, because they crucified Christ daily. Given that the only Jew in the Bloomsbury group was Leonard Woolf, whom Jacques had never met, his denunciations had only the most slender connection with reality, which did not prevent Rupert from taking them seriously. It was a streak of rottenness within Neo-paganism, even if Jacques, Gwen, and Rupert were the only ones in the group who professed the anti-Semitic creed.

Going for a Ride

In the spring of 1912, Maynard Keynes had taken a fancy to ambling around the Cambridge countryside on the back of a horse. He liked it so well that he decided to organise a riding party in the summer. As a bachelor fellow of King's he was now prosperous enough to take over a small country hotel for several weeks, and invite his friends to stay for a week or two at a time. It would be more luxurious than the previous year's camp at Clifford Bridge, and this time Keynes would be host rather than guest. With Rupert in eclipse, Keynes could take over as the patron and master of ceremonies for young Cambridge. He was carrying on a mild flirtation with Bryn, inviting her up to Cambridge to go riding with him. Everleigh would again mix Neo-pagans and Apostles, but this time on Keynes's terms rather than Rupert's.

On 18 July Bryn and Noel met Justin at Waterloo (Daphne was to follow in a few days) and went down to Pewsey in Wiltshire. They were met at the station by Maynard, resplendent in a new riding outfit and boutonniere, and driven five miles across Salisbury Plain to the Crown Hotel at Everleigh. It was a big white foursquare house with a walled garden, stables, and croquet lawn, looking directly out to the Plain. Bryn and Noel were given a whole suite of panelled rooms with several large four-poster beds. During the day there were four horses to ride; in the evenings they all read *Emma* aloud.

When the Oliviers and Justin arrived, the other guests were two Apostles – Gerald Shove and Gordon Luce – and Frankie Birrell. It was a cosy little male coterie, with the lively and campy Birrell setting the pace. He was being looked over as a potential Apostle, but did not manage to get elected. After Rupert turned up on Wednesday the 24th, Maynard complained to Duncan Grant that he enjoyed his old friends better than his new ones: "I don't much care for the atmosphere these women breed and haven't liked this party nearly so much as my last week's. Noel is very nice and Daphne very innocent. But Bryn is too stupid – and I begin to take an active dislike to her. Out of the window I see Rupert making love to her – throwing a tiny [illegible] in her face, taking her hand, sitting at her feet, gazing at her eyes. Oh these womanisers. How on earth and what for can he do it."[22]

Rupert was not just flirting with Bryn; he was quarrelling with her too. Earlier in the month, he had invited her to go boating for a week in August. He still had tender memories of their cruise on the Broads three years before, with Dr Rogers as chaperone. Why not do it again on the Ouse, Rupert proposed – with Goldie Dickinson, who was keen to go, or perhaps just the two of them? The day she left for Everleigh, Bryn agreed to go, for the week of 4 August. But she preferred Beaulieu River, where they had camped in 1910, to Norfolk. Rupert should bring Dickinson, and Bryn would meet them there, with a companion who knew how to sail a boat. Since Rupert had spent several days sailing on the lake at Feldberg with Ka, he must have been miffed by Bryn's news that she was bringing an expert with her. At Everleigh he learned that the other sailor would be Hugh Popham. Having quietly scuttled Dickinson's participation, Rupert was now less than delighted to find that his romantic cruise with Bryn was going to be "chaperoned" by Hugh. With some other part of his mind, he was upset by Bryn's plan to leave Everleigh on Monday and walk across country to Poole Harbour – a jaunt of some sixty miles, which she expected to cover in five days. He thought it quite unseemly for a young woman to wander around unaccompanied like that.

Bryn spent the whole day arguing with Rupert about these arrangements. Exhausted, she finally told him that she and Hugh were going to be married: "I found it almost necessary to give him some explanation of *you* and bless me if I didn't make a comprehensive statement about my feelings and intentions such as would have amazed you to hear! So there's another peg to this queer web one has drawn over oneself. Don't mind my putting it like that – it seems a little true sometimes – tho' its of course only one aspect and an unimportant one … I'm sorry about Rupert, but he knows his own bloody character best, I suppose."[23] Bryn had turned down Hugh's proposal in October 1910, and then pointedly avoided him for a year or more. But somewhere around her twenty-fifth birthday – 20 May 1912 – she took stock of her life and decided that marriage was the sensible thing for her to do. Despite her beauty, or even because of it, she had never formed any deep romantic attachment. She could easily have married into society or into the intellectual aristocracy, but she was not comfortable in either realm. Within the Neo-pagan circle, only Rupert and Justin Brooke were possible matches for her. Though she was fond of both of them, in 1912 neither of them was fit to make a husband. Rupert was tapering off from a nervous breakdown, his £150 per year or so from his mother was not enough to marry on, he had no regular employment and no fixed home. Justin was potentially rich, but he was at least as nervous as Rupert, and even more uncertain about his career.

Hugh, on the other hand, had just established himself in London with a flat and a job in the Prints Department of the British Museum. He had not shone intellectually at King's, but he was nice-looking, outdoorsy, and sensitive. Most people liked him, though he was already known for being painfully tongue-tied. When he first fell in love with Bryn he was still an undergraduate, two years younger than her and far less mature. By the time he renewed his suit he was more sure of himself, while Bryn had become more vulnerable and uncertain. She had more or less abandoned her training as a jeweller. Perhaps she was simply tired of all the excitable young men of the past five years, and thought that Hugh's quiet devotion would ballast her life. Whatever her reasons, she told him, early in July, that she was in love with him. Hugh needed no further invitation:

I think it is almost impossibly much to ask you to marry me. It means so much more to you, to lose and somehow you seem a being God never intended to marry. But if you love me as you do, you must. There is no intermediate stage, which is satisfactory or convenient, do you think? So do. I don't know at all what you feel about having children and sexual matters generally: one must come to some conclusion on the subject. Do tell me. I don't think you are a person of very strong passions: but it is rather futile to try and separate one's body from one's heart in this way. I don't think I am either ... Does it sicken you of marriage looking at it coldbloodedly in this way?[24]

This had none of the throbbing sentiment in Rupert's letters to Bryn. On the other hand, it was a straight question that required, and got, a straight answer. Hugh did not trail any clouds of promised glory. A modest flat, a suitable job, and a conventional marriage set the bounds of his ambition. Still, Bryn was dissatisfied with her single life, she was halfway through her twenties, and she wanted children. Hugh must have impressed her as more serious and potentially a better father than any of her other suitors. And so Helen was won.

Rupert was deeply upset by Bryn's news. He flatly refused to come boating at all; in fact, he feared he was again going mad. When she left on Sunday he refused to say goodbye, and the boating trip fell through because she and Hugh couldn't find anyone to chaperone *them*. Instead, they went climbing in North Wales with Oscar Eckhardt. Noel and Daphne left for the mountains too, for three weeks in the Bernese Oberland with their cousin Ursula Cox. Given the way Rupert had been acting, Noel probably thought that the best way to deal with him was from the other side of the Channel. The night after the Oliviers left Everleigh, Rupert sat disconsolately in his room. What could he do but summon up all his eloquence for a final appeal to Noel:

Oh, Noel, Noel, Noel, my dearest; think! Remember all that has been! It's more than four years since that evening in Ben Keeling's rooms, and the days on the river – when we were so swiftly in love. Remember those days on the river; and the little camp at Penshurst, next year, – moments then; and Klosters; and the Beaulieu camp; and one evening by that great elm clump at Grantchester; and bathing in early morning by Oxford; and the heights above Clifford Bridge camp; and a thousand times when we've gone hand in hand – as no other two people could; – and twice this year I felt your tears, Noel's tears, on my hand. There are such things, such things that bind us ... I cannot live without you. I cannot indeed. You can make anything of me – For you I'll do anything, or make myself anything – anything in the world.[25]

Sorrow in love begets insomnia, so Rupert reached for another sheet of paper. Time for a letter to Bryn. Could they go away together one more time, before everything "closed down" for her?[26] They would have to act quickly, since the marriage date had been set only two months ahead. Having placed his bets on both red and black, Rupert filled up the days by playing poker with Maynard and Geoffrey Keynes. Two days later, it was Elisabeth van Rysselberghe's turn. She was going to be in England again in a couple of months, and Rupert wanted to see her. "If I can't give you the love you want," he wrote, "I can give you what love and sympathy and pity and everything else I have. And I have a lot ... I've had a lot of pain, infinite pain – I know what it's all like ... I'm not worth your loving, in any way."[27]

Meanwhile, Ka was staying with two aunts at the Swan Hotel, Bibury, in the Cotswolds. Keynes had invited her to Everleigh too, though not until after Rupert had left. She had not seen Rupert for two unhappy months and she simply couldn't stop crying, she wrote pathetically to Frances. All Ka asked was for Rupert to make up his mind about their relationship, and then meet to tell her. What *she* wanted had already been settled, a fortnight after she returned to England in June:

I love Rupert – I'm quite clear – and I'm waiting quietly now and getting as strong as I possibly can. To see if he has strength and love enough to heal himself and love me again. I have broken and hurt and maimed him – I see. O my dear – apart from me – it was wicked, it was awful to hurt so lovely a thing and so lovely a person. If I've destroyed love and strength in him (not for me particularly – but for everyone) there is no atonement and no help – I feel. I'm being very quiet – and I don't want to bother him now at all. He knows what it is and what there is to decide.[28]

The day after Bryn left Everleigh, Rupert wrote to tell Ka that he was ready to see her. Justin came by in his Opel and drove Rupert to meet Ka in the woods near Bibury. They talked for three hours while Justin waited in the car. When they returned, Ka was taken back to her aunts, while

Rupert and Justin drove on to spend the night at a hotel in Witney. This time, it really was the end of the affair. "I can't love her, you see," Rupert told Frances. "So now it's all at an end. And she's passed out of my power to help or comfort. I'm so sad for her, and a little terrified, and so damnably powerless." He went on to Rugby, and wrote Ka a letter that renounced his love, but not his grievance against her:

It's no good. I *can't* marry you. You must see. If I married you, I should kill myself in three months. I may, I daresay I shall, anyway. But if I marry you, I'm certain to. ... You keep comparing your coming to Germany then [i.e., in February], with my marrying you now; and my emotions then, with yours now. There is no comparison. You had two ways before you, a dirty one and a clean one; coming to Germany was not even deciding; it was only giving the clean one a chance. You refused to marry me. You refused to forswear filth.

I felt ashamed because you were better and honester than I (ashamed – and yet superior, because you are a woman.). Yet it's not my lack of strength that makes me want not to marry you. It is my strength ... When I found that I wasn't too dead for a sort of love, – but that it wasn't for you, that you *had* killed my love for you too dead, – it seemed to me useless to prolong waiting any longer.[29]

To break with Ka cleanly would not have been in character for Rupert. He remained obsessed with the sexual wound that she had inflicted on him, and went on trying to punish her for it. But the hope of marriage was gone, the child was gone and, except for one accidental collision, he would not see her again for two years.

Raymond Buildings
August 1912–May 1913

Friends and Enemies

"I was once in love with 3 people," Rupert said later, about the events of 1912, "and that wasn't all jam."[1] It wasn't all jam for others, either. Rupert's vacillations between Ka, Noel, and Bryn broke the easy companionship that the Neo-pagans had once shared. No one had the heart to make a summer camp in 1912, nor would they ever assemble again with Rupert at their head. After five years, most of them wanted to reduce their stakes in the group. Several now believed in marriage more than in friendship; all had seen too much grief within their circle to have faith in their old dream of lives without age or care. They disagreed about politics, religion, the suffrage, and many other things. Some had simply realised that they didn't like each other much. "Youth is a very deceitful thing," Jacques had told Frances a year before. "It makes one think so many people so much nicer than really they are, just because of that insolent flush of hot young blood. Middle age finds them all out in all their nakedness of soul – and body."[2]

Frances felt that the immediate need was to get all the emotional invalids on their feet, which also meant keeping them apart from each another. When Rupert came to her after his painful farewell to Ka, she told him bluntly that he should leave England for at least a year, and go far beyond reach of Ka or Noel. Picking oranges in California, or similar unthinking manual work, was the best thing for him. He was, she felt, "all jangled and neurotic and terrified of everything … If he doesn't go off and work hard (till he's so tired at night he can only just crawl to bed and sleep) I feel he'll become contemptible and drifting or lose his self-respect irrevocably."[3] In principle, Rupert agreed, though it would be nearly a year before he actually set sail. He was not going to marry Ka or Noel, but neither was he going to leave them alone; and he also had his vendetta with Bloomsbury to pursue. He was supposed to go on a restful holiday in Scotland with James, but as the time approached Rupert bombarded him with abusive letters:

> To be a Strachey is to be blind – without a sense – towards good and bad, and clean and dirty; irrelevantly clever about a few things, dangerously infantile about many; to have undescended spiritual testicles; to be a mere bugger; useless as a baby as means, and a little smirched as an end ... Buggery, with its mild irresponsibilities and simple problems, still hangs about you. You can't understand anything being really important – except selfishly – can you? So you'll not understand the possibility of "He that is not with me is against me" being occasionally true ... It becomes possible to see what was meant by the person who said that seeing you and any member of the Olivier family together made them cold and sick. But then I suppose you can't understand anyone turning cold and sick to see anybody with anybody else – except through jealousy, and that makes hot – ; can you? It doesn't happen in buggery.

Soon James was invited to Rugby for the coup de grâce. "The explosion," he reported to Lytton, "has had every motive assigned to it except the obvious one. Oh lord there *have* been scenes. And the dreadful thing is that he's clearly slightly cracked and has now cut himself off from everyone. It's all a regular day-out for a cynic – but unluckily I'm not one."[4]

The "obvious motive" was James's dogged and unfruitful courtship of Noel. Once Rupert had cast off Ka, he was filled with remorse that he had ever faltered in his ideal love for Noel: "I fell in love again with Noel with the frenzy of weakness and the desperate feeling that, after the impossible filth and pain, things might yet go well with me – a mad vision – if that came off. So it was bad with me when it appeared how utterly she'd fallen out of love with me. I felt I *couldn't* live. All August and half September I'd tossed about among things; but generally coming back to that plan of suicide." Noel, however, was casting off any love she had

had for Rupert. "He thought I wouldn't mind if he went off with Ka," she confided to Mary Newbery, "but I did."⁵ Later in the summer, when she went to visit Gwen and Jacques at Prunoy, Rupert spilled before Jacques the accumulated sour grapes of his involvement with the Oliviers:

[Noel] got tired of me about a year ago, and also she's extremely romantic, in the young woman's way, of conceiving love as only possible towards a person you don't know. She's rather frightened, now, I think, of going on flirting; so she wants to be rid of me, very much. She's one of these virgin-harlots of modern days; a dangerous brood.

Yes, Margery is the only decent one of the family (though Bryn's been extraordinarily nice to me.)⁶

By mid-September Noel was back in England, and willing to give Rupert as much time as he needed to come to terms with their being "just friends": "I won't be argumentative now. And when we talk, I'll try not to be harsh and dogmatic ... But you *must* try not to be too upsetting. You can reduce me to dumb helplessness through despair, when you explain all your misery. I *must* help you, if I can."⁷ Like so many other meetings, this one at Limpsfield was no help, either in changing Noel's mind, or making Rupert accept that change was not on the menu. "She refused for hours," he told Ka, "to consider seriously even the possibility she might love me again. It was only the sight of my agony (she's rather soft, besides stupid) that made her offer to wait a year before finally deciding against me. I've gone off on that."⁸

During her stay with the Raverats, Noel probably learned more about how deeply and compromisingly Rupert had been involved with Ka. Noel could only repeat, over and over, that she was the last person qualified to save Rupert from his loneliness and despair. When she was a child, Edward Garnett had looked her over and said: "Heart – hard. Hard as nails!" Noel heard, and "grinned with pride."⁹ Apart from her hard heart, Noel pointed out that as she had got to know Rupert, she had discovered qualities that she had come to hate. His emotional demands were relentless, as was his fury when they were not satisfied. "Yes you *want* marriage," Noel said, "and you almost need it; but you shouldn't have it till you can do without it."¹⁰ This was good advice, though not of a kind that Rupert was willing or able to hear. From his point of view,

Noel's firm resolution to "do without it" had tarnished their relationship from the beginning: "There's one other thing, I see about myself. That waiting wouldn't ever quite have done. For other people, perhaps; but not for me. I've too much burning inside. You scorn males for it, and dislike it. But it's there. I need marriage or some equivalent: and I should only rage till I get it. Don't curl your maiden lip. It's you that are unpleasant: not me."[11]

Another bitter pill was that when Rupert went to Limpsfield, his usual room was now reserved for Hugh Popham. In three weeks, he and Bryn would be man and wife – a pill even more bitter. Rupert had told her that he was going to go to America, or shoot himself; in either case, they should meet for a last walk before she got married and never saw him again. Bryn replied that he wrote a lot of nonsense; but since they were both to be in Scotland, she agreed to meet him at Carlisle to go walking for a day or two at the end of August. "If they object to us in inns," Rupert joked, "I shall say you're my aunt." At the last moment, though, Bryn stood him up. She got a mild case of flu and found she couldn't face any more emotional sessions with Rupert: "I'm better now and think it was rather disgraceful of me – but no good could have come of my seeing him. He's evidently got to get through this – what ever *this* is, by himself. I cant help being slightly muddled by his rhetoric even after all these years and dont say the things I meant to when I'm with him, so what's the good? One comes away feeling baffled and exhausted."[12]

On 3 October 1912 Bryn became Mrs Hugh Popham, after an engagement of two and a half months. She had got married briskly enough, but already her friends were hearing about her misgivings. The wedding itself was a little pinched: Sir Sydney and Lady Olivier were in Jamaica, and Rupert's antics discouraged Bryn's friends from making any great celebration. Though she had wanted a church wedding, she settled (at Hugh's insistence) for the registry office, with a going-away supper afterwards at the Richelieu restaurant on Oxford Street. Bunny Garnett, James Strachey, Arthur Waley, and Ka were among the guests, but Rupert stayed in his tent at Rugby. Garnett recalled Bryn, in a rust-coloured tweed dress, "glowing with beauty" as she went off with Hugh from Paddington. Later, however, she confessed that she had sat in the train and "looked at her husband with a sinking feeling."[13]

Rupert must have contributed to her depression by sending her an unconventional wedding present: a long letter bewailing their five years of lost opportunities. In this secretive, shy, and ignorant world, he told her, he was queerer and shyer than most – and with "more to be dishonest about." So, in all, they had barely come within hearing distance of each other:

> Oh but come, don't even you, my dear "sensible" unmorbid straightforward Bryn, think that everyone *is* infinitely incomprehensible and far and secret from everyone, and that approach is infinitely difficult and infinitely rare? One tells, some times, some people, a *few* things, – in a misleading sort of way. But any *Truth!* – – Oh, Bryn! One of the great difficulties, and perils, you see, in ever telling anyone any truth, is the same as in ever loving anyone, but more so. It gives them such a devilish handle over you. I mean, they can *hurt.* If I love a person and say nothing, I'm fairly safe. But if I tell them, I deliver myself bound into their hands.[14]

Rupert would not claim that he had loved only her all this time, but his joy in seeing her beauty and knowing her had been one of the good things in his life. After Bank, especially, he had wanted passionately to explore the joys of the body with her, and he knew she had the courage to carry off an affair finely. But he was sick, and too shy to ask her directly. His hopes of going away with her in August had collapsed when she told him, at Everleigh, that she was engaged. Rupert had lectured her on the importance of marriage in a way that she found "dreadfully conventional." At the same time, he now admitted, he had wanted to inveigle her into an affair before the wedding came and made it too late. Bryn's caution had prevented that, and here was Rupert sitting in his mother's house at Rugby, consumed with jealousy of Hugh – for possessing Bryn's fineness and beauty – and lonely envy of their shared life. But Bryn, during Rupert's lifetime at least, had made her bed and settled into it.

Ka, unfortunately, was left alone through all this, and deeply unhappy. Ottoline Morrell saw her in July, and thought her "evidently devoted to Rupert – and missing him very much after having lived with him as his wife ... She says she feels so tied to him – and that is I believe the effect on women *much* more than on men. – I don't know if once or twice would have that effect but I think any length of time would."[15] Ka's closest friends, the Raverats, still cared deeply for her, but they no longer respected her. They agreed with Rupert that she was, for the time being, incapable of making her own decisions. Gwen did not even want to see her at Prunoy – because of the danger that Ka might fall in love again with Jacques! Frances felt the Raverats should have been more sympathetic to Ka, and "not pressed her so hard to marry Rupert." But she agreed that Ka should be kept away. "She's got a frightening amount of sex," observed Frances, "and it isn't under control. She ought never to have lived this strange modern life." Though friends and family gave her some help, mainly Ka had to get through the aftermath of Rupert's rejection on her own resources – "honestly and truly suffering," Frances felt, "and bearing it with real courage and simplicity."[16]

By the autumn of 1912, most of the Neo-pagans were embarked on separate lives. Ka was living mainly in London, and trying not to cross Rupert's path. After a honeymoon in Holland and Belgium, Bryn set up house with Hugh in Regent Square – around the corner from the London School of Medicine for Women, where Noel was studying. Gwen and Jacques took their own advice and went to live in the country, at Croydon near Cambridge. Before they came back to England from Prunoy, Gwen admitted that she had no desire to take in lame ducks, as Frances always seemed willing to do: "I don't a bit want to see anyone ever again. I feel as if I'd only just left them a minute ago, all grovelling and wallowing about like tadpoles in a pool. When you look at each one of them separately, they're very very nice, but as a whole they're incredibly wearisome ... I don't want to see poor turbid Rupert or sad Ka."[17]

From now on, Rupert vowed to denounce the "miasmic atmosphere" of intellectual London. Asked to speak to the Apostles in October, he gave a talk that amounted to a declaration of war. His theme was his new-found passion for active goodness, rather than ethical contemplation as he had learned it from Moore:

> I think, now, that this passion for goodness and loathing of evil
> is the most valuable and important thing in us. And therefore it
> must not be in any way stifled, nor compelled to wait upon exact
> judgement. If, after ordering your life and thoughts as wisely as
> possible, you find yourself hating, as evil, some person or thing,
> one should count-five, perhaps, but then certainly hit out ... I see
> the world as two armies in mortal combat, and inextricably con-

fused. The word "He that is not with me is against me" has gone out. One cannot completely distinguish friend from foe. The only thing is to thwack suspicious heads in the neighbourhood. It may contribute to winning the battle. It is the only battle that counts.[18]

This was really a picture of Rupert's own emotional state, out of which he created a similarly disordered world. But he could not go on as he had done over the past year. He had to deny his own darker impulses, or else go down into his underworld and perhaps never come out. If he could no longer be a happy pilgrim, he must turn into a crusader. He could still have allies and, when war came, comrades; but the ideal of a life based on friendship, which he had tried to live for the past five years, had gone out of him. Also, a life based on the Platonic worship of Noel. In October he told Ka he hated Noel, and by January 1913 she was marked down for the snub direct. At the Shaw/Belloc debate, he informed Ka, he "unluckily ran into that swine Noel. However we put up our noses and cut each other, which was good fun."[19]

Wandering

For the rest of 1912 Rupert pursued an erratic course, driven by two compulsions: never to be alone, never to stay in one place for more than a week. His first refuge after the showdown with Ka was the usual one: back to Bilton Road, where he spent a dismal twenty-fifth birthday on 3 August. He fired off letters to half the people he knew, setting up a round of visits, and left on 8 August. The first stop was Beckhythe Manor at Overstrand, Norfolk. Gilbert Murray, the Regius Professor of Greek at Oxford, was spending the summer there with his numerous family. His daughter Rosalind had met Rupert when she had a small part in *Faustus* at Cambridge, in August 1910. They got on well, though Rosalind did not become one of Rupert's obsessive loves. He saw her a few times more in September, and went to stay with the Murrays again in Oxford the following March. Nothing was made clear about his feelings for Rosalind, except that he reported to Ka, "my sexual egoism makes me believe that all young women I know are oozing for me."[20] Three months after that Rupert was taken aback to hear that Rosalind had become engaged to a promising young academic, Arnold Toynbee, who had just been made a fellow of Balliol. While Rupert was at Overstrand another of his women friends was removed from circulation: on 10 August a marriage took place, at St Pancras Registry Office, between Virginia Stephen and Leonard Woolf. Rupert did not see Virginia until the beginning of November, when she and Leonard had moved to Clifford's Inn. "She seemed calmer for her marriage," he told Noel, "I felt infinitely removed from her."[21]

After five days with the Murrays, Rupert went to stay with Justin Brooke at Leylands, the family home near Dorking. Justin had troubles of his own: he was supposed to be studying law but spent most of his time laid up with colitis and nervous indecision. Rupert had an anxiety attack at Leylands too, and crawled back to Rugby. He was living in hope of the prenuptial walking tour near Carlisle with Bryn at the end of the month. When she called it off, Rupert had to settle for a much less exciting northern journey: a tour of Scotland with Harry Norton and his aunt. Norton was one of the Apostles, like Eddie, who were good at soothing Rupert. He had been in love with Rupert for a while, in 1908, and simultaneously with Vanessa Bell; neither passion had reached any tangible conclusion. James Strachey called Norton "the affable eunuch," which probably made him the right kind of company for Rupert at that moment.[22] Like Rupert he also suffered from manic depression – treated by Dr Craig – which cut short his career as a mathematician.

Rupert trailed around Dumfries and Galloway with the Nortons for ten days, sending off plaintive or angry letters to Noel as he went. Failure on the Olivier front coincided with a critical decision about his future domestic life. Since his nervous breakdown he had only made brief visits to Grantchester, finding it too haunted by painful memories. But if the Old Vicarage could no longer be his home, and Bilton Road was his mother's home, where could he find a secure resting place? The idea of having his own flat, and being responsible for his own cooking and washing up, was never on his horizon. One possibility remained, Eddie Marsh's rooms at 5 Raymond Buildings, Gray's Inn: "Brooke came to London in August, and wrote his name on an envelope and affixed it with a drawing-pin to the dark green outer door at the top of the spiral steps at Raymond Buildings. He now had first claim on the spare room, which he filled with his books and luggage and made the place his London home. Mrs. Elgy was delighted, in spite of the extra work, for Marsh was out all day and Brooke, she said, was a 'stoojius [studious] type', who caused no trouble."[23] It may have been September rather than August, and Rupert did not date his letters from "Eddie's" until the following spring (before that he used the National Liberal Club). But he was content to have a regular share in Eddie's flat, and Eddie was more than content to have him. What Rupert did not share was expenses, and this was no small consideration. He could live comfortably rent-free in central London, with Mrs Elgy's excellent cooking as a bonus. The package was worth at least £120 per year.[24] Eddie was not wealthy, but his income and capital were more than enough for his needs, and he took pleasure in helping artists and writers to make ends meet. That goodwill was not always returned. His epicene manner, monocle, and snobbish devotions could easily make him a figure of fun. Jacques Raverat was cruel but deadly in calling Eddie "a valet to his heroes." Yet he had shrewd tastes, and many rising young talents benefited from his patronage.

Still, it was Rupert who benefited most, which poses the question: what did Eddie get in return? Almost certainly no physical gratification beyond, perhaps, an occasional hug or holding of hands. Eddie seems to have been impotent all his life, due to a childhood attack of mumps.[25] The relationship was a mixture of intellectual mentoring, like Rupert's earlier ties to St John Lucas, Arthur Eckersley, and Charles Sayle, and a curious kind of pseudo-marriage. Apart from the platonic relationship with Cathleen Nesbitt, later in 1912, all the young women who mattered to Rupert were kept secret from Eddie. In that respect, Eddie was like Rupert's mother: someone whom he loved, and who gave him emotional security, but who was usually kept in the dark about his erotic affairs. Rupert hardly ever appeared socially in London accompanied by a single young woman. In all his life he never "dated" in the contemporary sense, and never had an unsupervised domestic space where he could reliably be alone with a woman. Instead, he went about as Eddie's partner (and Eddie never appeared with a woman either). Eddie was the established and solicitous older man, Rupert the beautiful consort who raised Eddie's status. This was the unwritten contract. Eddie looked after Rupert financially and emotionally; in exchange, he was admired and envied for having Rupert under his wing. Effectively, it was a society marriage without sex. Seven months after Rupert's death, Eddie would establish a similar relationship with another beautiful and talented young man: Ivor Novello. The only difference was that Novello was unambiguously and exclusively gay.[26]

Eddie took care of business as well as pleasure. He had money, a nose for literary talent, and an impressive gift as a cultural entrepreneur. He recognised that "The Sentimental Exile," the long poem from Rupert's stay in Berlin earlier in the year, was likely to boost his reputation beyond the slighter work in the 1911 *Poems*. The title was changed to "The Old Vicarage, Grantchester," and Eddie set about constructing an anthology around it. This would be a promising move in the old game of poetic back scratching (and, of course, back stabbing too). Eddie was as skilled a player here as he was in the bureaucratic manoeuvres of his day job in Whitehall. He and Rupert would make a collection of the emerging younger poets who suited their taste. The result was *Georgian Poetry*, a five-volume series that became the wildly successful house organ of what Orwell skewered as the "beer and cricket" school of English poetry. Rupert was a better poet than most of the Georgians, and less simple-minded about his enthusiasms, but they were the birds of a feather with whom he chose to flock.

On 19 September the venture was launched over lunch at Raymond Buildings, with Rupert, W.W. Gibson, John Drinkwater, Harold Monro (who edited the *Poetry Review*), and his assistant Arundel del Re. As the host, Eddie was also the natural choice to be the editor. He was also neutral, in the sense of not being a poet himself. A rival gang was led by Ezra Pound, who had just met in the British Museum tearoom with Hilda Doolittle and Richard Aldington and claimed the name "Imagists."[27] *Georgian Poetry* signalled a break with the sententiousness of late Victorians, and with the Decadents of the turn of the century. The poetic figure who loomed over their enterprise was Thomas Hardy; the Georgians paid him homage, while falling short of the astringent originality of his vision. Hardy himself was never going to appear in such company, nor was the other great poet of the moment, W.B. Yeats. But Eddie rounded up seventeen contributors, most with shared styles and values, except for such outliers as G.K. Chesterton and D.H. Lawrence.

Positively, the Georgian movement was fuelled by the traditional sights and emotions of English country life. "The Old Vicarage, Grantchester" was the central statement of *Georgian Poetry* thanks to its exploitation of nostalgia, and it was nostalgia that set the tone for the whole Georgian movement, even though its new young poets were supposed to be breaking with the past. A further irony was that in October Rupert went to stay at Grantchester for the last time. Having glorified it as the great good English village, he had to admit that it was no longer a good place for him.

Phyllis

Rupert's two weeks at the Old Vicarage were set aside for work on revising his fellowship thesis, away from the distractions of London. As solitude began to pinch, he would go into Cambridge and wander around the colleges, seeing if any of his old acquaintances might be available to share a meal. One of them was A.C. Benson, fellow of Magdalene, known today for composing the imperialist anthem "Land of Hope and Glory." Like Eddie, he was an asexual older gay man, an admirer of Rupert from a distance. Rupert needed such male company, but it did not exclude "womanising," so long as one sphere of action did not overlap with the other. "One can't – I can't – be properly and permanently all right till I'm married," Rupert told Frances Cornford, "Marriage is the only thing. But, oh dear! One's very reluctant to go into it without love – the full business."[28] That meant being able to feel love within himself, since Ka and others had been quite ready to love him. In any case, he believed that "love's more important for men than for women," because women could find half their fulfillment in loving their children.

The only woman Rupert had really loved – Noel – did not love him, and was now unattainable. If love was so elusive, desire was all too present and pressing, whenever Rupert found himself alone. From Grantchester he wrote to Elisabeth van Rysselberghe at Swanley, asking her to go away together for a long weekend in the country. She agreed, but that left a few days to wait; and Rupert had another young lady who might be willing to come to him at the Old Vicarage. Phyllis Gardner had first laid eyes on Rupert on Armistice Day, 1911, in the tea-room at King's Cross station. Struck by his beauty, she made a sketch of him on the train to Cambridge, though they did not speak. Phyllis was just twenty-one, and had been a student at the Slade since 1908, where she was a classmate of Gwen Raverat. Her background might easily have made her a Neo-pagan, but something had kept her apart from Rupert's circle. Ernest Gardner, her father, was a former fellow of Caius; he was now professor of archaeology at University College, London. Mary Gardner, her mother, aspired to be both a poet and a friend of poets; these ambitions would play a role in her daughter's romance with Rupert. In 1911 the Gardners were living at Tadworth, a leafy suburb near Epsom, rather like the Oliviers' base a few miles away at Limpsfield.

Before making any approach, Phyllis started to do some research on Rupert or, in modern terms, stalking him. She found a student at Newnham who knew him, a "dark, tragic-looking creature." This must have been Margery Olivier, who was beginning her long mental collapse. Back in London, there was more to be winkled out from Noel, whom Phyllis already knew through the Women's Union at University College. On 4 December 1911 she went to tea at the Olivier house in St John's Wood, where she spotted a copy of Rupert's poems, just published. Noel sensed Phyllis's eagerness, and told her that Rupert was "very difficult to catch."[29] That had never been Noel's problem, but it amused her to see how many young women had pursued Rupert in vain. Her own relations with Rupert were at a critical point: he was demanding a deeper commitment, she was holding back. But Noel was not going to help Phyllis become her replacement.

While recovering from his nervous breakdown in Cannes, Rupert entertained Ka with news of Phyllis's campaign: "You know about the Romance of my Life. I know I told you, because I remember how beastly you were about her – Miss Phyllis (is it Phyllis?) Gardner. Everyone was so beastly that I hadn't the heart to meet her. She went to tea day after day in St John's Wood, and I was always too sulky and too *schuchtern* to go ... Oh, I've put it in the hands of my solicitor (Miss Noel Olivier) who has been acting for me in this matter throughout."[30]

Phyllis's infatuation made her a laughingstock to Neo-pagans, even as they fed her hopes that they would produce Rupert for her. He did not become available until 25 June when he came back from Germany after the final shipwreck of his affair with Ka. Phyllis's mother then tried the direct approach by inviting him to lunch at her club, with Phyllis in tow. Rupert was now turning again to Noel, with a side bet on Elisabeth van Rysselberghe. But an ardent, red-haired Slade student was at least worth an interview. For her part, Phyllis was head-over-heels from their first meeting. Rupert was flitting between London, Rugby, Scotland, and other points of attraction; but over the next three months he saw Phyllis intermittently, and went to stay with her parents at Tadworth. The major step was when he invited her to Grantchester, where he went on 12 October and stayed until the 30th. She could have her own room at the Old Vicarage, which paid lip service to propriety. But in Rupert's room was something less decorous: a photograph of a friend standing naked in a willow tree, ready to dive into the river. If it was Noel, Phyllis would have recognised her, though it might have been some other Neo-pagan, or even Virginia Stephen from her visit a year before. In any case, Phyllis took up the challenge when Rupert proposed going down to Byron's Pool. If nudity helped to get his attention, nude she would be.

A month before, Rupert had told Jacques that he was reluctant to go back to Germany: "At present I feel more like going to bed or into an asylum for three months. I feel half mad, most of the time."[31] With Phyllis, it was closer to being mad all the way. They swam at the pool, then went into the meadow on the other side:

> He seized hold of me by the throat and pressed his thumbs on my Adam's apple, and laid me back on the grass, and said: – "Supposing I were to kill you?" And I smiled up at him and said: – "Supposing you did? Then I should be dead..."
> He said: – "I want to see you," and spread me out flat. And he looked at me, and felt me, and then said in an off-hand kind of way: – "You've rather a beautiful body." And then quite suddenly he bent over and kissed me.
> And then we got dressed.[32]

Rupert didn't really want to murder someone, but he wanted to feel what it was like to be a murderer. It was not just the trouble with Ka that sent him over the edge, though that was trouble enough. Bryn was lost to marriage with Hugh; Noel was still indispensable, and still impregnable. And as he was trying to seduce Phyllis at Grantchester, Rupert was finalising plans for a weekend away with Elisabeth van Rysselberghe. Some of this was just a frantic attempt to try every door, in the hope of finding one that wasn't locked. But if Rupert managed to get through a door, he was likely to become more frantic on the other side. The women he chose were all well-brought-up young ladies who cherished their virginity, and whose sentimental idealism left them ill-equipped to handle a flagrant neurotic like Rupert. They thought that sex should wait until marriage, or at least that it should come with the kind of love that would guarantee marriage soon after.

The trip with Elisabeth required careful planning, Rupert told her: "England's a queer place, and I mustn't be seen by my relations spending the weekend with a young woman ... Dress Englishly ... have you a ring that looks like a plain gold one? If it has a gold band you can wear that outside and the rest inside – turned round. It's only England!" To avoid another kind of mishap, he would send her a book on contraception.[33] Elisabeth came up from Swanley on Friday afternoon, 1 November. Her instructions were to get a taxi at Victoria – telling the driver to go to Hampstead if anyone she knew was in earshot – and meet Rupert in the tea room at Waterloo. From there they would leave to spend the weekend in Devon.[34] Everything went according to plan, except for the bodily joys that Rupert had been looking forward to so eagerly. As had happened with Ka at Neu Strelitz, the sex was incomplete and disappointing. Rupert was angry, or indifferent, or impotent, or simply beastly; he left Elisabeth broken-hearted, though still in love with him. Unhappily for her, it was precisely her love and desire for Rupert that stirred up his old resentments.

As usual, Rupert's instinctive response to difficulties with girls was to make himself unavailable. Once Elisabeth was back in Kent, he left for a month in Berlin, to stay with the Wards and finish his thesis. He told Hugh Dalton that he hadn't written a word, but spent his time making love – unsuccessfully – to female dancers.[35] This would be either Annemarie Ward's sister Clotilde, or friends of hers. Another escape from the thesis was to meet T.E. Hulme at the station, on 22 November, and spend several days showing him around Berlin. Hulme had come because of a curious predicament, which he kept secret from Rupert and from everyone else. He had been the house guest of a wealthy Fabian called Wilson Carr and started an intrigue with his daughter Joan, who was a sixteen-year-old prefect at Roedean. Hulme was extremely keen on sex: not just doing it, but also talking or writing about it. He drew Joan into a correspondence where he taught her all the four-letter words, and the actions that went with them. Although he failed to actually seduce Joan, some of the correspondence fell into her father's hands. He had his solicitors send Hulme a stern warning about his "letter of an unspeakably disgusting character." Hulme promised that he would go to Germany as soon as he finished a translation he was working on, and would have no further contact with Joan. This was not enough for Wilson Carr, who wrote to the master of St John's College, Cambridge, where Hulme had just been re-admitted (he had been sent down in 1904 for riotous behaviour and immorality).[36] That ended Hulme's second attempt to get a Cambridge degree. The price of his escape from prosecution was a promise to stay in Germany for at least a year. He actually stayed in Berlin for six months and returned to England in mid-May 1913, just before Rupert would leave for the United States.

Like Rupert, Hulme had a considerable stake in German culture (which did not affect his eagerness to fight as soon as the war began). Rupert described Hulme as "an amiable creature," but they remained acquaintances rather than friends.[37] For Hulme, Rupert was too much the despised "Romantic" type, both poetically and personally. Hulme's ideals of Classicism, Toryism, and "dry hardness" could not have been Rupert's cup of tea. His coarse ideas about relations with women would not have helped either. Still, it was a conversation in the street with Hulme that inspired one of Rupert's most powerful but least typical poems, "The Night Journey."[38] The blind purposefulness of a night train stands for a man's half-conscious encounter with his fate:

> Sure as a flood, smooth as a vast wind blowing;
>   And, gathering power and godhead as he goes,
> Unstumbling, unreluctant, strong, unknowing,
>   Borne by a will not his, that lifts, that grows.
>
> Sweep into darkness, triumphing to his goal,
>   Out of the fire, out of the little room! ...
> –There is an end appointed, O my soul!

The deep fatalism of this vision may connect with Rupert's work on the tragedies of Webster and other Jacobean dramatists, which he discussed with Hulme. Beyond that, the weak foundations of his personal identity left him vulnerable to external powers – including, of course, those of August 1914.

Rupert did finish his thesis in Berlin, and came back to submit it at King's in mid-December. If he succeeded this time, he would have a respectable position in the world; that might soften his mother's anxiety about whether he could recover from his collapse at the beginning of the year. The immediate success of *Georgian Poetry* also boosted his morale. His reputation was growing, and the anthologies would bring a steady flow of cash to their contributors. Still, Rupert felt the need for a radical break with everything he had been doing for the past two years. As soon as the Christmas holidays were over at Rugby he went off to spend ten days with the Cornfords in Cornwall, and take stock of his prospects for 1913.

Frances was a firm believer in resolution by separation and a complete change of environment. Rupert and Ka had become a toxic pair, and any contact between them could only increase their pain. While Rupert was with the Cornfords at the Lizard, Ka finally left for Berlin to stay with Dudley and Annemarie. She would go on to St Petersburg, and not return to England until the summer. Absence rarely did much to soothe Rupert's amorous turmoil, and he kept skirmishing with Noel by letter, worrying about her safety in a half-mad way: "I say, there's one thing … So many people get kidnapped nowadays: and you're always drifting about alone. Please, I'm perfectly serious – be careful … Don't ever, on any pretext, go off with people you don't know, however well authenticated, or get into cabs – it's impossible to be too careful. I demand this."[39] He was not giving up his obsessions with dangers to Ka and Noel, and he was building up new ones about pre-emptive strikes against people he disagreed with. His talk to the Society in October had been a scattered attack against people he considered evil. In February 1913, talking to The Heretics in Cambridge, he concentrated his fire on the feminists who were upsetting the natural order between men and women.[40] There was little distinction between his intellectual opposition to feminism and his frustration with the two women he was trying to get into bed – Phyllis and Elisabeth. The only real cure for that trouble was to remove himself from temptation.

When Rupert came back to Eddie's from Cornwall he knew that he would be leaving for the United States some time before the year was out. He brought with him a poem, "The Funeral of Youth," that was an epitaph for his days of innocence. His inspiration came from Hardy's "God's Funeral," which had been published in the *Fortnightly Review* two years before. Both poems describe a line of symbolic mourners following a coffin; but Hardy's is a solemn meditation on the death of belief, Rupert's a cynical jest at his own expense. Everything that once gave him joy has gone: "*Laughter … Pride … Love …* [and] *Contentment*, who had known *Youth* as a child / And never seen him since."

There seemed to be little reason for discontent in the first two months of 1913. *Georgian Poetry* was flying off the shelves, and likely to have a sequel.[41] Eddie's social campaign on Rupert's behalf reached every corner of fashionable London. At the Russian Ballet's *Les Sylphides*, Rupert was introduced both to the late King Edward's Queen, Alexandra, and to his mistress, Mrs Keppel.[42] Rupert had already met Hardy at Cambridge; now Eddie brought in A.E. Housman and Yeats, who came up with the delirious judgment that Rupert was "the handsomest man in England."

Rubbing shoulders with literary giants was pleasing, even if Rupert was never going to be in their league. But the other fruits of Eddie's snobbery helped to widen the breach between Rupert and his earlier friends. The Apostles, Bloomsbury, even the Neo-pagans, still felt some loyalty to the Cambridge tradition of "plain living and high thinking." They held themselves superior to the aristocratic and socialite circles to which Rupert was transferring his allegiance. His new fondness for queens and duchesses struck them as both a betrayal and a degeneration. His shift to aggressively conventional views on patriotism and personal relations confirmed their feeling that he was no longer "one of us" but "one of them."

The only Neo-pagans that Rupert was now seeing regularly were Jacques and Gwen at Royston and Frances in Cambridge (where her husband was a fellow of Trinity). He felt safer with married people, if not safe about getting married himself. Rather, he was trying to get sex in a less official way, meeting regularly with both Phyllis and Elisabeth. When he was alone during the day at Eddie's, Phyllis was free to visit, hoping to pick up where they had left off in October: "We discovered that we wanted to see one another again with nothing on ... we gently ran our hands over one another."[43] Neither of them, however, was ready to go further. Rupert's hesitation may have been connected to fallout from his weekend with Elisabeth. He wrote to her on Christmas Day from Rugby: "I did you wrong. I'm sorry. I was very tired those days; and you made me very angry ... I am a beast."[44]

Cathleen

By Christmas there was yet another turn of the wheel. Four days after his failed confrontation with Noel on 17 September, Rupert went to the first night of *The Winter's Tale* at the Savoy theatre. Harley Granville-Barker was the director and the matinée idol Harry Ainley played the jealous king, Leontes. Cathleen Nesbitt, an unknown young actress from Ulster, had auditioned for a small part and then been given the lead when Granville-Barker became dissatisfied with his original Perdita. At twenty-three, Cathleen became a star overnight. She charmed audiences as the shepherdess who was really a king's daughter; and she charmed Rupert with her artless femininity. After his string of mishaps with the demi-virgins of 1912, infatuation with a real virgin was the obvious antidote.

Cathleen's virginity was already under siege when Rupert met her. Harry Ainley was only nine years older, but forceful enough to be credible playing her father. He set about wooing Cathleen and she fell in love with him, while drawing the line against actually going to bed. Before long she learned that her caution was well advised. Ainley had a mistress who was in a nursing home with a difficult pregnancy; he also had a wife, who showed up at Cathleen's dressing room and accused her of being pregnant with Ainley's child. By the time of this confrontation, Cathleen had moved on to her next part, as a parlourmaid made pregnant by her master's son.[45] Life and art were getting confused.

Eddie Marsh was an avid theatregoer, with a wide acquaintance among actors. He invited Cathleen to dinner on 20 December so that Rupert could meet her. Cathleen accepted because she wanted to meet Gilbert Cannan, a young playwright and novelist who was currently in the limelight. He was married – to the former wife of J.M. Barrie – though he came alone to Eddie's. To stir the pot, Harry Ainley came too. Eddie enjoyed the company of glamorous or aristocratic women, but that was as far as it went. He once asked a friend, "Why is it harder to fall in love with women the more real they are?" He could fall in love with women in novels, or famous women of the past, "next with an actress in a part and hardest of all with actual women in real life."[46] Perhaps he felt that Cathleen was not real enough to threaten his closeness to Rupert.

Rupert and Cathleen did manage to fall in love, though on both sides it was largely a passion for appearances. He told her she was "incredibly, inordinately, devastatingly, immortally, calamitously, hearteningly, adorably beautiful." But their admiration never brought them to sexual union, as Cathleen explained (and there is no reason to doubt her), "When we spent the night at a country inn we had separate rooms. He would come in and sit on the edge of my bed and talk almost until dawn, but strange as it may seem to anyone of this generation, we never actually became lovers in the sense that he 'seduced' me, as the contemporary phrase would have it. We both had very serious views on marriage and we both wanted to be very sure that we would have a good one."[47]

Fair enough, but there were two things Cathleen did not know. One was that saying "wait until we are married" allowed Rupert to hide how fearful he was about getting married at all. He would reveal this to his male confidants like Eddie or Jacques, but there is no record of his telling Cathleen herself. His other evasion was about his habit of separating love from lust. When away from her, he campaigned relentlessly to get Elisabeth van Rysselberghe or Phyllis Gardner into his bed. Paying that debt to lust made possible his ethereal love for Cathleen. In a hyacinth wood, he told her that they were experiencing what Donne had described in "The Ecstasy":

> Our souls (which to advance their state,
>   Were gone out,) hung 'twixt her, and me.
> And whilst our souls negotiate there,
>   We like sepulchral statues lay;
> All day, the same our postures were,
>   And we said nothing, all the day.

Cathleen wrote later that she wanted a lover who would "caress her soul" rather than her body. She seems to have remained a virgin until she married, in her early thirties.[48] Rupert could restrain himself too, but only when he was with her. His affair with Phyllis was coming to a point of decision. She was beginning to scent danger in Rupert's friends: "he had been drawn into a vortex of would-be original people, who to satisfy their own base natures had made inconstancy a principle."[49] Her knowledge of these people was limited because Rupert had sealed her off from any contact with them. The Cornfords were the opposite of inconstant, nor were the Neo-pagans base. Rupert must have told Phyllis something about the Henry Lamb/Strachey/Keynes vortex, but he was in the process of escaping from it. He did not need instruction in how to be inconstant – and also how to keep Phyllis in the dark about Elisabeth and Cathleen. But his was the inconstancy of a fractured self, quite different from the avant-garde promiscuity of Bloomsbury.

What Phyllis wanted was constancy in legal form. No woman was going to put salt on Rupert's tail there, so a crisis was not long in coming. The occasion was another session of exploration at Eddie's:

> "I must have you *here*," he said, laying a hand over what is delicately referred to by artists as "the central point of the figure."
> "Yes – sometime," I said.

Impatient with any delay, Rupert took to addressing Phyllis as "a rotten female." "All women are beasts!" he announced, "and they want a vote – but they'll never get it!"[50] What Rupert wanted was "the central point of the figure"; but would he ever get it? He asked Phyllis to go away with him for a weekend, but upset her by trying to explain about contraception, to which she replied, "I don't see how any female who isn't a beast can consent to the thing which you asked me to consent to: practically the murder of her possible offspring ... But if going on seeing you means that: intercourse without result – I do definitely refuse it. Why don't you want me enough to do so much as consider the possibility of marrying me?"[51] If Rupert was going to marry anyone at this point, it would be Cathleen. But he said nothing to Phyllis of her rival; instead, he treated her to a philosophical disquisition on the "two ways of living: the normal and the wandering."[52] Since his was the wandering way, it was useless for Phyllis to expect commitment from him. They should take their pleasure, then wander off in different directions.

Phyllis did neither: she went home to Tadworth at the beginning of March with a nervous breakdown. Rupert went to Rugby with the flu. Phyllis's mother fired off angry letters to him about his caddish behaviour, which convinced him that leaving the country was the best way of dealing with female beasts of various sorts. An angry mother was especially fearsome; hopefully her arm would not reach as far as California. "I'd better go, you know," he told Ka on 7 March, "I'm not doing anyone any good here, myself nor nobody."[53] In fact he was doing harm, to at least two young women. Getting the news of his fellowship success, a day later, did nothing to change his mind. It gave him a welcome £120 per year, and King's did not require anything in return for the money. Instead of taking up rooms in college in October, California was where he would be. It would take him nearly three months to actually get on the ship, but there was no tie strong enough to keep him in England.

Cathleen, lovely as she was, belonged in that "not enough" category. To convince himself of this Rupert wrote a cynical little poem, "The Young Man in April":

In the queer light, in twilight,
In April of the year,
I meet a thousand women,
But I never meet my Dear.

If he did not meet his Dear, it was not for want of trying by Eddie. On 11 March he gave a dinner to celebrate Rupert's fellowship. W.B. Yeats was the guest of honour, but Eddie also invited three new ladies (and no Cathleen). Lady Cynthia Asquith was married to the prime minister's son Herbert, and Clementine Churchill was married to Winston. The third lady was Violet Asquith, the prime minister's daughter by his first marriage. She was good-looking, literary, highly strung, and the same age as Rupert. She had carried a torch for Winston and may have attempted suicide when he became engaged to Clementine. Since she was the only single woman there, Eddie may have marked her as a good match for Rupert. They did become close, but if there were romantic feelings they were only on Violet's side, and she remains one of the might-have-beens in Rupert's life. The Asquiths were not an aristocratic family, so he would not have been jumping too many rungs of the ladder in marrying one of them. Eddie's plan succeeded to the extent that Rupert and Violet became friends, and Violet probably would have liked them to be more than that. But Rupert had his hands full elsewhere. A month later she invited him to her birthday dinner at 10 Downing Street, where the other guests included George Bernard Shaw, Edmund Gosse, J.M. Barrie, and John Masefield. Violet liked to have writers and artists around her, though Rupert was the only one who was young, handsome and single.

In early April, Rupert's status as a celebrity was recognised by an invitation to have his picture taken by the American photographer Sherrill Schell.[54] His casual clothes, and the informal setting of Schell's Pimlico flat, made for a new style of portraiture. In time, the pictures would do as much as the poetry for Rupert's romantic image. He tried to laugh off the results, especially the profile shot for which he had stripped to the waist: "very shadowy and ethereal and poetic, of me in profile, and naked-shouldered. Eddie says it's very good. I think it's rather silly." Rupert sent these comments from a stately home at East Knowle where he and Eddie were staying with George Wyndham, Lady Cynthia Asquith's uncle.[55]

On 10 February Rupert had lunch with Hugh Russell-Smith, Geoffrey Marchand, and their fiancées.[56] Marchand was a former president of the Cambridge Liberal Society. It was a reminder that when marriage began, friendships were likely to end. Russell-Smith had been Rupert's closest chum in Rugby days; his brother Denham, dead for seven months, had been more than that. Hugh had been a visitor at Harvard and was getting ahead in his academic career at St John's, his old college. His career would be cut short on the Somme in July 1916.

In mid-April Rupert moved temporarily to Albert Rothenstein's studio flat at 5 Thurloe Square, behind the South Kensington Tube station. Though he would sneer at him behind his back, Rupert kept Rothenstein as his token Jewish friend. He was, after all, an artist rather than a financier.[57] Possession of the studio would make it possible for young ladies to visit privately, and even spend the night. But the field was dwindling. Cathleen was away on tour, and in any case not a candidate for sex. The friendship with Violet Asquith was flourishing, but had not ripened into an affair. Phyllis Gardner was secluded with her mother at Tadworth. That left Elisabeth van Rysselberghe, and Rupert kept up his siege during April and May. "I want more," he told her, "I want to 'complete' our memories."[58] But that was not what Elisabeth wanted. She had been shocked and hurt by Rupert's behaviour when they went away to Devon. Probably that resembled what had happened with Phyllis – that Rupert had attempted intercourse, but had not managed to complete it. Elisabeth may have loved Rupert, but she wanted true love and marriage in return. Once he was at sea, at the end of May, Rupert explained why she was not going to get it from him:

I'm in love, in different ways, with two or three people. I always am. You probably know this. I'm not married to anybody, nor likely to be. A year and a bit ago I was violently in love with somebody who treated me badly. The story is a bloody one: and doesn't matter. Only, it left me for a time rather incapable of loving anybody.

As for you, child: I have two feelings about you now, which alternate and mix and make confusion. I like to be with you ...

But quite apart (in origin) from all that, you – move me to passion ... The fire in you lights the fire in me – and I'm not wholly responsible. Only, my dear, that's all there is: those two things. I don't want to marry you. I'm not in love with you in that way.[59]

He would like to live with her sometime for half a year, Rupert continued, so long as it was on his own terms. Meanwhile, he advised her to get over her love for him and become independent. "I have been so great a lover," he would begin a poem, later; but the poem is about beloved things and sensations, rather than people. Rupert's letter to Elisabeth was belated, but at least it let *her* know where she stood.

The rest of May was taken up with the list of things to be done before Rupert sailed for New York. He had to spend time in Rugby, to placate his "bitter and enraged" mother.[60] She was furious both that Rupert was leaving her alone, and not following in his father's footsteps by taking up his fellowship at King's. He could hardly explain that Phyllis Gardner's mother was even more bitter and enraged, which settled his internal argument about whether to stay or to go. In March he had told Gwen Raverat that he was torn between two passions: for "various women in London," and for escape to the South Seas.[61] By the middle of April he had decided that he must leave the country for some time. One reason was to be away before Ka came back from Germany. But more pressing, surely, was a direct demand from Mrs Gardner that Phyllis's nervous state made it essential that he should go. This would be the context for the way Rupert broke the news to Cathleen: "I do love you so: and yet I'm going to leave England in May. I've got to go, for a bit. Because I promised. I got mixed up with a woman. Do you know how human beings tear each other? I've been so torn, and torn so. But everything's very complicated, and one day I'll explain, maybe."[62]

The practical concern about travelling was eased by Naomi Royde-Smith's commission for a series of travel articles for the *Westminster Gazette*. Most of the payment was in the form of expenses, including return tickets by ship and train from London to California. Nonetheless, Rupert would come back from his travels with a substantial overdraft at his Rugby bank.[63] Eddie Marsh left England before Rupert, on 9 May, to tour the Mediterranean with the Churchills and Asquiths. He held a farewell dinner for Rupert and Cathleen before going, also inviting two of her old flames, Gilbert Cannan and Harry Ainley. If this was designed to extract a commitment from Rupert by making him jealous, it did not succeed. He was worried about how Cathleen might manage without him, but not worried enough to cancel his trip. The same went for Ka and Noel, exposed to the temptations of London. Ka was still in a bad way, he felt, and not getting better. He could only ask the Raverats and Cornfords to do their best: "I think the sooner she gets quite clear of me, the better. But I think the idea of 'leaving her to work out her own fate' is silly. It doesn't apply to young women ... Be gentle with her; remembering she's a feeble fool."[64] Noel had better defences, and the problem there was more on Rupert's side: how was he to cure himself of being dependent on her? She agreed to have dinner with him the night before he left, after he promised to keep himself under control: "I get along very well without you: and lead a fairly happy life. I have a dreadfully consistent and faithful disposition, I'm afraid; ... However, as time goes on Love grows potential and not actual. A comfort. And I've succeeded in hardening my heart against you."[65]

As usual, at dinner they could not articulate what had gone wrong. Rupert did achieve clarity in one quarter: he had been forbidden to write to Phyllis, but the day before he left England he told her mother that he was "sorry it has all been like this; and that you think me so disgusting. Goodbye."[66] The next day Denis Browne saw him off at Euston, and at Liverpool the RMS *Cedric* was docked, ready to take him to New York.[67]

Rupert and Phyllis met again once, in October 1914, when he was in the Royal Naval Division and just back from Antwerp. They had lunch, with Phyllis's mother, at Gatti's in Covent Garden. By this time Mrs Gardner had transferred her lion hunting to Robert Frost, who became contemptuous of her ambitions – both poetic and social. Phyllis had become a devout Christian, and accepted Rupert's death with resignation. She never married, and devoted herself to breeding Irish wolfhounds. At her death in 1950 she left the records of her love for Rupert to the British Library, not to be opened until 2000.

13

Stepping Westwards
May 1913–May 1914

Letters from America

Rupert sailed from Liverpool on the RMS *Cedric* on 22 May 1913. She was a relatively slow ship, taking nine days to get to New York. There were more than two thousand emigrants below in steerage but Rupert, in first class, had nothing to say about them. His main concern, as the ship plowed on at sixteen knots, was to make firm his relationship with Cathleen.[1] That forced him to say more about what had happened with Ka a year earlier, and about his resolution to make a clean break with her:

> It's bitter destroying and breaking things two have built together
> – intimacies and trusts and friendliness. It's like cutting something
> out of oneself ...
>   Child, beyond a certain point men and women shouldn't go,
> unless they marry. Not if they're people of human feelings. Or
> they pay overmuch in irretrievable ways ...
>   I cling more and more to the peace and comfort, I find more
> and more in loving you and being with you ... I pray you love
> good and keep away from the evil things of the world, for my
> sake and for your sake and for both our sakes.[2]

It was good that Rupert laid some of his cards on the table, and explained what he had learned from his misfortunes with Ka. But he was also holding back his ace. Cathleen might well assume that they would get married when he returned, but Rupert's letters said everything *except* that. And when would he return? He had told Eddie that he would probably be back by January 1914, but that was not a promise. Cathleen thought he was going because of Ka, not realising that it was mainly because of Phyllis Gardner and her mother that he needed to get out of town. Once he was in America he could not be pressured by Cathleen to take any decisive action about their future. Cathleen herself seems to have accepted Rupert's strategy of delay. She could have demanded a commitment from Rupert, as Phyllis had, and seen what the outcome might be. Instead, she kept playing out more line, all the way to Tahiti. When Rupert returned a year later he would still be unwilling to decide, until the war ended all decisions.

Meanwhile, his immediate task was to come to terms with America. Henry James would note that Rupert's dispatches to the *Westminster Gazette* became "steadily more vivid and delightful as he continues his travels from New York."[3] James complained that Rupert's idea of New York focused on the pervasiveness of advertising, and especially of giant neon signs: "we feel him not a little lost and lonely and stranded in the New York pandemonium – obliged to throw himself upon sky-scrapers and overspread blackness pricked out in a flickering fury of imaged advertisement for want of some more interesting view of character and manners."[4] James regretted Rupert's limited human contact with New Yorkers, apart from the usual clichés about Americans being boastful and simple-minded. But he was right about Rupert being "lost and lonely." He had managed to leave his letters of introduction behind, and was stuck in the gloomy Broadway Central Hotel.[5] Although he managed to knock out his three articles on the visit, he was indeed homesick and suffering from culture shock. "I'm crying," he wrote Cathleen, "I want you. I don't want to be alone." The next day he was ashamed, but sent the letter anyway: "After all I wrote it – one of the 'I's. And you'd better see them all." Even the sturdier "I" of the day after was convinced that "this is *not* a land for a civilized man."[6] Rupert went up to Boston to see the Harvard Commencement, and enjoyed the welcoming style of the undergraduates. When he returned to New York he was no longer feeling so much at a loss. Part of his trouble was that he had come for a negative reason, to put an ocean between himself and Ka, Phyllis, and Noel. The *Gazette* assignment had got him out of England, but hadn't given him any pleasure in being in the United States.

Rupert spent only the month of June in New York and Boston, followed by two and a half months in Canada.[7] He was not exactly an imperialist, but it was important to him that North America still had a country ruled by the king and looking in many things to the motherland. He did not much like Canada or Canadians, in the eastern part at least. But he grasped that it was a country oriented to the future, and dominated by a vast and unpeopled natural world. About that future, his record as a prophet was mixed. In Montreal, he encountered the primary difference between Canada and the United States: the "French fact," and the "complete separateness of the two races." "Inter-marriage is very rare. They do not meet socially; only on business, and that not often. In the same city these two communities dwell side by side, with different traditions, different languages, different ideals, without sympathy or comprehension."[8] "Racial difficulties are the most enduring of all," Rupert concluded. He had a letter of introduction to the former prime minister, Sir Wilfrid Laurier, but predicted confidently that no francophone would ever be prime minister again. He was wrong about that, but right about the persistence of "two solitudes" a hundred years later.

Rupert went on to Ottawa, which he liked better than Montreal, and where he formed his only real friendship with a Canadian. Duncan Campbell Scott was a poet who celebrated his young nation in verse, complete with stereotyped Indians and Québécois peasants. Twenty-five years older than Rupert, he was deputy superintendent of the Department of Indian Affairs. Today, he is condemned for his aggressive policies of cultural assimilation. Scott took a schizoid view of the Aboriginal question, not unusual for his time. He took regular canoe trips into the wilderness and romanticised the Native heritage, but his assimilation policy was carried out with singular ruthlessness. "I want to get rid of the Indian problem," he wrote, "I do not think as a matter of fact, that the country ought to continuously protect a class of people who are unable to stand alone ... Our objective is to continue until there is not a single Indian in Canada that has not been absorbed into the body politic and there is no Indian question, and no Indian department."[9]

Since the Jesuit missions of the seventeenth century, Europeans had tried to Christianise Native Americans. Canada's assimilation policy went further. Its main – and most notorious – instrument was the residential school, which Indian children were persuaded or forced to attend. The schools were run by either Protestant or Catholic clergy. In addition to religious instruction, the children were separated from their traditional culture, made to wear European clothes, and punished for speaking any language except English. No doubt Scott praised the policy to Rupert; so far as we can tell, he accepted the need for assimilation, while also taking a romantic view of Indians he happened to meet on his travels. But that would not be until he had travelled further west.

Noel wrote to Rupert in June, after their awkward dinner just before he left England. She admitted that she had little idea of how she wanted to live, or should live. But she knew where Rupert was likely to go: "You, an English gentleman, having become le grand indifferent, will have the success of the man who pockets his heart and can devote his energies to prattle and flash. Then ... you will drop all that and very determinedly set up a family in England; bully them rather, and write pamphlets; and all the old friends will say you found your level and visit you from time to time." In reply, Rupert spent most of July writing a letter in installments. He vowed that he no longer loved Noel, and was going to marry and have children very soon: "I've tried loving a woman who doesn't love me, you; and I've tried loving a woman who isn't clean, Ka; and it doesn't pay. I'm going to find some woman who is clean, and loves me."[10]

Rupert's formula might even have worked, if the third woman was Cathleen. But things in that quarter were not straightforward, starting with the problem that if a woman went to bed with Rupert, she would stop being clean. Nor, he admitted, was it easy to be truthful about his plans: "It's so very hard, trying to write humanly. All these damned affectations get in the light – they leap from the end of the pen."[11] The affectations were camouflage for the submerged conflict between them: that Noel had held on implacably to her virginity, while Rupert found this both necessary and intolerable. The open conflict was about Lytton Strachey. Noel found him "a good-natured, slightly dotty buffoon; and in so far as the ridiculous makes the world brighter – an excellent fellow." To which Rupert countered: "I know he is Judas Iscariot. So let it rest."[12] Noel did not let it rest, though: she went on peppering her letters with cheery mentions of her Bloomsbury chums. This was a way of annoying Rupert but also a point of principle. Unlike Rupert, she did not believe in living her life in compartments, each walled off from the other.

Rupert continued his journey westwards, finding little to spark his imagination in Toronto, but something hugely impressive in Niagara

Falls. It caused "great cloudy thoughts of destiny and the passage of empires [to] drift through the mind ... the river, with its multitudinous waves and its single current, likens itself to a life, whether of an individual or of a community ... In such places, one is aware, with an almost insupportable and yet comforting certitude, that both men and nations are hurried onwards to their ruin or ending as inevitably as this dark flood."[13] In July 1913, such thoughts were dangerous.

In Winnipeg, Rupert found an Old Rugbeian, who took him to the wilderness east of the city. On the way they encountered a motley crowd of immigrants, whom Rupert saw with a jaundiced eye: "The problem of immigration here reveals that purposelessness that exists in the affairs of Canada even more than those of other nations. The multitude from South or East Europe flocks in ... The most remain, often in inassimilable lumps. There is every sign that these lumps may poison the health of Canada as dangerously as they have that of the United States."[14] Despite his chauvinism, Rupert perceived what would, in the long run, make Canada one of the most successful multicultural countries. "Purposelessness" is another name for the lack of a rigid national identity, to which newcomers are required to conform. From his nativist perspective, Rupert saw only "the peril of too large an element of foreign blood and traditions in a small nation already little more than half composed of British blood and descent." That perspective remains a force today – more in Britain than in Canada, surely – but Rupert did not see Canada's potential for hybrid vigour. Holding on to his racial categories, he equated immigration with mongrelisation: "Canadians regard this influx [of immigrants] with that queer fatalism which men adopt under plutocracy."[15] Early Fabians like Rupert often supported eugenics, which meant hostility to immigration and ethnic intermarriage.

When he got to Calgary, Rupert could take into account the only people in Canada who were not immigrants. His chapter on "The Indians" recognises the partial success of the government policy of assimilation. "Not the best Indians these, say lovers of the race. I have met them, as clerks or stenographers, only distinguishable from their neighbours by a darker skin and a sweeter voice and manner ... So we finish with kindness what our fathers began with war." Rupert visited the Stoney Indian Reserve, outside of Calgary, and felt sentimental about their attempt to keep living in a traditional way, "more in touch with permanent things than the America that has succeeded them."[16] The further away from cities they were, the better their chances of sustaining a nomadic life of hunting and trapping. But Rupert foresaw the problems ahead for either choice: assimilation, or life on a reservation.

Rupert did not find it easy to produce his travel pieces to order, and this showed in the result. Noel Olivier pointed out the limitations of going rapidly from town to town. "And in the people you meet," she noted, "it is only the superficial, queer and obvious things you look for; and if you find them to be what you like to think is typical of the country, you are satisfied and leave them."[17] A fair criticism, except that Rupert did not put everyone he met into the *Westminster Gazette*. On 19 August he left Calgary for Lake Louise, in the Rockies, where he would "rest awhile and try to write."[18] Well, not exactly.

Back in New York, Rupert had reminded Eddie of his offer to introduce him to "a rich widow in Canada." This was the Marchesa Mannucci Capponi, whose husband had recently died. He came from a storied Tuscan family, established in the Villa Capponi at Barberino Val d'Elsa. The marchesa was an American, née Agnes Smith, daughter of a Midwestern physician. She had taken a degree in English as a mature student at Stanford in 1898, then married a German and gone to live in Berlin. In 1906 they had a son who died two days after he was born. Agnes was a widow when she married Mannucci Capponi, and now was a widow again, living in Minneapolis. She became acquainted with Eddie Marsh around 1911–12, thanks to whom she and Rupert could meet at the Chateau Lake Louise hotel.[19] The many letters he wrote to her over the next year make it almost certain that they became lovers over the fortnight that they were together at the lake.[20]

Rupert wrote to Agnes affectionately and at length. He found her an oasis of sophistication in the Canadian wilderness, but it is hard to get a sense of what she was like, or how deeply he cared for her. When she came back to the United States on the ss *Celtic* in 1912 she took eight years off her age on the ship's register.[21] Did Rupert realise that she was forty-one, not thirty-three? In any case, she was clearly older than he was, whereas all his previous lovers or half-lovers were younger. We can only assume that she knew what she wanted, sexually, and that Rupert was happy to give it to her. Even allowing for the expurgation of his letters, there is no hint of the usual hysteria and ambivalence in his love affairs. His previous relationships had been plagued by various kinds of uneasiness around virginity, pre-marital sex, contraception, and secrecy.

Up in the mountains, where no one knew him, with an experienced and eager partner, Rupert could turn the page on the past.

How much did it matter that Agnes was almost old enough to be Rupert's mother? She had been twice married and had given birth, so it would be pointless for Rupert to tee up his obsessions about "dirtiness," female vulnerability, or woman-as-child. Yet his interlude with Agnes did not change the deep structure of his feelings about women. If she tried to deflect his puritanism, she failed. Still, they succeeded in becoming friends as well as lovers, the first time Rupert had managed that.

Rupert and Agnes left Lake Louise in different directions: he westward to Vancouver, she eastward to her home and later to England. While there, around March 1914, she went to visit Mrs Brooke in Rugby. An occasion, probably, where everything important remained unsaid. Yet how much had Rupert *encouraged* Agnes to go and see his mother, with motives we can only guess at? He waited to write to Cathleen Nesbitt until Agnes had left Lake Louise, and then his report was a masterpiece of omission: "I've been 'down' for a week and a half – submerged – but oh! Very happy. Just lounging and staring at the lake and the mountains and the snow. It is the most beautiful place in the world ... So I eat and chatter and roam and look."[22]

When Rupert arrived in Vancouver, a letter from Eddie suggested that Cathleen expected him to marry her on his return. Under the heading "PRIVATE," he tried to sum up the state of play:

> Then, am I engaged to Cathleen? Well, one's always being engaged to *someone* you know. And I recollect saying a lot about marrying her, to her ... My dear, I don't know if we shall marry. I might die. WE might feel differently ...
>
> My general position, you know, is queer. I've had enough and too much of love. I've come to the conclusion that marriage is the best cure for love. If I married, perhaps I could settle down, be at peace, and WORK ... Cathleen's character is very good, and I'm very fond of her. Why not her? – On the other hand, she's an actress ...
> (This is the sort of letter that doesn't look well in a Biography.)[23]

Eddie was the only person that Rupert really confided in at this time – someone gay, and an Apostle, like James Strachey (who had now been discarded). Still, Rupert held back from Eddie whatever he had learned from his just-concluded episode with Agnes Capponi. Writing to her in November, he asked, "When, as these months and years clatter on, shall I be able to spend some months in peace with you, working and seeing you?" On Christmas Day, his message was, "I'm writing now – I always do, to you – in one place and one condition. I wonder if you know what it is?"[24] Reading between the lines, we can guess that sexual frustration was agony for Rupert, except that living with a woman provoked agonies of another kind.

In his piece on "The Rockies" Rupert included two lyrical pages on the beauty of Lake Louise. But the beauty did not make up for the size and desolation of the North American landscape: "It is an empty land. To love the country here – mountains are worshipped, not loved – is like embracing a wraith. A European can find nothing to satisfy the hunger of his heart ... The land is virginal, the wind cleaner than elsewhere, and every lake new-born, and each day is the first day."[25] There were no "ghosts of lovers in Canadian lanes," Rupert lamented. There were lovers in flesh and blood at the hotel, but that was not to be shared with his readers. The chapter on "The Rockies" in the *Westminster Gazette* marked the most westerly point for Rupert's travel writings. He did not write about Vancouver, nor about San Francisco or Tahiti. When he went to Lake Louise he had some half-finished poems but, he told Eddie, he had "an Episode with a Widow" instead of finishing them. They may have been in the notebook he lost somewhere in British Columbia, never recovered. One poem was to be called "Aeterna Corpora," probably linked to what he later wrote to Agnes: "There are only two things in the world I think beautiful. One is a woman's head and body, and the other is goodness."[26] Two different things, we note.

Rupert told Eddie that Vancouver was "a wicked city," but he gave no reason. He may have objected to the dens of vice downtown or to the presence of so many Asians whom, like a good Fabian, he blamed for driving down the wages of the "white man." In all, he was happy to leave Canada behind. Despite their faults, the Americans had more vitality, while Canadians had no interest in anything beyond making the most money in the shortest time. He arrived in San Francisco around 15 September, and at once found it more agreeable than the north, and also more interested in *him*. "Their wide-mouthed awe at England is so touching," he reported to Eddie, "they really are merely a colony of ours still."[27] After a couple of weeks Rupert went across the bay to Berkeley where Charles Mills Gayley, the chairman of the English Department, took him in as a house guest. He arranged for Rupert to read at both Berkeley and Stanford, and encouraged undergraduates to come and see the visitor at his house on Piedmont Avenue. One of them was John Schoolcraft, who set down his impressions of this shy and unknown young poet:

> I have seen some handsome Englishmen, particularly through service with the British army, but none who could come up to Brooke. Actually, he was a combination of the perfect English school boy, and the perfect English man, with a real overlay of beautiful girl ... The best comparison I can think of is the young Garbo. His skin was like that of a girl, his coloring pink and white. He wore his dark-gold hair long, parted in the middle and flowing over the ears, but not offensively. Yet there was no effeminacy in speech or manner or in the management of his tall, strongly-built body.[28]

On his way back from Tahiti Rupert stayed in Berkeley again, and read some of his new poems to great effect – though, Schoolcraft notes, "Nor was anyone moved to tears, as Scott Fitzgerald was when Brooke read from his earlier verse to a group of undergraduates at Princeton in the fall of 1913."[29] Rupert was in San Francisco and Hawaii in September and October 1913, so he cannot have been at Princeton that fall. If Fitzgerald did hear him read, it was more likely in May 1914, when Rupert was staying with Russell Loines in New York. But there is no record of such an occasion at Princeton. Fitzgerald certainly went through an intense Rupert Brooke phase, writing imitative poems as an undergraduate and taking the title of his first novel, *This Side of Paradise*, from "Tiare Tahiti." Was the phase so intense that he convinced himself he had seen Rupert in the flesh?

Rupert would later grumble about California, as he did about most things American, though the "young Apollo" side of his personality should have been a good fit with the emerging culture of Berkeley, Stanford, and Marin County (where he went hiking on Mt Tamalpais). He lingered in the Bay Area, uncertain whether to set a return course for England or continue further west. "How perfectly imbecile I am to wander over here," he told Eddie, "when Europe is infinitely more romantic!"[30] Nonetheless, he tossed a coin, which pointed towards the South Seas. A few days later, he got a cautionary letter from Naomi Royde-Smith. The *Westminster Gazette* never printed more than six articles in a travel series, she said, and they were just printing Rupert's first one. The fee of four guineas was paid on publication, not on delivery, so only now would money start to trickle into Rupert's account in Rugby.[31] They had paid his fare to New York and, presumably, a substantial travel advance. There was not going to be a lot more coming from that quarter.

Even with his £150 from Mrs Brooke and £120 from King's, Rupert did not have cash on hand to keep going. Nothing daunted, he got Russell Loines to send him a loan, covered by a check on Rupert's bank (where the manager was an accommodating sort). His puritanical streak did not extend to financial affairs, where he never seems to have worried about running short or not having a job. Staying on the road was better than facing the complications he had left behind in England, including the tricky question of whether he could or should marry Cathleen. So he would take his cue from Robert Louis Stevenson and Gauguin. The South Seas were not a solution to his problems; they were a way of making his problems irrelevant. If myths could be believed, in the South Seas there *were* no problems.

The Idea of South

Rupert sailed for Hawaii on the ss *Sierra* on 7 October. He had told Eddie that he found it impossible to write poetry while travelling, but on the ship he started again. He thought of composing two sonnet-sequences; only seven sonnets made it into the *Collected Poems*. Most of them tried to deal with the failure of his love for Noel. His model may have been George Meredith's *Modern Love*, though Rupert could not match that sequence in scale or intensity. One sonnet, "Mutability," may have been addressed to Agnes Capponi rather than Noel:

> Dear, we know only that we sigh, kiss, smile;
>   Each kiss lasts but the kissing, ...

Poor straws! On the dark flood we catch awhile,
　Cling, and are borne into the night apart.
The laugh dies with the lips, "Love" with the lover.

That was an argument for snatching kisses when offered, knowing they
could not last. But the other sonnets added up to an argument *against*
consummation. Rupert explained to Cathleen how he had come to realise
this with Noel, probably when he was staying at her house in Limpsfield:

> I crept along ... to her room, some little while before dawn ...
> I knelt down by her, ... and put my head on her hand; and she
> woke, and felt fond of me I suppose, and pulled my head against
> her heart and held me a minute. And I thought I had found
> heaven ... [But] she was too wise, and something in her heart too
> strong, for her to give herself to me, because she loved and pitied
> me in that way; nor did I love her little enough to want it given –
> in that way. Else it would have been a thousand times worse; as
> I know from later things.[32]

Love, for this side of Rupert, was all about a woman taking pity on some
needy and troubled man. Or not even that because, as Rupert went on
to say, "a man is a child." The trouble was, "a woman is a child too."
One needed comfort; the other needed protection, when her longing to
give herself led her astray. What followed, though Rupert could not consciously express it, was that the primal relationship was between
woman/mother and man/child. A few months on, Rupert started to read
D.H. Lawrence's *Sons and Lovers*, which he found "hectic" but impressive. Did the novel's message ever sink in? Paul Morel must either break
his attachment to his mother or die. Rupert never really tried to make the
break. Concealment and cunning were his strategies in the oedipal wars.
　Rupert arrived in Hawaii on 15 October, and stayed at Waikiki. He
went over to Kauai for four days, where he had an introduction to a
plantation owner, and enjoyed a trek to Wailua falls.[33] The warmth and
tropical vegetation made their usual impact, but Hawaii was too tourist-
infested for a long stay. On 27 October Rupert sailed for islands where
his longing for romance had a better chance of being satisfied. He arrived
at Samoa on 2 November, and immediately recognised that this was

what he had been looking for. He wandered through villages, living among "naked people of incredible loveliness, perfect manners, and immense kindliness."[34] The women, especially, were staggeringly attractive: "Samoan girls have extraordinarily beautiful bodies, and walk like goddesses ... in carriage and face they remind me continually and vividly of my incomparable heartless and ever-loved Clotilde. Fancy moving among a tribe of Clotildes!" That was Dudley Ward's sister-in-law, Clotilde van Derp, a pioneer of modern dance. But Rupert told Edmund Gosse that sex remained in the background: "The idea of the South Seas as a place of passion and a Mohammedan's paradise is but a sailor's yarn. It is nothing near so disturbing. It is rather the opposite to alcohol, according to the Porter's definition; for it promotes performance but takes away desire."[35]

In the last of his travel pieces, he called the Samoans the happiest and healthiest of God's children:

If you live the South Sea life, the intellect soon lapses into quiescence. The body becomes more active, the senses and perceptions more lordly and acute ... It is part of the charm of these people that, while they are not so foolish as to "think," their intelligence is incredibly lively and subtle, their sense of humour and their intuitions of other people's feelings are very keen and living ... A white man living with them soon feels his mind as deplorably dull as his skin is pale and unhealthy among those glorious golden-brown bodies. But even he soon learns to *be* his body (and so his true mind), instead of using it as a stupid convenience for his personality, a moment's umbrella against this world. He is perpetually and intensely aware of the subtleties of taste in food, of every tint and line of the incomparable glories of those dawns and evenings, of each shade of intercourse in fishing or swimming or dancing with the best companions in the world. That alone is life; all else is death.[36]

Western Samoa was a German colony when Rupert arrived there, but on 29 August 1914 the New Zealanders invaded to reclaim it for the British Empire. As soon as he heard the news Rupert wrote about his stay there for the *New Statesman*, which printed his piece on 19 September.[37] The chronology counts because by then Rupert had both read

Sons and Lovers and recently met D.H. Lawrence (on 27 June and 30 July). It seems likely that they discussed the primacy of body over mind – what Lawrence later defined as "blood consciousness."[38] Yet whatever they had in common, their responses to the war were diametrically opposed. Lawrence hated it from the first, and refused to participate in any way. Rupert, just as he was writing in praise of the only true life – in Samoa – was choosing its alternative: "all else is death."

Robert Louis Stevenson had died in Samoa, and Rupert made his pilgrimage to the grave on the hill above Vailima. Its epitaph, "This Be the Verse," was another boast about embracing death:

Under the wide and starry sky,
Dig the grave and let me lie.
Glad did I live and gladly die
And I laid me down with a will.

After following in Stevenson's footprints, Rupert wanted to follow Gauguin's, having seen an exhibition of his paintings in London in December 1911. One of them, *Manao Tupapau*, shows Gauguin's thirteen-year-old mistress lying nude on a bed as an evil spirit watches her. Rupert might have liked the idea of re-enacting the picture, though his ostensible motive for the voyage to Tahiti was to snap up any of Gauguin's art that might still be lying around. He could not get a direct ship from Samoa, so after a month in Fiji he left for New Zealand, where he had to spend three weeks waiting for the ss *Tahiti* to take him to Papeete. He found New Zealand a "desolate place," but also "almost exactly like England." The difference was that they had "got all the things in the Liberal or mild Fabian programme – eight hours' day (or less), bigger old age pensions, access to the land, minimum wage, insurance, etc. etc. – and yet it's not Paradise. The same troubles exist in much the same form ... I suppose there'll be no peace anywhere till the rich are curbed altogether."[39] One item was missing from this list. New Zealand was the first Western nation to have female suffrage, in 1893. Rupert was writing to his mother, so we can assume that she would not welcome fulminations about women having the vote. New Zealand also had Maoris, who had come from Tahiti about nine hundred years earlier, and still spoke a similar language. But, in the absence of a Gauguin, they had no sexual mythology that might entice Rupert.

Practical Fabianism mattered little to Rupert when he was eager for the climax of his travels, Tahiti. He left New Zealand on 7 January, arriving in Papeete a week later. There was one obvious place for a European to stay, the Hotel Tiare Tahiti (Tiare was the Tahitian gardenia flower). It was a ramshackle bungalow with a large veranda and various outbuildings. The rooms had curtains rather than doors, the better to pay visits without knocking. The proprietress was a well-known and loved figure, Lovaina Chapman. Her ancestry was one-quarter Tahitian, three-quarters American. She weighed three hundred pounds, and ran the hotel with a set of strict rules that were often broken. She would die in the 1918 flu epidemic. After a few days at Lovaina's hotel, Rupert wanted to live more freely in the countryside, away from the beachcombers of Papeete. In Auckland, he had heard that someone had just found some Gauguin paintings on glass and carried them off.[40] Why not go to Gauguin's old haunts, and see if there was anything left, whether of the paintings or the way of life?

Gauguin's account of his life at Mataiea, *Noa Noa*, was published in Paris in 1901, but Rupert probably never saw it. He was following the same impulse, though: to flee the half-European capital and live in a purely Tahitian culture. Gauguin had rented a thatched hut between the sea and the mountain. For Rupert there was a substantial guesthouse belonging to the village chief, Tetuanui, and his wife Haamoeura.[41] They were childless but had adopted twenty-five children from local families who hoped to benefit from the chief's patronage. Tetuanui spoke French fluently and was in favour with the authorities, who had rewarded him with a trip to Paris in 1889. He had met Gauguin in Papeete and invited him to Mataiea, where he stayed for two years from 1891 to 1893. The chief lived in another house nearby, and the guesthouse was run by a local man who had married an Australian woman. Rupert would sit on the broad veranda overlooking the turquoise lagoon, with the surf breaking on the distant reef. Behind were the mountains, in their endless different shades of green. On the veranda Rupert wrote "The Great Lover" and "Retrospect," both nostalgic poems about England, on the other side of the globe. But he spent most of his time with the locals, swimming in the lagoon, fishing, gathering fruit.

Frederick O'Brien was there too, and wrote about it in *Mystic Isles of the South Seas*. He and Rupert would paddle a canoe out to the reef to fish or just watch the creatures that lived in the coral:

Brooke and I swam every day off the wharf ... The water was
four or five fathoms deep, dazzling in the vibrance of the Southern sun, and Brooke, a brilliant blond, gleamed in the violet radi-
ancy like a dream figure of ivory. We dived into schools of the
vari-colored fish, which we could see a dozen feet below, and
tried to seize them in our hands, and we spent hours floating and
playing in the lagoon, or lying on our backs in the sun ... We remarked that while we plunged into the sea bare, Tahitians never
went completely nude, and they were more modest in hiding their
nakedness than any white people we had ever met.[42]

Both men and women wore the *pareu* around their loins at all times.
When Gauguin was there, the local gendarme had threatened to arrest
him for swimming nude in the river.

O'Brien and Brooke went to a wedding where the bride had a dress
from Paris and the groom a frock-coat. After a Christian ceremony,
everyone went to a traditional feast that ended in a pagan orgy of drink-
ing and sex. "We are on Mount Parnassus," Rupert whispered to O'Brien,
"The women in faun skins will enter in a moment, swinging the thyrsus
and beating the cymbals." Another day, O'Brien and Rupert went back
towards Papeete to see the Marae, the ruins of a great pyramid that had
been visited by Captain Cook. Once a place of human sacrifice, now it
was fallen and overgrown. The chosen victims were killed, but not eaten.
When the first white men came and asked the Tahitians if they ate people, they replied, "Do you?"[43]

O'Brien is tantalisingly reticent about love affairs between European
men and Tahitian women. He does record a visit by Atupu to his bedroom at Lovaina's hotel: "Seeing me alone in Tahiti, and kind-hearted,
she said, she had thought to tell me of the Tahitian heart and the old
ways of the land. She had robed, perfumed, and adorned herself, and entered my sleeping-place, as she said was the wont of Tahitian girls."
When O'Brien turned down the invitation, he was waited on by a tear-
stained Atupu at breakfast. A Tahitian princess explained to him the local
rules of love:

The woman of Tahiti exercises the same sexual freedom as the
average white man does in your country and in England or
France. She pursues the man she wants, as he does the woman.

Your women pursue, too, but they do it by cunning, by little lies, by coquetry, by displaying their persons, by flattery, and by feeding you.

The Tahitian woman makes the first advances in friendship openly, if she chooses ... She does not take from the Tahitian man or from the foreigner his right to choose, but she chooses herself, too.[44]

In her travels, the princess had told the feminists of London and Washington that the women of Tahiti were in advance of them. Eventually the rest of the world would come around to loving in the same way. If it did, that would be Rupert's worst nightmare; yet in Tahiti he felt that he should do as the Tahitians did.

In early February, when he was at Mataiea, Rupert told Eddie that he was having "astonishing medieval adventures with Tahitian beauties."[45] The plural is significant, and has created confusion for biographers. Rupert's great love poem, "Tiare Tahiti," is addressed to "Mamua." This is not a recognised word or proper name in Tahitian; most likely it was Rupert's transcription of "Maimoa," which means the favourite or chosen one. Robert Keable went to Mataiea in 1923 and said that Mamua's correct name was Maaua, and that she was an adopted or illegitimate daughter of the local chief, Tetuanui.[46] But Maaua is not a recognised name either. In any case, by the time Keable arrived, she and her father were both dead, Tetuanui in 1916 and Mamua probably in the flu pandemic of 1918, which killed 20 percent of the Tahitian population. Eight people died at Mataiea in 1917 and thirteen in 1919. In 1918 there were 199. More people died of disease from 1914 to 1918 than in battle, so both Mamua and Rupert could be thought of as indirect casualties of the war.[47]

Gauguin left the world his paintings; Rupert's "Tiare Tahiti" gives us the best of his poetic legacy. It follows the greatest *carpe diem* poem in English, Marvell's "To His Coy Mistress": first the philosophical statement, then the demand to seize the day of sensual fulfillment. But Marvell's poem attacks the beloved's reluctance head-on, while in Rupert's we know that Mamua won't need persuasion to plunge into the lagoon. The poem first describes the Platonic paradise that the "ungainly wise" believe in:

Songs in Song shall disappear;
Instead of lovers, Love shall be;
For hearts, Immutability.

Everything particular to the here and now will fade into the eternal types
of Plato's dream. Part of the poem's humour is the impossibility of explaining Plato to Tahitians, for whom the world of the senses is the only
one that counts.[48] Mamua never left that world, and it is the poet who
is seduced at the end into abandoning his search for the ideal:

Tau here, Mamua,
Crown the hair, and come away! ...
Hasten, hand in human hand,
Down the dark, the flowered way,
Along the whiteness of the sand,
And in the water's soft caress,
Wash the mind of foolishness,
Mamua, until the day ...
Well this side of Paradise! ...
There's little comfort in the wise.[49]

The poem succeeds wonderfully in refuting Plato, or Platonic love at
least, and it leaves behind the puritanism and misogyny that had poisoned Rupert's relations with Noel, Ka, Elisabeth van Rysselberghe, and
Phyllis Gardner. With Mamua he was able to live in the moment, and
make fun of Western philosophy; what he could not do, though, was reconsider the values that caused his string of erotic disasters before he
came to the flowered way of Mataiea. The sensual lagoon of Mataiea
had been left behind when, ten months later, Rupert wrote his most famous poem about the cleansing leap into war.

By the middle of February, Rupert had a bad case of sunburn and coral
poisoning, and had to go back to Lovaina's hotel to have it treated.
"Tiare Tahiti" is dated "Papeete, February 1914," but it was already an
exercise in nostalgia for Mataiea and Rupert's beloved there. Lovaina's
hotel was in the middle of a bustling city, with no "flowered way" to
nighttime swims in the lagoon. It was here that "Taatamata" entered the
plot: "I have been nursed and waited on by a girl with wonderful eyes,

the walk of a goddess, and the heart of an angel, who is, luckily, devoted to me. She gives her time to ministering to me, I mine to probing her queer mind. I think I shall write a book about her – Only I fear I'm too fond of her. Oh dear, its a relaxing place and I feel alarmingly out of track with Europe."⁵⁰ Frederick O'Brien adds a snippet of information: "Taata Mata, the name of a charming Tahitian woman I knew, signifies 'Man's Eye,' her own large eyes, perhaps, explaining the name."⁵¹

At Lovaina's, Rupert experienced both pain and pleasure: "I've been lying on my back for eight or nine days suffering intensely while I swab my skinless flesh with boiling disinfectant. However, I've got over it now, and have started hobbling about. At first I had a bit of fever: but I feel very spry now, I think I've been doing too much fucking. Shaw says its bad for one's work. Do you think that's true?"⁵² Eddie Marsh's opinion on Shaw's warning has not survived. Once Rupert was well enough, he and Taata-mata went back to Mataiea together, and he took a blurry picture of her on the verandah of his guesthouse. In March he described his life as "knocking about with Conrad characters in a Gauguin *entourage.*"⁵³ When Gauguin first arrived at Mataiea, no local young women were willing to share his hut. He went back to Papeete and picked up Titi, who returned with him. That did not end well, and Gauguin went further south, to the back country of Little Tahiti. He brought back the thirteen-year-old Teha'amana, his temporary bride, model, and muse.

Who was Rupert's Taatamata? Her name was Tumatataata Tapoto-farerani, and she was two years older than Rupert. When she took him under her wing at Lovaina's she already had four children; no father was recorded for any of them.⁵⁴ Her family was an important one in Moorea, the storybook island facing Tahiti. In the 1920s she returned to Moorea and became the common-law wife of an American musician and beach-comber from San Francisco, Mike Fogel, with whom she had two more children. She died in May 1947.

The occasion for Rupert's third Tahiti poem, "The Great Lover," was his imminent departure from the island. It starts, again, with a philo-sophical question: How can the things we love resist change and death? With Mamua, the sensual moment overwhelmed any other anxieties. In "The Great Lover" sexual love gives way to a catalogue of Georgian and Neo-pagan minor pleasures – some of them so minor as to be bathetic. "The comfortable smell of friendly fingers"(?); "The rough male kiss of blankets"(??); "Holes in the ground"(???!). Rupert prepared himself for going home with an all-too-English pipe dream of woodsmoke and crusty bread. He was running short of money and scraping together loans from his American friends. His mother might rebel against subsidising a beachcombing son, and King's was going to expect something from him in exchange for his fellowship stipend. "I'll never never never go to sea again," he told Eddie, "All I want in life is a cottage and the leisure to write supreme poems and plays. I can't do it in this vagabondage."[55] It was time to set his course for the land of horse chestnuts and wet roofs.

When Gauguin left in 1893, he was two years older than when he came and, he said, twenty years younger in spirit: "Yes, the savages – these ignorant people – had taught many things to this old civilised man, many things about knowing how to live and about how to be happy. Above all, they made me know myself better, they had shown me my own truth."[56] Gauguin went back to Europe to sort out some financial affairs. He did not even meet the wife and five children he had left behind. Two years later he was back in Tahiti, though not at Mataiea. After six years he moved on to the Marquesas, a place he hoped would be more "savage," and died there in 1903. What he had discovered in Tahiti he followed out to its end, both in life and in art. Rupert agreed with everything Gauguin said about life in the South Seas, but still went back to civilisation, and died in uniform. He had failed, also, with his quest to get rich by finding a Gauguin painting. Somerset Maugham turned up three years later and asked Lovaina if there were any Gauguin's still around. She directed him to a house in Mataiea where Gauguin had stayed; Maugham found a painting of a young woman holding a breadfruit on a glass door, and carried it off for two hundred francs.[57] How did Rupert miss it?

"I was sad at heart to leave Tahiti," Rupert said, "but I resigned myself to the vessel, and watched the green shores and rocky peaks fade with hardly a pang." Yet he also said that he "got out ... not without tears." So the tears must have been Taatamata's, who called Rupert her "dear Love darling."[58] In 1893 Gauguin's beloved Teha'amana had cried every night before he left. His farewell gesture was his great portrait of her, *Merahi Metua*.

One reason for Taatamata's tears might have been that she was pregnant; if so, that could have been an incentive for Rupert to leave, in less than gentlemanly fashion. In mid-January 1915 Rupert returned from a day in the field at Blandford Camp to find a letter from Taatamata, which she had sent off on 2 May 1914, a month after he left. The liner *Empress of Ireland* had sunk after a collision in the St Lawrence at the end of May, with the loss of over one thousand lives. Some months later, divers recovered her mailbags and Rupert got his letter, which was extremely difficult to read:

> I wish you here that night I get fat all time Sweetheart you know I always thinking about you that time when you left me I been sorry for long time. whe have good time when you was here I always remember about you forget me all readly oh! Mon cher bien aimé je t'aimerai toujours ...
>
> Je me rappeler toujour votre petite etroite figure et la petite bouche qui me baise bien tu m'a percee mon coeur et je aime toujours.[59]

Lovaina had also used the phrase, "she get very fat," to describe a pregnant woman. "I can't decipher any reference to prospects of a baby," Rupert told Dudley Ward, "So that dream goes with the rest."[60] Mike Read has identified one "Arlice Rapoto" as Brooke's daughter. But Alice Tapotofarerani was born on 20 October 1908, so she cannot have been Rupert's child, and Taatamata had no other children between 1912 and 1920. If she was pregnant in April 1914, the baby was not carried to term.[61] In any case, a month later she had dried her tears and was enjoying all-night parties at Lovaina's hotel with a hundred cadets from an Argentinian training ship.

Rupert left Papeete around 5 April on the ss *Tahiti* again, headed this time for San Francisco.[62] There were English newspapers on the ship, and his political irritations immediately started to fizzle. His prejudices had hardened into an ill-assorted bundle of dislikes: of plutocrats, especially Jewish ones, who were grinding down the working man; of the feminists who were now running New Zealand and the United States, and trying to run Britain; of, worst of all, "hermaphrodites and eunuchs, Stracheys, moral vagabonds, pitiable scum."[63] The common thread in these rants was anxiety about sex. Apart from the usual charges about Jewish affinity for money, Rupert saw them as a sexual threat to Anglo-Saxon womanhood. Feminists were perverting the "natural" role of women; Stracheys were despicable because a hermaphrodite was nothing like a real man. Reading such letters, one sees that Rupert's 1912 break-down had also been a conversion experience, like those of people who go from extreme left to extreme right with no delay in the middle. Things that had been incidental annoyances for Rupert before 1912 were now consolidated into a comprehensive worldview – in effect, a character suffused by paranoia.

Rupert was trying to forget his bisexual past by asserting a stern, one-dimensional masculinity. Since his encounter with Denham Russell-Smith in 1909 he may have renounced further interest in gay sex. But he had set up his homosocial ménage with Eddie Marsh in the autumn of 1912, and never broke away from it until he went into barracks with the Royal Naval Division two years later. All the while, he would be saying how eager he was to marry and father a son, but there was always something he preferred to actually doing it. Marriage was a proof of masculinity, yet also a danger to it, because a wife was bound to have some power over you. With his parents, the wife's power had been total, but Rupert respected his mother's petticoat rule. Now he was eager to get back to Rugby.

The journey back, halfway around the world, took two months. On arrival in San Francisco, Rupert went back to his friends in the Berkeley English department: C.M. Gayley, Chauncey Wells, and Leonard Bacon, who all lived on the same block of Piedmont Avenue. After a week, during which Rupert gave another poetry reading, he left on the California Limited for Chicago. En route, he treated Jacques Raverat to a tirade against American women, who must have been the students or faculty wives he had been meeting in Berkeley: "I see with intense clearness exactly what all those unovaried spectacled precise dirty minded Newnham bitches (an insult to an honest word) are coming to ... 'Tis the one boast in America that's true, that she's twenty years ahead of England on the slimy downhill path. I know what my daughters will be like ... There is no young woman in America who could, under *any* circumstances, give a self-respecting penis an erection."[64] There was one exception, perhaps because she was not really young. As his train left the Bay Area, Rupert received a letter from Agnes Capponi, telling him that she had just returned from Europe and was now in Washington, DC. He replied saying he would meet her there: "I want to lie on a sofa and talk," he told her, "There's lots of things I want."[65]

Rupert first stopped over for a few days in Chicago, kept there by his

liking for Maurice Browne and his wife, the actress Ellen van Volken-
burg.[66] Together they ran the Chicago Little Theatre. They had put on
plays by Wilfred Gibson and Lascelles Abercrombie, and Rupert now
read to them his play *Lithuania*, which he had written in Berlin in May
1912.[67] He was starting a phase of being stage-struck, hoping that he
could establish a theatre in Cambridge on his return. The Georgian poets
dreamed of reviving the Elizabethan spirit in a great popular theatre – a
will-o-the-wisp, as it proved.

After a grim day in Pittsburgh, Rupert arrived in Washington on 5
May, where he stayed for nine days. He dined with the British ambassa-
dor and saw the usual sights, but his main purpose was to be with Agnes
again. The letters he sent afterwards suggest that it was an affectionate
reunion, though the transcripts have been expurgated. That Rupert could
conduct affairs with Maaua, Taatamata, and a forty-three-year-old
American widow, a month or two apart, shows versatility at least. While
in Italy Agnes had become a disciple of Maria Montessori, and she now
hoped to promote her educational methods in the United States. In principle, Agnes was the kind of do-gooder that Rupert abhorred. But she
gave him a motherly warmth that soothed his irritable passions. Perhaps
she had learned something when she visited Rugby two months before.

For his last fortnight, Rupert visited friends up and down the east
coast. He went back to Boston, gave a reading at Yale, and spent time at
the McAlpin Hotel in New York (at that time the largest in the world).
Much of this was arranged by Russell Loines, the successful lawyer who
was a patron of poetry and also a poet himself. If Rupert read at Princeton, and was heard by the freshman F. Scott Fitzgerald, it must have been
during these two weeks.[68] But his business with America was over, no
more travel articles had to be delivered, and everything now focused on
what he was coming back to on the far side of the Atlantic.

14

The Soldier
June–December 1914

Home Ground

When the *Philadelphia* docked at Plymouth on 25 June 1914, Rupert was twenty-six years old and eager to return to English life. But what sort of life? For a young man in his position it should include a place to live, a job, a set of old friends, and a suitable woman to marry. In a year or two, he could put down roots, making the transition from wanderer to householder, from uncertain youth to an established man. The war would cut across his course, but without that intervention from history Rupert would still have had great difficulty in finding his place or, to put it bluntly, growing up.

Rupert's rooms at the Old Vicarage had been let, so he had no home of his own to return to. When the train from Plymouth arrived in London, at two o'clock in the morning, Eddie Marsh and Cathleen Nesbitt were there on the platform to take Rupert to Gray's Inn for the night. The next day he went up to Rugby to spend five days with his mother; but he would only tell her about his life in London on a "need to know" basis. After Rupert's death, when Marsh showed Mrs Brooke a draft of his *Memoir*, she said, "Who is Cathleen Nesbitt?" The two most important women in Rupert's last two years of life had been kept strictly apart.[1] After Rugby, Rupert went back to Eddie's flat. This would remain the closest thing to a home for the rest of his life; though there was much to be concealed from Eddie too.

One way of looking at Rupert's alternatives in May 1914 is to follow the money. The *Westminster Gazette* had paid a share of his expenses for his year of travel, and four guineas more for each of his thirteen articles.

Still, he had to borrow money and run up an overdraft at his bank. He had his fellowship income from King's, where he planned to claim his rooms in the autumn and assist Professor Quiller-Couch with some teaching. His mother refused to increase his income, and sometimes reduced it when he had a windfall from his writing. Not only that, she could cut him off at any time. He had to keep her in the dark about anything that might offend her, and especially his relations with women.

Eddie was happy to give Rupert his free board and lodging. In exchange, he could show off Rupert as the "flower in his button hole," a supremely decorative young man who could be taken to 10 Downing Street and dine with Eddie on his left, the prime minister on his right. Rupert had to do everything to cast reflected glory on Eddie – except go to bed with him, which, so far as the evidence goes, neither of them wanted. Nonetheless, Phyllis Gardner cannot have been the only one who saw Rupert and Eddie together and thought that she "never saw a worse-assorted pair."[2] But being admired, or even desired, by men had never troubled Rupert. Male worship, by St John Lucas or James Strachey or so many others, could either be accepted or laughed off. Female worship was the problem, unless it came from his mother. A woman could not show that she loved him without violating his instincts about how women should behave (other than in Tahiti).

Before Rupert's year of travel, having his rooms at Grantchester kept Raymond Buildings in the category of a London pied-à-terre. Now it was unquestionably his home. For a freelance poet and journalist, a London base was a great advantage. The success of the first Georgian anthology had launched a group of younger poets whose work suited the times. Indeed, from about 1912 to 1918, it seemed that the Georgians represented the future of English poetry. Rupert was happy to join forces with them, even though his better poems had more of an edge than the Georgians' often flaccid celebrations of rural life. Some of Rupert's edge came from his admiration for Hardy's poetry, which dated from the appearance of *Time's Laughingstocks* in 1909. Hardy showed the potential grandeur in Georgian themes, even as he refused to be seen as a member of their group.[3]

Rupert aligned himself with a core group of Georgians whose talents proved fairly slight: W.W. Gibson, Lascelles Abercrombie, Walter de la Mare. These were also the poets who would enjoy a small fortune from

Rupert's literary estate.[4] Stronger poets either remained on the fringes of the group (Lawrence, Graves, Sassoon) or were excluded on grounds of nationality (Pound and Frost). Gibson, Abercrombie, and de la Mare were also replacements for friends that Rupert wanted to leave behind: some Neo-pagans, all Bloomsberries. Georgians had in common lower-middle-class origins, lack of Oxbridge education (except for Rupert), scrambling for a living in the literary marketplace, long-suffering and unglamorous wives with flocks of children in tow.[5] Rupert's Georgian friends wrote about the countryside, but it was also the only place they could afford to live.

On 24 June Rupert went to stay with Wilfred Gibson at his cottage, the Old Nailshop, near Dymock in Gloucestershire. This was, first of all, a business meeting about the Dymock journal *New Numbers*, which had proved both popular and financially successful. As always, poets were joining forces in pursuit of money and fame. But it was also a happy moment of fellowship in that last pre-war summer, with five of the poets present.[6] Gibson commemorated their first evening together in "The Golden Room":

> Do you remember the still summer evening
> When in the cosy cream-washed living-room
> Of the Old Nailshop we all talked and laughed
> Our neighbors from the Gallows, Catherine
> And Lascelles Abercrombie; Rupert Brooke;
> Eleanor and Robert Frost, living awhile
> At Little Iddens, who'd brought over with them
> Helen and Edward Thomas? In the lamplight
> We talked and laughed, but for the most part listened
> While Robert Frost kept on and on and on
> In his slow New England fashion for our delight,
> Holding us with shrewd turns and racy quips,
> And the rare twinkle of his grave blue eyes.
>
> We sat there in the lamplight while the day
> Died from rose-latticed casements, and the plovers
> Called over the low meadows till the owls
> Answered them from the elms; we sat and talked

Now a quick flash from Abercrombie, now
A murmured dry half-heard aside from Thomas,
Now a clear laughing word from Brooke, and then
Again Frost's rich and ripe philosophy
That had the body and tang of good draught-cider
And poured as clear a stream.

Rupert had already met Frost in London, but now he came to know him more intimately, the way one can in the country rather than in the town. Gibson's poem recognises Frost's dominance. He was the oldest person there – thirteen years older than Rupert – and had made a brilliant debut on the British literary scene with *A Boy's Will* (1913) and *North of Boston* (just published, on 15 May). Abercrombie and Ezra Pound, along with many others, hailed Frost's poetic talent. But it was Edward Thomas who reviewed the volume in three different places, and best defined Frost's distinctive gift: "This is one of the most revolutionary books of modern times, but one of the quietest and least aggressive. It speaks, and it is poetry ... Many, if not most, of the separate lines and separate sentences are plain and, in themselves, nothing. But they are bound together and made elements of beauty by a calm eagerness of emotion."[7]

About half of the seventeen poems in *North of Boston* – including the seminal "Mending Wall" – had been composed in England since Frost's arrival there a year and a half before. What the Dymock poets admired in Frost was how he combined common speech with fathomless depths of irony and philosophical complexity. Frost was partly a disciple of Hardy but he used his poems to work through a problem rather than being content, as Hardy usually was, to leave the problem with no possible resolution. On long country walks together, Thomas absorbed Frost's cast of mind and was liberated to himself become a poet in a similar vein.

The effect on Rupert of the Dymock gathering is harder to define. Frost responded to Rupert's charm, but cast a cold eye on his verses. "Neither is Brooke worth bothering with," was his comment on Rupert's contributions to *New Numbers 3*.[8] This was fair comment on "Retrospect," a poem written at Mataiea. Rupert's aim was to bring his four years with Noel into perspective, but the result is an awkward mixture of condescension and sentimentality. It harks back to the time Noel had taken him to her breast at Limpsfield, and imagines her doing so again:

O mother-quiet, breasts of peace,
Where love itself would faint and cease!
O infinite deep I never knew,
I would come back, come back to you,
Find you, as a pool unstirred,
Kneel down by you, and never a word,
Lay my head, and nothing said,
In your hands, ungarlanded;

Love does not end in delight, but in the oblivion of sleep and a quasi-maternal bosom, while nothing is said about what Rupert had been up to while he was away.

Frost's dislike of the poem may also have stemmed from a misunderstanding. He had become friendly with Phyllis Gardner and her mother while Rupert was on his travels, and may have thought that the poem was a shot against Phyllis: "We know this hardly treated girl oh very well. Her beauty is her red hair. Her cleverness is in painting. She has a picture in the New English Exhibition. Her mother has written a volume of verse in which he gets his. Very funny. No one will die."[9]

Mrs Gardner's salvo was *Plain Themes*, with woodcuts by Phyllis, published the year before. Several poems are spoken in Phyllis's voice and directed at her faithless lover. Robert Frost said that Rupert "gets his" in the poems, but they are more rueful than resentful. "Rejected" sets the tone:

Death calls me to him, and with heart on fire,
Although I long for death, from him I fly.
Bound unto earth by this one sweet desire,
To kiss your lips again before I die.

Now Madness beckons, yet it is in vain,
My every thought is centred now in yours;
Clinging to reason is my aching brain,
The wish to meet your eyes again endures.
Despair may take my hand, her tear-stained eyes
And pale drawn face I can as yet gainsay;
For hidden in my breaking heart there lies
The hope to hold your hand again one day.[10]

Elsewhere, Frost dismissed Rupert as a would-be metaphysical, trying to produce Edwardian variations on Donne.[11] The real difference between them was that Frost's poems were built on conflicting points of view, while Rupert's displayed just one set of feelings: his own. Frost's judgment softened after Rupert's death: "I was struck sad for Rupert. But he chose the right way. Your letter telling of his death came right on the heels of another from Smith saying how much the war had done to make him a better poet. The war saved him only to kill him."[12] The Dymock gathering showed Rupert gravitating to two likeable individuals but minor talents: Gibson and Abercrombie. Frost and Thomas could have helped his poetic development, but he was less comfortable with them and they never became mentors.

At Dymock the other poets had their entourages of wives and children; Rupert was still single and still conflicted about sex and love. He could see the appeal of the Dymock way: cheap rent in a cottage, the responsibilities of family life, husband and wife working as a team to support a steady flow of poems and reviews. Steadiness, though, was never part of Rupert's temperament. When he told Jacques that he "*must* marry soon," he at once veered around by saying that he prayed continually: "Twelve hours a day, that I may, sometime, fall in love with somebody. Twelve hours a day that I may *never* fall in love with anybody. Either alternative seems too Hellish to bear." Either alternative also seemed to rule out being in love with Cathleen Nesbitt. But if Rupert didn't fall in love, that left an endless round of what he called "cunt-sniffing."[13] Presumably that was the right category for Agnes Capponi, and for the young woman Rupert hoped to go away with the weekend after his Dymock meeting. "One hangs hopelessly around young women one doesn't care for a scrap," he told Jacques, "and – at this date – sees through entirely. And if one *doesn't* do that: one's too bally restless to work."[14] He does not name the woman, but most likely it was Elisabeth van Rysselberghe, to whom he had written on 8 June and 10. He had lunch with her at Simpson's in July, but did not succeed in re-kindling their affair.

Needless to say, a rendezvous with a former lover was not, in Rupert's view, something that Cathleen Nesbitt needed to know about. They had been a couple for a year and a half now. Nominally they were in love, and they had just gone away to stay at the Pink and Lily in the Chilterns, but they had yet to kiss each other on the lips. As with Noel, chastity made Cathleen safe to love, because to make love was not required. In spite of all, both women remained possible candidates for Rupert to marry. But a major obstacle was that they had embarked on professional careers that they had no intention of giving up. Rupert had always ignored the clause in the Fabian "Basis" that recognised equal citizenship for men and women, but over the years he had become an ever fiercer opponent of feminism in all its forms, whether personal or social. "I loathe the idea of women acting in public," he had told Cathleen.[15] Some of this came from personal frustrations in his relations with Ka and other advanced young women; some from his dislike of the young women he had observed in the United States. All his resentments found a focus in August Strindberg, for Rupert the exemplary misogynist of the age.

Rupert had first worked on Strindberg in the summer of 1911, helped by the Newnham student Estrid Linder. In February 1913 he had given a lecture on Strindberg and Ibsen to the Heretics Society in Cambridge. Strindberg's generation, he argued, had rejected the sentimentality of their predecessors and sought refuge in its opposite: "The morbid symptom of lovelessness is that denial of sex called feminism, with its resultant shallowness of woman and degradation of man. Feminism disgusted Strindberg, who was born with a curiously high standard of emotional and intellectual morality; its accompaniments of natural and unnatural vice shocked him. We know what Shakespeare suffered through one light woman. Strindberg was plunged into a generation of light women."[16]

Rupert's aim in 1912–14 was to become an English Strindberg, if in a minor key. His one play, *Lithuania*, was about a homicidal young woman who kills her brother by mistake. Strindberg's history had points of contact with Rupert's. He also lived in the shadow of his puritanical mother, and was in his youth an enthusiast for socialism and female emancipation. He became embittered by the Swedish feminists who denounced the "immorality" of his plays, and by conflicts with his first wife, Siri von Essen. Strindberg accused von Essen of infidelity, and assaulted a woman he suspected of being her lesbian lover. Years of paranoia and nervous breakdowns followed. Ever consistent, he was a hysterical anti-Semite to match his other hysterical hatreds.

The crux, for both Strindberg and Rupert, was that feminism revealed women's desire to be like men, to compete with them, and to neglect their traditional roles of nurturing their mates and children. Once the historic polarity between the sexes was broken, there would be a chaotic loss of identity for both men and women. Homosexuality and lesbianism were sure to be part of this. Rupert tried to explain his fears to Frances Cornford, a woman who was safely married and with a new baby: "I am not insulting women. There *was* a period when I despised them a little, perceiving what fourthrate men they made. But lately I've cheered up, noticing what supreme women they make ... Think of Gwen."[17] Gwen was safe too, in her marriage to Jacques where she did not challenge his prejudices. That was another of Rupert's fixed ideas: that women could never be trusted unless they had a man who guided and protected them. When Geoffrey Keynes accused Rupert of being cynical about women, he replied, "It's about as cynical to hold my views about females, as it is to put fire-guards in front of a nursery fire."[18]

Rupert's obsessions about women did not manage to be consistent. He feared the hordes of New Women, so militant that they would even be willing to die for equality, as Emily Davison did when she ran onto the Derby course in June 1913. But he also feared the vulnerability of young women, exposed as they were to a corrupt milieu full of intellectuals, perverts, and Jews. Did he fear women because they were strong, or because they were weak? And what could he do about his own desire and need for women? He admitted, to Cathleen, that there was no consistency in his views: "I've been dodging the young ladies who are in love with me. I wish I were a decent man. I suppose no unmarried man is decent and only 50 per cent of the married ones. My subconscious is angry with every dreary young woman I meet if she doesn't fall in love with me; and my consciousness is furious with her if she does."[19]

The most important of the young ladies that Rupert was dodging in August was Lady Eileen Wellesley, a daughter of the 4th Duke of Wellington; except that he didn't always dodge. Eddie took Rupert to dine with the Duchess of Leeds on 24 July, where he sat between Eileen and the duchess's daughter Gwendoline. Both had been debutantes nine years before, when a society column described Eileen as "very good-looking in a somewhat picturesque style, with her fair hair loosely dressed, and a slight, elegant figure. Like her mother, Lady Eileen is literary in her tastes, and has greatly enjoyed the months she has spent abroad in study." Patrick Shaw-Stewart found her "nice though spoilt and exacting."[20] Eileen was the same age as Rupert, and had some resemblance to Cathleen Nesbitt in looks. She had been "finished" at Dresden with a group of young aristocrats that included Violet Asquith, Cynthia Charteris (who would marry Violet's brother Herbert), and Mary Vesey (who married Aubrey Herbert). Later, Eileen studied art, and worked in watercolours. Nigel Nicolson reports that she was "half-engaged" to Harold Nicolson before he met Vita Sackville-West.[21] Eileen and Violet were still in that somewhat aimless time, for women of their class, between debut and marriage. Both were attracted to Rupert, while recognising the obstacles to marrying a middle-class young man with no money, poet or not.

After the dinner at the Duchess of Leeds, Eileen sent Rupert a Tahitian-style note: "Dear Mr Brooke, I'm afraid you left your cigarette-case behind the other day. Would you care to come to tea to collect it?" He did go to tea, though he didn't smoke.[22] A few days later they went out for the day to Richmond Park, where they seem to have found a secluded corner to make love. Cathleen had gone away, touring in a play called "A Butterfly on a Wheel." It was a tiresome society drama, but she needed the money. Rupert did not approve, and that may have fuelled his readiness to fall into bed, or into the long grass, with Eileen. A further attraction, probably, was that this was like going to bed with a piece of English history. Eileen's blood was deepest blue, and she lived at 1 Hyde Park Corner in Apsley House, acquired by the Iron Duke after Waterloo. But we need hardly speculate about Rupert's motives. He slept with Eileen because she was present and willing, and because he saw no need for Cathleen to know about it. After his death, Cynthia Asquith summed it up: "Mary Herbert ... told me Eileen Wellesley claims very serious love affair with Rupert Brooke saying that quite unsuspected of everyone else they used to meet in Richmond Park and in Eddie's flat. No doubt Rupert Brooke had the thoroughly polygamous instincts of most poets."[23]

Eileen was surely in love with Rupert; just how deeply we cannot know because he ordered her letters to be burnt after his death. It was probably Eileen who shocked Mrs Elgy by seizing Rupert by the neck and exclaiming, "Oh you gorgeous piece of flesh!"[24] She agreed to keep their affair a secret because he was fit to dine with duke's daughters but not to marry them. They could have their trysts at Eddie's flat, but not at Apsley House. If Rupert cherished any ambition to marry into the aristocracy, there is no sign of it in his surviving letters to Eileen. "Do you know how real you are?" he wrote in his second letter to her, "The time with you is the only waking hours in a life of dreams. All that's another way of saying I adore you."[25] In fact, his time alone with Eileen was the dream because his many other commitments took precedence over his erotic life. That life had always been conducted secretly, away from his mother's inquisition, since its start in the upstairs dormitory at School Field. Secrecy was intrinsic to sexuality, and all of Rupert's secrets were guilty secrets. That meant that the women he slept with were guilty too – except for Maaua and Taatamata, who were outside Mrs Brooke's radius of action. Rupert told Eileen that California had "'Flowers without scent, birds without song, men without honour, & women without virtue' – and at least three of the four sections of this proverb I know very well to be true."[26] Rupert's Californian without virtue must have been Agnes Capponi.

Rupert's liaison with Eileen would continue until he sailed for Gallipoli at the end of February 1915. It helped him to postpone indefinitely the marriage question, so long as he had Eileen to meet his sexual needs. But what if she became sufficiently infatuated with him to want him for her husband, unsuitable match or not? To head that off, Rupert used the same line he had tried on Phyllis Gardner:

> I find in myself two natures – not necessarily conflicting, but – different. There's half my heart which is normal & English – what's the word, not quite "good" or "honourable" – "*straight*," I think. But the other half is a wanderer and a solitary, selfish, unbound, and doubtful ...
>
> Oh, it's all right if you don't *trust* me, my dear. *I* don't. Never trust me an inch.
>
> Oh, I'm rather a horror. A vagabond, drifting from one imbecility to another. You don't know how pointless and undependable and rotten a thing you've got hold of.[27]

Rupert was asking forgiveness in advance for future disappointments. If Eileen should complain, he could always reply, "I warned you, didn't I?" "I'm very selfish and horrible towards you," he wrote in October, "I expect it will be the best thing for every one if a stray bullet finds me next year, – for myself and for the rest of the world."[28]

Eileen was no ingénue, and had jumped into the affair as impulsively as Rupert had. Still, the fragmentary correspondence suggests that her relationship with him, which lasted seven months altogether, might have been happier and more mature than anything he had managed before he met her. There is no sign in the letters of the hysteria and posturing that poisoned his relations with Ka, Noel, or Phyllis; he seems to have cared for Eileen as she was, and tried to make an honest connection with her. "It's true," he wrote, six weeks after they met, "what you said, that there was a great *advance* in knowing each other last night. I feel it so definitely. I think that sort of thing's *easier* to see and measure in absence – especially in writing a letter – than in presence. Do you see that?"[29] Perhaps Eileen was able to draw out qualities in Rupert that no previous lover had managed to find. Alternatively, he felt obliged to be on his best behaviour with someone who was his social superior, unlike the previous lovers who were on the same rung of the ladder as him.

Disgusting People

Rupert's conquest of Eileen was part of a wider social campaign in the summer of 1914. It was ironic that his biggest triumph – going to bed with a duke's daughter – was also the one he had to keep quiet about. He had been gravitating towards the Establishment in the months before he left for North America. Despite his effete manner, Eddie Marsh was taken seriously in the corridors of power, both public and private. It was a reason for Rupert to stay in his orbit: he might have been a wandering young poet, but it was seductive for him to be close to the centre of affairs, even if no one wanted to give him any actual responsibilities. He could feel superior to Bloomsbury and Cambridge just by being "in the know" about high politics. And rubbing shoulders with the great fostered the belligerent nationalism that he had brought home from his travels.

Travel is supposed to broaden the mind, but for Rupert it had the opposite effect. Contempt for foreigners implied going on the offensive against former friends who did not conform to his idea of how English men – and women – should behave. That included cutting ties with the two women who had meant most to him before 1913: Ka Cox and Noel Olivier. After his stern goodbye letter to Ka of June 1913, silence had fallen between them. Back in England he continued to avoid her, until his enlistment would bring about a tentative reconciliation. From the Grand Canyon in April 1914 he had laid down terms to Noel: "You *do* shine in comparison with the American female. Noel, I do not think you clever. I have given up every kind of admiration for you – everything, indeed, except a sort of affection ... I shall come back to England – I intend to live the rest of my life with my mother who is the only person I really like. But I shall take occasional holidays in London or Cambridge: so I may run across you again."[30]

When they did run across each other, at the ballet on 18 June, neither of them was in an affectionate mood. Noel later called it "our very stern meeting in a theatre corridor"; Rupert called it something worse: "Noel is *not* a bloody little bitch. At least ... not *quite*. I feel very kindly towards her just now. I met her the other day & didn't recognise her for some minutes. That *was* a triumph. Haven't felt so pleased with myself since Father died. I went home & laughed about it for an hour."[31] The triumph, for Rupert, was no longer being under the spell of someone whose self-possession had proved stronger than his own. In his whole life, only Noel and his mother had got the better of him. Now, once he had renounced his desire for Noel, his main grudge against her was one of guilt by association. Just around the corner from her medical school was 38 Brunswick Square, where Maynard and Geoffrey Keynes lived with Adrian Stephen, and various others. Noel refused Adrian's love, but she was happy to stop by for tea, or go to the ballet with James Strachey or other Bloomsburyites living nearby. These everyday friendships infuriated Rupert. "One of the less creditable periods of my life enmeshed me with the intellectuals," he told Cathleen, "I hover on their fringes yet: dehumanized, disgusting people."[32] With James and Noel it had become more than a friendship. James had wooed her passionately in 1913, until in September Noel had drawn a line and said they should stop seeing each other. After Rupert's death they became intimate again, for everything except complete intercourse. In 1916, for example, James was looking forward to Bedalian pleasures at Limpsfield: "We'll have a bath together each evening and it'll be nicer than it's ever been."[33] Rupert had managed that in a river, but never in the closer quarters of a bathtub.

It was not just a question of avoiding the intellectuals; Rupert launched a campaign of insults and ostracism against them. The only softening of his private war was in his attendance of the annual dinner of Apostles at the end of June. The presence of Keynes and the Stracheys was diluted by such other guests as G.E. Moore, Gerald Shove, H.T. Norton, and John Sheppard (Brooke's former tutor at King's). Sir Arthur Quiller-Couch, the Cambridge professor of English, had asked for Rupert's help with his teaching in the autumn term. But even without the war it is hard to imagine Rupert settling down to a don's life. He had bigger fish to fry than were served at High Table. Moreover, living in Cambridge would mean being surrounded by intellectuals. He no longer cared that some of his fellow Apostles were among the seminal thinkers of his time – Keynes, Russell, Moore, Wittgenstein. He was reverting to type: the Rugby ethos that not only was character more important than brains but that brains, in themselves, were objects of suspicion. After his last evening out with James Strachey, Rupert told him, "I may not have explained to you how much I was grieved at your opinions. I had hoped you had got rid of them. They seem to me not only eunuch & shocking, but also damned silly & slightly dangerous."[34] His rants against Bloomsbury expressed what has been called "anti-Judaism." Former friends like the Stracheys were to him equivalent to Jews because of their rootlessness, their sterile intellectualism, and their lack of true masculinity. In Rupert's paranoid vision, you didn't have to be Jewish to sap the foundations of native English virtue.[35] Feminism was equally threatening, as an abstract idea of equality that denied the biological imperatives of male and female. It scarcely occurred to him that the primacy of blood, soil, and genitals was an idea too, one that would begin its terrible blossoming in August.

The removal from his life of Neo-pagans and Bloomsberries was part of a thorough changing of the guard in Rupert's intimate circle. Pride and resentment accounted for the removal of Noel. With Ka, the chief motive was guilt. He refused her invitation to stay with her in her cottage at Woking, saying that any contact was unwise: "The thought of you ... makes me deeply and bitterly ashamed of myself. I don't know *why* – I mean, it's not that my mind condemns me, especially, in any way. I only know that – inevitably or not – through me you have been greatly hurt, and two or three years of your life – which can be so wonderful – have been changed and damaged."[36] The only Neo-pagans that Rupert was still close to were the Raverats and Frances Cornford. Jacques was his particular confederate for outbursts against women, Jews, intellectuals, and other disturbers of the peace. Unfortunately, Jacques was trapped with Gwen in their country house at Royston, as MS tightened its grip on him. Frances was busy with her baby daughter Helena.

What kind of new group could Rupert assemble around himself? On the female side, Eddie Marsh had introduced him to all three of Cathleen Nesbitt, Eileen Wellesley, and Violet Asquith. For male friends, the picture was less clear. Eddie was promoting Rupert in all the best London circles: political (Asquith and Churchill), aristocratic (Lady Leeds) or literary

(Yeats, Barrie, Henry James). Almost everyone was won over by Rupert's charm and good looks. But if it was obvious how this helped Eddie, how much did it really help Rupert? As with a beautiful woman, being admired provided only a passive identity, laid on from the outside. His literary connections were now well established, but further success depended greatly on publishing a second volume of poems, at least a year or two in the future. Meanwhile, there was only the long march through journalism, for which he had no great talent.

Rupert's launch into a more glittering social world was bound to stir up sneers and jeers from those who considered themselves both more serious and more solid than his new friends. Virginia Woolf and Lytton Strachey were not immune to the glamour of lords and ladies, but they did not enter those circles until after the war, when they had achieved a wider reputation. Rupert was part of an emergent celebrity culture, where the daughters of the aristocracy were fawned upon as archetypes of English beauty and breeding. Their faces were on display around London, in society magazines and even newspaper placards. It hardly mattered that they did little but dress fashionably and go to one social event after another. Their fathers had never cared for them to be properly educated. That was no concern for Rupert, who now looked with a jaundiced eye both at women with university education (Ka, three out of four Olivier sisters) and at women who had a career (Cathleen).[37]

How might Rupert take advantage of the connections he was making in the political realm? He could enjoy intimate chats with Churchill, and know what went on in Cabinet; but a serious start on a political career required much more. Rupert was not inclined to take the civil service exam and follow in Eddie's footsteps. Hugh Dalton, his contemporary at King's, was studying economics and law. In 1914 Ben Keeling had published a book on child labour and was now an assistant editor on the *New Statesman*. This was how one moved on from Cambridge to a real career in politics. How could Rupert expect to climb the ladder of power – even if he wanted to – without serving any apprenticeship?

Two months after Rupert landed at Plymouth, Britain was at war, and what he had done since his return ceased to be relevant. But the broad strokes of a likely future had been laid on in June and July. They involved a base in London, the acceptance of Eddie as his mentor, and the cutting off of his former intimates. When he had moved to Grantchester in 1908, it had been a theatrical gesture of protest against upper-middle-class conventionality. In 1914 the audience for that role had largely disappeared, and Rupert was no longer interested in playing it. He still complained about London as a foul and immoral place. But the central figures in his life – Eddie, Cathleen, Eileen Wellesley – were firmly rooted there, and so would he be unless some great event invaded his life.

The Fight

On 4 August 1914 Rupert's life did change, regardless of what he himself might have chosen. The war would be both the making and the ending of Rupert Brooke, in less than nine months. But how should we judge the individual who, in some degree by mere chance, becomes a participant in great events? When D.H. Lawrence considered the Easter Rising in 1916, he weighed in on the side of events. Ottoline Morrell "thinks the Irish of the late rebellion all poets and fine fellows," he told E.M. Forster. "I think them mostly windbags and nothings who happen to have become tragically significant in death."[38] By this standard, the personal stature of such figures was irrelevant. But Rupert was neither a windbag nor a nothing. If his poetic talent was not of the highest rank, it still had qualities that made him the most popular English poet for ten years or more. With his romantic appearance thrown into the balance, he became the individual whose death made him the tragic symbol of the sufferings of his class: the roughly one hundred thousand public school boys who went through school Officers Training Corps (OTC) and served in the British army from 1914 to 1918.

However historians may debate the origins of the Great War, Rupert cannot be blamed for lacking a foresight that was lacking everywhere else, including among those who had an actual power to shape events. Everyone looked to the precedent of the Franco-Prussian war of 1870, which was settled by a single battle, two months after hostilities began. They might have considered rather the American Civil War, a war of attrition that dragged on for four years. Yet both precedents were largely irrelevant. In 1914 what mattered was, first, the global scale of a complex system of national alliances; second, the extraordinary industrial and technical advances of the previous four decades. There were revolutionary improvements in communications and logistics, and in the mass production of artillery (which accounted for more than half of all deaths on the Western Front), machine guns, tanks, poison gas. About a million men had fought on the Paris–Berlin axis in 1870. In August 1914, ten million were mobilised by Germany, France, and Russia alone. The enormous civil and military cost of twentieth-century warfare should have been evident – and also the enormous mistakes that would be made. One of the first of these mistakes, which sealed Rupert's fate, came from his most powerful patron, and was called Gallipoli.

If history cannot be determined, at least individuals can determine how they will respond to it. Rupert was a hugely privileged young man in the summer of 1914, not destined to be mere cannon fodder. He knew the rational case for staying out of the war, articulated by fellow Apostles like Bertrand Russell and Lytton Strachey. But for several years he had dedicated himself to a process of reversion to type. We meet that type in the chapter of *Tom Brown's Schooldays* called "The Fight." Tom Brown and Slugger Williams have it out behind the Rugby School Chapel, much to the author's satisfaction:

> After all, what would life be without fighting, I should like to know? From the cradle to the grave, fighting, rightly understood, is the business, the real highest, honestest business of every son of man. Every one who is worth his salt has his enemies, who must be beaten, be they evil thoughts or habits in himself, or spiritual wickednesses in high places, or Russians, or Border-ruffians, or Bill, Tom, or Harry, who will not let him live his life in quiet till he has thrashed them.
>
> It is no good for quakers, or any other body of men, to uplift their voices against fighting. Human nature is too strong for them, and they don't follow their own precepts ... The world might be a better world without fighting, for anything I know but it wouldn't be our world.[39]

Tom's closest friend, Harry East, becomes a professional fighter, and is badly wounded in the 1857 Indian Mutiny.

Rupert would have been a most unusual Rugbeian if he had opposed the war.[40] Almost all the public school volunteers became infantry officers. The Navy required more extensive training, and the Army had always been favoured as a profession for younger sons of the aristocracy or upper-middle class. It was assumed that five or six years at a public school was enough preparation for going into battle, sometimes with only a few weeks of actual military training. Such amateurism contributed to the appalling casualty rates for infantry subalterns, about twice as high as the rank and file under their command. Rupert had put in his time with the Officers Training Corps at Rugby, but it was not taken too seriously when for the last hundred years Britain had fought only wars of choice in distant lands, with a professional army of less than 250,000.

Once the war began anyone who gained an infantry commission could expect to see action in short order. Joining the army as an amateur meant getting on a train at Victoria and learning your trade on arrival, if you lived long enough. In *Goodbye to All That*, Robert Graves gave an expectancy of six weeks before an infantry officer was wounded or killed.[41] The odds at Gallipoli would be worse than that. But in the sacrificial mood of 1914, volunteers took for granted the prospect of death, and still went in search of any regiment willing to take them.

Rupert might have just floated along with the tide of enthusiasm for war, an enthusiasm that ran equally high in other countries besides Britain. Patriotism and national rivalry were the obvious collective forces that drew young men into battle. Less visible, but equally compelling, were the individual compulsions that pushed them to the front. There was a long tradition of seeing war as the best remedy for the existential crisis of any young male. The hero of Tennyson's *Maud* goes off to the Crimean War to purge himself of guilt over his beloved's death. Vronský goes to war, seeking an honourable death, after Anna Karenina's suicide. His war is a crusade to liberate the Christian Serbs from the Turks (1876–78).

Although Rupert would memorably describe his mission as "into cleanness leaping," it is not clear what was the dirt he hoped to wash off. He had apologised to Ka for the wrong he had done her in 1912, and told her it was best if they did not meet. If there was sexual "dirt" he needed to remove, he might have acquired it from Eileen Wellesley (or Agnes Capponi or certain Tahitians before her). Cathleen Nesbitt remained "clean" because their relationship was Platonic. The deeper sense of guilt in Rupert lay in the internal enemies called "evil thoughts and habits." At the Rugby and Oxford of Thomas Hughes, those sins were masturbation, homosexuality, and lusting after barmaids. All of them were the sort of thing Rupert would be most concerned to hide from his mother. A sexual revolution had been smoldering since he left school, though with many hesitations and dead ends. It seems disproportionate to blame the war on the sexual confusion of young men at the turn of the century. Yet the idea of war as a purging of sexual sin was not just Rupert's. It appealed to many young men of his class, along with the related idea of war as an antidote to the greed and anomie of commercial society.

Rupert's beliefs about the positive value of war were distilled into poetry later in the year, after he had a taste of combat in the Antwerp expedition. His first plan in August was to become a war correspondent, but he soon decided to enlist as soon as he could find a regiment. His service with the Rugby OTC guaranteed that he could enter the Army with a commission. Not surprisingly, his path was smoothed by Eddie Marsh. Churchill's military background was as an officer in the regular army, but as First Lord of the Admiralty he found a way to create a miniature army of his own. This was the Royal Naval Division (RND), cobbled together from eight battalions of sailors who were not needed at sea and four existing battalions of Royal Marines. The eight battalions each needed about thirty officers, to command a thousand men. The officers were seconded from other army units or, like Rupert, taken in off the street. He sent in his application for a commission on 15 September, spent a few days gathering his kit, and joined the Anson Battalion at Betteshanger Park on 27 September. One of his fellow sub-lieutenants was Denis Browne, a professional musician who had been his contemporary at Rugby and King's. Another was Arthur Asquith, son of the prime minister.

Churchill was thirty-nine years old at the outbreak of war. He liked rapid action, and the RND was one of his hasty enterprises. It provided a place to put Rupert but also sent him to his death, along with scores of ill-prepared other officers. One who survived was Rupert's commanding officer in the Anson Brigade, Colonel George Cornwallis-West. The same age as Churchill, he was also his former step-father: he married Lady Churchill after Lord Randolph died, then left her in 1912 to marry the actress Mrs Patrick Campbell. Cornwallis-West was a man about town, a handsome spit-and-polish officer in the Scots Guards. He was not pleased with his transfer to the RND, and his young officers were not pleased to be serving under him. For his part, Rupert had to absorb his first real contact with the working class: thirty former stokers, mostly from Scotland and Ireland: "Occasionally I'm faintly shaken by a suspicion that I might find incredible beauty in the washing place, with rows of naked, superb men, bathing in a September sun or in the Camp at night under a full moon, faint lights burning through the ghostly tents, and a distant bugler blowing *Lights Out* – if only I were sensitive. But I'm not. I'm a warrior. So I think of nothing, and go to bed."[42]

Antwerp

They may have been superb when naked, but most of the RND were ill-equipped and unprepared for the first mission Churchill sent them on. The German Third Reserve Army had invaded neutral Belgium, and found it more difficult than they expected to crush Belgian resistance. By the beginning of October they had laid siege to Antwerp. The British Expeditionary Force to the south was fully committed against the German advance in France. Churchill went to the Belgian front in late September, and made an impulsive decision to send the RND to the aid of the Belgian army. The division had no artillery, while the Germans were shelling the Belgian forts with "Big Bertha," the world's largest gun. Cornwallis-West told his officers that they were sure to be wiped out soon after they arrived. Allegedly, Prime Minister Asquith had told Churchill it would be "idle butchery" to send the raw troops of the RND (including his son Arthur) to Antwerp. Churchill lied, telling Asquith that only the four trained Marine brigades would be sent.[43]

Rupert had been in uniform for exactly a week when the Anson battalion sailed from Dover for Dunkirk. His men had been issued semi-obsolete charger-loading rifles three days before. They went to Antwerp by train and marched through the streets on the morning of 6 October, welcomed with apples and chocolate, and cries of "Vivent les Anglais." Cornwallis-West had lost his maps, and was stopping pedestrians to ask if they had a map of the city. The Ansons eventually found their way to Vieux-Dieu, southwest of the centre, but by the time they got there Churchill's gambit was already a lost cause. The forts protecting the city were crumbling under the German heavy artillery, and the city itself was being shelled at random. The rape of Belgium, as it came to be called, was well under way.

The Marine battalions of the RND had arrived earlier and been put in the front line on 4 October at Lierre, southeast of Antwerp. Churchill considered them trained and battle-ready. Their job was to buy time until reinforcements could arrive: the British 7th Division from England and French forces who had sailed from Le Havre. Churchill himself had arrived the evening before, in the hope of stiffening Belgian resistance. He was still there on the morning of the 6th, when the Anson Brigade was cheered through the streets, and may have seen Rupert march by. With his usual bumptiousness, Churchill had offered to resign as First Lord of the Admiralty in order to take command of British forces in Belgium.[44] His offer was refused. General Rawlinson arrived on the afternoon of the 6th to take command, and Churchill returned to London.

After an uncomfortable and frightening night in an abandoned chateau, the Ansons marched to trenches on the southern approaches to the city. Churchill had decided to place them in an "intermediate position." They would hold "a support and rallying line for the Belgian troops who were falling back ... Solidly dug in with their rifles and plenty of ammunition, these ardent, determined men would not be easily dislodged."[45] As the German advance continued, the Ansons were moved back, without actually engaging the enemy. They dug in next to Fort 7, one of the inner ring of forts around the city.

The German heavy howitzers were able to destroy the Belgian forts in a matter of hours. The next step would be to destroy the city itself, and the Belgians prepared to surrender it instead. Their army, along with the British contingent, retreated westward across the river Scheldt. Some elements of the RND strayed across the Dutch border and were interned for the duration. Churchill could have ordered the remaining battalions of the RND to join the 7th Division at Ostend and Zeebrugge; from there they would have entered the First Battle of Ypres on 19 October, where the British Expeditionary Force would lose almost one-third of its strength. Eileen Wellesley's brother Richard would be killed there with the Grenadier Guards on 29 October. Fortunately for the RND, Churchill ordered it back to the UK, "to refit, reorganise and resume its interrupted training."[46] The Ansons marched twenty-five miles to the station at St Gilles, where they entrained for Ostend. Rupert was back at Dover on 9 October, five days after he had left. He had not fired his rifle, or seen the enemy face to face. But he was wearing an eye-patch for an outbreak of pinkeye, and the crowds cheered him as a wounded hero.

The formative experience for Rupert at Antwerp was not battle or the red badge of courage. It was the destruction and civilian suffering that were the byproducts of war:

> After a bit we got to the land by the river, where the Belgians had let all the petrol out of the tanks and fired it. Rivers and seas of flame leaping up hundreds of feet, crowned by black smoke that covered the entire heavens. It lit up houses wrecked by shells, dead horses, demolished railway stations, engines that had been taken up with their lines and signals, and all twisted round and pulled out, as a bad child spoils a toy ... [Hoboken] was like Hell, a Dantesque Hell, terrible. But there – and later – I saw what was a truer Hell. Hundreds of thousands of refugees, their goods on barrows and hand-carts and perambulators and wagons, moving with infinite slowness out into the night, two unending lines of them, the old men mostly weeping, the women with hard white drawn faces, the children playing or crying or sleeping. That's what Belgium is now: the country where three civilians have been killed to every one soldier ... It's queer to think one has been a witness of one of the greatest crimes of history. Has ever nation been treated like that? And how can such a stain be wiped out?[47]

It would make little sense to criticise Rupert for failing to foresee the Somme in 1916 or Passchendaele in 1917. No one foresaw them in October 1914. Rupert's response to the war was emotional, but it was not naive. It was a response to what he had seen with his own eyes, one of the first Englishmen to see it. He respected Goldie Dickinson, a sweet-natured pacifist don, but told him, "I hope you don't think me very reactionary and callous for taking up this function of England. There shouldn't be war – but what's to be done, but fight Prussia? I've seen the half million refugees in the night outside Antwerp: and I want, more than before, to go on, till Prussia's destroyed. I wish everyone I know were fighting."[48]

Britain had entered the war because of its pledge to defend Belgium. The Schlieffen Plan, years in the making, ignored Belgian neutrality. The German road to Paris lay through Brussels, and that was just bad luck for Belgium. Ford Madox Ford claimed that Frieda Lawrence said to him, in March 1915, "Dirty Belgians! Who cares for them!"[49] Whether

Frieda said it or not, in effect the German government had said it. There were only two arguments that English people could make against the war. One was that Germany had suffered great injuries in the years leading up to 1914, sufficient to justify any pain inflicted on Belgium. This was not an argument likely to convince anyone who was not German. The second and stronger argument was to accept the lesser evil. Germany had done wrong to Belgium, but resisting Germany would do more wrong to more people than standing aside and letting Germany conquer France once again.[50] This might become convincing by 1916, but in 1914 no one knew how great an evil was yet to come.

In the early months of the war, Rupert was a militant patriot, but he was not a mindless one. Like most British intellectuals, he had formed a rational commitment to resist Germany by all means necessary. The old questions about his sexuality or his purpose in life could be set aside for the duration of the war. He continued to divide his attentions between virginal Cathleen and sensual Eileen without any great qualms of conscience. What did trouble him was whether he should marry before going out again to the front. Many young soldiers grappled with this, though Rupert was more indecisive about it than most. On his way to Antwerp he had thought "What *Hell* it is that I shan't have any children – any sons." But a couple of months later he confessed that he was still unable to act: "If the war *hadn't* happened, I'd have gone on eyeing the brink, hesitating, and deferring, never quite blinded enough to say 'Well, tomorrow'll do –' until I relapsed into a friendly celibate middle-age, the amiable bachelor, a Dent or livelier Sayle, or less distinguished Eddie, with my rooms and bedder and hosts of young friends."[51] This was either disingenuous, or an admission of his true inclinations. E.J. Dent, Charles Sayle, and Eddie Marsh were all aging gay men who cultivated sentimental friendships (for Sayle and Marsh, with Rupert himself).[52] Did Rupert's fear of marriage mask a gay identity that he expected to prevail in the long run? It was hardly unusual for a gay man to be eager for children, but not for marriage. After the war, Elisabeth van Rysselberghe, of all people, bore a child for André Gide without marrying him. Rupert saw the same conflict between having a child, and having a wife: "If I *knew* I'd be shot, I'd marry in a flash – oh any of two or three ladies – and do my best to leave a son. How comforting it would be to *know*: and what delicious snatches of domesticity I could steal before January 20! But, oh, if I came back in a year, and found myself caught. It's easy to select a wife for a month: but for a lifetime – one must be a little more certain."[53]

When trying to avoid marriage with Phyllis Gardner – as with others – Rupert made much of his wandering nature, unable to settle down. But what if "wandering" was really a compulsion to get away from any woman who gave herself to him, and who therefore made a claim on his love? At the least, Rupert was quite open that for him marriage meant the death of freedom. How he summed it up to Jacques was how it turned out: "The only horror is that I want to marry in a hurry and get a child, before I vanish. There's the question ... Insoluble: and the weeks slip on. It'll end in my muddling that, as I've muddled everything else."[54] Rupert never did propose to Cathleen, or to Eileen. He had a partial reconciliation with Noel after he came back from Antwerp, and went with her to a play-reading at Bryn's house on 16 October. But Noel's closeness with the Bloomsbury pacifists excluded her from Rupert's list of possible wives. Nor, he realised, was she ever going to bend to his will.

Another loose end to be settled after Antwerp was the quarrel between the Anson Battalion subalterns and their commander, Colonel Cornwallis-West. It is not clear whether they objected to his military orders, or just his pessimism and his peremptory manners. On his side, he could not be expected to defer to a group of young varsity men with minimal military experience. But Arthur Asquith was ready to take him down a peg: "Papa Asquith ... suddenly took the idea that his son had been insulted and ill used (as he had), sent for Winston, cussed him, and told him to put it right. So Winston damned an Admiral, who made blue Hell for the G.O.C. Marines, who wiped the floor with [Cornwallis-West], who – and finally two Sub-lieutenants Browne and Brooke were wired to, to join the Hood, where Asquith was ... It's worth while, being the P.M.'s son."[55] By the beginning of December, Cornwallis-West was in a nursing home with a nervous breakdown. In January his solicitors wrote to the *Times* to deny "persistent rumours that he had been shot in England as a spy."[56] Either he was the victim of a cruel joke, or he was suffering from delusions of persecution. Rupert and Arthur Asquith succeeded in transferring to the Hood Battalion at Blandford Camp, Dorset. Denis Browne joined them later. Living in huts was far from pleasant, but at least Rupert was with his friends, and able to get away regularly to London.

The Poetry of It

The return from Antwerp had consolidated Rupert's identity in more ways than one. He was completely loyal to his military commitment; his dislike of Cornwallis-West did not lead to any disillusionment with the general conduct of the war, or with Churchill's decision to throw untrained battalions of the RND into battle. Another conviction was that the purpose of the war was to defend a certain idea of England, embodied in the English countryside. The Georgian poets had done much to popularise this ideal; the war made the land more precious because it was now vulnerable to a Prussian invasion. Never mind that the ideal left out both the industrial north and London, which were the actual strategic prizes of the war. The glorification of hedgerows, old churches, rooks calling in the elms, and all the rest played a powerful role in mobilising public opinion against Germany. In France, similarly, "la terre de France" was personified as a motherland laid waste and violated by its invaders.

Rupert's commitment to the war was also deeply personal. The enemy within was the Bloomsbury male: intellectual, pacifist, cosmopolitan, effete, cowardly, and physically repulsive. The supreme example of the type, and therefore the focus for Rupert's hatred, was Lytton Strachey. Homosexuality was also included in Rupert's gibe at the "half-men" in the first of his war sonnets. But, paradoxically, his personal ideal was now almost exclusively masculine. Much of the jingoist war rhetoric played on the idea of England, like Belgium, as a defenceless maiden being raped by Prussian soldiery. For Rupert, the awakening into manliness was virtue enough, and the women of England remain only shadowy figures.

The war sonnets were composed between Rupert's return from Antwerp on 9 October and the Christmas holidays he spent at Rugby. Their publication in *New Numbers IV* was delayed until the beginning of March 1915.[57] Rupert's romantic and sacrificial vision of the war created, in due course, a reaction. Now the five poems seem to sum up every false sentiment provoked by the war, and to legitimise the terrible suffering of the years after Rupert's death. As with Kipling, though, the success of nationalistic poetry rests on the values and tastes of its mass audience. The emotional history of its creators is not yet available at the time when it first appears. Today we can see how Rupert's neuroses found an outlet in the sonnets; in 1915, they were simply an eloquent expression of collective values and myths.

We could go further and say that the sonnets both revealed Rupert's emotional conflicts and, for the first time in his life, showed a way of overcoming them. The fundamental questions of identity that had led to his 1912 breakdown had now been resolved, two years later. For Rupert, as for many young men of his sort, the war was the best of therapists. He might well have relapsed in two years more – perhaps ending up at Craiglockhart with Sassoon and Owen – but that remains unknown.

A peculiarity of Rupert's war sonnets is that they say nothing about weapons, the enemy, military life, or even aggression of any sort. Everything that drives Kipling's war poetry is absent in Rupert's. The suffering or mutilated body appears nowhere. Instead, three words keep recurring, markers for the poet's destination: Peace, Safety, Death. D.H. Lawrence found in Rupert's poems "the great inhalation of desire" for death. Death is the great cleanser; it is the distinguished thing, unlike the "little emptiness" of heterosexual love, and the worse than emptiness of the "dirty songs" of the "half-men." Joseph Bristow has argued that Rupert's entire career centred on his "poetic engagements with death."[58]

The first four of the war sonnets are spoken as a "we" rather than an "I." They are the collective voice of all the young men "who have known shame," and are now to be awakened and purged. Rupert makes his own case that of his class, the infantry subalterns of 1914. It was a bold gambit, but one confirmed by the poems' reception. Those who remained in England were told that their beloved sons had been absolved of their sins and made perfect by going to war. Because they were all volunteers, they were making a purely moral statement. Conscription, which posed a different concept of duty, would not come until 1916. That it existed from the start for the French, German, and Russian armies made England a special case: a country where war was not a duty of citizenship, but a voluntary self-sacrifice. To think of it so obscured the reality of war. Rupert's soldiers were not just going to meet a noble death; they were also going to inflict as much death as possible on the enemy. "The central purpose of my life," Rupert said to Cathleen, "the aim and end of it, now, the thing God wants of me, is to get good at beating Germans."[59] But in the war sonnets, a soldier is for England, not against a Germany that is not even mentioned.

Another kind of war poem imagines gaining honour in the field in order to come back to one's beloved in triumph. But Rupert's soldier has been "proudly friended," rather than passionately loved. The second sonnet seems to recall Rupert and Cathleen's "ecstasy" in the Chilterns, when they were mystically but not sensually united:

> We have built a house that is not for Time's throwing.
> We have gained a peace unshaken by pain forever.
> War knows no power. Safe shall be my going,
> Secretly armed against all death's endeavour;

This is the opposite of a carpe diem poem. Their love is eternal because unconsummated, and therefore never tainted by the kind of pain Rupert had suffered with Ka. Nor is it harmed by running parallel with his affair with Eileen Wellesley – an affair that is also made safe by not aiming too high. In any case, Eileen is excluded from the war sonnets, as an inconvenient secret that would compromise their message.

Only in the last sonnet, "The Soldier," does Rupert's "I" make an entrance:

> If I should die, think only this of me:
>   That there's some corner of a foreign field
> That is for ever England. There shall be
>   In that rich earth a richer dust concealed;

So it continues its sonorous and irresistibly emotional way. The individual Rupert did find his foreign field on Skyros, even if it was a stony rather than a fertile earth. But the "I" here is any British soldier who rests in a foreign field, as tens of thousands would do in Flanders or the Somme. What counts is the mystical claim that English soil grows its own precious form of manhood – dreaming, laughing, washed by rivers. The mass appeal of the sonnets rested on what they chose to leave out: the filth and mutilation of death as it actually happened in modern war. Yet the sonnets succeeded perfectly in depicting war the way those at home wanted to imagine it; not the way Wilfred Owen would know it, "the old lie: *Dulce et decorum est / Pro patria mori.*"

In Rupert's defence one can say that when he composed the sonnets he had no personal knowledge of trench warfare, as it would be fought from late 1914 on. His 1914 letters have many sayings along the lines of "Come and die, it'll be great fun," but he was not alone in his careless-ness. Julian Grenfell, notoriously, wrote home, "I adore war. It is like a big picnic but without the objectivelessness of a picnic. I have never been more well or more happy."[60] In January 1915 Churchill could still say, "I would not be out of this glorious delicious war for anything the world could give me."[61] The war sonnets were the most powerful statement, in their time, of the eternal message that death and suffering are noble, meaningful, and redemptive. Rupert was nominally an atheist, but his sonnets provided an essentially religious consolation. When he wrote them he knew nothing about Gallipoli, and expected his sacrifice to be consummated in Flanders. Only after his death did the sonnets take on a further weight of myth: of the siege of Troy, the Crusades, and Byron's death at Missolonghi for the liberation of the Greeks.[62]

15

Gallipoli
January–April 1915

Breaking Crockery

Rupert met his fate in the Gallipoli expedition, which was Churchill's war and the worst of his many strategic blunders. He conceived an attack on the Dardanelles as a giant flanking movement around the Western Front. It also had the attraction of giving a central role to the forces he controlled personally: the Navy and the Royal Naval Division (RND). Asquith was guilty of egging him on. A few days after Antwerp had surrendered, he suggested to Churchill that it was "time that he bagged something, and broke some crockery."[1] Britain and France were about to declare war on the Ottoman Empire, so the Turkish china shop was the obvious place for Churchill to send in his bull.

War with Turkey came from another of 1914's disastrous chain reactions. Two powerful German warships, the *Goeben* and the *Breslau*, had taken refuge at Istanbul in August 1914. On 27 September the Turks closed the Dardanelles to all shipping; this was aimed at their historic rival, Russia, which sent 90 percent of her trade through the Straits. A month later, the *Goeben* and *Breslau* entered the Black Sea to attack Russian ports and warships. Germany and Turkey appeared to be hand in glove, so the Allies responded by declaring war. That implied making war, through a naval counterstroke against the Turks. Churchill was happy to oblige though many others, from Asquith on down, were ready to give him support.

On 3 January 1915, Churchill formally asked Admiral Cardan if the Mediterranean fleet could re-open the Dardanelles. In an ominous phrase, Churchill suggested that "Importance of results would justify severe loss." Losses would indeed come, but not the hoped-for results, and a more level-headed strategist could have seen this in advance. But Churchill took pride in drawing no lessons from Antwerp. "I care for nothing but the future in war," he would write in *The World Crisis*.[2] In any case, the loss of Antwerp could be blamed on the failure of the French to arrive in time. Then there were the rich prizes of victory in the Dardanelles. As soon as the British and French fleets arrived in the Sea of Marmara, bringing Istanbul under their guns, Turkey would have to sue for peace. Istanbul would go back to being called Constantinople because the Allies had promised to hand it over to Russia. The Orthodox mass would again be celebrated in Hagia Sophia. British and French munitions would flow to the Eastern front, while Russian grain could be sold in the west for ready cash. There were obvious flaws in Churchill's plans, not least that the Allies were barely holding their own on the Western Front and could not spare any guns or ammunition to send east. But everything else depended on whether it was feasible to open the Dardanelles. That was a question of tactics rather than strategy and the Allies, under Churchill's influence, got it disastrously wrong.

Such was the background in high politics to Rupert's five months as a soldier in England after Antwerp. His war sonnets assumed that as soon as the RND was trained it would go to France to join the British Expeditionary Force. The need for reinforcements on the Western Front was acute, but Churchill held back the RND, in part because he wanted them for combined operations with the Navy. Once they were committed to Gallipoli the prime minister, thinking of his son, confided to Venetia Stanley: "How lucky [the RND] are to escape Flanders and the trenches and be sent to the 'gorgeous East.'"[3] If the Dardanelles could be opened by naval bombardment only, the RND might land unopposed to occupy Istanbul after its surrender. Knowing nothing of these pipe dreams, Rupert had his mind set on France. A staff officer told him to expect 75 percent casualties for his battalion when they got there. In January there was still no news of the Hood's deployment. "It's TOO bloody," Rupert commented, "to have THREE more months of life, when one hoped for three weeks."[4]

Having staked his claim to heroic martyrdom with the war sonnets, Rupert now faced an indefinite stay in the damp and dismal huts of Blandford Camp, though with frequent leaves to Rugby and London. Between August 1914 and February 1915 he met often and intimately with Churchill. He was fond of Rupert, though this never prevented his putting him in harm's way. Violet and Arthur Asquith took Rupert twice to Walmer Castle: "a divine and Paradisal interlude ... a moment of peace."[5] His host there was the Earl of Beauchamp, a member of Asquith's Cabinet and warden of the Cinque Ports. Beauchamp, the supposed model for Lord Marchmain in *Brideshead Revisited*, maintained a flagrantly gay domestic establishment, with decorative footmen and louche hangers-on. He was finally driven into exile in 1931 by his brother-in-law, the duke of Westminster, who threatened to expose him. Of contact between Beauchamp and Rupert there is, unfortunately, no record.

Rupert's closeness to Liberal aristocrats did not soften his hostility to another key group of Liberal supporters: wealthy or otherwise prominent Jews who found more acceptance among Liberals than among Tories. Rupert had long fulminated against the presence of Jews in the National Liberal Club. They were there because most of the older-established clubs would not admit them. Herbert Samuel and Rufus Isaacs had been attacked by Belloc and Chesterton for their alleged corruption in the Marconi scandal, but Asquith kept them in his government. In November 1913, when he was in the Pacific, Rupert told Eddie Marsh that he wanted to resign from the National Liberal Club because Isaacs was a member.[6] In December 1914 he was "all in favour of shooting the rich and tyrannical *here*, beginning with Sir Edgar Speyer."[7] Born in New York, Speyer was of German Jewish origin; he was a financier, patron of the arts, and a Liberal supporter. In 1914 there was a McCarthyite campaign against him as a German fifth-columnist. Other Jews, such as Ernest Cassel, felt obliged to make public professions of loyalty to England. In Rupert's eyes, Jews were both enemies of the old England of the greenwood, and friends of Germany, where many of them had their roots. Christopher Hassall, in his biography, suggested that Rupert's anti-Semitism was little more than a private quirk that he indulged in with Jacques Raverat.[8] Insofar as it had any rational basis, Rupert's prejudice aligned him with the guild socialism of Belloc and Chesterton, which held that financial capitalism was destroying the traditional order of artisans and peasants. But hatred of Jews was more than Rupert's secret vice. Jews were one of the five horsemen of his demonology, the others being feminists, eunuchs, pacifists, and intellectuals. They should all be purged from that "forever England" for which Rupert wanted his friends to fight and die.

Blandford Camp had none of Rupert's bugbears, but in January it was cold, wet, and muddy. For most of the month he suffered from colds and flu. "They've discovered," he told Violet Asquith, "that no one *ever* gets better in these miasmic huts."⁹ At the end of the month he went up to Eddie's to be nursed by Mrs Elgy. But he still got worse, and Mrs Elgy went home at night, so on 4 February Violet carried him off to 10 Downing Street. Blandford Camp was a nasty place in winter, but Rupert suffered more illness than his fellow officers. His lifelong vulnerability to infection was probably being made worse by a weakened immune system. It would only need one more major attack for his health to break down altogether.

In the warmth and comfort of a bedroom at Downing Street Rupert managed to get back on his feet. By 7 February he was trying to make an assignation with Eileen Wellesley; this was difficult because a "Jew artist" – Mark Gertler – had taken his place at Eddie's flat. For the 5th, Violet Asquith had arranged for Rupert to have lunch with Henry James; he had to come to Downing Street because Rupert was not yet strong enough to go out. James had not seen Rupert since they had gone punting at Cambridge in 1909. It had been a tremulous occasion for the Master, though this second encounter was equally moving: "Nothing certainly could have been called more modern than all the elements and suggestions of his situation for the hour, the very spot in London that could best serve as a centre for vibrations the keenest and most various; a challenge to the appreciation of life, to that of the whole range of the possible English future, at its most uplifting."¹⁰

This was part of James's posthumous tribute to Rupert, in the Preface to *Letters from America*. The tribute would be a lavish one, though with the usual Jamesian indirection. It was typical that he did not identify the "centre for vibrations" as 10 Downing Street. "Rupert expressed us *all*," James wrote, "at the highest tide of our actuality." It is fair to say that James was infatuated with Rupert, as he had been with other handsome young men. Yet he wondered about the chances of Rupert's "development," when he was so much shaped by the glow of admiration, and by his own wandering inclinations: "Why shouldn't the art of living inward a little more, and thereby of digging a little deeper or pressing a little further, rather modestly replace the enviable, always the enviable, young Briton's enormous range of alternatives in the way of question-begging movement, ... the enormous habit of holidays?" James cannot have known much about Rupert's question-begging movement from one woman to another, but he sensed how far Rupert's boyish pose may have covered a fundamental lack of purpose – life itself as one long holiday. Except, of course, the sacrificial purpose of April 1915, to which James could only respond, when told of his death: "of course, of course!"[11]

Caught up as he was in the national cause that led him to take British citizenship three months after Rupert's death, James saw him as the finest flower of British culture. In the essay "An Unusual Young Man," Rupert had described his conversion experience in August 1914: "With a sudden tightening of his heart, he realised that there might be a raid on the English coast ... The idea sickened him. He was immensely to perceive that the actual earth of England held for him a quality which he found in A_____, and in a friend's honour, and scarcely anywhere else, a quality which, if he'd ever been sentimental enough to use the word, he'd have called 'holiness.'"[12] James would praise the "noble beauty" of Rupert's war sonnets, and his whole tribute endorses the myth of sacrifice: that a nation may only survive by offering up its most perfect youth to death in battle, "the consecration of the event."[13]

That death, as James sat by Rupert's bedside, was now less than three months off. Rupert had dinner with Churchill at the Admiralty on 14 February, and found him "very confident about the Navy and our side of Europe." A week later, with no concern for security, Rupert was telling his mother and friends that the division was going to the East: "It will be much more glorious and less dangerous than France." He was thrilled to follow in the footsteps of both the Crusaders, and of Lord Byron. "I've never been quite so happy in my life, I think," he told Violet Asquith, "Not quite so *pervasively* happy; like a stream flowing entirely to one end. I suddenly realise that the ambition of my life has been – since I was two – to go on a military expedition against Constantinople."[14]

Journey to the East

Both Churchill and King George V came down to Blandford on 25 February to review the RND. Two days later they marched across country to Shillingstone, where they entrained for Avonmouth. The Hood and the Anson battalions boarded the *Grantully Castle*, a small liner that had been converted into a troopship. On 28 February the ship sailed, with

Violet Asquith on the quay, waving to Rupert and to her brother Arthur ("Oc"). On boarding the ship Rupert had been given an amulet with a note from Eddie: "My dear, this is from a very beautiful lady who wants you to come back safe – her name is not to be divulged ... It's a very potent charm."[15]

From Malta, Rupert wrote to Eddie, asking him to thank the donor, though saying that he wasn't sure what kind of luck her gift might bring: "I can well see that life might be great fun: and I can well see death might be an admirable solution. At that, quote to her something appropriate from the *Apology*, & leave her to her prayers."[16] In the *Apology*, one of Socrates's arguments is that we cannot know for certain whether death is a good or an evil thing. The amulet might be a blessing whatever happened, so Rupert was happy to wear it round his neck with his identity disk. It was a pentacle: a circular medal with a five-pointed star inscribed within it. The early Christians believed that it protected against demons. In the twelfth century it was adopted by the Templars, which suited Rupert's mission since they were the first warriors to enter Constantinople in 1204, during the Fourth Crusade.

Who was the woman who sent Rupert the amulet? Most likely it was Lady Gwendoline Churchill, who sat next to him at his farewell dinner on 24 February. Anonymity was prudent because she was married to Churchill's younger brother John. She was a renowned society beauty and a Catholic, who might like the medieval symbolism of the pentacle. The medal itself was not mentioned by Rupert's burial party; presumably it lies with his bones in the grave at Skyros.

The Crusades were being revived, Rupert told Jacques, and should be carried out in the same style: "The early Crusaders were very jolly people ... when they got East, to the Levant and Constantinople, were they kind to their brother Christians they found there? No. They very properly thwacked and trounced them, and took their money, and cut their throats, and ravished their daughters and so left them: for that they were Greeks, Jews, Slavs, Vlachs, Magyars, Czechs, and Levantines, and not gentlemen."[17] On his ship, Rupert had been reading up on the history of Constantinople, so he knew that what the Crusaders did there was a hundred times worse than anything the Germans had done to Belgium. He enjoyed competing with Jacques to see who could come up with the most bloodthirsty rubbish, rather like Kingsley Amis and his cronies in recent times. Neither Rupert nor Kingsley actually did anything terrible, so is it fair to harp on their terrible words? On the other hand, we could argue that Rupert said to Jacques what he really felt, whereas with others he held back out of fear of offending them. At the least, we should mind the gap between the ideal English soldier of the war sonnets, and the Rupert who boasted about how many wogs he hoped to rape and kill.

As the *Grantully Castle* steamed into the Mediterranean, and past the site of ancient Carthage, Rupert vowed to come to Africa after the war. He had plenty of time to write to his ladies: most profusely to Violet Asquith, but also to Cathleen, to Eileen, and to Ka. But not Noel; they had exchanged their last letters. Noel had kept telling him about her meetings with the Bloomsbury pacifists. She knew that this would infuriate Rupert, and perhaps that was just what she wanted to do. He went to see *Tosca* at the Malta opera house, and re-embarked on the troopship. On 11 March they sailed into Mudros Bay, on the island of Lemnos, where they would spend two weeks. Rupert had time to address his literary and sentimental legacy. He chose Dudley Ward to sort out his affairs – a solid, married man, not a literary intellectual. Rupert's first concern was to preserve the reputations of Elisabeth van Rysselberghe, Eileen Wellesley, and Ka by ordering Dudley to destroy all their letters. None have survived, so we can assume that Dudley did as he was asked.[18]

A week before, Rupert had tried to atone for his romantic misadventures by returning Ka to the place of honour:

I suppose you're about the best I can do in the way of a widow ... Let [Mrs Brooke] think we might have married. Perhaps it's true.

My dear, my dear, you did me wrong: but I have done you very great wrong. Every day I see it greater.

You were the best thing I found in life. If I have memory, I shall remember ... I hope you will be happy, and marry and have children. It's a good thing I die.[19]

Even when Rupert is doing his utmost to speak the plain truth, he cannot. The "wrong" that Ka committed was no more than an inconclusive flirtation with Henry Lamb, followed by sleeping with Rupert because she was sorry for him. Neither act would have made marriage to Rupert impossible. His problem was not Ka, who loved him deeply, but marriage itself, with anyone. Ka did marry, have children, and become a beloved member of her little community in Zennor, Cornwall. After her period of youthful angst she led a normal life. Rupert knew that this was beyond reach for him, hence the fatal attraction of a warrior's death.

· A great Allied fleet had assembled off Lemnos, just a few miles away from Turkish waters and the entrance to the Dardanelles. Churchill's plan for the fleet was a signal piece of folly. The entrance to the Dardanelles was about five miles wide, narrowing steadily to less than a mile at Canakkale, where there was a fort on each side. There was high ground on both sides of the strait, lined with shore batteries and mobile howitzers. The gun crews were directed and trained by German officers. The Allied fleet had many semi-obsolete ships, considered expendable by Churchill. They did not have armoured decks, which made them vulnerable to plunging fire coming down on them from the heights. Between the entrance to the strait and the narrows, a distance of about ten miles, the Turks had placed a gauntlet of ten rows of mines, plus another row on the right side of the strait that the Allies had not detected. Their ships would be advancing into a naval Valley of Death.

On 18 March, sixteen capital ships steamed into the strait, with three French ships in the lead. Minesweepers manned by civilians were supposed to clear a way for them; not surprisingly, their crews did not like being shelled from the heights, and they retreated without completing their task. The warships then had to turn back as well. The French battleship *Bouvet* hit a mine and turned turtle, drowning more than six hundred of her crew, with only about fifty survivors. Five other Allied ships were either sunk or crippled by the end of the day. "They ought to have gone on," Churchill told an American journalist, "What did it matter if more ships were lost? The ships were old and useless." If they had gone on, even more sailors would have died and the attack would still almost certainly have failed.[20]

While the naval battle went on, Rupert and his comrades were embarked with full battle gear. They spent the day offshore, kept in ignorance of the disaster that was unfolding in the straits, then returned tamely to Mudros Bay. The Turks now knew that the Allies had a landing force ready, which gave them six weeks to thicken their defences against invasion. The *Grantully Castle* stayed at Lemnos until 24 March, then sailed for encampments near Port Said. There was no room on Lemnos for troops to train; in Egypt they could march around in the desert and practise their musketry. At no time, though, did Rupert's division practise landing under fire, which was supposed to be a standard mission for marines. The price of unreadiness would be paid a month later.

As soon as he could, Rupert left his fly-infested tent for a night at Shepheard's Hotel in Cairo. He managed to fit in the Pyramids, the Sphinx, and a camel ride, but was feeling unwell by the time he returned to camp. He spent the next day in the desert regardless, marching and firing at targets. In the night he was sick and the next day, 2 April, he could do nothing but lie on his camp bed under an awning. At this point his illness was probably no more than heatstroke and the shock of being in a subtropical climate. As he lay there, feeling feverish and generally miserable, General Sir Ian Hamilton paid him a visit. He was the commander of the Mediterranean Expeditionary Force, all the British and Anzac divisions whose objective was Istanbul.

Hamilton was an unusual general, a poet and intellectual who had also been twice recommended for a Victoria Cross. In his *Gallipoli Diary* he wrote the epitaph for his own career: "There is nothing certain about war except that one side won't win."[21] In the 1930s he became an admirer of Hitler. Hamilton had met Rupert before but did not know him well. Nonetheless, he offered him a position on his staff, which was the closest thing to a guarantee that Rupert would survive the war. The proposal probably started with Churchill, nudged by Eddie. They may have decided that Rupert's health could not hold up at the front; they certainly knew that after 18 March there was going to be a bloody struggle on the ground against the Turks. Rupert sensed his commander's misgivings. He told Violet Asquith that Hamilton was "a little fearful – not *fearful*, but less than cock-sure – about the job."[22] To his credit, Rupert knew that he must resist temptation and stay with his friends in the Hood. He left open the possibility that he might accept later, after he had proved himself in combat. How would it look if the man who wrote "The Soldier" dodged the coming battle to become an *aide-de-camp* with no clear duties, and no previous training as a staff officer? Hamilton had thrown Rupert a lifeline, but his poetry made it impossible for him to grasp it.

One respite Rupert was willing to accept was to move from his camp, with its heat and blowing sand, to the large and luxurious Casino Palace Hotel in Port Said. Rupert shared a room with Patrick Shaw-Stewart, a friend since Antwerp. A year younger than Rupert, Shaw-Stewart had been a brilliant classicist at Eton and Balliol. Elected to an All Souls fellowship, he then made a career at Barings Bank. A snob of the first water,

Shaw-Stewart complained that his men smelled, and boasted that "He had never met a Duke he didn't like." He and Rupert suffered constant fever and dysentery for a week.

After two days – on 4 April – Rupert was bothered by a sore on his upper lip, which the battalion medical officer said was of little importance. If it was a mosquito bite, this was an ironically trivial cause for a fatal illness. By scratching the bite, Rupert might have given infection access to his system. But he might have picked up a staphylococcus infection in other ways – for example, from his hotel dinner on 1 April, after which he had vomited during the night. In the past he had often suffered from conjunctivitis, normally a staph infection. In any case, the combined shock of dysentery, fatigue, and the Egyptian climate had weakened him enough for the infection to take hold. Without antibiotics, septicemia was virtually untreatable; even today, it can often be fatal. Rupert was not a special case. One of his men had died on the ship on the way to Egypt, and in the Gallipoli campaign, bloody as it was, two-thirds of the two hundred thousand Allied casualties were caused by disease rather than enemy action. Going to hospital in Port Said might have helped Rupert, but he was determined to get better on his own and be with his men for the coming offensive.

Meanwhile, the powers that be proceeded on their fatal course. After the naval failure of 18 March, the Allies had three choices. One was to send the ships in again, hoping that this time they could force the narrows and arrive in front of Istanbul. Even Churchill realised that the risk of another debacle was too high. The second choice was to admit that Turkish defences were too strong, given their favourable terrain and short lines of communication, and give up the dream of taking their capital. The Mediterranean forces of ships and men could then be redirected towards the Western Front (this happened in 1916, after the RND and the Anzacs had been withdrawn from Gallipoli). The third choice was to make a landing on the Gallipoli peninsula, so as to control the western side of the Dardanelles. Once the Allied army had been moved to the Turkish front there was great psychological pressure to bring it into action, rather than quietly withdraw it for use elsewhere.

Somewhere in these calculations lay the Homeric precedent of the Trojan War. It should not have carried any weight in the strategic planning for Gallipoli. But the public schoolboys of the RND were thrilled to be following in the tracks of Agamemnon and Menelaus, some thirty-one centuries ago. "Do you think *perhaps* the fort on the Asiatic corner will want quelling," Rupert asked, "and we'll land and come at it from behind and they'll make a sortie and meet us on the plains of Troy?"[23] His fellow invalid at Port Said, Patrick Shaw-Stewart, had accepted a staff position as liaison officer with the French First Division, which would land near Troy as a diversion from the main effort on Gallipoli.[24] After Rupert's death he went ashore on Imbros, some twenty-five miles from the site of ancient Troy. Having a copy of *The Shropshire Lad* with him, he wrote his own poem on the end-papers:

> Achilles came to Troyland
>   And I to Chersonese:
> He turned from wrath to battle,
>   And I from three days' peace.
>
> Was it so hard, Achilles,
>   So very hard to die?
> Thou knewest, and I know not—
>   So much the happier I.
>
> I will go back this morning
>   From Imbros over the sea;
> Stand in the trench, Achilles,
>   Flame-capped, and shout for me.

The chosen objective for the invasion force was the west side of the Gallipoli peninsula. This was a long, narrow hog's back, rising to 971 feet at its highest point. The Allied troops would have to climb up to the top of the ridge, then go down the other side to knock out the Turkish guns that dominated the straits. There were only a few small beaches where they could land, thick with barbed wire and swept by concealed machine guns. Even if they gained control of the peninsula the Turks would still have their minefields, and their batteries on the other side of the straits. The Allies had a poor opinion of the enemy, thinking of them as Orientals who would turn tail at the first whiff of cordite. In fact, they were brave and capable troops, well led by a mixture of German and Turkish officers. But Churchill was driving the enterprise ahead, and there was no one with power or will to hold him back.

On 10 April the Hood battalion re-embarked on the *Grantully Castle*. They steamed very slowly because they were towing a barge for putting the troops ashore when the time came. Rupert had lost weight and was still semi-invalid, excused from standing watch and spending hours in his cabin. He was mulling over another long poem about England, to be called "an Ode or Threnody: a very serene affair, full of major chords and larger outlooks, like an English lawn at sunset."[25] It sounds like a reconsideration of "Grantchester," but taking on darker questions than whether there will still be honey for tea. Perhaps Rupert had realised that the Edwardian summer was over, and even if Britain won the war it would be a different country. The poem remained unwritten.

In the evenings Rupert joined the little group of friends who called themselves "the Latin Club." As they sailed by Lemnos, they would be remembering that the Greeks had left Philoctetes there as they approached Troy because he had an infected wound that stank unbearably. Later they had to go back, having learned that without Philoctetes and his bow they would be unable to take Troy.[26] Whether or not the club would make the connection between Rupert and Philoctetes is unknown, but without doubt they were excited by the connections between the classical myths and their present expedition. Their club had seven members: Rupert, Shaw-Stewart, Oc Asquith, Denis Browne, John Dodge, F.S. Kelly, and Charles Lister. All had gone to Oxford or Cambridge except Dodge (a cousin of Churchill's), who had been born in the United States and went to McGill in Montreal. Lister, Kelly, and Shaw-Stewart were Etonians; Rupert and Browne Rugbeians; Asquith a Wykehamite; Dodge went to St Mark's, where the curriculum was almost entirely Latin and Greek. The "glittering prizes" of the Latin club are too many to list. Shaw-Stewart won so many awards at Eton that he was written up as "the cleverest boy in England." Kelly had a gold medal from the 1908 Olympics, where he rowed in the British eight. He would die on the Somme in 1916. Shaw-Stewart returned to the front line when the RND moved to France, and was killed at Cambrai in 1917. Browne and Lister would die on Gallipoli. Only Asquith and Dodge survived the war. Asquith lost a leg and Dodge went on to serve heroically in the Second World War. Between the two of them, they earned four Distinguished Service Orders, a Distinguished Service Cross, and a Military Cross.

For a week the *Grantully Castle* shunted aimlessly around the Aegean, until it dropped anchor in Trebuki Bay at Skyros. Mail came aboard, and

Rupert heard from Eddie that Virginia Woolf had published *The Voyage Out* and that Henry James was deeply impressed by the war sonnets. "I think of [Rupert] quite inordinately," he said.[27] This was private worship; more significant for Rupert's immortality was the service in St Paul's Cathedral for those who had already died in the war, held on Easter Sunday, 4 April. The sermon was by Dean William Inge, an Etonian and fellow of King's. He read Rupert's "The Soldier," and said that "the enthusiasm of a pure and elevated patriotism had never found a nobler expression."[28] No longer buried in the pages of *New Numbers*, "The Soldier" had become the anthem of the hour, and Rupert the epitome of all soldiers. Anchored off a Greek island, and expecting to go into battle in a few days, he paid little attention to the first echoes of his coming fame.

Rupert was far from well but was still determined to keep up with the rest of his battalion. Two days after arriving at Skyros he went ashore with his men, who amused themselves by shooting adders and trying to stage a tortoise race. The next day, 20 April, was more serious, a rehearsal for what awaited them on Gallipoli. The Hood battalion deployed from the beach into the stony interior of the island. It was hot and exhausting work. In the afternoon Rupert and three of his fellow subalterns rested in the shade of a small olive grove, where he remarked on the beauty of the place. That led his comrades to return, three days later.

The divisional field day went on for eight hours, and Rupert had also been on watch for four hours during the night. At the end of the day, Bernard Freyberg, Oc Asquith, and Charles Lister proposed a swimming race back to the ship. Rupert was too tired to take up the challenge – a sensible decision since Freyberg had been champion of New Zealand at one hundred yards. He came back in a fishing boat, dined with the Latin club, and went to bed early. In the morning he was too weak to get up; the swelling on his lip was worse, and he had pains in his chest and back. Five doctors came to examine him. They agreed that Rupert was dying and there was little that could be done. The ship's surgeon, Dr Goodale, was a bacteriologist; he identified Rupert's infection as *Streptococcus pneumoniae*. This could produce various major and minor ailments and could be fatal to anyone with a weakened immune system.[29] It may seem odd that for three weeks none of Rupert's doctors seemed alarmed about his condition, then became concerned only two days before he died. But they were not necessarily incompetent. Infections were endemic, given how the soldiers lived, and they ran their course in unpredictable ways.

And once sepsis took hold there was little that the medicine of 1915 could do.

All that remained was palliative care, which was hard to provide in Rupert's cramped and stuffy cabin. In the same bay on Skyros was the *Duguay-Trouin*, a French three-master now converted into a hospital ship. It had a full surgical team for six hundred beds, but no patients until the French went into battle. Rupert did not want to leave his comrades, but a transfer to the French ship was in his best interest. Oc Asquith went over with him, to see him settled as comfortably as possible. He asked Rupert if there was anything he wanted, to which he replied "water" – his last coherent word.

Rupert lapsed into unconsciousness that evening. The next morning the French surgeons operated to drain and cauterize the abscess on his lip, but with no expectation that this could save his life. When Oc Asquith asked the chief surgeon about Rupert's condition, he replied, "*État désespéré.*" The French surgeons and nurses were all male, so Rupert went to his end with no touch of a woman's hand. Denis Browne was the only one of his comrades with him when he died, at a quarter to five in the afternoon of Friday, 23 April. He and Rupert were the two Rugby boys in the Latin Club. In six weeks Browne would be gone too.[30]

The *Grantully Castle* was due to join the invasion early the next morning (in the event, it was postponed until the following day, Sunday, 25 April). If they took Rupert's body with them, he would have to be buried at sea. To make a known resting place, a burial party would have to go ashore at once, while Asquith had Rupert dressed in his uniform and placed in an oak coffin. Browne and Lister took a contingent from Rupert's platoon to the grove where they had rested three days before. By the time the coffin had been landed and carried up a dry stream bed, the grave had been dug and lined with branches of wild olive. Asquith reported the scene to his sister Violet: "the moon thinly veiled: a man carrying a plain wooden cross and a lantern leading the way: some other lanterns glimmering: the scent of wild thyme: a dim group of French and English officers: the three volleys: the Last Post."[31]

The ship's chaplain intoned the sonorities of the Anglican burial service, then the firing party fired their three shots – traditionally, a signal that a truce to bury the dead was over and war could resume. The olive branches in the grave were for Rupert the poet, and dead poets before him. On the cross that Rupert's platoon had made, the Greek interpreter wrote an epitaph in his own language: "Here lies the servant of God ... Who died for the deliverance of Constantinople from the Turks." F.S. Kelly wrote in his journal, "It was as though one were involved in the origin of some classical myth."[32]

The burial service includes these words: "If thou, Lord, wilt be extreme to mark what shall be done amiss, who shall abide it?" No one in that grove on Skyros would care about Rupert's feet of clay. He had paid his price, whatever his sins, and they knew all too well that they were likely to pay it too. More than half of them were dead men walking, including the Battalion commander Colonel Quilter. Rupert's stately funeral affirmed the high meaning of their expedition; nothing like it could follow, once they encountered the horrors of trench warfare on Gallipoli. The myth of Rupert's death and burial might be considered a delusion, in the light of what was to come. But how could men fight as bravely as they did, unless they had a belief? What Rupert's death meant to them came from the immediate experience of seeing his body and carrying it to its grave. This was of a different order from the Rupert Brooke myth being stirred up in Britain. That was a dubious blend of genuine feeling and official opportunism, trying to make palatable a ghastly and static war of attrition.

When the first landings were made on Gallipoli, the Hood battalion was still in reserve. Their only action was a solo diversion by Freyberg at the northern end of the front.[33] The Anzacs had gone in about halfway up the peninsula; the main British and French effort came at Helles Bay, at the southern tip. Here the troops could be well supported by naval guns, but they only managed to advance about three miles. Their main objective, the village of Krithia, remained beyond reach. The Hood battalion came in as reinforcements on 30 April, in time for the second attempt to take Krithia from 6 May to 8 May. This was another futile, literally uphill battle against well-entrenched Turks. The commander of the Hood, Colonel Quilter, was killed on the first day.

General Hamilton renewed the assault on 4 June, with even worse results. The second brigade of the RND, which included the Hood and three other battalions, lost sixty of its seventy officers – killed or wounded. The Collingwood's losses were so heavy that the battalion had to be disbanded. Oc Asquith was wounded in the leg in second Krithia and evacuated to Egypt, where Violet went to look after him. He told her that it was "simply a choice between being killed and being disabled for life –

one or the other *must* happen in time."[34] If we ask what might have happened to Rupert, we can only note that the Hood subalterns led their
men into murderous fire from the Turks, who were on higher ground
and well-entrenched. Rupert would have gone forward with his comrades until he was wounded or killed. Siegfried Sassoon, the most prominent of the officers who turned against the war, did not do so until
1917.[35] He had won his Military Cross in 1916, and went back to the front
in 1918. Rupert might have come to share his sentiments, but not in May
1915. The subalterns of Gallipoli knew their leaders had blundered, but
none are known to have flinched from their duty. In the entire war only
two British officers were executed for desertion, both of them on the
Somme in 1916–17.[36] More typical of Gallipoli was George Moor, who
received a Victoria Cross for stopping a retreat by shooting four of his
own men, then leading the rest back into the attack.

The making of Rupert into a mythic hero depended on ignorance both
of the facts of his life, and of the reality of Gallipoli. D.H. Lawrence was
the most astute of the mythmakers, though his judgment was a private
one, in a letter to Ottoline Morrell a week after Rupert's death:

> He was slain by bright Phoebus' shaft – it was in keeping with his
> general sunniness – it was the real climax of his pose. I first heard
> of him as a Greek god under a Japanese sunshade, reading poetry
> in his pyjamas at Grantchester – at Grantchester upon the lawns
> where the river goes. Bright Phoebus smote him down. It is all
> in the saga.
>   O God, O God, it is all too much of a piece: it is like
> madness.[37]

Lawrence had seen the early reports that Rupert died of sunstroke. The
satyr Marsyas picked up Athena's flute and challenged Apollo, the sun
god, to a competition. When he lost, Apollo had him flayed alive. His
blood became the river Marsyas, which flows into the Aegean not far
from Gallipoli. Lawrence captures the paradox of a "real climax" to a
"pose." The pose is an inauthentic way of being; reality both destroyed
Rupert's pose, and confirmed that the pose was all there was to him. For
Lawrence, Rupert's death was the extreme case of how young Englishmen of his class were dying in style, in a war that gave them a significance
they had not been able to find in peace.

Lawrence still mourned Rupert, if not in the conventional way. One of his unkind party pieces was an imitation of Eddie Marsh lamenting Rupert's death over his evening whiskey.[38] Eddie was the one who did most to make Rupert a national symbol, if it was he who actually wrote the tribute published under Churchill's name in *The Times*:

> He expected to die; he was willing to die for the dear England whose beauty and majesty he knew; and he advanced towards the brink in perfect serenity, with absolute conviction of the rightness of his country's cause, and a heart devoid of hate for fellow-men ...
>
> Joyous, fearless, versatile, deeply instructed, with classic symmetry of mind and body, he was all that one would wish England's noblest sons to be in days when no sacrifice but the most precious is acceptable, and the most precious is that which is most freely proffered.[39]

Edgar Allan Poe had said that the death of a beautiful woman was the most poetic subject in the world; for Eddie, and for the whole nation, it was the death of a beautiful man. Britain was paying its tribute to the Minotaur and the true hero, like Theseus, was one who offered himself to save his people.

A great issue was coming to a head, with Rupert's death at the centre of it. Unlike the Continental great powers, Britain had never had a conscript army. The Liberals, especially, felt that volunteerism was a keystone of British identity. As news sank in of the butcher's bill at Gallipoli and in France, the number of volunteers for the army started to dwindle. Old-style Liberals, and the Labour Party, still felt that conscription was "against the spirit of British democracy and full of danger to the liberties of the people."[40] Lord Northcliffe, through *The Times* and *The Daily Mail*, ceaselessly banged the drum for conscription: winning the war was the point, not abstract ideas about liberty. By the end of 1915 Lloyd George and Churchill had come to support conscription, and Asquith had to resign as prime minister in December 1916. By 1939 conscription was taken for granted in Britain from the beginning of the war.

Rupert's death would have counted for much less if he had been a conscript. As a volunteer, it mattered little that he had died of illness just before his fellow officers were mowed down by the Turks. He had chosen to face death for his country; his country had not chosen for him. And he had volunteered as a poet, who in his war sonnets had expressed the volunteer's creed of self-sacrifice. Nor did all war poetry need to be of that kind: the poets of disillusion – Sassoon, Graves, Owen – had been volunteers too. The 1914–15 generation of volunteers had a unique moral authority, sandwiched between the professionals of the British Expeditionary Force and the conscripts of 1916–18. No other belligerent country had met its wartime needs for soldiers in the British way; not coincidentally, none of those countries produced a comparable generation of poets. Whatever the excesses of Rupert's war poems, he still has his place in that lyrical flowering, without precedent before or since.

When Sassoon, Graves, and Owen went to enlist, they did so in much the same spirit as Rupert. Their later poetry came from experiences that he did not share, but that was just the product of chance. If Rupert had gone to the Somme with the remnants of the RND in November 1916, his poetry would surely have evolved from the glory of it all to the pity of it all.[41] His war poems were so much a distillation of the passions of 1914 that his personal responsibility for their sentiments becomes almost irrelevant. Rupert's voice, for that moment, had become the voice of his time and of his country. If figures like Churchill or Henry James lost their sense of proportion in canonising Rupert, that was because an individual fate could be understood but not the impersonal and ultimately inexplicable collective forces of 1914. Rupert Brooke or Edith Cavell made sense; what did not was that an Austrian nobody called Hitler would become, thanks to the war, a world historical figure. To believe in the public school hero was to keep society's reference points in their proper place, from playing fields to Flanders Fields. Who could grasp that the next war would arise from places with different rules: the beerhalls of Munich, the Finland Station of St Petersburg?

The question of what Rupert might have done as poet or statesman after the war has to remain open, which is not the same as calling it an idle question. His actual legacy is known: that he left his capital from his father and the royalties from his poems to Wilfred Gibson, Lascelles Abercrombie, and Walter de la Mare. The massive sales of the poems provided all three with comfortable lifetime incomes. Rupert hoped that what they wrote after the war might compensate for his own death. Unfortunately, their best work was already behind them by 1915, and they gradually sank into eclipse.[42] Better poets might have benefited, but

Rupert preferred those who were both personal friends, and most likely to write poetry in his own Georgian vein.

Two months after Rupert another poet, Apostle, and Kingsman died, at Bukovina on the Eastern Front.[43] Feri Békássy made his way out of England after the declaration of war to enlist in the cavalry and fight for the Austro-Hungarian Empire. Like Rupert he wrote a poem, in English, with the title "1914":

He went without fears, went gaily, since go he must,
And drilled and sweated and sang, and rode in the heat and the dust
Of the summer; his fellows were round him, as eager as he.
While over the world the gloomy days of war dragged heavily.

"I am sure to get something good out of the war unless I die in it," he wrote to Noel Olivier.[44] The cavalry had its own form of fatal glamour – and fatal illusion, as the painter Oskar Kokoschka discovered:

Our uniforms, red, blue and white, stood out only too well, and as I rode out, I felt spied upon by an unseen enemy in the dense, dark foliage of the forests.

The first dead that I encountered were young comrades-in-arms of my own, men with whom, only a few nights earlier, I had been sitting round the camp-fire in those Ukrainian forests, playing cards and joking. Not much more than boys they were, squatting there on the moss in their bright-coloured trousers, a group of them round a tree trunk.

From a branch a few paces further on a cap dangled, and on the next tree a dragoon's fur-lined blue cloak. He who had worn these things himself, hung naked, head downward, from a third tree.[45]

Békássy was killed four days after he arrived at the front. He and Rupert made the poetry of innocence; the poetry of experience was yet to come.

Notes

ABBREVIATIONS

BA   Rupert Brooke Archive, King's College, Cambridge
Berg Berg Collection, New York Public Library
BL   The British Library, London
CUL Cambridge University Library
LRB *The Letters of Rupert Brooke,* ed. Geoffrey Keynes
SOL *Song of Love: The Letters of Rupert Brooke and Noel Olivier, 1909–1915,* ed. Pippa Harris

INTRODUCTION

1 Lawrence, *Collected Letters* 1:456; Brittain, *Testament of Youth,* quoted in Caesar, *Taking It Like a Man,* 3.
2 Orwell, "Inside the Whale," 117.
3 Egremont, *Some Desperate Glory.*
4 Bond, *The Unquiet Western Front,* 1.
5 Clark, *The Sleepwalkers,* 359–61.
6 Clarissa Dalloway feels a kinship with Septimus, the shell-shocked veteran of the trenches, more than with her society friends. The model for Clarissa, Kitty Maxse, was the sister-in-law of Ivor Maxse, the general in Siegfried Sassoon's poem:

"He's a cheery old card," grunted Harry to Jack
As they slogged up to Arras with rifle and pack
  . . . .
But he did for them both by his plan of attack.

Maxse was also an Old Rugbeian. Small world.

CHAPTER ONE

1   Calling Mrs Brooke "The Ranee" began as one of Lytton Strachey's jokes in 1905. Sarawak, which was part of the island of Borneo, had been ruled by a dynasty of Brookes since 1842, known as the "White Rajahs." Charles Brooke (no relation) was the rajah during Rupert's lifetime; his wife was the Ranee of Sarawak, equivalent to queen. Rupert picked up the joke, and called his mother "The Ranee" behind her back from then on.

2   Simpson, *Rugby since Arnold*, 36–7. £1,600 would be at least sixteen times the average Victorian wage. Average earnings in the UK in 2014 were about £26,000, so Rugby housemasters earned the rough equivalent of £400,000 now. They also had free housing and paid almost no income tax.

3   Orwell, review of *The Backward Son* by Stephen Spender, quoted in Crick, *George Orwell*, 67. Orwell considered his memoir of St Cyprian's, "Such, Such were the Joys," to be "too libellous to print." It appeared after his death, in 1968. Orwell, *Collected Essays* 4:330.

4   One hundred and eighty pounds is equivalent to about £75,000 today. Fees at Eton in 2014–15 are about £34,000. Orwell had a scholarship at St Cyprian's, which reduced his fees to £90, though this was a shameful secret, to be kept from his classmates. His father's pension from the Indian Opium Department was £438 per year.

5   Before the 1870s, masters of colleges could marry, but not fellows. Plato's guardians were drawn from both genders, but Jowett ignored that.

6   Nick Duffell, "Why Boarding Schools Produce Bad Leaders," *The Guardian*, 9 June 2014.

7   Brooke, *Song of Love: The Letters of Rupert Brooke and Noel Olivier, 1909–1915* [hereafter *SOL*], 21. Lucas had gone to Haileybury, and the novel shows the public school system from the point of view of a boy who is a sensitive outsider.

8   Hassall, *Rupert Brooke*, 29.

9   Ibid.

10   Ibid., 159.

11   Ibid., 33.

12   Ibid., 30.

13   Crick, *George Orwell*, 51.

14   Graves, *Goodbye to All That*, 23.

15   Ibid.

16   Seymour-Smith, *Robert Graves*, 13. Eden is still there in a 1906 school photo, but his disgrace must have come soon after.

17   Roche, *With Duncan Grant in Southern Turkey*, 47. Grant had left the school long before Eden's disgrace.

18 An English "public school," in the nineteenth century, meant a school to which anyone could be admitted if they passed the entrance exam, and which was not run for profit by its proprietors. There was also an implied contrast with the usual schooling of the aristocracy by private tutors. The nine major public schools, as identified by the Clarendon Commission in 1861, were Eton, Charterhouse, Harrow, Rugby, Shrewsbury, Westminster, Winchester, St Paul's, and Merchant Taylors'.

19 Connolly, *Enemies of Promise*, 260.

20 Honey, *Tom Brown's Universe*, 3.

21 Simpson, *Rugby since Arnold*, 5–6.

22 Quoted in Honey, *Tom Brown's Universe*, 17–18.

23 Eckersley, *Odds and Ends*, ix.

24 Lehmann, *Rupert Brooke*.

25 Caesar, *Taking It Like a Man*, 6.

26 Sedgwick, *Between Men*, 173.

27 Woolf, *Letters*, 3:155.

28 Hickson, *The Poisoned Bowl*, 20.

29 One of them, Edwin Dyett, served in Rupert Brooke's unit, the Royal Naval Division. See Herbert, *The Secret Battle*.

30 Hickson, *The Poisoned Bowl*, 35, citing Peter Ustinov's memoir (though Ustinov did not go to Rugby, and may not be a reliable source).

31 Hughes, *Tom Brown's Schooldays*, 169–70.

32 Brooke, *Letters of Rupert Brooke* [hereafter LRB], 23 Feb. 1906, 41. Sadler later changed his name to Sadleir to avoid being confused with his father, Sir Michael Sadler.

33 LRB, 43, 46. Rupert's letters to Sadler have not survived. They were probably destroyed by Sadler himself, or by Geoffrey Keynes (who suppressed Sadler's name in his edition of Brooke's letters). Sadler married in 1914 and had a distinguished career as a bibliographer and book collector.

34 Ibid., 52.

35 Ibid., 46.

36 Ibid., 49.

37 Rupert Brooke to Ka Cox, "Friday evening," [1 March 1912], BA.

38 "The Beginning," *Poetical Works*, 166. This poem is dated "January 1907" in the *Poetical Works*, but it was enclosed in a letter of July 1906. LRB, 58.

39 LRB, 60; Hale, *Friends and Apostles*, 250.

40 The high point in Lascelles's theatre career was a part as Prince Giglio in *The Rose and the Ring* at Wyndham's Theatre, in December 1923.

41 Rupert had lunch with Lascelles in London on 9 July 1909 (Hale, *Friends and Apostles*, 67–8). He wrote to Geoffrey Keynes on 26 April

1913, asking for Lascelles's London address; presumably he wanted to see Lascelles before leaving for the United States a month later.

42   Rupert Brooke to St John Lucas, *LRB*, 77.

43   *LRB*, 258.

44   J.M. Keynes to Duncan Grant, 8 Feb. 1909, BL. Could this master have been the "lewd and bearded Jove" of p. 24 above?

45   Cotterill, an aspiring playwright, is remembered now for her infatuation with George Bernard Shaw.

46   *LRB*, 81.

47   Quoted in Hastings, *Handsomest Young Man in England*, 71.

CHAPTER TWO

1   Demolins's work was translated into English, *Anglo-Saxon Superiority: To What It Is Due*, in 1898.

2   Raverat, Memoir, 3:2, my translation.

3   Gwen Raverat, Novel, 1.1.3.

4   Raverat, Memoir, 2:7.

5   *LRB*, 73.

6   Ibid., 576.

7   Keynes, *The Gates of Memory*, 87.

8   *LRB*, 116–17.

9   Mary Newbery Sturrock, interview with the author, June 1980.

10   *LRB*, 118.

11   Olivier, *Letters*, 9.

12   Garnett, *Golden Echo*, 100.

13   Ibid., 17.

14   Hassall, *Rupert Brooke*, 175.

15   The Pye sisters were a few years older than the Oliviers but constant companions for Neo-pagan camping and boating trips. Sybil, the elder, became a bookbinder of some renown; Ethel was an artist. Neither of them married. Their brother David, another Neo-pagan, studied engineering at Trinity College, where he became a fellow and a fellow of the Royal Society. Later he was Provost of University College, London.

16   Such vows drive the plot in *Much Ado about Nothing* and in *Love's Labours Lost*. They end up being broken, naturally.

17   Cornford, "Youth," in *Collected Poems*, 15.

18   Cornford, Memoir, 31.

19   *LRB*, 136; Hassall, *Rupert Brooke*, 163.

20   Hassall, *Rupert Brooke*, 165.

21   *LRB*, 339.

22   Lupton also built the Bedales School library, now a Grade I listed building.

23   Jacques Raverat to Ka Cox, 4 June 1908, in possession of Val Arnold-Forster, Ka Cox's daughter-in-law.

24 Jacques Raverat to Ka Cox, 20 Nov. 1908, in possession of Val Arnold-Forster.
25 *LRB*, 142.
26 Rupert Brooke to James Strachey, 7 Jan. 1909, Berg.
27 Hale, *Friends and Apostles*, 246.
28 Angela Harris, daughter of Noel Olivier, interview with the author, 1980.
29 *LRB*, 159.
30 Ibid., 164. Dowson was a decadent poet, known for the phrase "days of wine and roses."
31 Hassall, *Rupert Brooke*, 169.

CHAPTER THREE
1 Rupert Brooke to Elisabeth van Rysselberghe, 3–5 Jan 1912, private collection.
2 Speaight, *The Life of Hilaire Belloc*, 110.
3 Until 1906, membership was limited to seven hundred. This clause was repealed at the urging of H.G. Wells.
4 *LRB*, 116.
5 Its founder was the daughter of the Oxford historian S.R. Gardiner.
6 F.M. Wilson, "Friendships," in Phillips, *A Newnham Anthology*, 67; *LRB*, 308.
7 *LRB*, 117.
8 Its younger members included two future prime ministers: Ramsay MacDonald and Clement Attlee.
9 Wells, *New Worlds for Old*, 242–3, 303, quoted in N. and J. MacKenzie, *The Time-Traveller*, 228.
10 Wells, *New Worlds*, Chapter 2.
11 Wells, *A Modern Utopia*, 303, 316.
12 The socialist had no chance of winning, and the Tory was William Joynson-Hicks (Jix), a notorious enemy of writers and artists.
13 Amber told her parents that she needed to go away on a reading party to prepare for her finals; in fact she went to lodgings in Southend with H.G. Returning to Cambridge in high spirits, and armed with useful tips from her mentor, she took a First in Part II of the moral science tripos. Wells's formal resignation from the Fabian Society, six months later, was made inevitable when news of his affair with Amber started to leak out.
14 Webb and Webb, *Letters*, 2:316.
15 Waley, a friend of Rupert's from Rugby, was then going by his birth name of Schloss; he became a prominent translator from the Chinese. Shove was reading economics at King's.
16 Webb and Webb, *Letters*, 2:316.
17 Or the Webbs themselves. "One only becomes thoroughly 'adaptable'

after 50," Beatrice observed, "before that age, one is so terribly handicapped by one's body." *Letters*, 2:332.

18 Beatrice Webb, *Diary of Beatrice Webb*, 3:77; Webb and Webb, *Letters*, 2:280.

19 Webb, *Diary* 2:142. Allen became chairman of the No-Conscription Fellowship during the First World War. Foss was a friend of Rupert's from Emmanuel. Beatrice Webb's resentment of the Cambridge men may have been partly caused by her lack of a university education; she had educated herself, and supported her work on her private income of £1,000 per year.

20 Hale, *Friends and Apostles*, 132.

21 Webb and Webb, *Letters*, 2:372. The Webbs defined themselves as "B's" – Bourgeois, Benevolent, and Bureaucratic.

22 Hassall, *Rupert Brooke*, 168.

23 Webb, *Our Partnership*, 417.

24 Ibid., 419.

25 Hassall, *Rupert Brooke*, 227.

26 Jacques Raverat to Ka Cox, 19 Jan. 1910, in possession of Val Arnold-Foster.

27 *LRB*, 265.

28 Ibid., 258.

29 Holroyd, *Lytton Strachey*, 427. J.M. Keynes reported this to Duncan Grant.

30 *LRB*, 259.

31 These are the words of Franz Seldte, Nazi minister for labour.

CHAPTER FOUR

1 *LRB*, 85.

2 Hale, *Friends and Apostles*, 119.

3 The Uranians were inspired by a Greek ideal of love between older men and adolescent males.

4 Oates, "Charles Edward Sayle," 236–69. Sayle's "Diary" is in the Cambridge University Library, entry for 6 March 1908.

5 Sayle, "Diary," 22 Feb. 1908.

6 Holroyd, *Lytton Strachey*, 278, 124.

7 Harry Norton to Lytton Strachey, 18 Oct., 24 Oct., 9 Oct. 1906, BL.

8 The intellectual disappointment can be put down to rather narrow Apostolic ideas about cleverness, which required a particular style of wordplay derived from G.E. Moore. Except for Keynes, Hobhouse had more influence on British life than any other twentieth-century Apostle, through the "Hobhouse Report," which led to the establishment of the national park system in 1949.

9 Holroyd, *Lytton Strachey*, 281–2.

10 Gwen Raverat, Novel, 1.1.7, where James is given the pseudonym "Archie Hamilton."

11 Holroyd, *Lytton Strachey*, 168. "Taupe" (French for mole) was Forster's nickname.

12 The possible exception was an affair with Arthur Hobhouse. See Chapter 8.

13 James Strachey to Lytton Strachey, 7 April 1909, BL.

14 James Strachey to Duncan Grant, 16 April 1909, quoted in Taddeo, *Lytton Strachey*, 91. The year before, James was taken aback when Rupert told him about his love for Noel: "Oh God! He's in love with a woman. Why did we think him a sodomite? ... Don't you see now *why* he's kept everything so infernally dark? He's ashamed – because it's a woman."

15 *Whales* here refers to sardines. Rupert had just come from an Apostles meeting on Saturday, 30 October.

16 Hale, *Friends and Apostles*, 250–2.

17 Ibid., 155.

CHAPTER FIVE

1 *LRB*, 171.

2 *LRB*, 173.

3 Hale, *Friends and Apostles*, 249.

4 *LRB*, 139. The "elementalism" here consisted of four nights of camping out, while walking across Wales to the Fabian Summer School in August.

5 Carpenter, *Civilisation*, 46–7.

6 *SOL*, 13.

7 *SOL*, 16.

8 Raverat, Memoir, 3:8. The play, set in the American west, featured a good-hearted prostitute.

9 The first professor of English at Cambridge, A.W. Verrall, was appointed in 1911. He died soon after and was succeeded by Arthur Quiller-Couch. Rupert's stipend from his father was probably £150 per annum.

10 Although Rupert published nothing more in the *English Review*.

11 *LRB*, 188.

12 Brooke, *Prose of Rupert Brooke*, 173.

13 There is a picture of the picnic in Hastings, *Handsomest Young Man*, 87. Dorothy, a Newnham student, was Henry Lamb's sister. She became an archaeologist and civil servant. Robertson became a fellow of Trinity.

14 Hassall, *Rupert Brooke*, 188.

15 Holroyd, *Augustus John*, 362.

16 Ibid., 95.
17 The vacancy arose through the resignation of Leslie Stephen, who was suffering from grievous doubts about Christianity, and also wanted to marry.
18 Carpenter, *My Days and Dreams*, 72, 77.
19 Ward, *Reddie of Abbotsholme*, 56.
20 Ibid., 53.
21 Ibid., 72.
22 Brandreth and Hendry, *John Haden Badley*, 18.
23 E.L. (Peter) Grant Watson, "Bedales," in *The Old School*, ed. Greene, 215.
24 Greene, *The Old School*, 224, 27.
25 Raverat, "Memoir," 21B.
26 Ibid., 32–3.
27 Garnett, *Golden Echo*, 166.
28 Ibid., 170.
29 Badley, *A Schoolmaster's Testament*, 45.
30 *Bedales Record*, 1908.
31 Badley, *A Schoolmaster's Testament*, 169. Frances Partridge, who was at Bedales from 1915 to 1917, notes that Badley coached groups of naked teenage girls for their life-saving tests. She considered him, in retrospect, "an old hypocrite and a far from admirable character." *Memories*, 48.
32 Garnett, *Golden Echo*, 169.
33 "Sally" to Noel Olivier, 2 Feb. 1912, private collection.
34 *SOL*, 10 Feb. 1911, 81. Noel had not yet started at Bedales when she had these encounters in 1908, but the school culture certainly reinforced her habit of guarding her emotions.
35 *LRB*, 135. Misdated; should be August 1909.
36 *LRB*, 175; Rupert Brook to Dudley Ward, BA; Hassall, *Rupert Brooke*, 196.
37 Gwen Darwin to Frances Cornford, 25 Aug. 1908, BL.
38 *LRB*, 194.
39 Ibid., 184, 192–4. Ben Keeling was invited, but refused.
40 Ibid., 195.
41 Ibid., 181.
42 In January 1910 he would flee his office and set sail for six months in California and British Columbia.
43 Gwen Raverat, Novel, 2.1.4–5. Pseudonyms have been replaced with names of the real-life models.

CHAPTER SIX
1 *LRB*, 211.
2 In 1916 Allen served the first of several prison terms as leader of the No-Conscription Fellowship.

3   Hale, *Friends and Apostles*, 114.
4   *LRB*, 248.
5   However, Rupert said the income was scheduled to go up to £900 in 1911, without giving a reason. That would imply a capital of more than £20,000. When Mrs Brooke died in 1930 she left £20,753.
6   *SOL*, 36, 37.
7   Noel Olivier to David Garnett, Tuesday 22 (February or March 1910?), Northwestern University Library.
8   *LRB*, 212.
9   Ka Cox to James Strachey, 2 Feb. 1912, BL.
10 Raverat, Memoir, 3:22–3.
11 Hale, *Friends and Apostles*, 256.
12 *LRB*, 238.
13 Garnett, *The Golden Echo*, 222.
14 Mary Newbery Sturrock (who once accompanied her), interview with the author.
15 Hassall, *Rupert Brooke*, 230.
16 Raverat, Memoir, 3:24.
17 *SOL*, 10 Feb. 1911, 82. Noel's eccentric spelling has been preserved throughout.
18 Mary Newbery Sturrock to Noel Olivier, 24 April 1914, private collection.
19 Justin Brooke to Noel Olivier, 9 July 1916, private collection. Justin would have been twenty-seven in 1912. He married Doris Mead in 1917.
20 Pye, "Memoir," quoted in Hastings, *Handsomest Young Man*, 97.
21 Raverat, Memoir, 3:24. Raverat's pseudonyms in the memoir were "Yseult" for Noel and "Charles Rivers" for Rupert.
22 Rupert Brooke to Lytton Strachey, 11 Sept. 1910, Berg.
23 Gwen Raverat to Frances Cornford [Aug. 1910], BL.
24 Jacques Raverat to Ka Cox, 25 Aug. 1910, in possession of Val Arnold-Foster.
25 *LRB*, 256. Noel did not go on this occasion.
26 Jacques Raverat to Ka Cox, 29 Sep., 19 Jan., 29 Sep. 1910, in possession of Val Arnold-Foster.
27 *SOL*, 50.

CHAPTER SEVEN

1   Jacques Raverat to Ka Cox, 20 July, 29 Sept., 25 April [1910–11?], in possession of Val Arnold-Foster.
2   Gwen Raverat, Novel, 2.2.17; Mary Newbery Sturrock, interview with author.
3   See, for example, "Dust" and "The Life Beyond."
4   Rosalind's father was Hamo Thorneycroft, sculptor and son of sculptors. Her mother, née Agatha Cox, was Lady Olivier's sister.

302 NOTES TO PAGES 117–28

Rosalind divorced Baynes after the war and went to live in Italy, where she had an affair with D.H. Lawrence that was a partial inspiration for *Lady Chatterley's Lover*. She then married Hugh Popham, who had divorced Bryn Olivier.

5   Bryn Olivier to Hugh Popham, "Wednesday night" [12 Oct.? 1910], in possession of A.E. (Tony) Popham, Hugh's son.

6   Rupert Brooke to Ka Cox, 28 Nov. 1910, BA.

7   Jacques Raverat to Ka Cox, ?16 Dec. 1910, in possession of Val Arnold-Foster.

8   *LRB*, 265.

9   Ibid., 270.

10 Gwen Raverat, Novel, 2.3.24.

11 Ibid., 2.3.28. Pseudonyms have been converted: "George" to Jacques; "Hubert" to Rupert.

12 *LRB*, 269.

13 *LRB*, 270.

14 Lawrence, *Letters*, 1:416. One of those artists, a failed one, was Adolf Hitler. He moved to Munich in May 1913 to avoid conscription in Austria. He lived at the north end of Schwabing, and supported himself by peddling watercolours and postcards in coffee houses.

15 See Green, *Mountain of Truth*.

16 Grohmann, *Wassily Kandinsky*, 65.

17 *LRB*, 286.

18 Ibid., 286.

19 Ibid., 288.

20 Rupert Brooke to Ka Cox, 31 Mar. 1911, BA. The poem "Lust" is dated 1909 in the *Poetical Works*, but in an unpublished letter to Jacques (6 Dec. 1911) Rupert says it is about Elisabeth.

21 Rupert Brooke to Elisabeth van Rysselberghe, ?16 April 1911, private collection.

22 Rupert Brooke to James Strachey, 20 April 1911, Berg.

23 *LRB*, 301–2.

24 Rupert Brooke to Ka Cox, ?3 Mar 1911, BA.

25 *LRB*, 300. By the "writings of Jews," Rupert was thinking mainly of Schnitzler.

26 Jacques Raverat to Ka Cox, Monday [late 1910], in possession of Val Arnold-Foster.

27 Gwen Raverat, Novel, 2.5.36.

28 Ibid., 2.5.38.

29 Ibid., 2.3.28, 2.10.82.

30 Woolf, *Letters*, 1:463.

31 Jacques Raverat to Ka Cox, Gwithian [?April 1911], in possession of Val Arnold-Foster.

32 Gwen Raverat to Ka Cox, "Wednesday" [?April 1911]; Jacques
    Raverat to Ka Cox, "Monday" [May? 1911], in possession of Val
    Arnold-Foster.

CHAPTER EIGHT

1   Hale, *Friends and Apostles*, 112.
2   Raverat, Memoir, 3.17.
3   Ray Costelloe married Oliver Strachey; her sister Karen married
    Adrian Stephen.
4   Woolf, *Letters*, 1:450, 1:466.
5   *LRB*, 296.
6   See Delany, "The Death of a Beautiful Man: Rupert Brooke in
    Memory and Imagination."
7   Woolf, *Letters*, 1:446.
8   Ibid., 1:461. Woolf herself was "the Goat" to her sister Vanessa,
    who was "Dolphin."
9   Bertrand Russell to Lady Ottoline Morrell, 25 May 1911, Henry
    Ransom Research Center, University of Texas.
10 Woolf, *Letters*, 1:446, 1:461.
11 The Germans were Dudley's future wife, Annemarie von der Planitz,
    and her sister Clotilde "van Derp," a professional dancer.
12 *SOL*, 89, 91.
13 *LRB*, 310 (misdated; should be ?30 May), 291.
14 Gwen Raverat to Frances Cornford, [March 1911], 11 Nov. [1910],
    private collection.
15 *LRB*, 304 (misdated; ?11 July 1911), 305.
16 *SOL*, 100, 105.
17 *LRB*, 333.
18 Woolf, *Letters*, 1:475.
19 Feri Békássy and Gordon Luce became Apostles in January 1912.
    Frank Bliss and Ludwig Wittgenstein followed in November 1912.
    Rupert was out of the country for both elections.
20 Raverat, Memoir, 3:16–17.
21 Ibid., 3:25–6.
22 Hale, *Friends and Apostles*, 163.
23 Ibid., 129; James Strachey to Lytton Strachey, 18 Aug. 1910, BL.
24 L. Strachey, *Letters*, 227. Lytton continued his assessment of Noel
    with: "A great fish-wife's mouth, which it might be nice to ram one's
    prick into ... mais enfin – I could hardly be interested."
25 Holroyd, *Lytton Strachey*, 547; James Strachey to Lytton Strachey,
    12 Sept. 1910, BL.
26 Holroyd, *Lytton Strachey*, 466.
27 Hale, *Friends and Apostles*, 180.

28   Woolf, *Carlyle's House*, 8.

29   Michael Hastings, conversation with the author, citing Noel Olivier as source, 1984.

30   Woolf, *Letters*, 1:476.

31   Rupert Brooke to J.M. Keynes, 22 Aug. 1911, BA.

32   Skidelsky, *John Maynard Keynes* 1:259; Woolf, *Letters*, 1:477.

33   J.M. Keynes to Duncan Grant, 6 June 1910, BL. Keynes rented a house at Burford, in the Cotswolds, for August and September 1910.

34   Rupert Brooke to Ka Cox, ?16 Sept. 1911, BA.

35   *LRB*, 318.

36   Ibid., 307 (misdated; should be 13 Sept. 1911).

37   Rupert Brooke to Ka Cox, ?29 Feb. 1912, BA

38   *LRB*, 320, 323.

39   Ibid., 313.

40   Woolf, *Moments of Being*, 174.

41   J.M. Keynes to [James Strachey?], 19 Oct. 1911, BL.

42   *SOL*, 141.

43   Ibid., 147.

44   Ibid., 151.

45   Rupert Brooke to Ka Cox, ?29 Feb. 1912, BA.

46   Rupert Brooke to Ka Cox [28 Nov. 1910], BA.

47   Hale, *Friends and Apostles*, 217–19.

48   James Strachey to Lytton Strachey, 1 Nov. 1912, BL.

49   Hassall, *Rupert Brooke*, 292.

CHAPTER NINE

1   It is possible that the poem was a response to his affair with Elisabeth van Rysselberghe earlier in 1911.

 2   Frances Cornford to Gwen Raverat, [?18 Aug. 1912], CUL.

 3   Woolf, *Letters*, 1:378. When war began, Lamb qualified as a doctor and served with the Inniskilling Fusiliers. He was gassed, and awarded the Military Cross.

 4   Holroyd, *Lytton Strachey*, 505.

 5   Rupert Brooke to Ka Cox, "Thursday," ?29 Feb. 1912, BA.

 6   Rupert Brooke to Ka Cox, "Saturday noon" [?14 Dec. 1912], BA.

 7   The room did not become available because Leonard married Virginia Stephen instead of returning to Ceylon.

 8   J.M. Keynes to Duncan Grant, 31 Dec. 1911, 5 Jan. 1912, BL.

 9   Rupert Brooke to Ka Cox, ?29 Feb. 1912, BA.

10   Hale, *Friends and Apostles*, 260.

11   "The Obelisk has done me in, but eventually I'll subdue it." Henry Lamb to Lytton Strachey, "Thursday" [4 Jan.? 1912], BL. Lamb's frequenting of brothels may have contributed to Virginia Woolf's account of prostitution in *Jacob's Room*.

12   Holroyd, *Lytton Strachey*, 472.
13   Henry Lamb to Lytton Strachey, 6 Jan. 1912, BL.
14   Holroyd, *Lytton Strachey*, 473.
15   Ibid., 473.
16   *SOL*, 157.
17   He was also able to write coherently about other things. For example, he sent a long analysis of G.K. Chesterton's social views to Elisabeth van Rysselberghe, 3–5 Jan. 1912.
18   *LRB*, 671.
19   In contemporary terms, Rupert's diagnosis might be that he was in an acute episode of a longstanding bipolar disorder. But both his mania and his depression had a specific content belonging to the cultural obsessions of 1912 rather than 2012.
20   Rupert Brooke to Ka Cox, "Tuesday noon" [?27 Feb. 1912], BA.
21   Suetonius reported the rumour that Caesar was "every woman's husband and every man's wife."
22   Brooke, *John Webster*, 161–2, 99.
23   Rupert Brooke to Ka Cox, "Wednesday" [?April 1912], BA.
24   Brooke, *John Webster*, 102.
25   Craig, *Nerve Exhaustion*, 8, 21, 23, 79.
26   Rupert Brooke to E.J. Dent, 11 March 1912, BA. *Aber etwas langweilig*: but rather long drawn out. The Master of Magdalene was Stuart Donaldson.
27   Trombley, *'All That Summer She Was Mad,'* 186. When Daphne Olivier had a breakdown in 1915 she got the same treatment from Sir Henry Head: a course of "stuffing" lasting six weeks.
28   *LRB*, 333.
29   Ibid., 335.
30   *LRB*, 334; Rupert Brooke to Ka Cox, [24 Jan. 1912]; *LRB*, 339.
31   Rupert Brooke to Ka Cox, 25 Jan. 1912, BA.
32   Keynes prints this letter but omits this phrase in *LRB*, 347.

CHAPTER TEN

 1   He also would set the opening scene of *The Waste Land* in Munich, where summer arrives over the Starnbergersee. See Firchow, *Strange Meetings*.
 2   Hale, *Friends and Apostles*, 170.
 3   Rupert Brooke to Ka Cox [14?, 31? March 1912], BA.
 4   Rupert Brooke to Ka Cox, "Friday evening" [1 March 1912], BA.
 5   Hale, *Friends and Apostles*, 220.
 6   Rupert Brooke to Ka Cox [26 Feb., early March 1912], BA
 7   Rupert Brooke to Ka Cox [?27 Feb., 3 March 1912], BA.
 8   Hale, *Friends and Apostles*, 228.
 9   Keynes omits this passage in *LRB*, 365. On "Tuesday morning" [?2 April

1912] Rupert wrote to Ka, "I enclose a letter. Don't tell V. Keep it." This was probably Virginia's reply, now lost. Ka visited Virginia at Asheham in April.

10   *SOL*, 157–8.

11   Hale, *Friends and Apostles*, 230.

12   Hassall, *Rupert Brooke*, 333.

13   Rupert Brooke to Jacques Raverat [?26 March 1912], BA.

14   Rupert Brooke to Ka Cox [?24 March, ?28 March 1912], BA.

15   Rupert Brooke to Ka Cox [?22 Mar 1912], BA.

16   Gwen Raverat to Ka Cox [?27 March, 31 March 1912], in possession of Val Arnold-Foster.

17   Jacques Raverat to Ka Cox [April 1912], in possession of Val Arnold-Foster.

18   Gwen Raverat to Frances Cornford [?Aug. 1912], BL.

19   Oatine was a brand of face cream.

20   Rupert Brooke to Ka Cox [30 March 1912], BA; *LRB*, 367.

21   Rupert Brooke to Ka Cox [?1 April 1912], BA.

22   *LRB*, 370.

23   Rupert Brooke to Ka Cox [?16 March 1912]; Keynes omits this phrase in *LRB*, 366.

24   Cathleen Nesbitt, interview with the author, May 1981.

25   Woolf, *Letters*, 1.497.

26   *LRB*, 372.

27   Hale, *Friends and Apostles*, 247. A 6.35 mm Webley pistol could be bought at the Army and Navy Stores for two guineas.

28   Rupert Brooke to Brynhild Olivier [end September 1912], Eton College Library.

29   Woolf, *Letters*, 1:495.

30   Rupert Brooke to Ka Cox [?18 April 1912], BA.

31   *LRB*, 377.

32   Hale, *Friends and Apostles*, 241.

33   Rupert Brooke to Brynhild Olivier, [19 April 1912], Eton College Library.

34   On 5 June Virginia wrote to Noel Olivier, "you must congratulate me upon my engagement to Leonard Woolf – the strange black Jew –." Rupert's comment, to Ka, was "Woolf is, after all, a Jew" (Keynes omits this passage in *LRB*, 376).

CHAPTER ELEVEN

1   *SOL*, 167–8.

2   *LRB*, 378.

3   Brooke, *Prose of Rupert Brooke* 196. Rupert changed the details: it was May, not April, and the lake was north of Berlin, not south.

4   Hale, *Friends and Apostles*, 240–2. "Propose to by letter": in February

1911 James had received an invitation to tea containing an outline of the sender's penis, cut from tissue paper.

5 Rupert Brooke to Ka Cox [?24 April 1912], BA.

6 Rupert Brooke to A.E. Popham [?June 1912], BA; Hale, *Friends and Apostles*, 243.

7 Hale, *Friends and Apostles*, 246–7.

8 Hilton Young, an Eton and Trinity man, was the editor of the *Morning Post*. He figured in one of Geoffrey Keynes's emendations. Keynes printed "Hilton is with Alfred in the Black Forest"; what Rupert wrote was "Hilton is buggering Alfred in the Black Forest." *LRB*, 390.

9 *LRB*, 380.

10 Ibid., 386.

11 Hale, *Friends and Apostles*, 245–6.

12 Ibid., 232.

13 Known to its clientele as "Café Megalomania," it closed in 1915. The building was destroyed by the RAF in 1945.

14 Orwell, "Inside the Whale," 117.

15 *LRB*, 389.

16 Woolf, *Beginning Again*, 18–19.

17 *SOL*, 194.

18 In a letter to Bryn on 12 June, Rupert refers to "your Lawrence man," which suggests that she had met him when he came to visit Edward Garnett at The Cearne. In 1915 Lawrence told Bunny, "The Oliviers and such girls are wrong … You have always known the wrong people" (*Letters* 1:321–2). In his novel *Mr Noon*, Lawrence targeted the Neo-pagans as "that ephemeral school of young people who were to be quite, quite natural, impulsive and charming, in touch with the most advanced literature … the spoiled, well-to-do sons of a Fabian sort of middle-class, whose parents had given them such a happy picknicky childhood and youth that manhood was simply in the way" (*Mr Noon*, 255–7).

19 Rupert Brooke to Ka Cox [?18 July 1912], BA.

20 Hale, *Friends and Apostles*, 261.

21 Rupert Brooke to Ka Cox [?18 July 1912], BA.

22 J.M. Keynes to Duncan Grant, 26 July 1912, BL.

23 Hugh P. Popham to Brynhild Olivier [27 July 1912], in possession of A.E. (Tony) Popham, Hugh Popham's son.

24 Hugh P. Popham to Brynhild Olivier [?11 July 1912], in possession of A.E. Popham.

25 *SOL*, 197–8.

26 Rupert Brooke to Brynhild Olivier, Monday evening [29 July 1912], Eton College Library.

27 Rupert Brooke to Elisabeth van Rysselberghe, 31 July 1912, private collection.

28   Ka Cox to Frances Cornford, 21 June 1912, BA.
29   *LRB*, 390; Rupert Brooke to Ka Cox [?6 August 1912], BA.

CHAPTER TWELVE

1   *LRB*, 437.
2   Jacques Raverat to Frances Cornford [?April 1911], BL.
3   Frances Cornford to Gwen Riverat [?7 Sept. 1912], CUL.
4   Hale, *Friends and Apostles*, 258–9; James Strachey to Lytton Strachey, 17 Aug. 1912, BL.
5   Rupert Brooke to Ka Cox [?11 Oct 1912], BA. In an interview with the author, Mary Newbery remarked, "She was dead right to mind. He didn't love Ka deeply, but went off with her because someone else wanted to."
6   Rupert Brooke to Jacques Raverat, omitted from *LRB*, 397 [misdated; should be 7 Sept.].
7   *SOL*, 220.
8   Rupert Brooke to Ka Cox [?11 Oct 1912], BA.
9   *SOL*, 201.
10   Ibid., 210.
11   Ibid., 172.
12   Rupert Brooke to Brynhild Olivier, 21 Aug. 1912; Brynhild Olivier to James Strachey, 4 Sept. [1912], BL.
13   Anne Olivier Bell, interview with the author, 1980.
14   Rupert Brooke to Brynhild Olivier, end September 1912, Eton College Library.
15   Lady Ottoline Morrell to Bertrand Russell, 10 July 1912, Bertrand Russell Archives, McMaster University.
16   Frances Cornford to Gwen Riverat [?17 Aug. 1912], CUL.
17   Gwen Riverat to Frances Conford [?24 Sept. 1912], BL.
18   Brooke, "In Xanadu Did Kubla Khan," BA.
19   Omitted from *LRB*, 422.
20   *LRB*, 445, 30/31 March 1913.
21   *SOL*, 224.
22   Hale, *Friends and Apostles*, 55.
23   Hassall, *Edward Marsh*, 188. Mrs Elgy was Marsh's housekeeper and talented cook; she lived out.
24   Leonard Woolf was paying £11–£12 per month for his board and lodging at Brunswick Square.
25   Mumps can also cause testicular atrophy, which may account for Marsh's high squeaky voice.
26   Novello was not openly gay, though, given the state of the law before 1967. Novello lived with the actor Bobbie Andrews. Their house near Maidenhead, "Redroofs," became a centre for gay men in the arts, including Noel Coward. Marsh was a frequent visitor. Christopher Hassall, Brooke's biographer, had a similar relationship with Marsh.

27 At this stage, there was a good deal of fraternisation across the lines. For example, Rupert wrote a generally favourable review of Pound's *Personae* in December 1909: "he may be a great poet. It is important to remember his name." Brooke, *Prose of Rupert Brooke*, 113.

28 *LRB*, 402.

29 Gardner, Memoir, 7.

30 *LRB*, 340, ?19 Jan. 1912. "Schuchtern": coy.

31 *LRB*, 397.

32 Gardner, Memoir, 40–1.

33 Rupert Brooke to Elisabeth van Rysselberghe [30 Oct. 1912], private collection.

34 Rupert sent James a postcard from Exeter on 1 November. Probably he and Elisabeth went somewhere near Dartmoor.

35 *LRB*, 392. Letter is dated 7 August, but this must be a mistake; probably 7 November 1912.

36 Ferguson, *Short Sharp Life of T.E. Hulme*, 30.

37 Ibid., 137.

38 In his biography of Hulme, Ferguson misses the connection with "The Night Journey," and therefore finds Rupert's train metaphor inexplicable.

39 Noel made fun of the demand, to which Rupert replied, "don't joke about kidnapping." *SOL*, 231, 236.

40 The Heretics Society, co-founded by the Magdalene undergraduate C.K. Ogden, hosted many prominent speakers.

41 The second volume appeared in November 1915, after Rupert's death. By 1923 it had sold sixteen thousand copies at six shillings each, and the first volume had sold fifteen thousand.

42 *SOL*, 233.

43 Gardner, Memoir, 47.

44 Rupert Brooke to Elisabeth van Rysselberghe, 25 Dec. 1912.

45 The play was Galsworthy's *The Eldest Son*.

46 Hassall, *Edward Marsh*, 42.

47 Nesbitt, *A Little Love*, 63, 69.

48 Ibid., 68. Cathleen married Cecil Ramage, soldier, barrister, MP, and then actor. He had played Anthony to her Cleopatra in an Oxford production.

49 Gardner, Memoir, 69.

50 Ibid., 74, 77.

51 Phyllis Gardner, letters to Rupert Brooke, no. 48, 54, ?Jan.–Feb. 2013, BL.

52 Ibid., no. 55.

53 *LRB*, 427.

54 It is not known whether Eddie paid for this sitting, or whether Schell felt he could profit by adding Rupert to his roster of actors and

socialites. After Rupert's death, at least one of the portraits was published by Emory Walker of Clifford's Inn.

55   *LRB*, 447. Wyndham died prematurely two months later of a heart attack, in Paris.

56   Marchand's fiancée was Elsie Russell-Smith, Hugh's sister.

57   Rothenstein had been the designer for the Granville-Barker production of *The Winter's Tale*.

58   Rupert Brooke to Elisabeth van Rysselberghe, Wed. [16 April 1913?], private collection.

59   Rupert Brooke to Elisabeth van Rysselberghe, ?31 May 1913, private collection. However, Catherine Gide (Elisabeth's daughter) believed that Rupert and Elisabeth may have become lovers in a complete sense at Swanley in May 1913. Interview with the author, 1981.

60   *LRB*, 456.

61   Ibid., 421, misdated; should be 30 March 1913?

62   Ibid., 455, "Tuesday" ?15 April.

63   The total cost for this travel might be about £100. At his death, a year after his return, Rupert was overdrawn by about £400.

64   *LRB*, 457, misdated; should be mid-May.

65   *SOL*, 238.

66   Rupert Brooke to Mary Gardner, 21 May 1913, BL.

67   *Cedric* was built by Harland and Wolff in 1902 for the White Star Line. When launched she was the biggest ship in the world, though by 1912 the *Titanic* was more than twice as big.

CHAPTER THIRTEEN

1   He sent a snippy letter to Noel, saying he had been concerned by her "sallow and hideous appearance" when they met. This was not designed to rekindle any warmth between them.

2   *LRB*, 463; last sentence from Nesbitt, *A Little Love*, 70.

3   Brooke, *Letters from America*, xxxii.

4   Ibid., xxxii

5   Now demolished, Broadway Central Hotel was at Broadway and Bleecker St in Greenwich Village.

6   *LRB*, 468–9.

7   On Rupert's Canadian experience, see Martin and Hall, *Rupert Brooke in Canada*.

8   Brooke, *Letters from America*, 52.

9   Scott quoted in Leslie, *Historical Development of the Indian Act*, 114.

10   *SOL*, 240–1, 244.

11   Ibid., 245–6.

12   Ibid., 250, 255.

13   Brooke, *Letters from America*, 95–6.

14   Ibid., 111–12.

15 Ibid., 112, 113.

16 Ibid., 137–8, 143.

17 *SOL*, 263–4.

18 *LRB*, 500.

19 This Chateau Lake Louise hotel was not the present building but a mock-Tudor one designed by Francis Rattenbury, later destroyed by fire.

20 Rupert's letters to Agnes are in the Brooke Archive as expurgated transcripts, made either by her or by Geoffrey Keynes. The originals are not accessible.

21 She gave her date of birth as 7 December 1879, but a later ship's register gives 1871.

22 *LRB*, 502.

23 Rupert Brooke to Sir Edward Marsh, 6 Sept. 1913, omitted from *LRB*, 505.

24 Rupert Brooke to Agnes Capponi, ?23 Nov., 25 Dec. 1913, BA. One supposes that "one place" is in bed, naked?

25 Brooke, *Letters from America*, 155–6.

26 The phrase "Aeterna Corpora" (referring to the fixed stars) was used in the sonnet "Mutability," written before Rupert left for the United States.

27 *LRB*, 514.

28 Schoolcraft, "I Touched the Hand of Phoebus," 254.

29 Ibid., 256.

30 *LRB*, 513.

31 After the first article, the *Gazette* ran eight more at weekly intervals. The last four appeared from February to July 1914.

32 *LRB*, 516–17. The experience is re-worked in "Retrospect"; see Chapter 14.

33 Keynes transcribed the place incorrectly as "Kanai."

34 *LRB*, 525.

35 Ibid., 531. "The Porter" is an allusion to *Macbeth* II.3.

36 Brooke, *Letters from America*, 166–8.

37 The title was "Some Niggers," quoting an American woman who said on their arrival at Pago-Pago, "Look at those niggers! Whose are they?"

38 Lawrence, *Collected Letters* 1:393. After he had seen the South Seas, in 1922, Lawrence took a more skeptical view of the European myth, writing about Melville's *Typee*: "There on the island, where the golden-green great palm-trees chinked in the sun, and the elegant reed houses let the sea-breeze through, and people went naked and laughed a great deal, and Fayaway put flowers in his hair for him ... O God, why wasn't [Melville] happy? Why wasn't he? Because he wasn't ... The truth of the matter is, one cannot go back ... At the age of twenty-

five he came back to Home and Mother, to fight it out at close quarters. For you can't fight it out by running away." *Studies in Classic American Literature*, 148, 153.

39 *LRB*, 551, 553, 560–1.
40 Ibid., 550.
41 Tetuanui's legal name was Ariioehau Moeroa, b. Mataiea 1857, d. Pirae 1916. His wife was Haamoeura Moeroa, b. 1856, d. 1924, Mataiea.
42 O'Brien, *Mystic Isles of the South Seas*, 411–12.
43 Ibid., 421, 448. The thyrsus reference is to Euripides, *The Bacchae*.
44 Ibid., 66, 233.
45 Ibid., 564.
46 Keable, *Tahiti Isle of Dreams*, 115. Keable was a clergyman and Cambridge graduate. He became a propagandist for free love, and died in Tahiti in 1927.
47 At least seven young women died, presumably of the flu, at Mataiea in 1918. The only one with a name resembling Mamua or Maaua was Isabelle Alice Maraeura, b. 1897.
48 Tahitians did have a crowded Pantheon of Gods, demons, ghosts, etc., but there was nothing abstract about any of them.
49 "*Tau here*" means "My love."
50 *LRB*, 565, last sentence omitted by Keynes in *LRB*.
51 O'Brien, *Mystic Isles of the South Seas*, 381.
52 *LRB*, 564; Keynes omitted text after "very spry now."
53 Ibid., 568.
54 Hélène, born 1905; Louis, 1906; Alice, 1908; Charles, 1911. Mike Read comments that "the Tahitian records of births and deaths are fairly non-existent" (278). They are in fact existent and thorough, once you find the appropriate Mairie.
55 *LRB*, 565.
56 Gauguin, *Noa Noa*, X.
57 Maugham sold it at auction in 1962 for $48,000.
58 *LRB*, 570, 653. Taatamata did console herself with festivities set off by the arrival of an Argentinian training ship, *El Presidente Sarmiento*, with a hundred cadets on board. See O'Brien, *Mystic Isles of the South Seas*, 72–3.
59 *LRB*, 653–4. With conjectural emendations to Taatamata's French, "my dear sweetheart I'll always love you … I always remember your slender little body and the little mouth that kisses me nicely you have pierced my heart and I love always."
60 O'Brien, *Mystic Isles of the South Seas*, 390; *LRB*, 653–4.
61 Read, *Forever England*, 278.
62 In 1915 the ship was converted to carry Anzac troops to Gallipoli.
63 *LRB*, 573.

64 Rupert Brook to Jacques Raverat c. 23 April 1914. Cut from *LRB*, 581.
65 *LRB*, 583.
66 Rupert had a letter of introduction to them from Harold Monro of the Poetry Bookshop.
67 After Rupert's death, Browne and his wife mounted a production of *Lithuania* in Chicago, which was not a commercial or artistic success.
68 In *This Side of Paradise*, the hero Amory is said to "look a good deal like the picture of Rupert Brooke" (presumably one by Sherrill Schell). "To some extent Amory tried to play Rupert Brooke as long as he knew Eleanor. What he said, his attitude toward life, toward her, toward himself, were all reflexes of the dead Englishman's literary moods. Often she sat in the grass, a lazy wind playing with her short hair, her voice husky as she ran up and down the scale from Grantchester to Waikiki" (248).

CHAPTER FOURTEEN
1 When Cathleen Nesbitt and Mrs Brooke did meet, as mourners, they became good friends.
2 Gardner, Memoir, 12.
3 Marsh dedicated *Georgian Poetry (IV) 1918–19* to Hardy. However, D.H. Lawrence welcomed the first volume of *Georgian Poetry* as a reaction against "the nihilists, the intellectual, hopeless people – Ibsen, Flaubert, Thomas Hardy." *Phoenix*, 304.
4 The first installment of royalties, in 1915, was £500, and a steady flow continued for at least fifteen years. The three poets also shared the capital that had supported Rupert's annual income – probably about £4,000. Hassall, *Rupert Brooke*, 519.
5 Edward Thomas had gone to Oxford, but in June 1914 he had not yet started to write poetry.
6 John Drinkwater was absent. On the way to Dymock, Edward Thomas's train stopped at the hamlet Adlestrop. Six months later this inspired his classic "train window poem" of the same title.
7 Edward Thomas, *Daily News*, 22 July 1914. When Thomas was killed, Frost called it "the loss of the best friend I ever had." Frost, *Letters*, 1:592.
8 Hollis, *Now All Roads Lead to France*, 166.
9 Robert Frost to John Bartlett, in Frost, *Selected Letters*, 104.
10 Mary Gardner, *Plain Themes*.
11 Frost, *Selected Letters*, 104.
12 Robert Frost to John Haines, 15 May 1915, in Frost, *Letters*, 1:292–3.
13 *LRB*, 597 [misdated; ?20 June 1914]; 595, passage omitted by Keynes in *LRB*.
14 Ibid., 595 [misdated; 23 June 1914?].
15 Ibid., 449.

16   Brooke, *Prose of Rupert Brooke*, 176.

17   *LRB*, 592.

18   Ibid., 424.

19   Rupert Brooke to Cathleen Nesbitt, Aug? 1914, in Nesbitt *A Little Love*, 81.

20   Quoted in Jebb, *Patrick Shaw-Stewart*, 125.

21   Nicolson, *Portrait of a Marriage*, 141. Harold met Vita in June 1910.

22   Angus Macindoe (Eileen's grandson), personal communication with the author (email), April 2014.

23   Asquith, *Diary*, 50, 3 July 1915.

24   Hassall, *Edward Marsh*, 602. The other possible candidate would be Phyllis Gardner, but her style was more restrained.

25   *LRB*, 600, misdated; should be 2 August.

26   Ibid., 599.

27   Ibid., 608, 616.

28   Rupert Brooke to Eileen Wellesley, 23 Oct. 1914, BA.

29   Rupert Brooke to Eileen Wellesley, 5 Sept. 1914, BA.

30   *SOL*, 269.

31   Ibid., 273.

32   *LRB*, 613.

33   James Strachey to Noel Olivier, 20 July 1916, private collection. In the end, though, James married the Bedalian Alix Sargent-Florence and Noel her medical colleague Arthur Richards. Years after that, James and Noel had a long-running adulterous affair.

34   Hale, *Friends and Apostles*, 279.

35   See Nirenberg, *Anti-Judaism: The Western Tradition*.

36   *LRB*, 614.

37   Cathleen's mother was a suffragette who had gone to prison for breaking windows at a post office. Rupert may have been kept in the dark about this episode.

38   Lawrence, *Letters of D.H. Lawrence*, 2:611.

39   Hughes, *Tom Brown's Schooldays*, 206. Hughes uses "Russians" because the novel was composed during the Crimean War. "Border-ruffians" presumably refers to the tribal warriors of the North West Frontier, in present-day Afghanistan and Pakistan.

40   On the collective outlook of the war poets, see Caesar, *Taking It Like a Man*; and Egremont, *Some Desperate Glory*.

41   These survival odds are accepted by Lewis-Stempel, *Six Weeks*.

42   *LRB*, 621.

43   Beckett, *Making of the First World War*, 21.

44   Churchill was a major in the Reserves, but had never commanded a unit larger than two hundred men. He had also managed to send his own family regiment, the Queen's Own Oxfordshire Hussars, to Dunkirk, though they never reached Antwerp.

45 Churchill, *World Crisis*, 319.
46 Ibid., 328.
47 *LRB*, 624–5, 632–3.
48 Ibid., 627.
49 Nehls, *D.H. Lawrence*, 1:289.
50 A third argument, often made by pacifists, was that international conflicts should always be resolved by diplomacy rather than force of arms. But Germany had not given Belgium anything to negotiate.
51 *LRB* 633, 636.
52 Dent, a fellow of King's in music, was deeply attached to Clive Carey, another of Rupert's contemporaries.
53 *LRB*, 636.
54 Ibid., 637, omitted in *LRB*.
55 Ibid., 635–6. Keynes printed "X" for Cornwallis-West.
56 *Times*, 12 January 1915. Cornwallis-West did not return to active service; he went bankrupt in 1916 and died by his own hand in 1951.
57 *The Times* reviewed it on 11 March 1915.
58 Lawrence, *Letters* 3:38; Bristow, "Rupert Brooke's Poetic Deaths," 669.
59 *LRB*, 631.
60 Julian Grenfell's poem "Into Battle" was written six days after Rupert's death, and reads like a pastiche of his themes.
61 Quoted in Wilson, *The Myriad Faces of War*, 111.
62 Byron died in April 1824 and probably, like Brooke, of sepsis.

CHAPTER FIFTEEN

1 Wilson, *Myriad Faces of War*, 110.
2 Churchill, *World Crisis*, 339.
3 Wilson, *The Myriad Faces of War*, 130. Venetia Stanley was Asquith's mistress. The "gorgeous East" is a phrase from Wordsworth's sonnet on Venice.
4 *LRB*, 652.
5 Ibid., 663.
6 However, he also asked if Albert Rothenstein – about his only Jewish friend – would nominate him for the Savile Club. In 1916 Rothenstein changed his German-sounding name to Rutherston.
7 *LRB*, 639.
8 Hassall, *Rupert Brooke*, 438.
9 *LRB*, 658.
10 Henry James in Brooke, *Letters from America*, xxxviii.
11 Ibid., xiii, xxv, xl.
12 Brooke, *Prose of Rupert Brooke*, 199. "A" is the beloved of Rupert's semi-autobiographical protagonist – perhaps a blend of Noel and Cathleen?

13 James, in *Letters from America*, xl. James spoke informally of his admiration for Rupert in a letter to Eddie Marsh, 6 June 1915. James, *Life in Letters*, 547.

14 *LRB*, 660, 662–3.

15 Hassall, *Rupert Brooke*, 489.

16 *LRB*, 665.

17 Ibid., 668.

18 Rupert was unsure about James Strachey's letters, which he called "rather a pestilential heap." Dudley returned them to James, who held on to both sides of the correspondence. Geoffrey Keynes was eager to get them; James feared he might destroy ones that showed Rupert in a bad light, so he sold them to the Berg Collection of the New York Public Library. Rupert made no mention of Geoffrey in planning his literary legacy, beyond saying that he might like a keepsake. Geoffrey had never been part of Rupert's inner circle. He made himself a favourite with Mrs Brooke after Rupert's death, and she appointed him one of the estate's four trustees in 1930, when she cut Eddie Marsh out of her will.

19 *LRB*, 669–70.

20 Carlyon, *Gallipoli*, 320. The argument of the bitter-enders was that the Turks had lost many of their shore guns to naval bombardment and were running low on ammunition. But it was never likely that an entire battle fleet could be passed through the eye of the needle at Canakkale.

21 Hamilton, *Gallipoli Diary*, v.

22 *LRB*, 678.

23 Ibid., 662.

24 Kum Kale, where the French landed, was three miles from the ruins of Troy. They were withdrawn, and later fought next to the RND at Cape Helles.

25 *LRB*, 680. A threnody is a poem on the death of someone or something.

26 Philoctetes had been the lover of Heracles, and received his bow after his death.

27 Hassall, *Rupert Brooke*, 503.

28 Ibid., 502. Inge was an expert on Christian Platonism, but he objected to Rupert's claim that he would survive as "a pulse in the eternal mind."

29 *Streptococcus pneumoniae* was the proximate cause of death for many AIDS patients in the 1980s and 1990s. In this context, there seems little plausibility in the rumour that Rupert's fatal illness was connected with a bout of venereal disease when he was in Tahiti. There is no evidence for this, though the coral poisoning he suffered there probably weakened his constitution.

30 Browne died on 7 June. His body was never recovered for burial; his name is among the twenty-one thousand "missing in action" on the Helles Memorial.

31 Bonham-Carter, *Champion Redoubtable*, 2:42.

32 Hassall, *Rupert Brooke*, 513.

33 On the night of 24 April Freyberg made a one-man diversion, swimming ashore to set flares to deceive the Turks about the invasion point. He received the Distinguished Service Order for this feat. On 13 November 1916 he won a Victoria Cross at Beaucourt on the Somme. F.S. Kelly was killed there on the same day.

34 Bonham-Carter, *Champion Redoubtable*, 2:69.

35 His younger brother Hamo Sassoon was fatally wounded at Gallipoli. He died on a hospital ship on 1 November 1915, and was buried at sea.

36 One of them was Edwin Dyett, from the Nelson Battalion of the RND. See A.P. Herbert, *The Secret Battle*.

37 Lawrence, *Collected Letters*, 1:337.

38 Asquith, *Diaries*, 94, 28 Oct. 1915.

39 *The Times*, 26 April 1915.

40 Labour Party resolution, 1916. Bonham-Carter, *Champion Redoubtable*, 78

41 In July 1916 the RND was reformed as the 63rd Division, a regular infantry unit. In the attack on Beaucourt in November the Hood battalion again lost most of its officers. By 1917 Oc Asquith was commander of the Hood, which was mauled again in the second battle of Passchendaele.

42 After the death of his three beneficiaries, income from Rupert's literary estate has been distributed to other deserving poets by the Brooke trustees.

43 Another Apostle, Ludwig Wittgenstein, also served in Bukovina with the Austrian Seventh Army in 1916–17.

44 Gomori, "Ferenc Békássy's Letters to J.M. Keynes," 169.

45 Kokoschka, *My Life*, 36.

Bibliography

Adams, Michael C.C. *The Great Adventure: Male Desire and the Coming of World War I*. Bloomington: Indiana University Press, 1990.

Asquith, Cynthia. *Diaries 1915–1918*. New York: Knopf, 1969.

Badley, J.H. *A Schoolmaster's Testament*. Oxford: Basil Blackwell, 1937.

Beckett, Ian. *The Making of the First World War*. New Haven: Yale University Press, 2012.

The Bedales Record. Petersfield: Bedales School.

Bell, Adrian. *By-Road*. London: John Lane, 1943.

Bell, Quentin. *Virginia Woolf: A Biography*. London: Hogarth Press, 1972.

Belloc, Hilaire. *The Four Men*. London: Thomas Nelson, 1912.

Best, Robert. "A Short Life and a Gay One: A Biography of Frank Best, 1893–1917." Unpublished MS, Birmingham Public Library.

Boissevain, Jeremy. *Friends of Friends*. Oxford: Basil Blackwell, 1974.

Bond, Brian. *The Unquiet Western Front: Britain's Role in Literature and History*. Cambridge: Cambridge University Press, 2002.

Bonham-Carter, Violet. *Champion Redoubtable: The Diaries and Letters of Violet Bonham-Carter 1914–1945*, edited by Mark Pottle. London: Phoenix, 1999.

Brandreth, Giles, and Sally Henry, eds. *John Haden Badley, 1865–1967: Bedales School and Its Founder*. Bedales: Bedales Society, 1967.

Bristow, Joseph. "Rupert Brooke's Poetic Deaths." *English Literary History* 81, no. 2 (2014): 663–92.

Brooke, Rupert. *Democracy and the Arts*. London: Rupert Hart-Davis, 1946.

– *The Irregular Verses of Rupert Brooke*. Edited by Peter Miller. Lechlade: Green Branch Press, 1997.

– *John Webster and the Elizabethan Drama*. New York: Lane, 1916.

– *The Letters of Rupert Brooke*. Edited by G. Keynes. London: Faber & Faber, 1968.

– *Letters from America*. With a Preface by Henry James. Toronto: McClelland & Stewart, 1916.

– *Letters from Rupert Brooke to His Publisher, 1911–1914.* New York: Octagon, 1975.
– *The Poetical Works of Rupert Brooke.* Edited by G. Keynes. London: Faber & Faber, 1970.
– *The Prose of Rupert Brooke.* C. Hassall, ed. London: Sidgwick & Jackson, 1956.
– *Rupert Brooke: The Collected Poems. With a Memoir by Edward Marsh.* London: Sidgwick & Jackson, 1942.
– *Song of Love: The Letters of Rupert Brooke and Noel Olivier, 1909–1915.* Edited by Pippa Harris. London: Bloomsbury, 1991.
Caesar, Adrian. *Taking It Like a Man: Suffering, Sexuality and the War Poets.* Manchester: Manchester University Press, 1993.
Carlyon, Les. *Gallipoli.* London: Transworld, 2001.
Carpenter. Edward. *Civilisation: Its Cause and Cure.* London: Allen & Unwin, 1921.
– *England's Ideal.* London: Swan Sonnenschein, 1901.
– *My Days and Dreams: Being Autobiographical Notes.* London: George Allen & Unwin, 1916.
Churchill, Winston. *The World Crisis.* London: Butterworth, 1923.
Clark, Christopher. *The Sleepwalkers: How Europe Went to War in 1914.* London: Penguin, 2013.
Clark, Ronald W. *The Life of Bertrand Russell.* London: Jonathan Cape & Weidenfeld & Nicolson, 1975.
Clements, Keith. *Henry Lamb.* London: Redcliffe Press, 1984.
Connolly, Cyril. *Enemies of Promise.* New York: Doubleday, 1960.
Cornford, Frances. *Collected Poems.* London: Cresset Press, 1954.
– Memoir. Manuscript in the possession of Christopher Cornford.
– *Poems.* Hampstead: Priory Press, 1910.
Craig, Maurice. *Nerve Exhaustion.* London: Churchill, 1922.
Crick, Bernard. *George Orwell: A Life.* Harmondsworth: Penguin, 1982.
Delany, Paul. "The Death of a Beautiful Man: Rupert Brooke in Memory and Imagination." In *Virginia Woolf and the Common(wealth) Reader: Selected Papers from the Twenty-Third Annual International Conference on Virginia Woolf,* edited by Helen Wussow and Mary Ann Gillies, 50–8. Clemson, SC: Clemson University Digital Press, 2014.
– *D.H. Lawrence's Nightmare: The Writer and His Circle in the Years of the Great War.* New York: Basic Books, 1978.
– *The Neo-Pagans: Friendship and Love in the Rupert Brooke Circle.* London: Macmillan, 1987.
Dellamora, Richard. *Masculine Desire: the Sexual Politics of Victorian Aestheticism.* Chapel Hill: University of North Carolina Press, 1990.
Demolins, Edmond. *Anglo-Saxon Superiority: To What It Is Due.* London: Leadenhall Press, 1898.

Eckersley, Arthur. *Odds and Ends of a Learned Clerk*. London: John Lane, 1922.

Egremont, Max. *Some Desperate Glory: The First World War the Poets Knew*. London: Picador, 2014.

Ferguson, Robert. *The Short Sharp Life of T.E. Hulme*. London: Allen Lane, 2002.

Firchow, Peter. *Strange Meetings: Anglo-German Literary Encounters from 1910 to 1960*. Washington: Catholic University of America Press, 2008.

Fitzgerald, F. Scott. *This Side of Paradise*. New York: Scribner's, 1920.

Forster, E.M. *Arctic Summer and Other Fiction*. London: Edward Arnold, 1980.

Frost, Robert. *The Letters of Robert Frost*. Vol. 1, *1886–1920*. Edited by Donald Sheehy, Mark Richardson, and Robert Faggen. Cambridge: Harvard University Press, 2014.

– *Selected Letters*. New York: Henry Holt, 1964.

Furbank, P.N. *E.M. Forster: A Life*. 2 vols. London: Secker & Warburg, 1977–79.

Gardner, Brian. *The Public Schools: An Historical Survey*. London: Hamish Hamilton, 1973.

Gardner, Mary. *Plain Themes*. London: J.M. Dent, 1913.

Gardner, Phyllis. Unpublished Memoir. Manuscript, British Library.

Garnett, David. *The Familiar Faces*. London: Chatto & Windus, 1962.

– *The Flowers of the Forest*. London: Chatto & Windus, 1955.

– *The Golden Echo*. London: Chatto & Windus, 1953.

– *Great Friends: Portraits of Seventeen Writers*. London: Macmillan, 1979.

Gathorne-Hardy, Jonathan. *The Public School Phenomenon*. New York: Viking, 1978.

Gauguin, Paul. *Noa Noa: Gauguin's Tahiti*. Edited by Nicholas Wadley. Oxford: Phaidon, 1985.

Gomori, George. "Ferenc Békássy's Letters to J.M. Keynes." *New Hungarian Quarterly* 79 (Autumn 1980): 158–70.

Graves, Robert. *Goodbye to All That*. Harmondsworth: Penguin, 1960.

Green, Martin. *Children of the Sun*. New York: Basic Books, 1976.

– *Mountain of Truth*. Hanover: University Press of New England, 1986.

Greene, Graham, ed. *The Old School: Essays by Divers Hands*. London: Jonathan Cape, 1934.

Grohmann, Will. *Wassily Kandinsky: Life and Work*. New York: Abrams, 1958.

Hale, Keith, ed. *Friends and Apostles: The Correspondence of Rupert Brooke and James Strachey*. New Haven: Yale University Press, 1998.

Hassall, Christopher. *Edward Marsh*. London: Longmans, 1959.

– *Rupert Brooke: A Biography*. London: Faber & Faber, 1964.

Hastings, Michael. *The Handsomest Young Man in England: Rupert Brooke*. London: Michael Joseph, 1967.

Henderson, James L. *Irregularly Bold*. London: Andre Deutsch, 1978.

Herbert, A.P. *The Secret Battle*. Oxford: Oxford University Press, 1982.

Hickson, Alisdare. *The Poisoned Bowl: Sex, Repression and the Public School System*. London: Constable, 1995.

Hollis, Matthew. *Now All Roads Lead to France: The Last Years of Edward Thomas*. London: Faber & Faber, 2011.

Holroyd, Michael. *Augustus John: A Biography*. Harmondsworth: Penguin, 1976.

– *Lytton Strachey: A Biography*. Harmondsworth: Penguin, 1971.

Honey, J.R. de S. *Tom Brown's Universe: The Development of the Victorian Public School*. London: Millington, 1977.

Hughes, Thomas. *Tom Brown at Oxford*. London: Thomas Nelson, n.d.

– *Tom Brown's Schooldays*. London: J.M. Dent, 1906.

Hynes, Samuel. *The Edwardian Turn of Mind*. Princeton: Princeton University Press, 1968.

Ilfeld, Fred Jr, and Roger Lauer. *Social Nudism in America*. New Haven, CT: College & University Press, 1964.

James, Henry. *A Life in Letters*. New York: Viking, 1999.

Jebb, Miles. *Patrick Shaw-Stewart: An Edwardian Meteor*. Stanbridge, UK: Dovecote Press, 2010.

Keable, Robert. *Tahiti Isle of Dreams*. London: Hutchinson, 1925.

Keynes, Geoffrey. *A Bibliography of Rupert Brooke*. London: Rupert Hart-Davis, 1954.

– *The Gates of Memory*. Oxford: Clarendon Press, 1981.

– *Henry James in Cambridge*. London: W. Heffer, 1967.

Kokoschka, Oskar. *My Life*. London: Thames & Hudson, 1974.

Lawrence, D.H. *Collected Letters*. 2 vols. Edited by Harry T. Moore. New York: Viking, 1962.

– *The Letters of D.H. Lawrence*. Vols. 1–3. Edited by James T. Boulton. Cambridge: Cambridge University Press, 1979–84.

– *Mr Noon*. Cambridge: Cambridge University Press, 1984.

– *Phoenix: The Posthumous Papers of D.H. Lawrence*. London: Heinemann, 1936.

– *Studies in Classic American Literature*. New York: Doubleday, 1951.

Lehmann, John. *Rupert Brooke: His Life and His Legend*. London: Weidenfeld & Nicolson, 1980.

Leslie, John. *The Historical Development of the Indian Act*. Ottawa: Department of Indian Affairs and Northern Development, Treaties and Historical Research Branch, 1978.

Levy, Paul. *Moore: G.E. Moore and the Cambridge Apostles*. London: Weidenfeld & Nicolson, 1979.

Lewis-Stempel, John. *Six Weeks: The Short and Gallant Life of the British Officer in the First World War*. London: Weidenfeld & Nicolson, 2010.

MacKenzie, Norman, and Jeanne MacKenzie. *The First Fabians*. London: Weidenfeld & Nicolson, 1977.

– *The Time Traveller: A Biography of H.G. Wells*. London: Weidenfeld & Nicolson, 1973.

Marsh, Edward. *A Number of People*. London: Heinemann & Hamish Hamilton, 1939.

Martin, Sandra, and Roger Hall, eds. *Rupert Brooke in Canada*. Toronto: Peter Martin Associates, 1978.

Masterman, C.F.G. *The Condition of England*. London: Methuen, 1960. (1st ed. 1909).

McWilliams-Tullberg, Rita. *Women at Cambridge*. London: Victor Gollancz, 1975.

Moore, George Edward. *Principia Ethica*. Cambridge: Cambridge University Press, 1965. (1st ed. 1903).

Murray, Gilbert. *A Biography of Francis McDonald Cornford, 1874–1943*. Oxford: Oxford University Press, 1944.

Nehls, Edward, ed. *D.H. Lawrence: A Composite Biography*. 3 vols. Madison: University of Wisconsin Press, 1957–59.

Nesbitt, Cathleen. *A Little Love and Good Company*. Owings Mills, MD: Stemmer House, 1977.

Nicolson, Nigel. *Portrait of a Marriage*. London: Weidenfeld & Nicolson, 1973.

Nirenberg, David. *Anti-Judaism: The Western Tradition*. New York: W.W. Norton, 2013.

Oates, J.C.T. "Charles Edward Sayle." *Transactions of the Cambridge Bibliographical Society* 8 (1982): 236–69.

O'Brien, Frederick. *Mystic Isles of the South Seas*. New York: Century, 1921.

Olivier, Sydney. *Letters and Selected Writings*. London: George Allen & Unwin, 1948.

Orwell, George. *The Collected Essays, Journalism and Letters*. 4 vols. London: Secker & Warburg, 1968.

Partridge, Frances. *Memories*. London: Gollancz, 1981.

Pearsall, Robert B. *Rupert Brooke: The Man and Poet*. Amsterdam: Rodopi, 1974.

Phillips, Ann, ed. *A Newnham Anthology*. Cambridge: Cambridge University Press, 1979.

Poole, Roger. *The Unknown Virginia Woolf*. Cambridge: Cambridge University Press, 1978.

Pye, Sybil. "Memoir of Rupert Brooke." *Life & Letters*, May 1929.

Raverat, Gwen. Novel. Unpublished MS in the possession of Sophie Gurney.

– *Period Piece: A Cambridge Childhood*. New York: Norton, 1952.

– *The Wood Engravings of Gwen Raverat*. Selected with an Introduction by Reynolds Stone. London: Faber & Faber, 1959.

Raverat, Jacques. Memoir. Unpublished MS in the possession of Sophie
    Gurney.
Read, Mike. *Forever England: The Life of Rupert Brooke.* Edinburgh: Main-
    stream, 1997.
Roche, Paul. *With Duncan Grant in Southern Turkey.* London: Honeyglen,
    1999.
Rogers, Timothy. *Rupert Brooke: A Reappraisal and Selection From His Writ-
    ings, Some Hitherto Unpublished.* London: Routledge & Kegan Paul, 1971.
Rothblatt, Sheldon. *The Revolution of the Dons: Cambridge and Society in
    Victorian England.* New York: Basic Books, 1968.
Sayle, Charles. Diary. Unpublished MS, Cambridge University Library.
Schoolcraft, John. "I Touched the Hand of Phoebus." *Michigan Quarterly
    Review* 5, no. 4 (1966), 253–8.
Sedgwick, Eve Kosofsky. *Between Men: English Literature and Male Homoso-
    cial Desire.* New York: Columbia University Press, 1985.
Seymour-Smith, Martin. *Robert Graves: His Life and Work.* London:
    Hutchinson, 1982.
Simpson, John Hope. *Rugby Since Arnold.* London: Macmillan, 1967.
Sinclair, Andrew. *The Red and the Blue: Intelligence, Treason, and the Univer-
    sities.* London: Weidenfeld & Nicolson, 1986.
Skidelsky, Robert. *English Progressive Schools.* Harmondsworth: Penguin,
    1969.
– *John Maynard Keynes.* Vol. 1, *Hopes Betrayed 1883–1920.* London:
    Macmillan, 1983.
Spalding, Frances. *Gwen Raverat: Friends, Family and Affections.* London:
    Harvill, 2001.
Spater, George, and Ian Parsons. *A Marriage of True Minds: An Intimate
    Portrait of Leonard and Virginia Woolf.* New York: Harcourt, Brace,
    Jovanovitch, 1977.
Speaight, Robert. *The Life of Hilaire Belloc.* New York: Farrar, Straus &
    Cudahy, 1957.
Stansky, Peter, and William Abrahams. *Journey to the Frontier: Two Roads to
    the Spanish Civil War.* New York: Norton, 1970.
Stewart, W.A.C. *Progressives and Radicals in English Education.* London:
    Macmillan, 1972.
Strachey, James, and Alix Strachey. *Bloomsbury/Freud: The Letters of James
    and Alix Strachey, 1924–25.* Edited by Perry Meisel and Walter Kendrick.
    New York: Basic Books, 1985.
Strachey, Lytton. *The Letters of Lytton Strachey.* Edited by Paul Levy. London:
    Viking, 2005.
Stringer, Arthur. *Red Wine of Youth.* New York: Bobbs-Merrill, 1948.
Taddeo, Julie Anne. *Lytton Strachey and the Search for Modern Sexual Iden-
    tity.* New York: Harrington Park Press, 2002.

Taylor, A.J.P. *English History, 1914–1945.* Harmondsworth: Penguin, 1970.

Thomas, Edward. *Letters From Edward Thomas to Gordon Bottomley.* Edited by R. George Thomas. London: Oxford University Press, 1968.

Trombley, Stephen. *'All That Summer She Was Mad': Virginia Woolf, Female Victim of Male Medicine.* New York: Continuum Press, 1982.

Tsuzuki, Chushichi. *Edward Carpenter, 1844–1929: Prophet of Human Fellowship.* Cambridge: Cambridge University Press, 1980.

Van Rysselberghe, Maria. *Les cahiers de la Petite Dame: Notes pour l'histoire authentique d'André Gide. 1918–1929. Cahiers André Gide, IV.* Paris: Gallimard, 1973.

Ward, B.M. *Reddie of Abbotsholme.* London: Allen & Unwin, 1934.

Webb, Beatrice. *The Diary of Beatrice Webb.* Vol. 3. London: Virago, 1984.

– *Our Partnership.* New York: Longmans Green, 1948.

Webb, Sidney, and Beatrice Webb. *The Letters of Sydney and Beatrice Webb.* Vol. 2, *Partnership, 1892–1912.* Edited by Norman Mackenzie. Cambridge: Cambridge University Press, 1978.

Wells, Frank. *H.G. Wells: A Pictorial Biography.* London: Jupiter Books, 1977.

Wells, H.G. *H.G. Wells in Love: Postscript to an Experiment in Autobiography.* Edited by G P. Wells. London: Faber & Faber, 1984.

– *A Modern Utopia.* Lincoln: University of Nebraska Press, 1967 (1st ed. 1905).

– *New Worlds For Old.* London: Constable, 1908.

West, Anthony. *H.G. Wells: Aspects of a Life.* London: Hutchinson, 1984.

Wilson, Trevor. *The Myriad Faces of War: Britain and the Great War, 1914–1918.* Cambridge: Polity Press, 1986.

Wohl, Robert. *The Generation of 1914.* Cambridge: Harvard University Press, 1979.

Woolf, Leonard. *Beginning Again: An Autobiography of the Years 1911 to 1918.* London: Hogarth, 1972.

Woolf, Virginia. *Carlyle's House and Other Sketches.* Edited by David Bradshaw. London: Hesperus, 2003.

– *The Diary of Virginia Woolf.* 6 vols. Edited by Anne Olivier Bell. London: The Hogarth Press, 1977–84.

– *The Letters of Virginia Woolf.* 6 vols. Edited by Nigel Nicolson and Joanne Trautmann. London: The Hogarth Press, 1975–80.

– *Moments of Being: Unpublished Autobiographical Writings.* Edited by Jeanne Schulkind, London: The Hogarth Press, 1978.

Index

Heidelberg, 120
Henley, William Ernest, 44
Herbert, Aubrey, 255
Herbert, Mary (née Vesey), 255
Heretics Society, The (Cambridge),
216, 253
Herrick, Robert, 81
Hickson, Alisdare, 23
Hillbrow School, 12, 14–17, 130
Hitler, Adolf, 282, 291
Hobhouse, Arthur, 70, 138, 148
Hobson, Harold, 88, 107
Hobson family, 37
Holroyd, Michael, 21
Homer, 96, 283–4
homosexuality: in all-male schools, 16,
20–1, 85; and desire for children,
268; Higher and Lower Sodomy, 21,
27; as means for sexual satisfaction,
76; pederasty, 16, 22, 67, 85; RB's re-
lationships with older men, 20, 67–8,
209; RB's relationships with younger
boys, 23–7, 73–7, 100; RB's sexual
fluidity, 7, 66; sentimental friend-
ships, 21–2, 67, 268
Hood Battalion: at Blandford Camp,
269, 275, 278; at Gallipoli, 9, 281–9;
Latin Club, 6, 7, 285, 286, 287
Housman, A.E., 5, 44, 192, 217; A
Shropshire Lad, 284
Hubback, Bill, 93, 105, 107, 138
Hughes, Thomas, 263; Tom Brown at
Oxford, 21; Tom Brown's
Schooldays, 19, 22, 23, 262
Hulme, T.E., 124–5
Hungary, 87, 151, 292

Ibsen, Henrik, 253; John Gabriel Borkman, 124
Imbros, 284
infantry subalterns, 4, 6–7, 19, 22–3,
262–3
Inge, William, 286

Jamaica: Olivier family in, 34, 36, 93,
106, 116–17, 118, 136, 204
James, Henry, 81–2, 179, 260, 277–8,
286; Letters from America, 277
James, Herbert, 23
Jews and Judaism: Belloc's anti-Semi-
tism, 190; RB's anti-Semitic views,
50–1, 65, 125–6, 195, 222, 244, 259,
276; RB's Jewish friends, 123, 222
John, Augustus, 62, 82, 121, 154, 156
John, Dorothy (Dorelia; née McNeil),
82, 154
John, Ida (née Nettleship), 82
Jowett, Benjamin, 13

Kandinsky, Wassily, 121
Kauai, 235
Keable, Robert, 240
Keeling, Ben: and Fabian Society, 36,
46, 52, 58, 62; political career, 63,
69, 260
Kelly, F.S., 285, 288
Keppel, Mrs, 217
Keynes, Geoffrey: in Bloomsbury, 258;
at Cambridge, 81; and Grant's portrait of Ka Cox, 136; and Neo-pagans, 37, 142; and publication of
RB's letters, 159; and RB's anti-femi-
nist views, 254; at Rugby, 25, 130;
and Charles Sayle, 67
Keynes, John Maynard: in Apostles,
70, 71, 192; and Ferenc Békássy, 151;
in Bloomsbury, 147, 258; and Justin
Brooke, 140; at Everleigh, 195–200;
and Arthur Hobhouse, 148; and Neo-
pagans, 140, 141, 143, 156, 158; at
Overcote picnics, 81
King's College (Cambridge): RB at, 30–
49; RB's fellowship at, 220, 248; RB's
thesis for (John Webster and the Elizabeth Drama), 80, 119, 134, 150,
152, 173, 211, 215; W.P. Brooke at,
11, 49
Kipling, Rudyard, 271